Rhetoric of Masculinity

Rhetoric of Masculinity

Male Body Image, Media, and Gender Role Stress/Conflict

Edited by Donnalyn Pompper

LEXINGTON BOOKS
Lanham • Boulder • New York • London

Published by Lexington Books
An imprint of The Rowman & Littlefield Publishing Group, Inc.
4501 Forbes Boulevard, Suite 200, Lanham, Maryland 20706
www.rowman.com

86-90 Paul Street, London EC2A 4NE

British Library Cataloguing in Publication Information Available

Library of Congress Cataloging-in-Publication Data

Names: Pompper, Donnalyn, 1960- editor.
Title: Rhetoric of masculinity : male body image, media, and gender role stress/
conflict / edited by Donnalyn Pompper.
Description: Lanham : Lexington Books, [2022] | Includes bibliographical references
and index. | Summary: "Rhetoric of Masculinity lends depth and global nuance to
discourse associated with the masculinity concept as it bears on males' self-image,
role in society, media representations of them, and the gender role stress/conflict
they experience when they fail to measure up to social standards associated with
what it means to be manly"— Provided by publisher.
Identifiers: LCCN 2021051296 (print) | LCCN 2021051297 (ebook) | ISBN
9781793626882 (cloth) | ISBN 9781793626905 (paperback) | ISBN 9781793626899
(ebook)
Subjects: LCSH: Masculinity. | Masculinity in popular culture. | Masculinity in
mass media. | Sex role. | Men—Identity.
Classification: LCC BF175.5.M37 R447 2022 (print) | LCC BF175.5.M37
(ebook) | DDC 305.31—dc23/eng/20211215
LC record available at https://lccn.loc.gov/2021051296
LC ebook record available at https://lccn.loc.gov/2021051297

Contents

Acknowledgments

It is a pleasure to thank several people who supported this project. First, I am grateful to the authors published in this edited collection for their energy, creativity, talent, and passion for expanding GRC/S theory by interrogating fascinating subtopics and crossing into new territories. When I circulated the call for chapter proposals in 2019, I received an overwhelmingly positive response. Then 2020 happened with political unrest in the United States and a pandemic that affected everyone. So, I appreciate authors' willingness to meet internal deadlines and to revise proposals and chapter drafts until we were mutually satisfied that arguments were clear and compelling. Along the way, a few authors had to drop out for reasons related to overwhelming workloads in balancing teaching with service and research—and a personal life. I offer a special thanks to authors who came aboard later in the process to support colleagues.

I especially thank external reviewers who offered double-blind feedback for improving good work: Guillermo Caliendo, assistant professor of Instruction, Temple University; Stephen Charbonneau, associate professor, Florida Atlantic University; Amanda Cote, assistant professor, University of Oregon; Rahul Mitra, associate professor, Wayne State University; Suman Mishra, associate professor, Southern Illinois University Edwardsville; and Arthur Raney, professor, Florida State University.

For all book projects, I love to shower thanks and praise on libraries and librarians. They deserve so much. Thank you, University of Oregon Knight Library, for database access and support. I also thank the School of Journalism and Communication for endowed chair in public relations support and graduate students Hadil Abuhmaid and Majd Mariam for help with library research.

Finally, but not least, an extra helping of thanks to Tracy L. Tylka and Lexington Studies in Contemporary Rhetoric Series Editor Gary C. Woodward, Acquisitions Editor Nicolette Amstutz, and the support team at Lexington Books, including production editor Taylor Breeding, an imprint of Rowman & Littlefield. I also would be remiss if I didn't thank my J320 Gender, Media, & Diversity students who teach me much and help me to remain curious and open minded.

Introduction

Male GRC/S as Viewed through Psychology and Communication Lenses

Donnalyn Pompper

This edited collection has been in the back of my mind as I finished writing *Rhetoric of Femininity: Female Body Image, Media, and Gender Role Stress/ Conflict* (Pompper, 2017) to fill gaps in our understanding of the female experience with gender role conflict/stress (GRC/S) once O'Neil (1981b, 2008) and others had covered so much important territory in psychology before to explain male experiences. I had been thinking about how male GRC/S theory applies to communication phenomena and so opted to mold *this* project as an edited collection that would attract diverse researchers across academic disciplines. My goal is to expand male GRC/S theory by interrogating media representations and men's embodied experiences in response to modern man's masculinity "crisis" (e.g., Levant, 1997). As a psychologist, Levant (1997) framed the masculinity concept in this cautionary way to draw attention to the increasingly lower self-esteem men feel (and unwillingness to talk about it) in conjunction with socioeconomic conditions, changing gender roles, and "poor media images" based on critique of male behaviors among Clarence Thomas, William Kennedy Smith, Mike Tyson, Woody Allen, and others accused of raping women and other sexual misconduct (Levant, 1997, p. 221). Nostalgically longing for a time when masculinity was *not* in crisis is shortsighted, though, given that 1890s men feared the wane of Victorianism (Brod, 1987), 1930s men worried about being good family providers in a challenging economy (Bernard, 1981), 1950s men were concerned about automation (Brod, 1987), and 1940s–1980s men feared being less masculine than they should be (Pleck, 1987). By the 1990s, MacInnes (1998) declared that old masculine privileges had pretty much disappeared.

Our book's chapters open new space for identifying and demystifying how and why some forms of masculinity are prized and idealized while other forms of masculinity are marginalized and/or denounced. Frameworks and categories used for understanding femininity or masculinity must remain flexible if we are to be truly inclusive in our attempts to understand patriarchy and its effects. Like Michael Kimmel, I posit that analyzing patriarchy requires not only interrogating men's power over women, but "some men's power over other men" as a means to learn more about why men resist gender equality and feel like they're "complete losers in the gender game" (Kimmel & Wade, 2018, p. 237). With chapter authors advocating for resistance and social change to traditions and ideals dictating how boys and men *should* live and be, critiques are informed and thought provoking. Confusing perceptions about masculinity among boys and men reflect internal conflict/stress experienced while navigating media-constructed signs and representations (Lotz, 2014; Scharrer & Blackburn, 2018) which become *normalized* in our minds. The way boys and men were raised, how they feel about their own body, and the images they experience in their everyday lives do not always coincide.

What follows is groundwork for this edited collection: 1) What is masculinity? 2) Social change is constant, 3) Theory as a tool, and 4) Societal policing of masculinity.

WHAT IS MASCULINITY?

To explore this question, I take a social constructionist viewpoint, which means that *masculinity* is a human construct. That makes it a variable, slippery concept. For some, masculinity is the male sex role (Kimmel, 1987). For others, being masculine means having "a particular psychological identity, social role, cultural script, place in the labor force" (Stimpson, 1987, p. xi). There are as many masculinities as there are human beings, it seems. Generally, authors in this collection use *gender* when referring to a social construction and *sex* when referring to biology. Masculinity is a dynamic set of processes according to time, culture, norms, values, so like Kimmel (2001) and Connell (2005), I prefer the plural form of *masculinities*. It is a word socially constructed by people, and then embraced (or not)—and, hopefully, contextualized. Male gender roles do not emerge from nature, but are products imprinted by socialization patterns across generations (Zamarripa et al., 2003). Thus, even though masculinity is what a culture expects of men (Craig, 1992), there is significant confusion about what masculinity means, and the stakes can be high for men in public and private spheres who do not (or choose not to) measure up to others' expectations in the form of social standards.

Masculinity has been in the news a lot lately. *Toxic masculinity* characterizes the toll of males blocking their emotions and the outcomes of this behavior. Victims are males themselves and everyone else, too. Boys are pressured to adhere to a rigid boy code and to suppress their anxieties (e.g. Pollack and Shuster, 2000). Men fight and even die to live up to masculinity standards set up for them since childhood. Males are socialized to be stoic, reluctant to seek help, and to develop their own self-management strategies (Oliffe et al., 2012). If males suspect their sense of masculinity is being threatened, they can *man up* in an effort to live up to standards, ideals, and stereotypes—or lash out in anger that can take the form of self-harm or rage inflicted on partners, children, and others. Public health data assessed for "key outcomes or consequences" of harmful masculine stereotypes (the Man Box) and translated in measurable social and economic impact revealed that toxic masculinity costs the U.S. $15.6 billion annually in the form of traffic accidents, suicide, depression, sexual violence, bullying and violence, and binge drinking (Heilman et al., 2019).

The masculinity crisis is real because its rhetorical strategies can be discerned and its effects charted (Robinson, 2000). Specific impacts of male gender stereotypes suggest that the same hackneyed dictates that boys and men must act, look, and appear certain ways—as masculine and muscular, performing certain jobs such as police officer or manager, and being good at math and playing sports—inform stereotypes which continue to limit expectations about males (Ellemers, 2018; Fernandez, 2021). Words traditionally associated with men are aggressive, independent, rough, competitive, dominant, active—while women are emotional, submissive, passive, helpful, kind, gentle (Bhatia & Bhatia, 2021). Such binary oppositions along gender lines form a basis for bias and discrimination, keeping men and women compartmentalized and assigned separate spaces (Pompper, 2014).

Specific expressions of masculinity can become toxic if praised as a form of conflict resolution or when harmful behaviors like misogyny and homophobia negatively impact others (Kimmel, 2017). Masculinity can become toxic when turned inward, too. For example, boys and men are socialized to restrict emotions other than anger and are taught to avoid crying (Gesualdi, 2013) or showing emotion when they are ill—which can inhibit coping responses (Hoyt, 2009). Findings of a study of college men diagnosed with depression in Canada revealed three predominant "faux" masculine identities—the angry man who lashes out, the solitary man who self-isolates, and the risk-reliant man who self-medicates with substances—as depression-related deficits rather than positions of strength (Oliffe et al., 2012). Earlier, Connell (2005) characterized relational ways men connect with hegemonic masculinity, naming the categories of complicit, subordinate, marginalized, and protest masculinities. It seems that merely cataloging forms of harm related to the masculinities concept has not moved us closer to the level of systemic change required to assure positive gender equity and peace.

SOCIAL CHANGE IS CONSTANT

Large-scale entrance of women into the paid labor force in the twentieth century, the result of massive immigration, economic necessity, and new job opportunities in conjunction with World War II, created a climate of social change that continues to impact ways we think about expectations for men and forged new conflicts and stressors among them. Unfortunately, men are more likely to be involved in violence in their life course than women—whether it be suicide, homicide, imprisonment, fatal car crashes, substance abuse, or rage (American Foundation for Suicide Prevention, 2013; Federal Bureau of Investigation, 2010; Bureau of Justice Statistics, 2010; Insurance Institute for Highway Safety, 2013). Perhaps the most distressing outcome of twentieth century changes for men is that the breadwinner role as a basis for male identity (Tolson, 1977) has been destabilized. At the other end of the age continuum, older men's retirement or removal from the occupational breadwinner role negatively impacts their sense of sexual potency (Meadows & Davidson, 2006).

Men of today were not socialized to engage with domestic chores as boys and, generally, their fathers were not expected to perform them either. Hence, the stress of overcoming a learning curve is a reality for men, and the ideal of shared labor at home is a hotly debated issue (Sanbonmatsu, 2004). It became a source of contention during the 2020 COVID-19 pandemic, with research findings suggesting that women (especially mothers) still spent more time on childcare and household chores than their male partners in the United States, Canada, Denmark, Brazil, and Spain (Giurge et al., 2021). In the face of so much change, research findings suggest that men's *place* in U.S. society has not changed to the extent of women's, given that men still occupy the higher status jobs, earning more than women in these jobs—and with women still performing more housework in dual-income households (U.S. Bureau of Labor of Statistics, 2018). With so many women also working outside the home, the need for sharing domestic chores has increased for all adults at home (Sherman, 2009), particularly when children are involved. So, it seems that men are needed to play a greater role around the house, but they resist engaging with private sphere work traditionally associated with women.

Articulating inner emotional experiences is new territory for many men socialized to rely primarily on silence, anger, or grandiosity (acting the fool) (Dvorkin, 2015) and this dynamic has fueled media stereotyping of men. While media narratives about men appearing vulnerable due to being misunderstood or ineffective—in the kitchen, for example—has sustained comedic and dramatic television programming plotlines for several decades (Lotz, 2014; Scharrer and Blackburn, 2018), the sobering reality is that contemporary relational complexity requires greater emotional reflexivity from men (Holmes, 2015). These dynamics add new stressors to men's lives because they are socialized to *not* show emotion (e.g., Dvorkin, 2015).

To help men cope or feel better about such conflicts and stresses in their lives, consumer goods serve as stand-ins, defining and reinforcing what is masculine (Barthel, 1992). In recent decades, consumer package goods once reserved for women now are marketed to men in the form of body care products and services. The *spornosexual* characterizes (Simpson, 2014) "a new, more extreme, sex- and body-obsessed version" of a single man who contributes to industries like soap and body services which have increased 4.5 percent annually each of the past 20 years (Bano & Sharif, 2015). Paradoxically, what appears on the surface as pampering or a reward actually fuels insecurities that men are not good enough the way they are (Jhally, 1990). While people's beliefs, attitudes, and perceptions about gender roles and ways men and women should look and act are continually changing, society's ideas about males and masculinity are proving exceptionally resistant to change when males are expected to be tough and unemotional (Bhatia & Bhatia, 2021), or *not feminine*.

THEORY AS A TOOL

To help researchers understand and predict social change, we rely on theory building. Theory lenses from psychology, communication, and more, are integrated in this book. In psychology, Sandra Bem (1974) introduced a psychometric construct offering researchers benchmarks for assessing gender qualities—the Bem Sex Role Inventory (BSRI) measure—which has become the most frequently tested gender role instrument. Yet, to accommodate for regionality/culture (Endut et al., 2020) and other contexts, social construction theory (Berger & Luckmann, 1966) adds greater nuance as underpinning for social research. Vance (1989) persuasively argued that the history of sexuality has been greatly enriched by adding social constructionism to the field of sexuality, as it accommodates contexts of social movements like feminism and lesbian/gay liberation, labor market changes with economic restructuring and globalization, and technological innovation. Thus, I've always considered the communication and psychology fields as allied in theorizing about interpersonal, organizational, and mediated phenomena. Specifically, psychology research informs our study of ways gender plays out in and is represented by media.

Social constructionism provides the theoretical backbone for this book's attention to masculinity as a communication phenomenon that interplays with male GRC/S. Studying ways producers of media and other communicators seek to inform, persuade, or motivate people to think or behave with regard to normative masculinity ideals or in resistance to them can involve examining symbols and other representations to discern ways people make meaning. Who we are as human beings and how and why we relate to others is shaped by where we come from, how we live now, and how we shape all within our sphere of influence. Because scrutinizing language usage and thought processes are activities central to rhetorical criticism, communication media offer many clues for interrogating questions about influence and power. This means examining who constructs reality (especially from a standpoint of privilege) and why some particular constructions of reality gain traction in comparison to others.

For me, O'Neil's (1981a, 1981b, 2008) gender role conflict/stress (GRC/S) theory has proved exceptionally useful in understanding gendered concepts of femininity and masculinity. He developed theory to identify areas of stress in masculine behavior, cognitions, affective behavior, and the unconscious. Gender role conflict is "a psychological state in which gender roles (masculine, feminine, or androgynous roles) have negative consequences or impacts" on people (O' Neil, 1981b, p. 203) and can play out in limiting a person's ability to ascertain their or others' highest human potential. Male GRC/S theory includes attention to specific patterns (O'Neil, 2008): Success/Power/Competition (SPC), Restrictive Emotionality (RE), Restrictive Affectionate Behavior Between Men (RABBM), and Conflict Between Work and Family Relations (CBWFR). Perceptions of threats to masculinity among males who hold traditional gender ideologies can cause conflict and stress as they attempt to distance themselves from femininity (Chaffee et al., 2020) and homosexuality (Kimmel, 1987). Specifically, when boys and men internalize traditional ideals about what it means to be masculine—valuing toughness and rigid expectations for a gender role as father, breadwinner, protector—these dynamics may result in GRC/S when males strive to achieve such ideals or fail to achieve them.

Masculinity-threatened men enact specific behaviors to protect their manhood. Threats to masculinity often lead males to avoid feminine-typed domains such as childrearing, playing with dolls, learning a new language, cleaning, and cooking. Masculinity is *not* being feminine; a benchmark used to gauge degrees of masculinity (Connell, 2005; Kimmel, 2004) and a compulsion to avoid associations with homosexuality (O'Neil et al., 1986). Gender roles, when understood as a binary dualism (masculine/feminine), foments oppression that can manifest in male GRC/S (Pompper, 2010). As a therapist working with men experiencing depression, Dvorkin (2015) developed new techniques for enabling her male patients to express themselves.

Males' GRC/S can manifest in exaggerated, extreme masculine behavior (Cohn, Seibert, and Zeichner, 2009) as a defense against unconscious feminine identification (Cheryan et al., 2015). Male GRC/S and masculinities research has had a corollary benefit of helping to expand understanding of issues that greatly affect women—as male GRC/S effects can play out in domestic abuse, gendered salary disparity, and the organizational glass ceiling phenomenon. Understanding how the masculinity construct shapes men's negative attitudes about gender equality (Endut et al., 2020) will promote a drive toward gender justice, benefitting everyone.

Moreover, this book's attention to masculinity and male GRC/S underscores an approach and concept known as *intersectionality*, which contextualizes and acknowledges each person's social identity dimensions (e.g., age, culture, ethnicity, gender, race, religion/faith, sexual orientation) as integrated. The intersectionality approach means embracing multidimensionality of people's lived experiences. Researchers who embrace multiple social identity dimensions as constituting an individual posit that *each dimension is not some layer that is piled or added on*. This salient point has key implications for examining uneven power distribution in a society which firmly entrenches some people at the center and others in the margin (hooks, 2015). Consequently, using the intersectionality approach means extending respect to voices of people who live in society's margins (Crenshaw, 1989). I use the phrase *social identity dimensions* rather than just *identities* to emphasize the reality that no two boys or men are the same—even if they share the same age, ethnicity, gender, or sexual orientation, for example. Each facet or dimension of a male's social identity is unquantifiable and uniquely his, as it is intertwined with other dimensions. Often, males' social identity dimensions are intangible.

SOCIETAL POLICING OF MASCULINITY

Hegemonic masculinity is a cultural form of idealized manhood dominant over gay men, women, children, and the elderly that men use to compare themselves and to check one another (Connell, 2005) against behaviors considered un-masculine (Messerschmidt, 2010; Wellman et al., 2021). Idealized masculine identities are communicated to children at an early age, with boys learning about aggression from story books (Pompper & Merskin, 2020), action figures (Hart & Tannock, 2013), and video games (Anderson & Dill, 2000). Masculine ideals may be neither entirely good nor bad for males' health (Sloan et al., 2009) and boys learn early to suppress their emotions, be tough, and avoid the negative *mama's boy*, *sissy*, *pussy* tags, or others linked to sexuality such as *don't be a fag*. The *boys will be boys* trope describing boys' "alleged natural inclination" to be "rougher, more physical, and prone to higher rates of aggression and violence than what is thought to be true of girls" becomes a self-fulfilling prophesy (Keith, 2017, p. 71). Or, as Levant (1997) explained, some men respond to their sense of collapsing traditional masculinity very defensively with aggression. Indeed, messages to avoid emasculation, humiliation, and effeminacy (Kimmel, 2013) are communicated early and often throughout men's life course. Herein is rooted males' dread of abandonment which leaves them ill prepared to nurture themselves or others (Wright, 1994) and sometimes inhibits experiencing peace and comfort in their religious affiliation (Yoo, 2020). Socialized fear of appearing weak or powerless often is greater than any natural impulse to display emotions in the form of tears or desire to seek medical help for depression (Courtenay, 2004) since weakness is perceived as a female affliction (Riska, 2009).

Eminent masculinities scholar and activist Michael Kimmel has suggested that greater theorizing is needed to better understand patriarchy by "decenter[ing] the center" and making "straight, white, middle-class, able-bodied, cisgender men" more visible by naming them, their experiences, and effects of those experiences (Kimmel and Wade, 2018, p. 235). Inspired early in his career by women's studies and gender studies, he encourages researchers to interrogate masculinities' intersection with racism and backlash politics to explore why white men, as "arguably the most privileged people on the planet," do not feel powerful and are "so pissed off" (Kimmel & Wade, 2018, p. 236), or angry (Kimmel, 2013). In extremes, hypermasculinity involves exaggerated musculature that exposes rather than allays anxiety about masculinity (MacKinnon, 2003). Masculinity's intersection with sexual violence against women has increased in recent years as it relates to certain age and ethnic groups pressured to display their masculinity, such as among Latino youths (Haglund et al., 2019).

Other researchers have focused the masculinities lens on specific employment rankings and occupational fields, which are coded as being particularly masculine and featuring extreme constraint in expressing emotions. Conflict and stress is inherent in military service conditions, for example. So, psychological damage and fallout is more common among servicemen than the general population, but military toughness, stoicism, emotional control, and invulnerability makes men reluctant to seek psychological assistance (McAllister et al., 2019). In business, the chief executive officer (usually male) is expected to lead and generate profit. An advance in corporate social responsibility thinking, however, has included embracing humility as a valued quality for leaders who are virtuous and magnanimous (Petrenko et al.,

2017), by promoting a strong sense of professional will that is not attached to personal success (Collins, 2001), that can lead to empowerment and collaboration among management teams (Ou et al., 2014), and can serve as a model for participative leadership (Aime et al., 2014). Alternately, even in fields considered to be highly feminized like the floral trade, men are expected to be especially professionally competent florists (Zinn, 2019). So, it seems that some jobs have conflict and masculinity stressors inherently built in, making them even more challenging for men.

HOW THIS BOOK IS ORGANIZED

The book is organized according to fifteen chapters that cover several interrelated contexts for facilitating understanding of masculinities and how we make meaning about it—in terms of body image, media, and the gender role conflict/stress that may result.

Authors of five chapters in Unit I Masculinities in Nature or Nurture, consider masculinity as a social construct and the various contexts where it is shaped, ranging from social media sites on YouTube, through public discourse involving male public figures accused of sexual misconduct in the time of the #MeToo movement, in a Netflix animated series featuring characters of diverse sexualities, via strategic selection of male bodies for advertising products and services, and among a stigmatized community public work employment sector. Authors invoke a variety of research methods and techniques to examine male GRC/S around the world.

In chapter 1: Taking the Natural Red Pill: Conflicting Gender Roles through Nature and Antiquity in the Manosphere, Marcia Allison and Jesper Greve Kristensen perform a textual analysis of Roosh Valizadeh's (2015) *What is Neomasculinity* manifesto as a central manosphere doctrine which shows how this evolutionary ecological antiquity causes the manosphere male to experience gender conflict whenever encountering contemporary feminism that expresses non-classical and ruptured patriarchal gender norms. Their essay helps readers to examine ways misogyny undergirded the construction of masculinity online in 2020.

Whereas chapter 1's authors argue that male supremacy escalated in 2020 in the West, Robert Mundy's chapter 2: Case Studies of Male Rhetorical Mediation of Sexual Violence and Gender Role Stress/Conflict in the #MeToo Era, offers four case studies of ways male public figures—Brett Kavanaugh, James Franco, Aziz Ansari, and Louis C. K.—rhetorically pushed back against #MeToo movement effects, using a technique he calls *the comeback*. It is a strategy for reasserting hegemonic masculine authority in order to regain social standing by addressing the GRC/S experienced in the wake of being accused of sexual misconduct by women.

In chapter 3: When Nothing Changes into Something: Gender Role Stress/ Conflict Among Asexual Viewers of *BoJack Horseman*, ben Brandley and Katherine Mullé argue that despite more LGBTQIA+ representation on television, asexual (or ace) folks' identities and experiences remain under-examined. Undergirded by GRC/S theory, their critical thematic analysis of extant discussions about a *BoJack Horseman* character, Todd Chavez, offers findings on the interplay of GRC/S and masculine asexuality. They include future directions to address the unfortunate lack of attention to asexuality among mass media representations.

Next, Juan Mundel and Maria DeMoya share chapter 4: Pulling Back the Curtain on Advertisers' Perceptions of Male Images in U.S. Ads to rhetori-cally examine what happens behind the scenes when advertising executives select mediated images of men and how these processes, in turn, influence perceptions of how men should look and act. Based on interviews with advertising workers and their understandings of the masculinity construct as explained by GRC/S, these researchers discovered that men's appearance and men's character traits serve as themes in decision-making processes and conclude by advocating for greater diversity in male representations.

Akira Sai and Taro Yamauchi conclude the Unit 1 section with chapter 5: Dirty Work Masculinity and Coping Strategies among Garbage Collectors. While physical and mental toughness in a breadwinning context are well-regarded virtues among masculine men, social stigma attached to certain jobs—like collecting garbage—may reach abusive levels and workers may develop GRC/S. Their essay concludes by introducing the concept of *dirty work masculinity* as a stigma-coping, identity-enhancing, and conflict/stress-reducing strategy for better understanding the lived experiences of men who work in public health and sanitation jobs and may struggle to construct a satisfying masculine identity.

Unit II Masculinity and Social Identity Intersectionalities thematically binds the work of four chapters which explore ways the masculinity con-cept cuts across gender, sexuality, and geography social identity dimensions and interplays with GRC/S in contexts of athletics in the East, reality TV storylines involving military veterans in Britain, politically when a hyper-masculine Prime Minister was removed from office by Pakistan's Supreme Court and then bombarded with uncomplimentary memes/videos, and tweets among global Latinx audiences engaging with the video of a Grammy-winning reggaetón rapper, singer, and songwriter who creates and disaggre-gates machismo conflict.

In chapter 6: Exploring Masculinities in Ancient and Up-and-Coming Sports in South East Asia, Mark Brooke uses a mixed method research design to explore the masculinity concept in the context of South East Asia's ancient sport of wushu and other forms of athleticism for males. Using methods of content analysis, survey, and focus group, he expands upon male GRC/S theory building in the service of dismantling toxic hegemonic masculinity, as his findings suggest that masculinity in South East Asia offers a significant departure from ways masculinity is perceived in the West.

Next, Jenna Pitchford-Hyde's chapter 7: Masculinity, Identity, and Disabled Veterans: How British Audiences Respond to Representations of Military Veterans on Prime Time BBC Programmes, blends GRC/S theory with restricted emotionality and key perspectives in disability and media studies. She analyzes tweets about two BBC reality TV programs to discover that constructed narratives about disabled veterans' masculinised military identity feature men able to overcome their injuries and reclaim able-bodiedness—which adheres to an expected norm and can contribute greatly to GRC/S.

In chapter 8: Nawaz Sharif: The Rise and Fall of a Pakistani *Sher* (Big Cat), Sakina Jangbar analyzes Sharif's political imagery and the tweetstorm that followed his tearful exit as these elements took shape in memes and videos that thematically define masculinity in Pakistan in terms of cognitive dysfunction, feminization, and homophobia. She offers a rupture in the traditional view of masculinity and calls for a GRC/S model that presents a more nuanced picture of fears at the heart of masculinity.

Finally in Unit II, Nathian Shae Rodriguez offers chapter 9: The Machismo Conflict of Bad Bunny's *Yo Perreo Sola* in Reggaetón to expand ways of thinking about GRC/S theory by offering a textual analysis of a Latinx pop culture music video that runs counter hegemonic to cultural-gendered archetypes. Twitter reactions to Grammy-winning Bad Bunny provides context for exploring intersections of culture, gender, sexuality, and masculinities.

Unit III Masculinity and Emotionality features five chapters which explore ways the masculinity concept and GRC/S interplay across media forms by testing representations impacting perceptions about abused men, heteromasculine-emotionality as pathway for avoiding toxic masculinity contributors of restrictive emotionality (RE) and restrictive affectionate behavior between men (RABBM), expectancy violations of NFL athletes and their physical and emotional pain, a gender divide in face mask wearing behaviors during a pandemic, and rhetoric of YouTube influencers mentoring males through GRC/S. These authors rely on research methods of experiment, case study, critical discourse analysis, and rhetorical framing analysis.

In chapter 10: "Bitch-Ass Pussy!": Perceptions of Abused Men Predicted by Media, Educational, and Experiential Topic Exposure, Jessica J. Eckstein and Jessica Cherry explore GRC/S experienced by men abused by female romantic partners and variables influencing societal perceptions of abused men. They conclude that there are very few outlets currently portraying abused men in realistic, supportive, or otherwise positive ways.

In chapter 11: It's Not Unusual, or Is It? Tom Jones' Unique Blend of Heteromasculine Emotionality, I use erotic capital theory and male GRC/S theory to examine the career of global pop singer Tom Jones' unique blend of emotionality and heterosexuality that inspired female fans to throw their panties onstage as he performed across music genres. For nearly six decades, he has ruptured the heteromasculine ideal by showing emotions such as crying in public, which I suggest could affect positive social change enabling boys and men to express a wider range of emotions beyond just anger.

Similarly, Anthony V. LaStrape and Ann E. Burnette's chapter 12: Retire *Like a Man*: Peyton Manning, Andrew Luck, and Competing Masculinities examines careers of NFL superstars on the event of their retirement as each referred to physical and emotional pain associated with football quarterback work. They discovered that athletes who adhere to hegemonic masculinity norms are rewarded for silence about pain, injury, and hiding their emotions —while those who violate masculinity norms become targets for masculinity policing.

In chapter 13: A Critical Exploration of Pandemic Protection as a Threat to Masculinity: Facemask Usage and Gender, James Carviou and Jennifer A. Jackson were inspired by news reports of a gender divide in intention to wear a face mask to help prevent COVID-19 transmission. They examined a year's worth of tweets to discover how hegemonic masculinity shaped by a set of male opinion leaders' political ideologies may have played out during the pandemic.

Then in chapter 14: New Media Masculinities: How YouTube Influencers Incubate Masculine Ideologies and Mentor Males Through Gender Role Conflict/Stress, Gabriel Parks, Daniel Russo, and Jenni Simon use a male GRC/S lens to examine the ways three YouTube opinion-and-lifestyle influencers popular with large adolescent male audiences frame masculinity ideals and offer advice designed to support male gender identity development in the twenty-first century. Results suggest that each influencer's characterization of masculinity's problems offers a competing window on qualitatively examining perceptions of GRC/S inflicted upon or experienced by men.

Then, I offer a final chapter 15 to summarize recommendations for advancing GRC/S theory and offer suggestions for new research about the masculinities concept.

We hope you find this collection useful. Let me know if you'd like to collaborate on any future research projects by contacting me at pompper@uoregon.edu.

REFERENCES

Aime, F., Humphrey, S., DeRue, D. S., & Paul, J. B. (2014). The riddle of heterarchy: Power transitions in crossfunctional teams. *Academy of Management Journal*, 57(2), 327–352. doi: https://psycnet.apa.org/doi/10.5465/amj.2011.0756.

American Foundation for Suicide Prevention. (2013). *Facts and figures*. Downloaded June 25, 2021 from https://afsp.org/suicide-statistics/.

Anderson, C. A., & Dill, K. E. (2000). Video games and aggressive thoughts, feelings, and behavior in the laboratory and in life. *Journal of Personality and Social Psychology*, 78(4), 772–790. doi: 10.1037//O022-3514.78.4.772

Bano, S., & Sharif, M. A. M. (2015). Metrosexual: Emerging and lucrative segment for marketers. *International Review of Management and Marketing*, 6(4), p. 117. doi: http://www.econjournals.com/.

Barthel, D. (1992). When men put on appearances: Advertising and the social construction of masculinity. In S. Craig (Ed.), *Men, masculinity, and the media* (pp. 137–153). Sage.

Bem, S. L. (1974). The measurement of psychological androgyny. *Journal of Consulting and Clinical Psychology*, 42, 155–162. doi: https://psycnet.apa.org/doi/10.1037/h0036215.

Bernard, J. (1981). The good-provider role: Its rise and fall. *American Psychologist*, 36(1), 1–12. doi: https://psycnet.apa.org/doi/10.1037/0003-066X.36.1.1.

Berger, P. L., & Luckmann, T. (1966). *The social construction of reality*. Anchor Books Doubleday.

Bhatia, N., & Bhatia, S. (2021). Changes in gender stereotypes over time: A computational analysis. *Psychology of Women Quarterly*, 45(1), 106–125. doi: https://doi.org/10.1177/0361684320977178.

Brod, H. (1987). Introduction: Themes and theses of men's studies. In H. Brod (Ed.), *The making of masculinities: The new men's studies* (pp. 1–17). Allen & Unwin.

Bureau of Justice Statistics. (2010). *Correctional populations in the United States, 2010*. Downloaded June 25, 2021, from http://www.bjs.gov/content/pub/pdf/cpus10.pdf

Chaffee, K. E., Lou, N. M., Noels, K. A., & Katz, J. W. Why don't 'real men' learn languages? Masculinity threat and gender ideology suppress men's language learning motivation. *Group Processes & Intergroup Relations*, 23(2), 301–318. doi: https://journals.sagepub.com/home/gpi.

Cheryan, S., Cameron, J. S., Katagiri, Z., & Monin, B. (2015). Manning up: Threatened men compensate by disavowing feminine preferences and embracing masculine attributes. *Social Psychology*, 46, 218–227. doi:10.1027/1864-9335/a000239.

Cohn, A., Seibert, L. A., & Zeichner, A. (2009). The role of restrictive emotionality, trait anger, and masculinity threat in men's perpetration of physical aggression. *Psychology of Men and Masculinity*, 10, 218–224. doi:10.1037/a0015151.

Collins, J. C. (2001). Level 5 leadership: The triumph of humility and fierce resolve. *Harvard Business Review*, 79, 65–76.

Connell, R. W. (2005). *Masculinities* (2nd ed.). University of California Press.

Courtenay, W. (2004) Best practices for improving college men's health. *New Directions for Student Services*, 107, 59–74. doi: https://doi.org/10.1002/ss.133.

Craig, S. (1992). Introduction: Considering men and the media. In S. Craig (Ed.), *Men, masculinity, and the media* (pp. 1–7). Sage.

Crenshaw, K. W. (1989). Demarginalizing the intersection of race and sex: A Black feminist critique of antidiscrimination doctrine, feminist theory and antiracist politics. *University of Chicago Legal Forum 1989*, 139–167. doi: https://chicago unbound.uchicago.edu/uclf/vol1989/iss1/8.

Dvorkin, K. (2015). Working with men in therapy. *Group*, 39(3), 241–250. https://doi.org/10.13186/group.39.3.0241.

Ellemers, N. (2018). Gender stereotypes. *Annual Review of Psychology*, 69(1), 275–298.https://doi.org/10.1146/annurev-psych-122216-011719.

Endut, N., Bagheri, R., Azman, A., Hashim, I. H. M., Selamat, N. H., & Mohajer, L. (2020). The effect of gender role on attitudes towards inequitable gender norms among Malaysian men. *Sexuality & Culture*, 24, 2113–2136. doi: https://doi .org/10.1007/s12119-020-09740-6.

Federal Bureau of Investigation. (2010). *Expanded homicide data*. Downloaded June 25, 2021 from https:// www.fbi.gov/about-us/cjis/ucr/crime-in-the-u.s/2010/crime -in-the-u.s.-2010/offenses-known-to-law-enforcement/expanded/expandhomicide main .

Fernandez, I. (2021, March 24). What are gender roles? Downloaded June 27, 2021, from https://rb.gy/rh0uww.

Gesualdi, M. (2013). Man tears and masculinities: News coverage of John Boehner's tearful episodes. *Journal of Communication Inquiry*, 37(4), 304–321. doi: https://doi.org/10.1177/0196859913505617.

Giurge, L. M., Whillans, A. V., & Yemiscigil, A. (2021). A multicountry perspective on gender differences in time use during COVID-19. *PNAS Proceedings of the National Academy of Sciences of the United States of America*, 118 (12), 1–19. doi: https://doi.org/10.1073/pnas.2018494118.

Haglund, K., Belknap, R. A., Edwards, L. M., Tassara, M., Van Hoven, J., and Woda, A. (2019). The influence of masculinity on male Latino adolescents' perceptions regarding dating relationships and dating violence. *Violence Against Women*, 25(9), 1039–1052. doi: 10.1177/1077801218808395.

Hart, J. L., & Tannock, M. T. (2013). Young children's play fighting and use of war toys. *Encyclopedia of Early Childhood Development*, pp. 1–5, https://rb.gy/5x2agp.

Heilman, B., Guerrero-López, C. M., Ragonese, C., Kelberg, M., & Barker, G. (2019). The Cost of the Man Box: A study on the economic impacts of harmful masculine stereotypes in the United States. Washington, DC, and London: Promundo-US and Unilever.

hooks, b. (2015). *Ain't I a woman: Black women and feminism*. Routledge.

Hoyt, M. A. (2009). Gender role conflict and emotional approach coping in men with cancer. *Psychology and Health*, 24(8), 981–996.

Insurance Institute for Highway Safety. (2013). *Fatality facts, 2013*. Downloaded June 25, 2021, from http://www. iihs.org/iihs/topics/t/alcohol-impaired-driving/ fatalityfacts/alcohol-impaired-driving.

Jhally, S. (1990). *The codes of advertising: Fetishism and the political economy of meaning in the consumer society.* Routledge.

Keith, T. (2017). *Masculinities in contemporary American culture: An intersectional approach to the complexities and challenges of male identity.* Routledge.

Kimmel, M. S. (1987). The contemporary "crisis" of masculinity in historical perspective. In H. Brod (Ed.), *The making of masculinities: The new men's studies* (pp. 121–153). Allen & Unwin.

———. (2001). Global masculinities: Restoration and resistance. In B. Pease & K. Pringle (Eds.), *A man's world: Changing men's practices in a globalized world* (pp. 21–37). Zed Books.

———. (2004). Masculinity as homophobia: Fear, shame, and silence in the construction of gender identity. P. F. Murphy (Ed.), *Feminism & Masculinities* (pp. 182–199). Oxford University Press.

Kimmel, M. (2013). *Angry white men: American masculinity at the end of an era.* Nation Books.

Kimmel, M. S. (2017). *American masculinity at the end of an era: Angry white men.* Nation Books.

Kimmel, M. S., & Wade, L. (2018). Ask a feminist: Michael Kimmel and Lisa Wade discuss toxic masculinity. *Signs: Journal of Women in Culture and Society*, 44(1), 233–254. doi: https://doi.org/10.1086/698284.

Levant, R. F. (1997). The masculinity crisis. *The Journal of Men's Studies*, 5(3), 221–231. doi: https://doi.org/10.1177%2F106082659700500302.

Lotz, A. D. (2014). *Cable guys: Television and masculinities in the 21st century.* New York University Press.

MacInnes, J. (1998). *The end of masculinity.* Open University Press.

MacKinnon, K. (2003). *Representing men: Maleness and masculinity in the media.* Oxford University Press Inc.

McAllister, L., Callaghan, J. E. M., & Fellin, L. C. (2019). Masculinities and emotional expression in UK servicemen: Big boys don't cry? *Journal of Gender Studies*, 28(3), 257–270.

Meadows, R., & Davidson, K. (2006). Maintaining manliness in later life: Hegemonic masculinities and emphasized femininities. In T. M. Calasanti and K. F. Slevin (Eds.), *Age matters: Realigning feminist thinking* (pp. 295–312). Routledge.

Messerschmidt, J. W. (2010). *Hegemonic masculinities and camouflaged politics: Unmasking the Bush dynasty and its war against Iraq.* Paradigm.

Oliffe, J. L., Galdas, P. M., Han, C. S. E., & Kelly, M. T. (2012). Faux masculinities among college men who experience depression. *Health*, 17(1), 75–92. doi: https://doi.org/10.1177%2F1363459312447256.

O'Neil, J. M. (1981a). Male sex-role conflict, sexism, and masculinity: Implications for men, women, and the counseling psychologist. *Counseling Psychologist, 9,* 61–80. doi: https://doi.org/10.1177%2F001100008100900213.

———. (1981b). Patterns of gender role conflict and strain: Sexism and fear of femininity in men's lives. *Personnel and Guidance Journal, 60,* 203–210. doi: 10.1002/j.2164-4918.1981.tb00282.x.

————. (2008). Summarizing 25 years of research on men's gender role conflict using the Gender Role Conflict Scale: New research paradigms and clinical implications. *Counseling Psychologist, 36,* 358–445. doi: https://doi.org/10.1177/0011000008317057.

O'Neil, J. M., Good, G. E., & Holmes, S. (1995). Fifteen years of theory and research on men's gender role conflict: New paradigms for empirical research. In R. Levant & W. Pollack (Eds.), *The new psychology of men* (pp. 164–206). Basic Books.

O'Neil, J. M., Helms, B. J., Gable, R. K., David, L., & Wrightsman, L. S. (1986). Gender-role conflict scale: College men's fear of femininity. *Sex Roles, 14,* 335–350. doi: https://psycnet.apa.org/doi/10.1007/BF00287583.

Ou, A. Y., Tsui, A. S., Kinicki, A. J., Waldman, D. A., Xiao, Z., & Song, L. J. (2014). Humble chief executive officers' connections to top management team integration and middle managers' responses. *Administrative Science Quarterly, 59*(1), 34–72. doi: https://doi.org/10.1177%2F0001839213520131.

Petrenko, O. V., Aime, F., Recendes, T., & Chandler, J. A. (2017). The case for humbling expectations: CEO humility and market performance. *Strategic Management Journal, 40,* 1938–1964. doi: 10.1002/smj.3071.

Pleck, J. H. (1987). The theory of male sex-role identity: Its rise and fall, 1936 to the present. In H. Brod (Ed.), *The making of masculinities: The new men's studies* (pp. 23–38). Allen & Unwin.

Pollack, W. S., & Shuster, T. (2000). *Real boys' voices.* Random House.

Pompper, D. (2010). Masculinities, the metrosexual, and media images: across dimensions of age and ethnicity. *Sex Roles, 63,* 682–696. doi: https://doi.org/10.1007/s11199-010-9870-7.

————. (2014). *Practical and theoretical implications of successfully doing difference in organizations.* Emerald Group Publishing Limited.

————. (2017). *Rhetoric of femininity: Female body image, media, and gender role stress/conflict.* Lexington Books.

Pompper, D., & Merskin, D. (2020). The more things change? Social identity representations among "The 50 Best Kids' Books Published in the Last 25 Years." *Journal of Popular Culture, 53*(5), 1135–1159. doi: https://doi.org/10.1111/jpcu.12959.

Riska. E, (2009). Men's mental health. In A. Broom and P. Tovey (Eds.) *Men's health: Body, identity, and social context* (pp. 145–162). Wiley-Blackwell.

Robinson, S. (2000). *Marked men: White masculinity in crisis.* Columbia University Press.

Sanbonmatsu, K. (2004). *Democrats/Republicans and the politics of women's place.* University of Michigan Press.

Scharrer, E., & Blackburn, G. (2018). Cultivating conceptions of masculinity: Television and perceptions of masculine gender role norms. *Mass Communication and Society, 21*(2), 149–177. doi: https://doi.org/10.1080/15205436.2017.1406118.

Sherman, J. (2009). Bend to avoid breaking: Job loss, gender norms, and family stability in rural America. *Social Problems, 56*(4), 599–620. doi: https://doi.org/10.1525/sp.2009.56.4.599.

Simpson, M. (2014, June 11). Spornosexual is the new metrosexual. The Telegraph. Downloaded June 7, 2021, from https://rb.gy/rjktdy.

Stimpson, C. R. (1987). Forward. In H. Brod (Ed.), *The making of masculinities: The new men's studies* (pp. xi–xiii). Allen & Unwin.

Sloan, C., Gough, B., and Connor, M. (2009). Healthy masculinities/ How ostensibly healthy men talk about lifestyle, health and gender. *Psychology and Health*, 25(7), 783–803. doi: https://doi.org/10.1080/08870440902883204.

Tolson, A. (1977). *The limits of masculinity*. Routledge.

U.S. Department of Labor Statistics (2018). Women of working age. http://www.dol.gov/wb/stats/NEWSTATS/latest/demographics.htm#LF-SecRAceEthnicity.

Vance, C. S. (1989). Social construction theory: Problems in the history of sexuality. In A. van kooten nierkerk and T. Van Der Meer (Eds.), *Homosexuality, which homosexuality?* (pp. 13–34). An Dekker.

Wellman, J. D., Beam, A. J., Wilkins, C. L., Newell, E. E., & Mendez, C. A. (2021). Masculinity threat increases bias and negative emotions toward feminine gay men. *Psychology of Men & Masculinities*, advance online publication, doi: https://psycnet.apa.org/doi/10.1037/men0000349.

Wright, F. (1994). Men, shame, and group psychotherapy. *GROUP*, 18(4), 212–224. doi: https://psycnet.apa.org/doi/10.1007/BF01458098.

Yoo, W. (2020). Constructing soft masculinity: Christian conversion and gendered experience among young Chinese Christian men in Beijing. *Chinese Sociological Review*, 52(5), 539–561. doi: https://doi.org/10.1080/21620555.2020.1799347.

Zamarripa, M. X., Wampold, B. E., and Gregory, E. (2003). Male gender role conflict, depression, and anxiety: Clarification and generalizability to women. *Journal of Counseling Psychology*, 50(3), 333–338. doi: https://psycnet.apa.org/doi/10.1037/0022-0167.50.3.333.

Zinn, I. (2018). The truly creative florists: When creativity becomes a gendered privilege. *Journal of Contemporary Ethnography*, 48(3), 429–447. doi: https://journals.sagepub.com/home/jce.

Unit I

MASCULINITIES IN NATURE
OR NURTURE

Chapter One

Taking the Natural Red Pill

Conflicting Gender Roles through Nature and Antiquity in the Manosphere

Marcia Allison and Jesper Greve Kristensen

INTRODUCTION

The January 6, 2021 U.S. capitol riot was a global iconic media event (Sonnevend, 2016) that shook the world and brought doubt to the supposed infallibility of U.S. democracy. As the proliferation of images and videos from rioters, journalists, and onlookers become historical artifacts to this event, they also have come to symbolize the larger Western partisan political crisis of the so-called "culture wars." One striking visual that was shared across the media to capture the spirit of the event showed several rioters posing in the Capitol hallways in which the self-titled Q Shaman, Jake Angeli, stands prominently. Wearing a hybrid Viking-Native American hunting hat, a bare chest adorned with tattoos of Viking symbols, red-white-and-blue face paint, and an American flag hanging from a spear behind his back, Angeli's culturally appropriative aesthetic played upon multiple twenty-first century tropes of Western masculinity and U.S. patriotism. But these are not simply generic tropes of a Western masculine performativity. Rather, they represent a specific category of maleness related to the far-right fringe movement QAnon. Here, this notorious 8kun-chat board of unproven conspiracies pits itself against a supposed left-wing "deep-state cabal" of human traffickers, pedophiles, and general woke culture that promotes gender, racial, and other such equalities (Papasavva, 2020; Zuckerman, 2019). As a visual argument, Angeli's gendered performance thus serves as an embodied dogwhistle (Safire, 2008) to the intersectional role of ideology, gender, and online activism that has come to dominate Anglosphere politics.

In this chapter, we argue that this multi-layered and multimodal performance by Angeli represents the contemporary partisan divisions monopolizing current Western society. Although QAnon's conspiracy-driven narratives are continuously debunked, this fringe faction represents the deeper ideological conflict of the alt-right (Schmitz & Kazyak, 2016): a mostly online, far-right white nationalist movement founded in the U.S. Evans (2016) divided the alt-right into four factions: the natural conservatives drawn to the ideals of law, order, and hierarchy; the neo-Nazis; the "meme gang;" and finally, the intellectual manosphere (Farrell et al., 2019), which is the focus of this chapter. A conceptual blend (Fauconnier & Turner, 2003) coined by pornographer Ian Ironwood in the late 2000s (Nagle, 2017), this metonym refers to a nebulous, loosely connected set of alt- and far-right viewpoints shared through blogs, forums, and other social media channels. In particular, as argued by Zuckerberg's (2019) *Not All Dead White Men*, this amorphous network of disenfranchised men lamenting the supposed decline of traditional Western masculinity uses the ideas of Stoicism as the birthplace of democracy, free speech, and a logic that in classical antiquity was considered an inherently masculine trait. As significant manosphere proponent Roosh Valizadeh (2015) argues, logic is a treasured yet lost art due to the decline of inherently masculine, and thus superior, traits by the influx of feminism and other "woke" movements (Sharpe, 2018; Zuckerberg, 2019).

In this interdisciplinary study, we examine this rhetoric of a natural Sophist masculinity in the manosphere through the theoretical lens of the linguistic construction of reality combined with the humanistic methods of cultural criticism and textual analysis. This chapter consists of three main sections: 1) The red pill reality of natural masculinity, 2) An evolutionary rhetoric of ecological antiquity, and 3) A natural neomasculinity. First, we explore how sex and gender is linguistically constructed through binary opposition and the role this has played in the construction in the manosphere. Second, we posit that the manosphere bases its masculinity on an evolutionary rhetoric of *ecological antiquity* founded on narrow conceptions of what is biologically and socially "natural." We extend Zuckerberg's argument to account for this manosphere's rhetoric that proposes that society should return to its ancient—a metaphorical stand-in for "natural"—roots for an evolutionary, *ecological* antiquity. Here, men are the logical leaders of a deliberative democracy, women inhabit the role of Mother Earth, and humans should look to their evolutionary animalistic origins regarding gender roles. The manosphere male thus experiences a gender conflict when encountering feminism and other expressions of "non-traditional" gender norms that neither reflect sexed-based mammalian behaviors nor the patriarchal, hierarchical, and slavery-based birth of Western democracy. Third, we resolve that the manosphere creates a rhetoric of masculinity based upon a biological evolutionary logics combined with notions from classical antiquity as the birth of modern democracy.

Our argument is rooted in the first section with a case study to show how the language of nature, evolutionary origins, and gender intersect in the key document for the manosphere: former Pick Up Artist (PUA) Valizadeh's (2015) neomasculine doctrine, "What is Neomasculinity" manifesto. We therefore perform a textual analysis of the manifesto to show how the evolutionary ecological antiquity is central to the language of this key manosphere tenet. Moreover, we show how GRC is built into the language of the manifesto, thus risking serious psychological and physical conflicts in society as these restrictive gender roles based in a misogynistic rhetoric have dangerous and fatal consequences for both the individual and others (O'Neil, 2014). Ultimately, we show how this reveals further justifications for misogynist views of the construction of masculinity online, nevermore so then with the Western rise of male supremacy in 2021.

THE RED PILL REALITY OF NATURAL MASCULINITY

The Binary Opposition of Gender Role Conflict

The function of gender roles in Western society has been tested over the last 100 years. With the development of three Western waves of feminism that have sought the emancipation of women (Evans & Chamberlin 2015), citizens and academics alike have begun to explore how gender is a social construction separate from biological sex (Butler, 1980; Chambers, 2007; Hird, 2000; Lakoff, 2012; Pompper, 2017; Pompper, Soto, & Piel, 2007). Specifically, scholars have explored how gender is linguistically and thus socially constructed as binary of male and female (Allison, 2012, 2018), in turn leading to a dualistic construction of masculinity and femininity (O'Neil 1981a, 1981b; Pompper, 2010). This is a key cognitive linguistic maneuver developed from a Saussurean structuralism 100 years previously and its focus on binary oppositions (Danesi, 2009).

The cognitive linguistic role in perpetuating these binaries of both sex and gender combines O'Neil's work on GRC to create a unique rhetorical situation. As Charles Fillmore (1976) argued with his concept of Frame Semantics, words are cognitively framed in part through their connection to other words and concepts. Called an *encyclopedic knowledge* of related terms, Fillmore argues any word is in part denoted by its binary opposite by which to create an understanding of what *not* the concept/term represents. This linguistic construction then filters into the gender performance of masculinity and femininity, with the right type of cis heterosexual male pitted against what a woman should *not* be (cf. Menzies, 2017). This resonates with Connell's (1995) critique that such a binary approach to the men's movement oversimplifies the many different masculinities that exist.

This binary opposition of gender expectation is echoed by O'Neill's GRC, in which a negative psychological state is brought on by sexist and/or restrictive gender roles. This state manifests in three different ways. The first is the psychological domain in which cognitive, emotional, unconscious, and/or behavioral problems are caused by this conflict, thus causing both internal and external stress (O'Neil, 2008, 2010, n.d.). Secondly, GRC also is experienced in three situational contexts—either within the man, expressed toward others, or experienced from others. (O'Neil n.d.). As O'Neil (n.d.) argued, internal GRC is experienced through negative thoughts and emotions which, in interactions with others, can result in either feeling violated, devalued, and restricted. These two domains then are compounded by the third aspect—three types of personal experiences—that are caused by the restrictiveness, devaluations, and violations of the gender role norms of masculinity. Altogether, these three domains form a GRC as people experience, through policies and contact with others, challenges to traditional patriarchal gender expectations as a performance (Butler, 1990) that ultimately separates them from biological sex.

This discussion regarding GRC is key for examining the manosphere. We argue that GRC plays a significant role in forming the rhetoric and doctrine of the manosphere. Although much the literature on the linguistic and thus the social construction of language has focused on the construction of femininity as the altern "other" (Spivak, 2003) to the cishet white masculinity, we argue that masculinity, by its very definition as an oppositional binary category, needs further exploration. We turn to this next.

Taking the Red Pill of the Manosphere

The contemporary construction of masculinity begins with the development of various anti-feminist movements from the 1970s and 1980s (Ging, 2019) as a response to the second and third waves of feminism. The twenty-first century as the amorphous collection of masculinity-focused social movements became centralized with the development of the Web 2.0. As differing feminist movements (Banet-Wiser et al., 2020) proliferated, Men's Rights Activists (MRAs) formed across the various Internet platforms in order to counter what they saw as a misandrist culture. These discrete yet ideologically connected websites, fora, and other forms of social media became termed the "manosphere." Groups including Incels (involuntary celibates), fathers' rights groups, and Pick-Up Artists (PUA) use acronyms to give their particular group a sense of importance, consubstantiality (Burke, 2013), and to enable easier referencing within this co-dependent online space, thus enabling these fringe groups and terminologies to become established into mainstream discourses by 2014 (Jane, 2018).

Today, the manosphere allows disenfranchised men to share their subjective experiences to provide evidence that it is men, not women, who are subjugated and marginalized in a misandrist Western society (Zuckerberg, 2018). Believing themselves to be speaking a hidden truth, their role as truth tellers of a secret conspiracy has become encapsulated through the analogy of the "red pill"—the phrase developed on the antifeminist subreddit /redpill web forum (van Valkenburg, 2019) referring to a key moment in the cult classic *The Matrix* in which the protagonist must make a choice. First, he can take the red pill to lift the veil and see the illusion of reality—a concept reflected by Jake Angeli's self-imposed description as a Shaman. The other, lesser, option, is to take the blue pill and to remain blissfully unaware of the truth of his reality and to remain enslaved by an alien race. Referring to themselves as Red Pillers, numerous internal analogous references bolster the consubstantiality and internal cohesion (Kristensen, 2018) which creates their own evidence within their echo chamber (Cota, 2019). The existence of the manosphere is evidence of the injustice Western men perceive themselves facing.

The amorphous manosphere has many different sites offering educational artifacts by which to understand their discrete, yet connected, causes. One critical example of this Red Pill online movement is Valizadeh (2015) and his popular website *Return of Kings* (ROK): a name that implies manosphere men, as kings, are "returning" to their rightful place in society. Valizadeh presents his website as designed to "usher the return of the masculine man in a world where masculinity is being increasingly punished and shamed in favor of creating an androgynous and politically-correct society that allows women to assert superiority and control over men. Sadly, yesterday's masculinity is "today's misogyny" (Return of Kings n.d., para. 2). This concept of returning to a rightful, and thus natural, place is a rhetoric that is central to the manosphere masculinity that we explore next.

AN EVOLUTIONARY RHETORIC OF
ECOLOGICAL ANTIQUITY

The development of the manosphere reflects populist arguments of recent Western politics. Yet, politicians increasingly draw evidence and ethos from differing aspects of old, classical antiquity to suit their arguments. Here, deliberative democracy is not only idealized for its use of logic, evidence, and reason (Odida, 2019), but the Greco-Roman focus on oratory as part of the political process has become romanticized in Western culture. The democratic values of free speech, equality, the right to assemble and protest, and to vote for a political representative (Bessette, 1980) have become emblematic markers of cultural capital (Bourdieu, 2010). Democracy and its origins have become a symbol for Western society, so naming this political ideology strategically underscores a way of being that is inherently right, good, and politically superior.

This use of democracy as a signifier of value is significant to the consubstantiality and rhetorical work of the manosphere. As Zuckerberg (2018) argued, the manosphere is partly built around a contemporary (mis)reading of Stoicism that has also become a central part of the ideology of the alt-right. Evans (2016) argued that its culture of classical virtues alike Stoicism and morality have combined with an offbeat self-help ethos to create a movement driven by disaffected young college-educated men looking for a set of rules to live by; a "way to feel strong in a chaotic world" (Evans, 2016, para. 3). This is thus what Sharpe termed an "alt-Stoicism" (Sharpe, 2018); an alternative and general misreading of Hellenistic philosophy that engages in cherry-picking of important texts. From reading Ovid's Ars Amatoria as a manual for men asserting a sexual dominance over women, alt-right bloggers draw upon the Greco-Roman origins of democracy that only gave power and political representation to upper-class male nationals, thus "responding to and drawing on parts of Stoicism that advocates of the philosophy would prefer to ignore" (Zuckerberg, 2020). The Stoics are thus used to create a twenty-first century masculine life script (Berne, 1957; Steiner, 1990) of sexism, racism, and classicism that return to the origins of democracy by which to strategically communicate about contemporary life supported by supposed, "sometimes-erroneous 'quotations' from Marcus Aurelius" (Sharpe, 2018, p. 106).

Next, we examine two contexts central to exploring the impact of manosphere discourse on our understanding of masculinity today: 1) Nature as a noun, adjective, and metonym, and 2) the gender role conflict of masculinity.

Nature as a Noun, Adjective, and Metonym

Whilst recent scholarship on the manosphere has explored the use of classical antiquity as a figurehead for an inherent way of being human and evolved social animals, we posit that the use of nature as a qualifier in manosphere discourses is an important rhetorical maneuver that intersects with this alt-Stoicism. The adjectives ancient, classical, and traditional all become interwoven with the modified nature in its metaphorical understanding as implying an inherent moral imperative of the object. As Valizadeh argues in his manifesto, "Neomasculinity combines traditional beliefs, masculinity, and animal biology into one ideological system. It aims to aid men living in

Westernized nations that lack qualities such as classical virtue, masculinity in males, femininity in females, and objectivity, especially concerning beauty ideals and human behavior" (Valizadeh, 2015, para. 1). Here, the notion of naturalness refers to an encyclopedic depiction of evolutionary origins that can be read in two different ways coded as an inherent way of being with this moral imperative. The first is a heuristic for the evolutionary origins of our biology as mammals. The second is referring to our evolution as social beings, which for the alt-right is the Greco-Roman classical antiquity of deliberative democracy. Thus, this complex intersectional framework is what we call an *ecological antiquity*: a moral imperative to return to our evolutionary, natural origins as both mammals and social beings.

Valizadeh argues on ROK that men and women are genetically, mentally, and physically different, as humans have sex roles akin to other mammals (Valizadeh, 2015, n.d.). By using the Stoics to justify their argument for qualifying biological sex differences, gender performances of masculinity and femininity are consequently framed as an evolutionary binary that is morally correct. Here, the Stoics differentiated the masculine and feminine body as differing organisms, in which the cishet white abled-bodied Western male sat atop the hierarchy of humans with a supposed superior natural masculinity, logic, and athleticism. Conversely, women were framed as emotional, non-logical, motherly, defined by beauty, and the literal property of men (Irigaray, 2011).

This area of research bridges linguistic and conceptual connotations made between nonhuman nature and femininity. But such arguments become compounded by feminist and Marxist scholar Luce Irigaray's (2011) proposition for an intersection between Greco-Roman culture and nonhuman nature coded as female and women framed as being in tune with nature (as with the eponymous "Mother Earth"). For Irigaray, this has resulted in the cultural treatment of women as a non-agentic resource to be exploited by men as master.

The Gender Role Conflict of Masculinity

The notion of a natural order of things presents masculinity as a singular way of being in which it exists as a set of starkly defined categories on a spectrum of desirability. No matter where a man falls on the spectrum, he is defined both by his relationship to women and the manosphere itself. Each discrete category of masculinity thus relies on its encyclopedic framework of knowledge, engaging a set of binary oppositions that cause GRC (or stress) as these categories lead to specific expectations of a gendered performances of both masculinity and femininity that correlate beauty ideals with human behavior. Critically, men are expected to act according to the Red Pill doctrine that bases itself on "biological laws," while, conversely, women are painted as deceitful, untrustworthy, and attempting to deviate from these evolutionary logics. GRC or stress may therefore result when gender role expectancies are violated.

The Alpha/Beta Dichotomy

An Alpha/Beta dichotomy permeates manosphere rhetoric and contributes to significant GRC. Adapted from research on captive wolves by Rudolph Schenkel during WWII that was later debunked, this research was used as a neoliberal metaphor in which men who are dominant are healthier and *better* (Adrey, 1970; Mech, 1999). The Alpha male, as the ideal, is considered to be assertive, attractive, successful and lucky. As described in Donovan's (2012) *Way of Men*, the Alpha Western male is judged by their ability to be a "real man"—the physical defender of their group's safety and honor. In contrast, the lesser Beta male is understood to be submissive and subservient to women, lacking in assertiveness and self-discipline, and not physically attractive. Overall, in an unusual reclamation of oppression, many manosphere members only consider themselves to be Betas striving for Alpha status (Kristensen, 2018).

Like Fillmore's way of understanding words according to other associated concepts, this Alpha/Beta masculine distinction is framed by its binary opposite of femininity. For instance, a common myth expressed in manosphere circles is that women spend their "sexual prime" having sex with as many Alphas as possible and overall have control over sex which is inherently a male right. This therefore subverts the "normal" dynamic of men-women hierarchical relations (Kristensen, 2018). Despite women being framed as naturally submissive, less logical, and weaker than men, MRAs argue that a natural feminine agency can manipulate and control certain men. Such agency thus becomes framed as a negative trait in which women use men for their procreational, material, and emotional needs.

Such framing of female sexual agency creates significant GRC among men. The indecorous manosphere phrase, "Alpha Fucks, Beta Bucks," suggests that Alphas are pursued by women to have children with, but then settle for a Beta who will raise and financially provide for these children. With the majority of manosphere subscribers considering themselves Betas, this group frames itself as the good guys who love and respect women despite their hypergamous exploitation of men they deem to be weak and inferior. GRC is thus externally expressed through a manifold set of terms used to infer the violation and devaluation of men by women, including; *alpha widow, AWALT, cock carousel, comfort test, shit test, hamster, LMR, post-wall, pussy pass*, and *trickle truth* (Reddit 2020). Overly vulgar and insulting to both women and the Beta men that many manosphere proponents claim to be, usage of these terms implies a gender role conflict against some natural order of things. This evolutionary rhetoric thus becomes a self-fulling prophecy.

Consubstantiality In and Out of the Manosphere

Intersection of gender roles expectations and the manosphere's binary-linguistic logic includes even more disparaging categories used to describe people both in and outside the movement. One example is the "White Knight," a male who expresses views sympathetic to feminists. Because the Red Pill community interprets this as a strategy for attracting women, White Knights are expelled from the movement (Kristensen, 2018). Another insulting term "fag" is used to diminish someone or to describe manosphere occupants who have been victimized and degraded by other manosphere members (rather than a reclaimed term as used by queer community members). Moreover, despite Valizadeh's disclaimer that ROK is not for queer men, Red Pill posts have been penned by gay incel members, whose homosexuality creates GRC to the point of celibacy. Ultimately, while group members express overt homophobia, the act of having taken the red pill and expressing misogynist outrage ultimately trumps any masculine deviation (Kristensen, 2018).

These differing terms point to the complexity of belonging in the manosphere and overall consubstantiality in this patriarchal utopia. The manosphere has variations in masculinity but possesses a singular femininity that causes significant GRC when encountered. According to the manosphere, the most common GRC forms are caused by feminism and other expressions of non-traditional gender norms (O'Neill, 2014) that tell men they're anything less than their nature. Such manosphere men retreat further into their traditional male roles when they believe contemporary Western culture is invalidating their alt-right rage while elevating women's status. This dynamic is inconsistent with manosphere ideology which attaches lesser status to females considered to be overly emotional. Conflict thus arises between the perceived rationality of men, and the anger and outrage that underlies the men's rights movement, as both are ultimately co-signed by tenets of hegemonic masculinity. Both outcomes offer a source of affirmation and safety despite significant cognitive dissonance.

The notion of human behavior as natural is code for an evolutionary rhetoric that implies a purity in tune with our origins. However, the manosphere justifies conflict as a misjudgment by general society, and in order to progress, humans must regress back to their origins. But as our ability to create complex social and cultural systems differentiate us from other animals, this regression is Janus-faced: one face toward our biological origins, and the other pointing to the birth of modern society. In order to examine this in further detail, we turn next to a key manifesto within the manosphere for this rhetoric of masculinity. Using GRC alongside textual analyses, we critically unpack Roosh Valizadeh's manifesto for living that he calls *neomasculinity* and consequently explore how this rhetoric of masculinity has transformed from an idiom to a political philosophy.

A NATURAL NEOMASCULINITY

Former PUA Valizadeh has been a significant figure in the manosphere with its evolutionary ecological antiquity worldview—as exemplified in Valizadeh's (2015) manifesto, *What is Neomasculinity*. Hosted on his personal website, this manifesto is akin to a manual for men to learn about their masculinity and how to live authentically according to biological and social origins. Here, Valizadeh both visually and linguistically primes the audience with his use of *classical virtue* as moral conduct code. The website header reads as an artwork in its depiction of antiquity with images of a classical Greek sculpture with white marble, curly hair, and a god-like figure wrangling two mortals with a serpent. Moreover, this combines with an introductory paragraph and a table of contents that outlines the central role that gender conflict plays in his manifesto. Graphic representations alongside linguistic propositions of these virtues become their own scientific evidence for Valizadeh's claims.

The existence of something as being its own evidence of Valizadeh's interpretive truth is a key semiotic move that becomes central to his rhetorical strategy. His language is affirmative but lacking the linguistic signifiers that suggest this is opinion or interpretation. Rather, Valizadeh makes assertive propositions with hyperlinks by which to provide evidence to his claims. He moors the tenets of neomasculinity within Greco-Roman logics such as classical virtue and claims that his notion of masculinity, femininity, and their relationship to beauty ideals and human behavior are expressed as an objective fact. Consequently, Valizadeh (2015) proposes his tenets of neomasculinity as "an antidote for males who are being programmed to accept Western degeneracy, mindless consumerism, and immoral state authority" (para. 1).

Following an introductory section, Valizadeh (2015) uses the meta-communication tropes as seen in political manifestos to give credibility to his piece. His introduction is followed by a table of contents with chapters entitled "Traditional Sex Roles," "Sexual Marketplace Value," "Free Speech and Due Process," "Binary Sex Model," and "Male Virtue and Development." Valizadeh (2015) uses key terms and phrases to provide a conceptual framework for the reader, presenting this neomasculinity as an ideological system of being. Critically, phrases such as *binary sex model, due process,* and *free speech* echo both aspects of this ecological rhetoric.

Classical Biological Virtue

The biological origins of Valizadeh's argument begins with a simple premise: that classical virtues and traditional beliefs have been lost in contemporary Western society. This is not a new argument but it engages a conservative nostalgia for a long-gone time when, supposedly, life was simpler and life script ideals were clear. More specifically, this was a past in which white men were at the top of a Homosapien hierarchy and were able to control those below. As Valizadeh (2015) argues, "patriarchy does have its flaws in locking in roles for males and females who are outliers, but it was undoubtedly a superior societal system that catered to the innate abilities of the sexes and provided them with roles that not only furthered their own abilities and interests but civilization as a whole" (para. 22). Thus, whilst "traditional beliefs" often are associated with religious beliefs, Valizadeh's (2015) use of the term is a dog whistle (Saul, 2018) to conservatives and the alt-right that presume to be undefined by any particular ideology and religion. For Valizadeh, tradition, nature, and biology all become conceptual metaphors of moral righteousness.

This nod to nostalgia is not for a particular time period, but for any time period in which gender roles were clear and defined using a gender binary. Whilst we agree with feminist scholars that we still live in an era that supports certain traditional Western gender roles, we posit that the vernacular intersectional progress made in challenging patriarchy—such as with woke and cancel culture—presents the alt-right male with a GRC challenge. Valizadeh's desire for a simpler time is not a literal adjective. Rather, it is code for the desire of a person's preferred social hierarchy to be accepted unconditionally and without challenge. Thus, Valizadeh represents both the Red Pill and manosphere communities who strategically reject social constructionism and use our biological origins for gender role rigidity through an evolutionary rhetoric in which ecological words such as nature have become value ladened as a positive. Valizadeh's manifesto consequently creates a framework for understanding gender through an evolutionary rhetoric of both biological and social origins

Whilst Valizadeh focuses on creating a rhetoric of masculinity for the contemporary male, by its very nature, gender in the manosphere is based upon the biological binary of Fillmore's frame semantics. By framing masculinity in terms of sex/biology, Valizadeh argues for men to have certain evolutionary expectations of women. From the traits of "submissiveness, dependence, emotional nature, faster intuition, cooperative sharing" (Valiza-deh, 2015, para. 9), in the "Feminine Beauty Ideals" section he argues that elements such as symmetry and waist-to-hip ratio are genetically hardwired to create male attraction, thus making men morally good. Valizadeh supports the manosphere male to require a woman to be monogamous, but also empa-thizes with men's emotional distress caused by what he argues as contempo-rary hypergamous women. Thus, just as nature is simply a resource without agency, we argue that the manosphere male experiences GRC whether or not the women they pursue fulfils these expectations. If she does not defy biological expectations, she fails to fulfil the expectation that she will not meet her biological requirements. All thus experience significant situational and personal GRC.

Altogether, Valizadeh takes the pessimistic viewpoint that all people fail to live up to gender norms, "especially concerning beauty ideals and human behavior" (Valizadeh, 2015, para. 1). Valizadeh argues that the attraction to women who fall outside his idealized waist-to-hip ratio of 0.7 not only devalues men but must be caused by a biological deficiency such as a neuro-logical deficit or poor eyesight. And yet, he goes further to argue that women who attempt to modify their bodies to conform to these beauty standards are trying to ensnare men in an effort to continue their genetically inferior line (Valizadeh, 2015). By inference, Valizadeh even accuses the reader of violat-ing gender role norms that ultimately can be redeemed by adhering to tenets that unsurprisingly are laid out in books available for purchase through his website. Ultimately, by grounding attraction in such rigid and gender deter-ministic terms, not only does Valizadeh negate the spectrum of gender and attraction, but creates varying situational contexts that cause conflict for the many non-conformists.

The Social Manosphere

The evolutionary rhetoric of Valizadeh's neomasculinity may focus on individual expectations in relation to the opposite sex, but it also extends to the larger social framework that is central to humanity. The central conflict for the manosphere is that contemporary society is degenerate—feminized, decadent, and consumerist—and has deviated from natural gender roles that negate the Greco-Roman masculine logic. For Valizadeh, it is not only bio-logical natures that have been lost, but a sociological morality. He argues that contemporary societal structures deny basic, universal, and natural truths about human behavior that form the foundations for a natural state of social being for all people. With a rhetorical focus on the evolution of Western deliberative democracy, classical antiquity is thus framed as the social origins of what it is to be a man as a social mammal, framed as a moral goodness that aligns with both our biological and social natures. Valizadeh thus rejects the concept of gender as a social constructionism of gender in preference to the biology of sex to advance his ideology.

Although Valizadeh relies on biological examples of what it is to be in-line with one's biology, he qualifies his argument to suggest that men may go beyond the primal urges of survival and reproduction. Rather, he looks towards a different set of social norms that theorize ways of being. Here, he returns to ancient philosophies of being: "Aristotle's cardinal virtues were prudence, temperance, courage, and justice. Eastern philosophies teach self-control of desire. Stoicism tempers desire and aims for mental fortitude against misfortune" (Valizadeh, 2015, para. 87). Deliberative democracy is framed as the pinnacle of rational superiority with alt-Stoicism differentiating us from the wild animals we once were. Engaging Lakoff's (2014; 2016) conservative Strict Father Model of governance with discipline and training society members to be obedient yet self-reliant, men of the manosphere must strive for self-improvement, body development, hard work ethics, individual responsibility, and lifestyle optimization.

The alt-stoicism that forms the logics of the manosphere supports its biological origins which continue to define masculinity and femininity according to binary oppositions which Connell (1995) problematizes. Contemporary men and women are guaranteed to fit into one of Valizadeh's (2015) categories of gender through what he terms "a strength and weakness profile" that "allows them to either excel or be deficient in certain roles compared to the opposite sex" (p. 7). Here, as social animals, Valizadeh lays out the differences between sexes through gendered traits which are defined by their binary opposition displayed by the other sex. For men, they are considered to possess more independence, intelligence, rationale, analytical thinking, and dominance over women who instead inhabit dependence, emotional nature, faster intuition, cooperative sharing, and submissiveness. This then results in Validazeh defining career options based on these gender differentials. Men are better at leadership and hard physical labor; women are naturally better at domestic work and caregiving labor. In today's society, Valizadeh even argues that the neomasculine man should aim to become an entrepreneur as traditional workplaces have become hostile due to women and political correctness. And yet, despite this favoring, it is the supposed-masculine jobs that are culturally coded with more capital that within a neoliberal logics is rewarded by money. To not perform these gender roles is thus to experience conflict over gender roles, as it is the duty of men to create situational GRC.

We argue that we can ultimately consider the role of GRC in the manosphere as serving as a barometer for the male trying to adhere to this doctrine. To the manosphere male who views these strict gender definitions as a moral truth, GRC is an automatic warning signal of either gender failing to be their best biological selves. The strive for gender equality is thus framed as benefiting no one as it minimizes a person's innate strengths, maximizes their weakness, and decreases changes for reproduction, survival, and happiness, which ultimately minimize further when in an environment constrained with resources (Valizadeh, 2015). GRC thus results from internal stress if anyone deviates from both expectations but also the manosphere's argument at what behavior is socially normal but deviant from biological norms. The virtue of a true MRA in twenty-first society is thus to create cultural pushback against the feminist social structures that have challenged the power of cishet white men for centuries.

CONCLUSION

GRC plays a central strategic function in supporting this rhetoric used by Valizadeh (2015) and other similar pundits in the nebulous manosphere. By definition, the manosphere's creation was a response to the development of feminism and other movements that negate an alt-right set of ideological beliefs founded on evolutionary ecological antiquity. Here, metaphorical understandings of human origins become moral imperatives for being. In Valizadeh's manosphere, gender roles are clearly defined and based on both classical antiquity alongside primate hierarchies. GRC becomes enabled for the manosphere male as they go into on- and off-line combat with both women and white knights over social equality for women and other marginalized groups, arguing that we live in an evolutionary-wrong, misandrist society which privileges females. To be a male in this world is thus to face GRC everyday as they fight to expose their truth.

This promotion of truth continues with Valizadeh who, in 2018, underwent a religious awakening. Despite decrying his previous PUA status, Valizadeh has doubled down on his manosphere logics which are now supported by the ethos of religion. Moreover, he uses his previous PUA writings as an exemplar of the masculine biological behaviors that are natural and unconscious. By arguing for the degeneracy of society and its "fake news," Valizadeh and other manosphere community members turn directly to their own echo chambers to provide evidence to affirm their own beliefs in the superiority of Greco-Roman society. This self-assurity automatically becomes evidence of the truthfulness of their claims, alongside the manosphere sophist pundits (Zuckerberg, 2018).

One may question the importance of understanding how the classists are used by the manosphere to make their own arguments online. But we argue that the infiltration of this logic has potential regressive consequences in an ever-growing partisan, far-right Western culture. Moreover, we argue that this chapter expands O'Neil's (1981a, 1981b) initial construction of GRC alongside its latter developments (O'Neil, 2008, 2015; Pompper, 2007, 2017) as it explores how this gender role conflict and stress is experienced online, thus becoming the catalyst for *off-line* behavior. This is exemplified by the 2021 riots, in which President Trump's call to march on the Capitol saw many manosphere proponents engage in a particular gendered performance of masculine retrieval and defense of what is theirs: democracy as originated with classical antiquity.

This war-like approach continues in the so-called culture wars in which GRC forms a central role. The alt-right manosphere looks backwards to our human origins for guidance in how we should live, in which essential masculine behavior is regarded as the developmental cornerstone of society, thus legitimating patriarchal domination as the birthright of all men. In opposition, feminism is presented as doing harm not only to men but the natural order of things. The manosphere thus uses this essentialist view of gender as defense for the subjugation of women and as an attack on the feminist movement, by holding feminists as responsible for disrupting traditional gender roles and encouraging women to forego their femininity, stealing male jobs, and abandoning their responsibilities to their homes and families. Here, this GRC becomes a social construct that in turn reconfigures social reality in this ever partisan public sphere in which a solution for all viewpoints cannot be reached. This chapter thus both engages with GRC in which to explore this particular rhetoric of masculinity, while also expanding our understanding of this conflict as a self-perpetuating cycle in which the manosphere male intends to experience gender stress in order to confirm their beliefs and justify their behaviors that in turn reproduce further conflict. This is a Janus-faced operation of an ever-escalating heightening of experiences that risk serious real-world consequences.

In conclusion, we echo Irigaray's (2010) call for developing our democratic culture from this binary opposition of masculinity versus femininity. We argue that this use of an ecological, evolutionary metaphorical logics of nature is a serious misnomer that is abused in political rhetoric between another false equivalence that democracy is an untouchable idol (Irigaray, 2010). Instead, as Irigaray argues, in order for women to achieve full equality, we must break down this binary of gender roles. Otherwise, women can never enter into democratic culture as a full subject if their constitution is simply a response to the requirements of an individualization in the masculine. Ultimately, without addressing the GRC that this rhetoric of masculinity reveals, we risk only further divisions in our already partisan society.

REFERENCES

Adrey, R. (1970). Control of population. *Life Magazine.* February 20, 1970. Accessed from https://oldlifemagazine.com/february-20-1970-life-magazine.html.

Allison, M. (2018). G"hen"der Neutral—How Sweden is furthering gender equality through language. In J. Rice and C. Graham. (Eds.). *Rhetorics Change/Rhetoric's Change.* Parlor Press & Intermezzo. ISBN: 978-1-60235-502-6.

———. (2012). Other-sexed/other-gendered: Narrating a spectrum in a language of binaries. *Otherness: Essays and Studies, 2*(2). Aarhus University Press.

Banet-Weiser, S., Gill, R., & Rottenberg, C. (2020). Postfeminism, popular feminism and neoliberal feminism? Sarah Banet-Weiser, Rosalind Gill and Catherine Rottenberg in conversation. *Feminist Theory, 21*(1), 3–24. https://doi.org/10.1177/1464700119842555.

Berne, E. (1957). *A Layman's Guide to Psychiatry and Psychoanalysis.* Grove.

Bourdieu, P. (2010). *Distinction: A Social Critique of the Judgement of Taste.* Routledge Classics.

Burke, K. (2013). *A rhetoric of motives* (California ed., [Nachrdr.]). University of California Press.

Butler, J. (2006). *Gender Trouble: Feminism and the Subversion of Identity.* Routledge Classics.

Chambers, S. A. (2007). 'Sex' and the Problem of the Body: Reconstructing Judith Butler's Theory of Sex/Gender. *Body & Society, 13*(4), 47–75. https://doi.org/10.1177/1357034X07085537.

Connell, R. W. (1995). *Masculinities: Knowledge, power & social change.* University of California Press.

Copsey, N. (2013). "Fascism . . . but with an Open Mind." Reflections on the Contemporary Far Right in (Western) Europe. *Fascism,* 2(1): 1–17. https://doi.org/10.1163/22116257-00201008.

Cota, W., Ferreira, S. C., Pastor-Satorras, R., & Starnini, M. (2019). Quantifying Echo Chamber Effects in Information Spreading over Political Communication Networks. *EPJ Data Science,* 8(1): 35. https://doi.org/10.1140/epjds/s13688-019-0213-9.

Danesi, M. (2009). "Opposition theory and the interconnectedness of language, culture, and cognition." *Sign Systems Studies,* 37(1/2): 11–42. https://doi.org/10.12697/SSS.2009.37.1-2.02.

Donovan, J. (2012). *The Way of men.* Dissonant Hum.

el-Ojeili, C. (2019). Reflecting on post-fascism: Utopia and fear.*Critical Sociology, 45* (7–8), 1149–1166. https://doi.org/10.1177/0896920518768867.

Evans, E., & Chamberlain, P. (2015). "Critical waves: Exploring feminist identity, discourse and praxis in Western feminism." *Social Movement Studies, 14*(4): 396–409. https://doi.org/10.1080/14742837.2014.964199.

Evans, J. (2016). How the alt-right emerged from men's self-help. *History of Emotions Blog.* Nov 18, 2016. Accessed from https://emotionsblog.history.qmul.ac.uk/2016/11/how-the-alt-right-emerged-from-mens-self-help/.

Farrell, T, Fernandez, M., Novotny J., & Alani, H. (2019). Exploring misogyny across the manosphere in Reddit. In *WebSci '19 Proceedings of the 10th ACM Conference on Web Science*, 87–96.

Fauconnier, G., & Turner, M. (2003). *The way we think: Conceptual blending and the mind's hidden complexities*. Basic Books.

Fillmore, C. J. (1976). Frame semantics and the nature of language. *Annals of the New York Academy of Sciences* 280 (1 Origins and E): 20–32. https://doi.org/10.1111/j.1749-6632.1976.tb25467.x.

Hird, M. J. (2000). Gender's nature: Intersexuality, transsexualism and the 'sex'/'gender' binary. *Feminist Theory, 1*(3), 347–364. https://doi.org/10.1177/146470010000100305.

Irigaray, L. (2011). There can be no democracy without a culture of difference. In *Ecocritical theory: New European approaches*, A. Goodbody and K. Rigby (Eds.). University of Virginia Press. 194–205.

Lakoff, G. (2012). *Women, fire, and dangerous things: What categories reveal about the mind* (paperback ed., [Nachdr.]). The University of Chicago Press.

———. (2014). *The all-new don't think of an elephant! Know your values and frame the debate*. Chelsea Green Publishing.

———. (2016). *Moral politics: How liberals and conservatives think*. Third edition. The University of Chicago Press.

Lakoff, G., & Johnson, M. (2003). *Metaphors we live by*. University of Chicago Press.

Mech, D. L. (1999). Alpha status, dominance, and division of labor in wolf packs. *USGS Northern Prairie Wildlife Research Center. 353.* https://digitalcommons.unl.edu/usgsnpwrc/353.

Menzies, R. (2007). "Virtual backlash: Representations of men's 'rights' and feminist 'wrongs' in cyberspace." In *Reaction and resistance: Feminism, law, and social change*, edited by D. E. Chunn, S. B. Boyd, and H. Hessard. University of British Columbia Press.

Odida, A. (2019). "Book review: *Not all dead white men: Classics and misogyny in the digital age* by Donna Zuckerberg." *Feminist Review*, 123 (1): 140–42. https://doi.org/10.1177/0141778919878946.

O'Neil, J. (1981a). Male sex-role conflict, sexism & masculinity. *The Counseling Psychologist, 9*, 61-80. https://doi.org/10.1177/001100008100900213.

———. (1981b). Patterns of gender role conflict & strain: Sexism and fear of femininity in men's lives. *Personnel & Guidance Journal, 60*, 203-210. https://doi.org/10.1002/j.2164-4918.1981.tb00282.x.

———. (2008). "Summarizing 25 Years of Research on Men's Gender Role Conflict Using the gender role conflict scale: New research paradigms and clinical implications." *The Counseling Psychologist* 36 (3): 358–445. https://doi.org/10.1177/0011000008317057.

———. (2015). *Men's gender role conflict: Psychological costs, consequences, and an agenda for change*. American Psychological Association.

———. (n.d.) "An operational definition of gender role conflict and the gender role conflict scale" *University of Connecticut*. Accessed from https://james-oneil.uconn.edu/operational-definition-of-grc/#.

Papasavva, A., Blackburn, J. Stringhini, G., Zannettou, S. & De Cristofaro, E. (2020). "Is It a Qoincidence?": A first step towards understanding and characterizing the Qanon movement on voat.co. *ArXiv:2009.04885 [Cs]*, October. http://arxiv.org/abs/2009.04885.

Pompper, D. (2010). Masculinities, the metrosexual, and media images: Across dimensions of age and ethnicity. *Sex Roles*, 63, 682–696.

———. (2017). *Rhetoric of femininity: Female body image, media, and gender role stress/conflict*. Lexington Studies in Contemporary Rhetoric. Lexington Books.

Pompper, D., Soto, J. & Piel, L. (2007). Male body image and magazine standards: Considering dimensions of age and ethnicity. *Journalism & Mass Communication Quarterly 84*(3): 525–45. https://doi.org/10.1177/107769900708400308.

Reddit. 2020. The Red Pill. *Reddit*. Accessed from https://www.reddit.com/r/TheRedPill/comments/2zckqu/updated_glossary_of_terms_and_acronyms/.

Return of Kings. (n.d.) "About." *Return of Kings*. Accessed from https://www.returnofkings.com/about.

Safire, W. (2008). *Safire's political dictionary*. Oxford University Press.

Schmitz, R., and Kazyak, E. (2016.) Masculinities in cyberspace: An analysis of portrayals of manhood in men's rights activist websites. *Social Sciences 5*(2): 18. https://doi.org/10.3390/socsci5020018.

Sharpe, M. (2018). Into the heart of darkness or: Alt-stoicism? Actually, no. . . *Eidos. A Journal for Philosophy of Culture*, 6 (December): 106–13. https://doi.org/10.26319/6921.

Sonnevend, J. (2016). *Stories without borders: The Berlin Wall and the making of a global iconic event*. Oxford University Press.

Spivak, G. C. (2003). *Death of a discipline*. The Wellek Library Lectures in Critical Theory. Columbia University Press.

Steiner, C. (1990). *Scripts people live: Transactional analysis of life scripts*. 1st Evergreen ed. Grove Weidenfeld.

Valizadeh, R. (2015). "What is neomasculinity?" *Roosh Valizadeh. (*May 6, 2015). Accessed from https://www.rooshv.com/what-is-neomasculinity.

Vandiver, J. (2020). 'Alt-virilities: Masculinism, rhizomatics, and the contradictions of the American alt-right'. *Politics, Religion & Ideology, 21*(2): 153–76. https://doi.org/10.1080/21567689.2020.1763319.

Van Valkenburgh, S. P. (2018). Digesting the red pill: Masculinity and neoliberalism in the manosphere. *Men and Masculinities, December*, 1097184X1881611. https://doi.org/10.1177/1097184X18816118.

Zuckerberg, D. (2019). *Not all dead white men: Classics and misogyny in the digital age*. Harvard University Press.

Zuckerman, E. (2019). QAnon and the emergence of the unreal. *Journal of Design and Science*, (6). https://doi.org/10.21428/7808da6b.6b8a82b9.

Chapter Two

Case Studies of Male Rhetorical Mediation of Sexual Violence and Gender Role Stress/ Conflict in the #MeToo Era

Robert Mundy

INTRODUCTION

The #MeToo movement has disrupted patriarchy and its narrative. Through hashtag feminism and exposed spaces of "pain, narrative, and isolation" (Dixon, 2014, p. 34), the movement has interrupted generations of male taciturnity. Use of online platforms galvanized women in solidarity that brought attention to sexual violence, provided outlets and resources for survivors, and advanced further action to eliminate sexual assault (Langone, 2018). Disclosing their experiences of sexual abuse, women placed themselves at the forefront of a dialogue about misogyny, toxic masculinity, and rape culture. Women's collective stories of suffering and resilience served to break the silence that had shrouded sexual violence for generations, and their individual accounts put men on notice that sexual transgressions would be *called out* to a now vast and attentive audience in the most public way possible.

Language of abuse circulated freely, as women circumvented traditional media gatekeepers who, historically, have been predominantly male. Rape and assault were no longer spoken of in vague generalities or crafted second-party revisions of firsthand accounts, where the accused were afforded the ability to deflect or deny what had transpired. Whereas women of the #MeToo movement have challenged masculine norms that create and uphold a culture of gender-based violence, some men across masculinities have considered such language as a threat. Men were momentarily halted from marching forward unimpeded to dismiss or disavow allegations. In other words, men have found themselves in a defensive position where they've been required to account for allegations of sexual misconduct rather than relying on their privilege and simply ignoring charges. When growth of feminist advocacy outpaces hegemonic masculinity's ability to maintain strict gender order, some men may feel conflicted and stressed.

With women in control of the #MeToo narrative, men sought sympathy as they responded to potential conflict and stress associated with potentially being *cancelled*. This rhetorical maneuver was used to depict men as victims of a society that has gone too far; a sentiment shared by 40 percent of respondents to the NPR/Ipsos (2018) poll that examined views on sexual assault one year following #MeToo's inception. Some men claim that women use allegations of sexual violence to "gain attention," that the larger society had rushed to "judgment," and that "men are being wrongly accused" (Martin, 2018). Since #MeToo's onset with women amplifying their stories of sexual violence, I posit that four men accused of sexual assault who rhetorically characterized themselves as victims hoped to stage *a comeback* and restore their own reputation as well as support hegemonic masculinity.

My examination of selected cases is informed by New Literacy Studies (NLS), which suggests that literacy is ideological as a sociocultural construct that reflects and creates ongoing ways of knowing/composing the self and the world (Gee, 2015; Street, 2003). By exploring case studies of *the comeback*, I analyzed ways four men strategically used language to articulate their own sense of male gender role conflict (GRC). This is a psychological state of tension brought on by rigid, sexist, or restrictive socialized male gender roles (O'Neil, 1981). Similarly, male gender role stress (GRS) stems from a perceived threat to masculine standing (Copenhaver et al., 2000) and attempts to uphold hegemonic positions. *The comeback*, therefore, is a strategy of men moving past *has #MeToo gone too far?* and declaring that it had. In essence, *the comeback* is a narrative technique used to undermine the experiences of women in order to reclaim male privilege. Suggesting that their victimization is more worthy than women's accounts, men accused of sexual transgression rhetorically produced counternarratives steeped in claims of male GRC and GRS to reaffirm male authority.

LITERATURE REVIEW

Some men's responses to #MeToo offer an opportunity to examine dynamics shaped by relationships among language, perceptions of male GRC/GRS, and accusations of violence directed toward women. GRC theory suggests that male violence can happen when traditional gender roles prove contradictory or unrealistic (O'Neil, 1990), such as when subjective experience conflicts with male scripts (Reeser, 2010). Gender is socially constructed through "story, narrative, and ideological discourse" (Alexander, 2008, p. 1), often suggesting who is valued. Similarly, males learn what constitutes manhood through ongoing, contextual, social processes (Alexander, 2008) that ascribe worth to some bodies and marginalize others (Gee, 2012; Street, 2003).

Examining the power of language inherent in active resistance may offer a path forward in affecting social change (Butler, 1997). In particular, the ways that language has been used in the #MeToo movement reveals disrupted traditional gender roles and power abuses—wherein manhood has been deemed more powerful than womanhood. Being challenged for actions that historically warranted little or no public attention or scrutiny has left some men strategically using claims of internal/communal conflict/stress since systems of patriarchy make little provision for men experiencing power loss. Similarly, I consider the #MeToo movement as context to interrogate ways pent up male GRC/GRS may be directed at women accusers. This cycle has the potential to victimize women twice—first in conjunction with the sexual assault event and second in conjunction with defending themselves.

This review of literature unfolds in four parts: 1) Reading hegemony and enacted sexual violence, 2) Scrutinizing sexual violence as normative male behavior, 3) Examining #MeToo and digital defiance, and 4) Considering masculinity post-#MeToo.

Reading Hegemony and Enacted Sexual Violence

Gender is performative as an act that speaks more to social expectations than to an individual's sense of self (Butler, 1990) and males are socialized from an early age to perform their gender following hegemonic norms (Connell, 2005). Masculinity becomes hegemonic when men use it to dominate women and men who perform masculinity marginally or antithetically to its standard (Connell, 2005) and is realized through the "constant and unavoidable repetition" of "images, myths, discourses, and practices" (Reeser, 2010, p. 21). In other words, males learn via media and interpersonally what it means to be a *man* through endless interactions that shape and condition male gender performativity. Gender roles and boundaries are determined by associations between behaviors and expectations for what is expected as gender appropriate (O'Neil, 1981). Determining dominant and subordinated masculinity forms is an act of literacy that indexes who is *doing* gender *appropriately*, suggests who is not, and outlines consequences of these actions (West & Zimmerman, 1987).

Language mediates these dynamics through a sophisticated understanding of social context (Gee, 2012; Street, 2003) and identifies who is an insider and who is an outsider (Gee, 2015). Language is used to create and maintain hegemonic masculinity by benchmarking what is deemed feminine/inferior as a marker to establish that which is authoritative and masculine/superior. Antonymic logic defines masculinity as *not* being feminine and men as *not* being women (Connell, 1987; Murnen et al, 2002; O'Neil, 2008). Through sociocultural interaction, men learn to control women (Kivel, 2019) and avoid anything associated with femininity (Murnen et al. 2002; O'Neil, 2008) in conjunction with fear of the feminine (Blazina, 1997). Among what he called four basic rules of masculinity, Kimmel (2004) posited that masculinity is "the relentless repudiation of the feminine" (Kimmel, 2004); a mindset that also supports homophobia (O'Neil et al., 1986).

The power of hegemony is its ability to appear natural, normal, and as common sense. Hegemony is visible, both in terms of who disciplines and who is disciplined (Connell, 2005). Surveillance forms the groundwork for negative effects of this dynamic and plays out in male gender role conflict and stress when males' human potential is restricted (O'Neil, 1990). In other words, masculine norms limit individual agency (Smith et al, 2015). Through socialization, men develop and internalize anti-feminine attitudes as a means of gaining/preserving authority (O'Neil, 2008). Those who embody and practice hegemonic masculinity show greater "tolerance of sexual harassment" (Kearney et al. 2004, p. 78) and display hostility toward women (O'Neil et al. 1995), an attitude shown to be a strong predictor of sexual violence (Anderson & Anderson, 2008; Forbes et al., 2004; Murnen et al., 2002).

Scrutinizing Sexual Violence as Normative Male Behavior

Men across the masculinities spectrum engage in sexual dominance as part of their hegemonic position which is persuasive, "encouraging all to consent to, coalesce around, and embody . . . unequal gender" relations (Messerschmidt, 2019, p. 86). Group processes play a significant role in uniting masculine variances (Messerschmidt, 2005) to produce and uphold rape culture, as discovered among criminology research findings which suggest that violence targeting women is part of normative masculine identity (Godenzi et al., 2001). Masculine ideology is shaped by and, in turn, influences peer/institutional interactions that encourage gender inequality and support violence. Men who do not partake in hypermasculine associations are those considered to be deviant (Godenzi et al., 2001).

Males who perform masculinity in line with hegemonic male gender role norms and are challenged on those grounds—internally or externally—can experience male GRS (Eisler et al., 2000). Literacy of male gender role norms dictate communal awareness of ways males are expected to behave and decision-making processes become inherent, routine, and a benchmark against which they are judged—all, potentially, with stress-filled outcomes.

Boys and men constantly must decode their positionality and determine how to responsively code the self (Street, 2003), fully aware that they "are either in it or you're not" (Gee, 1989, p. 9), so that males either wholly embody the position or are a "pretender to the social role" (Chakrabarty, 2020, p. 2). Males can experience gender-based stress when they choose not to engage in violent behaviors even though they value their hegemonic social position (Gallagher & Parrott, 2011).

Males are products of gender hegemony, with its scrutiny and control to maintain gender-based status, toughness, aggression, and an anti-feminine position (Thompson & Pleck, 1986). Preserving social standing requires a state of constant alertness in which close watch is kept for moments when hegemonic masculinity is perceived to be under threat (Copenhaver et al., 2000). Sexual hostility and violence can result when men experience gendered stress with feelings of uncertainty and/or inferiority (Gallagher & Parrott, 2011).

Examining #MeToo and Digital Defiance

In 16 words, actress Alyssa Milano began the digital incarnation of Tarana Burke's Me Too movement: "If you've been sexually harassed or assaulted write 'Me Too' as a reply to this tweet" (Milano, 2017). To help female victims of sexual violence stand up for themselves, New-York activist Tarana Burke, founded the #MeToo movement in 2006. For men, the #MeToo movement's practice of advocating for destabilizing systems of oppression has had a profound effect. As women have engaged with the second-wave feminist ideal of *the personal is political* to connect personal experience with larger social and political structures (Hanisch, 2006), men have negotiated their gender role in ways they never have before. The #MeToo movement's narrative performed a political function (Clark-Parson, 2019) to educate women about rape culture (Keller at al., 2018; Phipps et al., 2017), to empower survivors to call out abusers and demand address, and to expose socioeconomic and sociocultural structures that uphold oppressive systems (Salter, 2013). Similarly, the naming of *rape culture* has exposed male hegemony to further scrutiny. Early documentation of rape culture featured survivor narratives that articulated sexual aggression and violence as mechanisms that sustain male dominance (Brownmiller, 1976; Lazarus & Wunderlich, 1975). Yet, for generations, a culture of silence has trivialized rape, stigmatized survivors, and suppressed women's accounts of sexual violence (Jacques-Tiura et al., 2010).

Women of the #MeToo era, however, have sought to break patriarchal subjugation by using social media digital messaging platforms to add their voices to the longstanding narrative of sexual violence (Clark-Parsons, 2019). Earlier, access to the traditional public remained obstructed by a patriarchal culture which regulates media space wherein gatekeepers (often male) determine which issues and stories are amplified. Members of the #MeToo movement use digital messaging to embrace "multimodal conceptions of literacy practices" (Street, 2004, p. 327) to amplify women's stories, creating what Powell (2015) called *counterpublics*, or liminal spaces that straddle private and social spheres so that survivors coalesce to disclose/expose abuse and provide/seek support (Clark-Parsons 2019; Gallagher et al., 2019; O'Neill, 2018). Thus, digital messaging platforms support "collective action for a collective solution" (Hanisch, 2006, p. 4). Online, women's stories magnify stigmatizing experiences (Gallagher et al., 2019). So far, outcomes of the #MeToo movement include 201 men facing accusations that range from sexual misconduct to multiple counts of rape (Carlsen et. al, 2018))—a result of the "silence breakers," *Time* magazine's "person of the year" (Zacharek et al., 2018).

Considering Masculinity Post-#MeToo*

By 2000, women's experiences of sexual violence could no longer be brushed aside in the public sphere. Their accounts spoke of collective and unique experiences, exposing multiple ways that male violence unfolds with men across socio-economic status groups using sexual violence. A society that believed only a small portion of men engage in sexual abuse had to reconcile the new numbers made public and that sexual violence and the men accused of using it is commonplace. For men, this dynamic of public disclosure of private events means systemic male hegemony regularly is called into question—with varying degrees of self-blame (O'Neill, 2018), stigma checked and undermined (Gallagher et al., 2019), and solidarity forged (Mendes et al, 2018). Among academic scholarship, connections between sexual violence and GRC/GRS outcomes have been known for decades. However, the #MeToo movement offers an opportunity to examine ways that some men struggle with admitting a role in gendered violence, or ways they work to fortify patriarchal culture as they watch heretofore fortified codes of dominance and marginalization begin to crumble. Because I contend that such work takes place through "language and symbolic meaning, all of which have material and ideological consequences" (Mundy & Denny, 2020), this chapter critically examines how men have used language to perform masculinity in post-#MeToo America. With four case studies, I seek to highlight and challenge dominant constructions of masculinity that negatively impact both women and men. The cases enable me to examine two general questions: How have the accused rhetorically framed *the comeback*? What does this discourse reveal about how men are experiencing and responding to GRC/GRS during the #MeToo era?

METHOD

The study reported in this chapter involves use of the case study method to examine interplay of male GRC/GRS in conjunction with the #MeToo movement. This approach is beneficial when investigating contemporary events with small samples of data and is useful for gaining a rich understanding of issues (Cresswell, 2013; Tellis, 1997; Yin, 2009). The study followed a collective approach (Stake, 1995) to review several cases related to a phenomenon that are not directly connected to one another—and reveal literal representation (Yin, 2009). *The comeback* outcome serves as a literacy event, or an observable episode (Barton & Hamilton, 2000) of what Halliday (2001) called "the environment of the text" (p. 190) where participants engage with language to provide context for their position (Halliday & Hasan, 1985). Each case reflects an evolution of *the comeback* narrative in response to perceptions of male GRC/GRS: 1) Brett Kavanaugh's Supreme Court nomination hearings, September 4–7, 2018; 2) James Franco's appearance on the Golden Globes, Stephen Colbert's *Late Show,* and Seth Meyers' *Late Night* in January 2018; 3) Louis C. K.'s return to the stage in December 2018; and 4) the Netflix premiere of the eponymous "Aziz Ansari: Right Now" on July 9, 2019.

I reviewed each case using a Critical Discourse Analysis (CDA) lens to sharpen focus on social practice and the multidirectional relationship between events and their situated contexts (Wodak, 2007). CDA takes into account the "public and semi-public" arenas where ideology is manifested, negotiated, or subverted through language (Wodak & Krzyżanowski, 2011). It examines how language is used to uphold existing power structures (van Dijk, 1995, who controls the narrative, and how they influence others in their own self-interest (van Dijk, 1995). CDA confirms "semiotic hegemony," an ability to dictate the course of interaction and the preferred meaning it prompts (Wodak, 2007). This method of analysis is grounded in social or political ethics," which is aimed at considering how "dominance and inequality . . . are reproduced or resisted by social group members through text and talk" (van Dijk, 1995, p. 18) so that sociocultural and socioeconomic change can be enacted (Wodak, 2007).

FINDINGS

As a movement rooted in challenging male power, #MeToo served as a locus for men to rally against. When pressed to account for their sexual transgressions, male GRC/GRS escalated among the experiences of four men examined in this chapter, causing them to construct counterarguments that endorse rape myths, obfuscate allegations, and leverage accounts of isolation, hurt, and victimization. In addition to defending themselves, accused males sought to maintain hegemonic masculinity by silencing women. These cases present *the comeback* through three distinct themes: 1) *Cancel Culture & Gender Role Affirmation,* 2) *(Non)Apology & Performative Allyship,* and 3) *Himpathy & Male Pain.* Each theme offers insight into ways language was used to evade responsibility and address conflict/stress through a reassertion of traditional gender order.

Brett Kavanaugh: Cancel Culture and Gender Role Affirmation

Brett Kavanaugh's U.S. Supreme Court confirmation hearing in 2018 included accusations of sexual misconduct in high school and college by three women. This event served as a pivotal moment when the #MeToo movement intersected with the rape culture phenomenon with blame of toxic masculinity. It inspired introduction of #HimToo, a hashtag used to support Kavanaugh against accusations that some believed were false. When confronted with being accused of attempted rape and sexual assault, Kavanaugh leveraged his male privilege, "categorically and unequivocally" denying the accusations without providing much of a defense besides his career/life record and religious faith (Carlisle & Paschal, 2018). Other than his high school calendar that Kavanaugh claimed exonerated him, his defense relied on indignation and belief that he was the victim of "last-minute smears" to halt his nomination (Carlisle & Paschal, 2018). As part of the confirmation hearing, Kavanaugh said: "This has destroyed my family and my good name" (Karson & Haslett, 2018). Kavanaugh directed anger at his accusers whom he perceived to be "lying in wait" to "take [him] out" (Kirby, 2018).

Political figures similarly defended Kavanaugh's nomination as the public discourse surrounding the hearing devolved into a referendum on *cancel culture* and served as a conservative talking point aimed at discrediting the #MeToo movement. Kavanaugh's supporters claimed men were being culturally erased by women and liberal interests. Then-U.S. President Donald Trump defended his Associate Justice of the U.S. Supreme Court nominee whom he had chosen to succeed retiring Justice Anthony Kennedy (The Latest, 2018). Trump argued: His "life is in tatters. A man's life is shattered" (Merritt, 2018). Trump disqualified voices of Kavanaugh's accusers, citing alcohol consumption and lapses in time between incidence and reporting (Malloy et al., 2018). Through populist rhetoric, he positioned himself as a similar victim (though an admitted sexual predator), and warned all men that they, too, could be wrongly accused: "It's a very scary time for young men in America, when you may be guilty of something that you may not be guilty of . . . somebody could accuse you of something . . . and you're automatically guilty" (Lind, 2018). For Trump, cancel culture means "decent Americans live in fear" (Santucci, 2020) of an exaggerated form of political correctness instead of the act of calling out injustice and holding the accused accountable. Fellow Republican Senator Lindsey Graham expressed his indignation as: "I'm a single white male . . . I've been told I should shut up, but I will not . . ." (Amatulli, 2018). To Kavanaugh, Graham added: "I cannot imagine what you and your family have gone through . . . "you are a victim" (Amatuli, 2018).

James Franco and Aziz Ansari: (Non)Apology and Performative Allyship

Two American actors who profess support for women's causes both have been accused of sexual impropriety and hypocrisy. In 2018, social media played a critical role in calling out American actor James Franco, who accepted the 2018 Golden Globe award on January 7 for best actor wearing on his lapel a Time's Up pin. Doing so suggested support of a charitable organization founded on January 1, 2018 by Hollywood celebrities in response to the #MeToo movement, with money raised to support sexual harassment victims. When American actor, Ally Sheedy (2018) saw this on the telecast, she used Twitter to question: "Why is James Franco allowed in?" followed by "[he] just won . . . never . . . ask me why I left the film/tv business." Similarly, Violet Paley (2018) alleged assault and reminded him of the two times he pursued 17-year-old women for sex, and Sarah Tither-Kaplan (2018) claimed how Franco had exploited and assaulted her on set. These tweets questioned Franco's transgressions. During media interviews, Franco admitted on *Live with Kelly and Michael* that he'd had "questionable" Instagram exchanges with a 17-year-old woman in 2014 and attributed the encounter to "bad judgment" (Robinson, 2018). As a guest on other talk shows, Franco stated: ". . . I completely support people coming out and being able to have a voice because they didn't have a voice for so long" and "There are stories that need to get out . . . people that need to be heard" (*Late Night*, 2018).

Another American actor and comedian, Aziz Ansari, spoke of sexual misconduct allegations directed at him as part of his Netflix standup comedy special, but has not publicly apologized to the female photographer who accused him of pressuring her for sex in his apartment after a date (North, 2019). Rather, in his comedy special *Right Now* (2019) Ansari focused on his own torment only seven months after he was accused of sexual misconduct: "There's times I felt scared, there's times I felt humiliated, there's times I felt embarrassed" (Right Now, 2019). As Franco supported Time's Up, Ansari similarly championed feminism on *Late Night with David Letterman* on October 6, 2014 (Marcotte, 2014; Kelly, 2018) and advocated for the #MeToo movement four years later with "I continue to support the movement that is happening in our culture. It is necessary and long overdue" (Steward, 2018).

Both men have spoken of having their own stories to tell about consensual relationships but have been unclear about they've learned. Repeatedly, both intimated allyship with women's causes but have used their own privilege to avoid culpability rather than to affect real change.

Louis C. K.: "Himpathy" and Male Pain

As reported in the *New York Times*, American comedian, actor, and writer Louis C. K. masturbated in front of "multiple women," including female colleagues and others who have alleged his sexual misconduct "for years" (Domonoske, 2017). Yet, Louis C. K. returned to the stage after confirming these reports (North, 2019). What seems to have garnered the most attention from the accusations/events—rather than trauma experienced by women— was the support of other men who lamented trauma that Louis C. K. experienced. For example, fellow American comedians Michael Ian Black tweeted: ". . . people have to be allowed to serve their time and move on with their lives . . ." (Black, 2018), Michael Che exclaimed: "OMG! Can you believe that guy went on with his life?!" (Wilstein, 2018), and Norm Macdonald argued: "victims didn't have to go through that," "losing everything in a day" as he believed C. K had (Hoffman, 2018). American actor Matt Damon stated: "I imagine that the price he's paid at this point is so beyond anything" (Valiente & Williams, 2017).

Not unlike Ansari, Louis C. K. returned to the stage shortly after the sexual misconduct allegations surfaced. As part of his comedy routine, he positioned himself as protagonist of the story and offered his embarrassment and pain to elicit himpathy. Men generate himpathy as a response to gender role disruption. According to Manne (2018), this is one way "powerful and privileged boys and men who commit acts of sexual violence or engage in misogynistic behavior often receive sympathy and concern over their female victims" (p. 5). Louis C. K. emphasized his own well-being, expressed worry that the accusations would destroy all he had worked for, and conjured fears of having his life ruined. Use of himpathy enabled Louis C. K. to rhetorically regain control of the narrative by exerting his male entitlement and reaffirm the traditional gender order.

DISCUSSION AND CONCLUSION

Examined together, these case studies involving four men accused of sexual misconduct suggest a common defensive thread that I call *the comeback* which was systematically supported in specific contexts. The men's response to negatively impacted reputation/social standing by using narratives designed to undermine the experiences of women in order to maintain/reclaim privilege reveals some ways hegemonic masculinity is maintained. Examining how one now Supreme Court Justice, one actor, and two comedians—Brett Kavanaugh, James Franco, Aziz Ansari, and Louis C. K.—responded to women's accusations and the GRC/GRS they expressed sheds light on defensive rhetorical work performed during a time when women's voices about sexual violence were being heard and acknowledged.

The timing, or context, of these events and the men's use of language is emblematic of self-defense in the wake of headline-making accusations by women during the #MeToo movement. When accused, each of the four men relied on what Kimmel (2017) called "aggrieved entitlement," or a feeling of humiliation brought forth when privilege is checked or denied. That the men chose to frame the sexual misconduct accusations in terms of their own GRC/GRS suggests that three Caucasian/White men (ages 56, 43, 53) and one Indian-American man (age 38) were united in relying on hegemonic masculinity to shield them from potentially career-ending defamation, cancelling in the court of public opinion, and/or criminal sentences in courts of law. Other male public figures like Trump and popular actors and comedians sought to rescue the accused with the old cliche of women "cry rape with ease and glee" (Brownmiller, 1976)—even though only between 2 percent and 10 percent of rape claims are said to be false (Lisak et al., 2010) and "1 in 6 women experience [sexual coercion] . . . in their lifetime" (Smith et al, 2018).

The context of public figures' socioeconomic status also must be considered part of men's defense arsenal when accused of sexual misconduct. Public figures have the financial, social, and political means to subvert allegations. With a litany of lawyers in tow, as part of their regular work and operations, they require nondisclosure agreements to be signed and have legal supports in place in anticipation of potential accusations. Such men are the courts, government, and media conglomerates. Their status and privilege as men shield them from taking responsibility or being accountable; standards otherwise expected of private individuals. Their access to the spotlight and public sphere means many women are hesitant to disclose such personal stories. Victims are aware that speaking out opens them up to scrutiny and further abuse, or a very public systematic interrogation and dismantling of their lives.

Moreover, the context of cancel culture considered by male public figures as threat to their livelihood serves as a dog whistle for other men who are not public figures, but private individuals. Rhetorically turning the tables to make themselves look like victims at the hands of women means that men who are private individuals hear and react to coded language suggesting that *all* men should be fearful of such action and fight back to ensure they, too, are not persecuted. At a time when social media fuels cancel culture, hegemonic masculinity is believed to be under attack and in need of fortification for traditional manhood to carry on. Social and economic shifts have taught these men that masculinity is always on the line (Faludi, 2000). Threats of cancel culture tap into ongoing anxiety men experience regarding their economic and familial standing. GRS for men intensifies when they perceive an inability to meet a breadwinner standard (O'Neil et al., 1995).

Taught from an early age that to apologize means to behave in ways inconsistent with the male gender role since it is females who are expected to show weakness (Kimmel, 1987), the closest that two of the four men examined in this chapter could come to acknowledging the allegations or apologizing was to communicate allyship. Such behaviors maintain benefits patriarchy affords (Kimmel, 1998). Rather, both Franco and Ansari presented themselves as being blindsided because they considered the events as consensual. Franco wore a Time's Up pin during a major television event and Ansari professed support of feminism on a popular talk show and the #MeToo movement in a public statement. Both entertainers seemed to use allyship to mitigate GRC/ GRS they experienced in conjunction with their own behaviors. Through the rhetoric of siding with *all* women, they could detach themselves from *the* women who accused them of sexual misconduct. They strategically deflected systemic sexism and gender violence away from themselves. Rather than verifying "the victim's experience" by admitting "wrongdoing" without "excuse, defense, justification, or explanation for the action," and pledging "that the act will not be repeated" (Regehr and Gutheil, 2002, p. 425), they opted for a pseudo apology in the form of general statements that lack specificity by engaging with a group and not a person in order to "avoid public condemnation" and to buy time that "heals, distorts, forgives, and forgets (Downey, 1993, p. 57-58).

The four case studies of men accused of sexual misconduct in this chapter offer an opportunity to examine ways that male gender roles are reinforced in terms of men being expected to be sexually prolific. The belief that women and sex are rewards for men who embody and perform hegemonic masculinity can lead to power abuses. Considering sexual relationships in terms of pursuit, or a game in which men chase coy, modest women who have been conditioned to rebuff sexual advances (while secretly long for them), enables men to fulfill a role as liberators—not violators. This dynamic sets up females to be victims of violence and men to experience GRS should they fail to meet this standard for masculine worth. Rebuked by other men and taught that female consent is subservient to male needs and boundaries, females who refuse sexual advances not only do not play an equal role in decision making, but can become victims of male aggression and violence integral to traditional hegemonic masculine behaviors. These dynamics reinforce among males that they have a right to enact power inherent in their masculine identity (Manne, 2018).

Emergence of the #MeToo movement has exposed a culture that remains without "ways of talking about . . . sexual violence in the lives of women" (Gilmore, 2018) and the case studies unwrapped in this chapter suggest that hegemonic masculinity proves exceptionally resilient and resistant to change—especially with regard to male gender power and violence as an adjunct for exerting that power. In a context of sexual violence, our public discourse sustains abuse and forgives abusive men. Male recourse has been to (re)assert patriarchal privilege in the face of feminist progress that is believed to cause instability, conflict, and stress for males. To bolster hegemonic masculinity and avoid disrupting male authority, men have leaned on *the comeback* narrative designed to undermine the experiences of women in order to reclaim privilege.

These case studies highlighted systemic fortification of hegemonic masculinity in a context of #MeToo movement gains in the public sphere. Male GRC/GRS inherent in hegemonic masculinity when boys and men feel incapable of measuring up to masculine ideals—sometimes resorting to aggression and violence toward women—now are used, rhetorically, to paint themselves victims of women's accusations about sexual misconduct. Like Connell and Messerschmidt (2005), I concur that we need a reformulation of the masculinity concept in terms of emphasizing the agency of women—and recognizing internal contradictions to support possibilities of movement toward gender democracy (Wedgwood, 2009).

More research exploring the systemic nature of deeply embedded ideas about masculinity that makes it hegemonic and toxic is vitally needed if we are to redirect masculinity and male gender roles toward inclusivity, respect, and justice. Developing a literacy of masculinity is not an altogether uplifting experience. To get to a place of civil discourse, toxic masculinity must be critically examined so that men may learn how women are impacted when their bodies are violated and stories and identities are invalidated. We must decode language of *the comeback* to read—not as men being ill-treated, as they have professed—but as women being forced to live through and endure ongoing exploitation from the violent act itself, through interplay across the judicial system and as part of public opinion discourse (Lees, 2002). Not long ago, women's stories were seldom heard. For a brief moment, they rose to prominence. To now ask "But what about the men?" risks acknowledging that women's stories may never be heard again.

52 Robert Mundy

REFERENCES

Alexander, C. (2020). Sorry (not sorry): Decoding #MeToo defenses. *SSRN Electronic Journal*. doi:10.2139/ssrn.3550207.

Alexander, J. (2008). Literacy, sexuality, pedagogy: Theory and practice for composition studies. https://rb.gy/0ietsv.

Amatuli, J. (2018, September 28). Lindsey Graham slammed for "single white man," "I will not shut up" remarks. *Huffington Post*. https://rb.gy/waq6ji.

Anderson, G. A. & Anderson, K. B. (2008). Men who target women: Specificity of target, generality of aggressive behavior. *Aggressive Behavior*, 34(6), 605–622, doi: 10.1002/ab.20274.

Ansari, A. (2019). Right now. *Netflix*.

AP News. The latest: Trump says Democrats trying to destroy Kavanaugh (2018, September 24). *Associated Press*. https://rb.gy/7fmbpm.

Barton, D., & Hamilton, M. (2000). Literacy practices. In D. Barton, M. Hamilton, and R. Ivanic (Eds.), *Situated literacies: Reading and writing in context* (pp. 7–15). Routledge.

Black, M. I. [michaelianblack]. (2018, August 28). Will take heat for this, but people have to be allowed to serve their time and move on with their [Tweet].

Blazina, C. (1997). The fear of the feminine in the Western psyche and the masculine task of disidentification: Their effect on the development of masculine gender role conflict. *The Journal of Men's Studies*, 6(1), 55–68. doi: https://doi.org/10.1177/1 06082659700600103.

Brownmiller, S. (1976). *Against our will: Men, women and rape*. Penguin.

Butler, J. (1990). *Gender trouble:* Feminism and the subversion of identity. Routledge.

———. (1997). *Excitable speech: A politics of the performative*. Routledge.

Carlsen, A., Salam, M., Miller, C. C., Lu, D., Ngu, A. Patel, J. K., & Wicher, Z. (2018). (2018, October 23). #MeToo brought down 201 powerful men. Nearly half of their replacements are women. *New York Times*. https://rb.gy/vdqwit.

Carlisle, M. & Paschal (2018, September 26). Brett Kavanaugh's prepared remarks. *The Atlantic*. https://rb.gy/hn9q82.

Chakrabarty, D. (2020). Theories of new literacy. *RJELAL*, 8(1), 1–8, doi:10.33329/rjelal.8.1.1.

Clark-Parsons, R. (2019). I see you, I believe you, I stand with you: #MeToo and the performance of networked feminist visibility. *Feminist Media Studies*, 21(3), 362–380 doi:10.1080/14680777.2019.1628797.

Connell, R. W. (1987). *Gender and power: Society, the person, and sexual politics*. Stanford University Press.

———. (2005). *Masculinities* (2nd ed.). University of California Press.

Connell, R. W., & Messerschmidt, J. W. (2005). Hegemonic masculinity: Rethinking the concept. *Gender & Society, 19*(6), 829–859. doi: https:// doi.org/ 10.1177/ 0891243205278639.

Copenhaver, M. M., Lash, S. J., & Eisler, R. M. (2000). Masculine gender-role stress, anger, and male intimate abusiveness: Implications for men's relationships. *Sex Roles*, 42(5–6), 405–414. doi: https://rb.gy/osaqdv.

Cresswell, J. W. (2013). *Qualitative inquiry & research design: Choosing among the five approaches.* Sage.

Dixon, K. (2014). Feminist online identity: Analyzing the presence of hashtag feminism. *Journal of Arts and Humanities*, 3, 34–40. doi: https://doi.org/10.18533/journal.v3i7.509.

Domonoske, C. (2017, November 9). Multiple women say Louis C. K. masturbated in front of them, New York Times reports. NPR. Downloaded June 22, 2021 from https://rb.gy/ofggnm.

Downey, S. D. (1993). The evolution of the rhetorical genre of apologia. *Western Journal of Communication, 57*(1), 42–64. doi:10.1080/10570319309374430.

Eisler, R. M., Franchina, J. J., Moore, T. M., Honeycutt, H. G., & Rhatigan, D. L. (2000). Masculine gender role stress and intimate abuse: Effects of gender relevance of conflict situations on men's attributions and affective responses. *Psychology of Men & Masculinity, 1*(1), 30–36. doi:10.1037/1524-9220.1.1.30.

Faludi, S. (2000). *Stiffed.* William Marrow.

Forbes, G. B, Adams-Curtis, L. E., & White, K. B. (2004). First- and second-generation measures of sexism, rape myths and related beliefs, and hostility toward women: Their interrelationships and association with college students' experiences with dating aggression and sexual coercion. *Violence Against Women*, 10(3), 236–261, doi: 10.1177/1077801203256002.

Gallagher, K. E. & Parrott, D. J. (2011). What accounts for men's hostile attitudes toward women? The influence of hegemonic male role norms and masculine gender role stress. *Violence Against Women*, 17(5), 568–583. doi:10.1177/1077801211407296.

Gallagher, R. J., Stowell, E., Parker, A. G., & Welles, B. F. (2019). Reclaiming stigmatized narratives: The networked disclosure landscape of #MeToo. doi:10.31235/osf.io/qsmce.

Gee, J. P. (1989). Literacy, discourse, and linguistics: Introduction. Journal of Education, 171(1), 5–176. doi: https://rb.gy/3twrad.

———. (2012). *Social linguistics and literacies: Ideology in discourses* (4th edition). Routledge, Taylor & Francis Group.

———. (2015). *The Routledge handbook of literacy studies.* Routledge.

Gilmore, L. (2018). *Tainted witness: Why we doubt what women say about their lives.* Columbia University Press.

Godenzi, A., Schwartz, M. D., & Dekeseredy, W. S. (2001). Toward a gendered social bond/male peer support theory of university woman abuse. *Critical Criminology*, 10, 1–16. doi: 10.1023/A:1013105118592.

Halliday, M. A. K. (2001). *Theory and resistance in education: A pedagogy for opposition.* Berginband Garvey.

Halliday, M. A. K., & Hasan, R. (1985). *Language, context, and text: Aspects of language in a social-semiotic perspective.* Deakin University Press.

Hanisch, C. (2006). *The personal is political: The Women's Liberation Movement classic with a new explanatory intrduction.* https://rb.gy/vvc98k.

Hoffman, A. (September 12, 2018). Norm Macdonald criticized for defending Louis C. K. and Roseanne Barr. *Time.* https://rb.gy/veezlm.

Ipsos (2018). Ipsos/NPR examine views on sexual harassment and assault. https://rb
.gy/8gnect.

Jacques-Tiura, A. J., Tkatch, R., Abbey, A., & Wegner, R. (2010). Disclosure of
sexual assault: Characteristics and implications for posttraumatic stress symptoms
among African American and Caucasian survivors. *Journal of Trauma & Dissocia-
tion*, 11(2), 174–192. doi: 10.1080/15299730903502938.

Karson, K. & Haslett C. (September 27, 2018). Kavanaugh hearing. *ABCNews*.
https://rb.gy/qn5d8j.

Kearney, L. K., Rochlen, A. B., & King, E. D. (2004). Male gender role conflict,
sexual harassment tolerance, and the efficacy of a psychoeducational training program. *Psychology of Men and Masculinity*, 5(1), 72–82. https://psycnet.apa.org/
doi/10.1037/1524-9220.5.1.72.

Keller, J., Mendes, K., & Ringrose, J. (2018). Speaking 'unspeakable things':
Documenting digital feminist responses to rape culture. *Journal of Gender Studies*,
27(1), 22–36. https://doi.org/10.1080/09589236.2016.1211511.

Kelly, M. (February 21, 2017). *Aziz Ansari on feminism* [Video]. *YouTube*. https://
rb.gy/o8pe9w.

Kimmel, M. S. (1987). The contemporary "crisis" of masculinity in historical perspective. In H. Brod (Ed.), *The making of masculinities: The new men's studies*
(pp. 121–153). Allen & Unwin.

———. (1998). Who's afraid of men doing feminism? In T. Digby (Ed.), *Men doing
feminism*. Routledge.

———. (2001). Global masculinities: Restoration and resistance. In B. Pease and K.
Pringle (Eds.), *A man's world: Changing men's practices in a globalized world*
(pp. 21–37). Zed Books.

———. (2004). Masculinity as homophobia: Fear, shame, and silence in the construction of gender identity. P. F. Murphy (Ed.), *Feminism & Masculinities* (pp.
182–199). Oxford University Press.

———. (2017). *Angry white men: American masculinity at the end of an era*. Nation
Books.

Kirby, J. (2018, September 27). Brett Kavanaugh's angry, emotional opening statement. *Vox*. https://rb.gy/xzupdq.

Kivel, P. (2019). The act-like-a-man box. In M. S. Kimmel & M. A. Messner (Eds.),
Men's lives (10th ed., pp. 16–18). Oxford University Press.

Langone, A. (2018). #MeToo and Time's Up founders explain the difference between
the 2 movements. *Time*. https://rb.gy/q16ihb.

Late Night. (2018, January 11). *James Franco addresses his sexual misconduct allegations* [Video]. *YouTube*. https://rb.gy/kt2d1b.

Late Show. (2018, January 10). *James Franco supports 'time's up,' addresses recent
accusations* [Video]. *YouTube*. https://rb.gy/6kahh6.

Lazarus, M, & Wunderlich, R. (Producers). (1975). *Rape culture* [Film]. Cambridge
Documentary Films.

Lees, S. (2002). *Carnal knowledge: Rape on trial* (2nd edition). Women's Press Ltd.

Lind, D. (2018, October 2). Trump: "It's a very scary time for young men in America." *Vox*. https://rb.gy/8td4hl.

Lisak, D., Gardinier, L., Nicksa, S. C., & Cote, A. M. (2010). False allegations of sexual assault: An analysis of ten years of reported cases. *Violence Against Women,* 16(12), 1318–1344. doi: 10.1177/1077801210387747.

Malloy, A., Sullivan, K., & Zeleny, J. (2018, October 3). Trump mocks Christine Blasey Ford's testimony. *CNN Politics.* https://rb.gy/ejngjz.

Manne, K. (2018). *Entitled: How male privilege hurts women.* Crown.

Marcotte, A. (October 7, 2014). Aziz Ansari is better than most celebrities at talking about feminism. Slate. Downloaded June 22, 2021, from https://rb.gy/hhjexr.

Martin, R. (2018). On #MeToo, Americans more divided by party than gender. *NPR.* https://rb.gy/wxh3ed.

Mendes, K., Ringrose, J., & Keller, J. (2018). #MeToo and the promise and pitfalls of challenging rape culture through digital feminist activism. *European Journal of Women's Studies, 25*(2), 236–246. doi:10.1177/1350506818765318.

Merritt, R. (October 3, 2018). Trump mocks Christine Blasey Ford after sexual assault testimony. *People.* https://rb.gy/svi3cw.

Messerschmidt, J. W. (2005). Men, masculinities, and crime. In M. S Kimmel, J. Hearn, and R. W. Connell (Eds). *The handbook of studies on men & masculinities* (pp. 196–212). Sage.

———. (2019). The salience of "hegemonic masculinity." *Men and Masculinities, 22*(1), 85–91. doi:10.1177/1097184x18805555.

Milano, A. [Alyssa Milano]. (October 15, 2017). If you've been sexually harassed or assaulted write "Me Too" as a reply to this tweet [Tweet]. https:// twitter.com/ alyssa_milano/status/ 919659438700670976?lang=en.

Mundy, R., & Denny, H. (2020). *Gender, sexuality, and the cultural politics of men's identity. Literacies of masculinity.* Routledge.

Netflix. (March 14, 2015). *Aziz Ansari: Live at Madison Square Garden* [Video]. *YouTube.* https://rb.gy/az5w8o.

North, A. (January 9, 2019). Louis C. K. and Aziz Ansari have an opportunity for redemption. They're squandering it. *Vox.* https://rb.gy/fdrjci.

———. (July 12, 2019). Aziz Ansari has addressed his sexual misconduct allegation. But he hasn't publicly apologized. *Vox.* Downloaded June 21, 2021, from https:// rb.gy/hsomzj.

O'Neil, J. M. (1981). Patterns of gender role conflict and strain: Sexism and fear of femininity in men's lives. *The Personnel and Guidance Journal, 60*(4), 203–210. doi:10.1002/j.2164-4918.1981.tb00282.x.

———. (1990). *Assessing men's gender role conflict.* In D. Moore & F. Leafgren (Eds.), *Problem solving strategies and interventions for men in conflict* (p. 23–38). American Association for Counseling.

———. (2008). Summarizing 25 years of research on men's gender role conflict using the gender role conflict scale: New research paradigms and clinical Implications. *The Counseling Psychologist,* 36(3), 358–445. doi:10.1177/0011000008317057.

O'Neil, J. M., Good, G. E., & Holmes, S. (1995). Fifty years of theory and research on men's gender role conflict: New paradigms for empirical research. In R. Levant & W. Pollack (Eds.), *The new psychology of men* (p. 164–206). Basic Books.

O'Neil, J. M., Helms, B. J., Gable, R. K., David, L., & Wrightsman, L. S. (1986). Gender-role conflict scale: College men's fear of femininity. *Sex Roles*, 14, 335–350.

O'Neill, T. (2018). "Today I speak: Exploring how victim-survivors use Reddit. *International Journal for Crime, Justice and Democracy*, 7(1), 44–59. https/doi .org/10.5204/ijcjsd.v7i1.402.

Paley, V. [@VioletPaley]. (January 8, 2018). *Cute #TIMESUP pin . . . Remember the time you pushed my head down . . . towards your exposed penis & that other time you told* [Tweet].

Phipps, A., Ringrose, J., Renold, E., & Jackson, C. (2017). Rape culture, lad culture and everyday sexism: Researching, conceptualizing and politicizing new mediations of gender and sexual violence. *Journal of Gender Studies*, 27(1), 1–8. doi: 10.1080/09589236.2016.1266792.

Powell, A. (2015). Seeking rape justice: Formal and informal responses to sexual violence through technosocial counterpublics. *Theoretical Criminology*, 19(4), 571–588. https://doi.org/10.1177/1362480615576271.

Regehr, C. & Gutheil, T. G. (2002). Apology, justice and trauma recovery. *The Journal of the American Academy of Psychiatry and the Law*, 30(3).

Reeser, T. W. (2010). *Masculinities in theory: An introduction.* Malden, MA: Wiley-Blackwell.

Rowley, J. (2002). Using case studies in research. *Management Research News*, 25(1), 16–27. doi: https://psycnet.apa.org/doi/10.1002/9781444317312.

Robinson, J. (January 7, 2018). Why did Ally Sheedy call out Golden Globe Winner James Franco on Twitter? *Vanity Fair*. Downloaded June 21, 2021, from https:// rb.gy/gklcht.

Santucci, J. (September 3, 2020). Trump decries 'cancel culture." *USA Today*. https:// rb.gy/iezb2e.

Salter, M. (2013). Justice and revenge in online counter-publics" Emerging responses to sexual violence in the age of social media. *Crime, Media, Culture*, 9(3), 225–242. https://doi.org. 10.1177%2F1741659013493918.

Sheedy, A. [@allysheedy1]. (January 7, 2018). *Why is James Franco allowed in?* [Tweet].

———. (January 7, 2018). *James Franco just won. Please never ask me why I left the tv/film business.* [Tweet].

Smith, R. M., Parrott, D. J., Swartout, K. M., & Tharp, A. T. (2015). Deconstructing hegemonic masculinity: The roles of antifemininity, subordination to women, and sexual dominance in men's perpetration of sexual aggression. *Psychol Men Masc.*, 16(2), 160–169.

Smith, S. G., Zhang, X., Basile, K. C., Merrick, M. T, Wang, J., Kresnow, M., & Chen, J. (2018). The national intimate partner and sexual violence survey. *CDC*. https://rb.gy/vobo5c.

Stake, R. E. (1995). *The art of case study research.* Sage.

Steward, E. (2018, January 15). Aziz Ansari responds to sexual misconduct allegations against him. *Vox*. https://rb.gy/csntrv.

Street, B. (2003). *Social literacies: Critical approaches to literacy in development, ethnography and education*. Longman.

———. (2004). Futures of the ethnography of literacy? *Language and Education, 5*(2), 77–91. https://rb.gy/in3afa.

Tellis, W. M. (1997). Application of a case study methodology. *The Qualitative Report, 3*(3).

Thompson, E. H. & Pleck, J. H. (1986). The structure of male role norms. *American Behavioral Scientist, 29*(5), 531–543. https://doi.org/10.1177/0002764860290050 03.

Tither-Kaplan, S. [@sarahtk]. (January 7, 2018). *Hey James Franco, nice #timesup pin at the #GoldenGlobes, remember a few weeks ago when you told me the full nudity* [Tweet].

Valiente, A. & Williams, A. (December 14, 2017). Matt Damon opens up about Harvey Weinstein, sexual harassment and confidentiality agreements. *abcNEWS*. https://rb.gy/fjwmoi.

van Dijk, T. A. (1995) Aims of critical discourse analysis. *Japanese Discourse (1)*, 17–27.

Wedgwood, N. (2009). Connell's theory of masculinity—its origins and influence son the study of gender. *Journal of Gender Studies*, 18(4), 329–339. doi: https://doi.org/10.1080/09589230903260001.

West, C. & Zimmerman, D. H. (1987). Doing gender. *Gender and Society, 1*(2), 125–151. https://doi.org/10.1177/ 0891243287001002002.

Wilstein, M. (August 29, 2018). Michael Che defends Louis C.K.'s 'right' to a come-back. *Daily Beast.* https://rb.gy/ytalac.

Wodak, R. (2007). Critical discourse analysis. In G. Weiss and R. Wodak (Eds.), *Critical Discourse Analysis: Theory and Interdisciplinarity* (pp. 302-316). Palgrave-MacMillan.

Wodak, R. & Krzyżanowski, M. (2011). Language in political institutions of multilin-gual states and European Union. In B. Kortmann and J. van der Auwera (Eds.), *The language and linguistics of Europe* (pp. 621–637). Mouton de Gruyter.

Yin, R. K. (2009). *Case study research: Design and Methods* (4th ed.). Sage.

Zacharek, S., Dockterman, E., and Edwards, H. S. (2017). The silence breakers. *Time Magazine.* https://rb.gy/q9xy8t.

Chapter Three

When Nothing Changes into Something

Gender Role Stress/Conflict Among Asexual Viewers of BoJack Horseman

ben Brandley and Katherine Mullé

INTRODUCTION

Sex, gender expression, and sexuality are inextricably connected. Historically, masculinity was reserved for categorizing heterosexual cisgender men, *real* men, while femininity was assigned to sexy yet demure heterosexual, cisgender women (Connell & Pearse, 2015). In the companion book, *Rhetoric of Femininity*, Pompper (2017) asserted that challenging this foundation was "long overdue" and a time for "social identity dimensions and their intersectionalities . . . [to] be embraced" (p. 237). In this chapter, we seek to complicate these social realities by calling attention to the material and rhetorical effects of gender roles, masculinities, and asexuality.

Many audiences are starting to see more masculine LGBTQIA+ representation across media (Eguchi & Kimura, 2020). Unfortunately, asexual (or ace) folks—a spectrum of individuals who feel little to no sexual or romantic attraction—remain underrepresented in the media and in research. In this chapter, we seek to explore this representation and examine how aces navigate gender role conflict and stress spurred by allonormative rhetoric imbued by the media. Allonormative rhetoric is the systems of discourse that forefront allosexuality (those who experience sexual attraction) as normative, thereby minoritizing and delegitimating asexual identities, relationships, and yearnings. We do this by examining perceptions held by AVENites (members of Asexuality Visibility and Education Network, or AVEN) on the character representation of Todd Chavez, a main protagonist from Netflix's *BoJack Horseman,* who is heralded as "TV's first out-and-proud asexual icon" (Nickalls, 2017, n.p.).

Using O'Neil's (1981) theory of masculine gender role conflict and stress (GRC/S), we analyze 359 posts and comments that center the perceptions of ace *BoJack Horseman* audience members from AVEN—the world's largest asexual online community. AVEN is a community for any and all ace folks (e.g., aromantic, demisexual, grey-A), allies and those questioning their orientation. A critical thematic analysis (Lawless & Chen, 2019) of the posts and comments written in various related fora by AVEN members allows us to address the unfortunate lack of asexuality research while forefronting the voices of this underrepresented group to understand how Todd Chavez's character influences perception, communication, and possibly behavior. Our goal is to not only bridge gaps of academic archival lacunas, but also to provide insights into the influences of media representation of minoritized sexual identities in hopes of assuaging some of the gender role conflicts and stresses they experience.

REVIEW OF LITERATURE

To guide in this study, we begin with exploring the rhetoric of (masculine) asexuality and allonormativity. As a foundation, we briefly establish the presence of asexual organizing in online communities. Next, we appraise media representations of masculine asexuality both broadly and then introduce the theoretical framework of GRC/S. Then, we provide an overview of the character of Todd Chavez and close this literature review by presenting our research questions.

Asexuality and Allonormativity

Asexuality is a spectrum of sexual orientation in which the individual feels little to no sexual attraction. As an orientation, it is different from one's deliberate choice to be celibate or chaste (Kelemen, 2007). Asexuality is usually represented by the letter "A" in the acronym LGBTQIA+ and is a catch-all term for individuals who exist on the asexual spectrum, recognizing that "there are many ways for people to identify" (Trevor Project, 2017, para. 2). However, for the purposes of this chapter, we position asexuality as an identity in which a person may wish to develop intimate relationships but not have sexual or even romantic interests. Simply put, asexuality is an orientation and not a harbinger of one's romantic/sexual knowledge or prowess.

In contrast with asexuality, allosexuals are people who experience sexual attraction or desire. Decker (2015) warns, however, that all sexual orientations, including asexuality, are "more like a range, [and] not a simple series of separate categories'' (p. 5). Thus, while there are many identities on the asexual spectrum (e.g., aromantic, demisexual, grey-A), it is important to recognize that various orientations exist in between. Decker (2015) further explains that "[o]rientation is complicated, and a person does not have to be free of all possible complicating factors to be asexual" (p. 100). Thus, we analyze content produced by people who use all gender and asexual identities as we seek to complicate ace masculinities as *feature of the self* that contend with and resist mainstream allonormative identities.

Allonormativity is the rhetorical and material structures which privilege allosexual being and behavior (Mollet, 2020). Allonormative rhetoric dominates most societies across the globe, manifesting in cultural expectations for one to desire romance and/or sex, raise families, and strengthen the sociopolitical power of families and communities. Emboldened by this hegemonic rhetoric, societies become allonormative and aces are erased, killed, exiled, or forced into compulsory allo/heterosexuality (Foucault, 1990). Scholars also have noted how rhetoric of whiteness plays a role in inappropriately ascribing asexuality—as in desexualizing the bodies of people of color, people with disabilities, and/or Others (Johnson, 2020). We emphasize the danger of whiteness rhetoric that ascribes or assumes asexuality as it further minoritizes ace identity legitimacy (Nakayama & Krizek, 1995).

Przybylo (2014) observed that men who resist allonormative rhetoric are "met with disapproval" by others, which can cause stress and conflict such as doubting "one's manliness and masculinity" (pp. 241–242). Thus, with one's sexuality intrinsically tied to their gender (one's psychological and sociocultural dis/connection with their sex), emasculation occurs when gender expectations of sexual bravado are unmet and their disinterest in romantic affection is revealed (Kelly, 2018). In this way, allonormative rhetoric looms over asexuals, infiltrating their relationalities and understandings of themselves, as media messages constantly reinforce sociosexual scripts that assume and privilege allosexuality. To this end, some scholars have recognized queer theory as a helpful lens to understand normative notions and sociosexual scripts regarding asexuality (Cerankowski & Milks, 2014). In this way, queer theory's examination of sociocultural assumptions, and its goals of survival and liberation, inform this work.

Brake (2012) makes a similar observation that sociocultural fetishizations of monogamy and marriage can marginalize ace spectrum intimacies. Przybylo (2014) adds that asexual men are distinctly at odds with Western discourses that have developed and reified a "sexusociety" which centers its "cultural prerogatives on sex as central to selfhood" (p. 242). This seemingly inescapable space marginalizes asexual men through "social exclusion and isolation, disbelief and invalidation of their (a)sexual identification, unwanted sex, bullying, teasing, and not fitting in" (p. 242). As such, allonormative rhetoric plays a key role in dictating gender roles and masculine expressions of sexuality, which can cause internalized and relational stress for those who do not meet its demands.

Opening Online Spaces for Alternate Sexual Identities

Since the advent of the Internet, scholars have noted the importance of online spaces for members of LGBTQIA+ communities to organize against normative rhetoric and expectations (Soriano, 2014). For example, Renninger (2015) notes how Tumblr was especially helpful in providing a counterpublic for asexuals, as the site dedicated blogs to ace resources, commiseration, and humor (p. 1,520). To provide an online space and community for asexuals, David Jay invented the Asexuality Visibility and Education Network, or AVEN, in 2001. AVEN has since become the world's largest asexual community with more than 130,000 registered members, replete with online resources and fora for ace individuals and others looking to discuss topics and issues dealing with (a)sexuality, gender, and life in general. In this way, online communities provide spaces for members to combat and/or escape allonormative messages in media and society.

AVEN undoubtedly has provided room for those on the ace spectrum to feel belonging, connect with others, and communicate frustrations, hopes, and shared experiences. However, Gupta (2016) observes that "members of the AVEN community face a paradox" because as they work "to increase the visibility of asexuality," their marginalization is reified by the "focus of the public on sexuality" (p. 1,009). In this sense, allonormative rhetoric that frames asexual as fascinating (via its ascribed abnormality) hampers genuine discussion about dismantling the issues of erasure. Mindful of this paradox, in this chapter, we focus on gender role conflict and stress experienced by members of AVEN and their reactions to a self-identifying asexual character, Todd Chavez, from Netflix's *BoJack Horseman*. Before discussing the show, we look at the role of media in cultivating images and rhetoric about asexuality and masculinity.

Asexual Representations in the Media

Media is a broad term that, in our modern era, includes traditional forms, as well as social media platforms, streaming services, films, shows, books, and music. BoJack Horseman was created by a relatively popular streaming service, Netflix, and as such, allows viewers with subscriptions to watch the show whenever, with minimal interruption. Many media content often perpetuate allonormativity—from Disney fairy tales to love songs, romance novels, and pornographic websites. Many convey essentializing messages convincing women to embody femininities of virtue and seduction, and men to embody masculinities that highlight vociferous sexual appetites (Elgie, 2020). While the past decade has seen LGBTQIA+ representations in television and film challenge storylines and tropes that center cisheteronormativity, for eample, reimagining the boy meets girl trope (Pompper, 2017), asexuality and ace issues remain relatively unseen (Simpson, 2017).

Fortunately, there are some examples of masculine ace representation in various films, shows, and books beyond our exploration of *BoJack Horseman's* Todd Chavez that have been confirmed by the creators or studios. Notable examples include *SpongeBob SquarePants*, Evan Waxman from *High Maintenance*, Raphael Santiago from the *Shadowhunters*, and *Jughead Jones* from Archie Comic.

Unfortunately, some asexual representations in media have reinforced harmful stereotypes of ace identity and orientation. As Renninger (2014) laments, "[i]n the mainstream media . . . there is almost always some skepticism or resistance to understanding asexuality as a legitimate identity" (p. 1524). One notable misrepresentation occurred on an episode of Fox television's popular medical drama *House*, in which a self-identified asexual couple is examined for their lack of sex drive, causing clamor in ace communities (Clark-Flory, 2012). As communication and media scholars have documented for decades, media can influence our identities and relationships by generating spaces of stress and conflict in regard to gender roles and sociosexual expectations (Eguchi & Kimura, 2020). O'Neil's (1981) masculine theory of gender role conflict and stress will be especially helpful in our project to locate these stressors and conflicts.

Masculine Gender Role Stress/Conflict Theory

Seeking to capture the fear of femininity in men and other learned norms that limit human potential, O'Neil's (1981) male-directed theory of gender role conflict and stress offers six patterns of men's gender role socializations and masculine value systems: 1) *restrictive emotionality*, or an affective performance that views certain emotional expressions as weak and therefore feminine; 2) *socialized control, power, and competition* in which the latter is seen as a "vehicle" to help promote "positive self-image" (p. 207) 3) *homophobia*, or the hatred of queer men (largely in part due to their femininity); 4) *restrictive sexual and affectionate behavior* that places sexual prowess as an achievement of true masculinity; 5) *obsession with achievement and success* (mostly in corporate spheres); and 6) *healthcare problems* that encourage men to downplay mental and physical health concerns so as not to appear weak (feminine). While O'Neil (2008) asserts that more research is needed in order to understand the functionalities and complexities of GRC across contexts, he also notes that "accepting a gay sexual identify while living in a heterosexist culture may force gay men to examine their GRC more proactively and resolve it earlier" (p. 381). Thus, we use O'Neil's (1981) masculine theory of gender role conflict and stress to further explore GRC in the context of sexual identity, recognizing the societal influences of masculinity as clearly coinciding with allonormative notions of sexuality and gender. The next section discusses *BoJack Horseman* and the show's representation of masculine asexuality through a main character, Todd Chavez.

Meet Todd Chavez

Todd Chavez is one of the main characters in Netflix's *BoJack Horseman*. He is a White-appearing, cisgender human man, who is a longtime friend of BoJack, a human-horse actor that the animated tragicomedy centers around. The series is set in Hollywoo, a fictional town that satirizes the toxicity of Hollywood celebrityhood in a place where humans and other animals coexist. Todd is in nearly all episodes and overwhelmingly portrayed as kind, bumbling, and affable with a desire to help others. The series ran for six seasons from 2014–2020, earned 25 professional awards, and garnered the number one spot on Indiewire's list of all-time best animated shows (Miller et al., 2020).

In the season three finale, Todd begins to come to grips with his sexuality at the behest of his friend, Emily. This important character development was applauded by fans and critics alike (Jackman, 2017). Though the studio never released a statement on waiting until the third season to disclose Todd's asexuality, perhaps this ambiguity symbolizes Todd's journey on understanding himself in an allonormative society and thus reflects experiences ace audience members may have in accepting themselves.

In a somber manner that deeply contrasts his usually upbeat cadence, Todd sighs, "I'm not gay. I mean, I don't think I am, but I don't think I'm straight either. I don't know what I am. I think I might be nothing" (Bob-Waksberg & Winfrey, 2016, 22:18). Emily supports his incertitude, and in the next episode calls Todd asexual, to which he gives a flustered response, but later accepts the term. Todd comes out for the first time as asexual to BoJack and afterwards attends an asexual community meeting by himself that night.

Another important moment comes when Todd sheepishly tells his group of ace friends that he is getting married, something unusual for an asexual. The group responds positively and affirms a variety of relationships occur along the ace spectrum, highlighting the diversity of ace identities under the overarching asexual label. Todd doesn't end up getting married, but later dates Yolanda to whom he clarifies that he is heteroromantic asexual. Due to their incompatibility outside of their asexuality, the relationship is short-lived. Todd later begins a relationship with Maude, whom he met on the asexual dating app he created. They are together from the last season to the series finale. Todd's journey highlights the gender role conflict and stress—first within himself and then socially with his peers—that arises when one's identity does not conform with allonormative understandings of sexuality. Todd's identity as a heteroromantic asexual cisgender man and his choice to enter a romantic relationship with women, challenges allonormative rhetoric that teaches sex and romance should be intertwined. This makes a space to recognize that there is no one way to be asexual.

In this way, the show offers insights into the intricacies and intragroup differences of the ace identities, describes definitions and manifestations of those frameworks, and invites viewers (ace and allo) to consider them via an entertainment platform—likely with the guidance of their asexual consultant (Kliegman, 2018). Thus, through the seasons, these segments provide educational moments to the viewers—particularly by providing in-depth moments of Todd's journey of self-discovery. As such, Todd Chavez became undoubtedly influential as one of the first openly ace characters in the media. Thus, we wish to understand how Todd Chavez's media representation of asexual masculinity is perceived by AVEN members, how O'Neil's GRC/S theory can guide us in understanding their navigations in allonormative societies, and ways in which we may expand GRC/S.

In this literature review, we have conceptualized asexuality and allonormativity, and covered some of the media's representations of asexual characters while introducing readers to Todd Chavez. We also have highlighted the importance of online organizing in asexual communities and presented the theoretical framework for this study, the theory of masculine gender role conflict and stress. In an effort to understand the relationships between asexual communities and Todd Chavez's asexual representation, we offer these research questions:

RQ1: How do ace individuals characterize Todd Chavez's representation of asexuality?

RQ2: In what ways do AVENites resist allonormativity?

METHOD

Data Collection

The focus of this research lies in our desire to forefront the voices and experiences of asexual viewers of a main character Todd Chavez from *BoJack Horseman*—as a means for expanding GRC/S theory. Recognizing that AVEN is the world's largest community for asexuals, we focused our attention on collecting data from already existing fora posts and comments written by AVENites' perceptions of the show and Todd. We followed Orbe and Allen's (2008) approach to examining large databases through keyword searches by seeking all relevant posts and comments to the phrase "BoJack." Not wanting to limit the data, we did not use any filters (e.g., who wrote the posts/comments or when); this resulted in 354 comments and posts that mentioned BoJack, which we recorded and catalogued in a spreadsheet. We then searched for either tacit or explicit mentions of Todd Chavez. We also analyzed five more comments/posts that discussed gender role conflict and stress, for a total of (N=359) texts analyzed. AVENites can choose which features of their identity they want to disclose under their avatar section, including gender pronouns. In the instances where the users share their pronouns (either on the profile or content), we use those pronouns. When the AVENite did not provide pronoun information, we use the neutral they/them/their.

Data Analysis

Upon identifying all germane posts and comments, we created a spreadsheet where the titles and the links of the data could be easily collected. As co-authors, we then divided the data to begin first-cycle coding. Wanting to highlight the qualitative richness of the data more so than quantitative happenings, we conducted a critical thematic analysis (CTA) of all extant discussions and posts about Todd to identify and organize common themes among the AVEN data. CTA is a burgeoning methodology which blends the use of critical approaches to thematic analysis methodologies (Lawless & Chen, 2019). While there are many iterations of thematic analyses, we relied on Braun and Clarke's (2006) six-step process: 1) familiarization with the data; 2) generation of initial, encompassing topical codes; 3) constant searching for themes across the texts; 4) reviewing the themes for accuracy and inclusion; 5) naming and defining the themes; and 6) reporting the themes as findings.

We constantly applied a critical approach, namely our desire to locate and critique rhetorical instances of allonormative masculinities, while coding the data. This critical approach also allowed us to attune the way media imbues cultural and sociosexual expectations (Ott & Mack, 2020). Throughout this process, we compared and contrasted our findings, discussing which category of themes to which data should belong. Our analytic process was iterative, as we went back-and-forth between the data and the theory, taking communal notes of how the theory applied to the data, and how our data could apply to the theory. Our intercoder cohesion resulted in only one minor disagreement, which was negotiated swiftly and thoughtfully. Together, we organized the data into three main themes that are shared below.

FINDINGS AND DISCUSSION

Our analysis revealed three common themes: viewing AVEN members' perceptions of Todd Chavez as: 1) a nuanced representation of asexuality; 2) a limited representation of asexuality; and 3) a challenge to allonormativity.

RQ1: How do ace individuals characterize Todd Chavez's representation of asexuality?

For RQ1, our findings revealed two themes that illustrate the major consensus of how Todd Chavez is characterized by AVENites. That is, most AVEN viewers characterize Todd Chavez as either a nuanced or limited representation of asexuality.

Theme #1: Todd Chavez as a Nuanced Representation of Asexuality

Given media's history of underrepresenting asexual folks, it is no surprise that *BoJack Horseman* is a popular topic of discussion on AVEN. Many posts discussing the show express support for Todd Chavez's character as providing a nuanced representation of the experiences that an asexual person may have, particularly in regard to gender role conflict and stress. In this way, many aces see Todd as representative of the AVEN community, which recognizes the importance of asexual representation. In Post 1, one user wrote:

> For the longest time, asexuality being represented didn't matter much to me, but these days I'm realizing how much better I would have felt about this [her experiences as an asexual female in an allonormative world] if my representation of happiness wasn't 100% shaped around successful sexual and romantic relationships.

In response to this powerful sentiment, another user shared that he had a similar experience in coming to realize the importance of asexual representation through watching *BoJack Horseman* and witnessing how Todd Chavez contributed to this representation. In Post 2, he stated:

> I watched *BoJack Horseman* at the beginning of quarantine and . . . watching it made me come to terms with some things that I didn't even realize I still hadn't come to terms with and ultimately, I . . . became more accepting of myself. . . .I thought representation didn't matter, but now I realize it really does, especially for people that haven't even realized they're ace yet.

This idea of representation being of particular importance to those who haven't realized their asexuality yet is supported by other members of the AVEN community. For instance, in Post 3, a user shared:

> Asexuality as an identity really needs to have a higher profile because many people either haven't heard about it or have misconceptions about it . . . .I never used to seriously consider that I might be ace because of inaccurate ideas of what I thought asexuality was.

This user's advocacy for more awareness is one of the key purposes of AVEN, as another user affirmed in Post 4. They wrote: "getting the news out there [is] . . . unfortunately slow going, but still better than before." They ended by sharing a Vox article on ace awareness and media representation that included Todd Chavez. These affirming experiences with ace representation can play a role in what O'Neil et al. (1987) call gender role transitions, "events and non-events" which stimulate changes one has about sexualities, "gender-role values and self-assumptions" (p. 77).

Indeed, this representation can help provide clarity on ace's gender role journey by helping them realize their perceptions of themselves and the values that they hold. For example, Post 5 is one of the AVEN posts containing detailed anecdotes of formally becoming aware of one's asexuality thanks to Todd Chavez. The author wrote:

> After years of trying to navigate through a relationship, feeling inadequate, broken and not enough, I have watched *BoJack* and stumbled upon this scene [where Todd describes that he doesn't think he is gay or straight, but perhaps "nothing"]. And when that "nothing" [feeling little to no sexual attraction] changed into something [an asexual identity], it was a huge relief for me. The relationship didn't survive this epiphany, but I did . . .

This epiphany is just one of the many stories found on AVEN that illuminate the importance of nuanced asexual representation informed by ace experiences—some AVEN users even created entire forums to discuss it. This open communication about the vulnerabilities of asserting their asexuality despite allonormative rhetoric is one way that restrictive emotionality, a key concept of masculinity for O'Neil (1981), is challenged. Many AVEN members share their tender feelings about the benefits of Todd's representation. As the theorist notes that restrictive emotionality can cause difficulties in interpersonal relationships, it seems that the AVENites who do speak up instead of lurking, or those who write posts in an online community instead of just reading them, are able to build positive connections with other members. They are also able to commemorate and opine with others about the importance (or lack thereof, for some) of media representation.

This discussion of this study's first theme, Todd Chavez as a nuanced representation of asexuality, contributes significantly in our exploration of RQ1 and how ace individuals characterize Todd Chavez's representation of asexuality. Indeed, it is difficult to overstate the importance of this first theme not only for asexual folks, but for all viewers of the show who may be learning of asexuality for the first time. Dyer (1993) notes "how social groups are treated in cultural representation . . . [influences] how they are treated in life" (p. 1), and for the author of Post 7 and other AVENites who saw themselves in Todd Chavez, this rings true. Todd Chavez not only helped many AVENites to feel normal and to provide a safe space for them to accept their aceness, but in reaching other viewers his character also serves as an important contribution in changing how aces are treated in real life, by themselves and others.

Theme #2: Todd Chavez as a Limited Representation of Asexuality

While members of the AVEN community expressed support for Todd Chavez, the limitations of his character as a representation of asexuality were also expressed, including AVENites finding his experiences unrelatable to their own. For instance, in Post 8, one user said he "could not relate to [Todd]," a disconnect "that made [him] question if [he is] ace." Such a statement centers the importance of multivocality in representation. Thus, while perceptions vary, representation seems to influence aces' sense of self—which is significant as asexuality disrupts dominant sociosexual scripts produced by allonormativity.

Similarly, some AVEN members still exploring their asexuality found themselves left with more questions after watching Todd Chavez when they did not find his character relatable. For instance, in Post 9, a user shared how they had been "wrestling with [their] sexuality for about 6 years now... [and] never considered the possibility of being ace until now. Heck I didn't relate to Todd from *BoJack Horseman* in the slightest."

In addition to these AVEN members who did not find Todd Chavez relatable, there are also members who took issue with other aspects of Todd's portrayal. For instance, the author of Post 10 opined,

> Todd Chavez from *BoJack* is great until you realize they write him as a buffoon sidekick who doesn't know how sex works . . . he makes a trash bucket into a sex bot for his best friend. I love him and his silliness but this isn't what we'd ideally get for the first mainstream [representation].

This post brings to light a possible noteworthy yet chilling interpretation of Todd's identity—that his asexuality may simply amount to an ignorance of sex, a harmful stereotype. Many asexuals know exactly how sexual intimacy works (some even do it), though some may be aware but averse to any coital and/or romantic acts. Simply put, asexuality is an orientation, not an indication of one's romantic/sexual competence.

Others took issue with how hypersexuality was portrayed in an episode that features Todd meeting Yolanda's high-libido family. Living in an allonormative society imbued with sex, for some ace folks, hypersexuality may represent a close opposite to their own experience (although it is important to note that some aces may still have libido). The author of Post 11 highlights the tensions that exist between the gaps of rhetorical attunements to allonormativity and how asexuals perceive them. They suggested the episode "could have also served as Todd's 'eyes opening moment' to realize how much his experience actually differs" from others. This author and other AVENites seem to agree that the cartoonish nature of hypersexuality can be misrepresented, just like asexuality. But Yolanda's porn star mother and homemade-lube-cherishing father may have overshadowed the nuances of living in a world crafted through allonormative rhetoric. It is from those messages in which interpersonal and internal conflicts can arise and where expectations of masculinity and sexuality can foment.

The findings presented in this second theme provide insights into RQ1 as they illuminate how ace individuals in the AVEN community recognize Todd Chavez's limitations in his representation of asexuality. The limitations presented here underscore that no media representation can perfectly capture the essence of an important feature of identity such as one's sexuality. After all, aces are not some monolithic group; instead, intersectional features of individual and group identities are key in understanding the intricacies to asexuality. However, these limitations further highlight the need for greater representation of asexuality in media, as more instances of representation can play a role in providing reprieve from allonormative rhetoric and gender role conflict and stress.

RQ2: In what ways do AVENites resist allonormativity?

For RQ2, we analyzed numerous posts where AVENites discuss their resistance of allonormativity, revealing tactics they use and ways in which they navigate an allonormative world.

Theme #3: Beyond Todd Chavez: AVENites' Tactics of Resisting Allonormativity

Allonormativity is inextricably woven into the themes and posts discussed so far, from the author of Post 5's story of feeling broken and inadequate for years in a relationship due to her asexuality, to the author of Post 2's story of how he was put off from identifying as asexual until college. Because allonormativity is incredibly prevalent in nearly all of the posts this chapter analyzed on AVEN, it deserves further exploration and explication here.

Allonormativity has effects on quotidian interactions on many aces, including causing intrapersonal and interpersonal stress as one "deviates from or conforms to masculinity ideology and norms" (O'Neil, 2008, p. 363).

In the AVEN community, gender role conflicts are observed in both the intrapersonal and interpersonal contexts. For example, the author of Post 12 shared how his lack of interest in romantic relationships led to his family and friends making assumptions about his sexual orientation. He wrote:

> Being born in a conservative family, [there was huge] expectations as a first son, and constant visits to psychiatrists . . . I've never developed attraction to anyone (and personally never cared to) and [since] . . . we are surrounded by super active sexual people I was seen as weird or cold or the common "C'mon, you're gay, right? Just admit it."

For this user, the interpersonal and societal expectations that led others to assume he was either gay, socially aloof, or mentally ill captures the discursive and material force of allonormativity, which also caused him to question on the intrapersonal level that perhaps he was "just sick" as he was led to believe. His experience also particularly illuminates the allosexist expectation of being sexual in some way, even if homosexually.

Such experiences of ace folks may be represented in O'Neil's (1981) GRC/S theory pattern of restrictive sexual and affectionate behavior, which is defined as "having limited ways of expressing one's sexuality and affection towards others" (p. 208). While the pattern addresses how traditional gender roles may result in relational and sexual conflicts, it could be expanded to address the underlying and prevailing expectation of sexual desire and behavior to start. As O'Neil (1981) elucidates, "sex is a primary means to prove one's masculinity. Affectionate, sensual, and intimate behavior are considered feminine and less valued" (p. 205). Including the experiences of aces in this sentiment is imperative because having decreased or absent sexual and/or romantic feelings is not only among behaviors that are less valued, but it also implies that men who do not have these feelings are not masculine. Thus, the pervasiveness of allonormativity is evident in stories like the author of Post 12's where others in his life assumed that he must be gay and encouraged him to "just admit it." His story exemplifies how allonormative ideals have impacted his life is just one of many such posts on AVEN.

In Post 13, another user shared they had to "play the part" of sexual/relational normalcy. Tears fell when they realized they were asexual a moment in "battling self-internalized acephobia" thinking their aceness was "something

. . . to feel ashamed of, or justify"—a feeling with which they still grapple. Sadly, those feelings of fear and shame many asexual folks may encounter. These findings offer an opportunity for the expansion of another GRC/S pattern, homophobia, "including beliefs, myths, and stereotypes about gay people" (O'Neil et al., 1986, p. 340). We suggest that this pattern should be expanded to queerphobia in order to include transphobia and acephobia, or the rhetorical and material discrimination produced by allonormativity. The author of Post 13 acutely described how acephobia and a lack of understanding, present both in herself and others, led to negative feelings surrounding her asexuality—feelings of loneliness, uncertainty, shame, and frustration—which underscore the hegemonic experiences of ace folks living in an allonormative world.

The stressors evoked by societal and media expectations of gender and masculinity can also hamper asexual identity. In Post 14, one user shared how gender role stressors impacted their self-acceptance because they were "in denial thinking [their] self-perception didn't matter to others" or that they weren't "'good enough at'" sex or masculinity to meet expectations," which they now admit was "dumb." Thus, the author offers insights into the always-messy web of gender, masculinity, and asexuality.

Similarly, the author of Post 15 shared how their experiences of being inculcated by allonormative rhetoric over the years has affected their sense of self and relationalities, sharing how acephobia "is so internalized, messy, and intimate, it's . . . difficult to confront and deal with." The author's somber experiences highlight the overlapping of power structures that spur the stressors of gender roles and expectations by which many asexual individuals are burdened. The self-hatred and internalization of acephobia was the most difficult and complex for them to bear. McDonald et al. (2020) note this phenomenon, claiming "[c]oming out of the closet is not universally liberating" because it "can be both oppressive and empowering" (p. 90). These findings provide disheartening examples of this reality.

Fortunately, for all that they have been through, AVEN members also have hope for a more inclusive future. For example, the author of Post 17 responded, "slowly but surely we are seeing more representation in the media" and listed Todd Chavez as one of her "personal favorites." She also offered discursive ways to combat allonormative utterances:

I do think talking to your friends more when it comes up is a great idea. Be gentle, but stand your ground and let them know when their words are hurting you or are incorrect. If they're good friends, they will learn and grow with you.

This AVENite's advice is perspicaciously aware of the moments in which allonormative rhetoric can cause gendered and sexualized expectations can be challenged through solidarity, and provides an answer to O'Neil's (2008) call for finding ways to cultivate "healthy masculinity" (p. 424).

This study's final theme has taken us beyond Todd Chavez in an exploration of how AVENites resist allonormativity (RQ2). These findings illuminate ways in which AVEN members resist allonormative rhetoric that labels them as odd, weird, or broken, and work toward replacing such rhetorics with ones of validity, acceptance, and respect. Thus, the experiences of AVENites in their resistance of allonormativity discussed in this section highlight the importance of such resistance in assuaging stress and conflict that can arise from masculine gender roles and expectations.

CONCLUSIONS

In this chapter, we have sought to bring awareness to the lack of research on the rhetoric and media representations of asexuality and masculinity. We used O'Neil's GRC/S theory to help us understand asexual viewers' perceptions of Todd Chavez from *BoJack Horseman* by analyzing 359 posts from AVEN containing rich commentary of life experiences. By analyzing posts from many self-defined asexual folks—both those identifying as asexual and those questioning, to those intimately aware of allonormative systems of oppression and those only coming to realize them—this study includes diverse anecdotes of asexual identity and experience while emphasizing the complexities of such. These data also illuminate how Todd's character has impacted asexual viewers in meaningful ways, by seeking to understand how ace individuals perceive Todd Chavez's representation of asexuality. In tandem with this endeavor, we desired to learn more about AVENites' experiences of gender role stress/conflict regarding Todd's character, we found that his representation influenced some AVEN viewers to challenge and struggle against allonormative expectations—if not often in heartbreakingly painful ways. Notwithstanding, this representation empowered many AVENites to feel more comfortable with themselves and seek out community of other aces.

We have sought to expand GRC/S and in doing so, have highlighted the theory's own allonormative assumptions, leading us to call for an expansion of the theory's "homophobia" pattern to become "queerphobia," which would include all identities under the LGTBQIA+ umbrella who have been historically silenced—asexuals included. Similarly, we also complicate the theory's assumption that sexual attraction is innate in masculinity. We hope that this study has illuminated the importance of expanding our understanding of theories such as GRC/S to inform and expand future research for a more just world more sufficiently.

In the first part of our chapter title, *When Nothing Changes into Something*, we reference the words of the author of Post 5 who eloquently describes a harrowing reality: that many aces have experienced feelings of being less than human—even nothing—because of their asexuality. This poignant discovery is a sentiment communicated by Todd Chavez as he came to terms with his asexuality and is one that resonated with many of the AVENites we encountered. In a society imbued with the allonormative ideal that sexual attraction is key to masculinity, feelings of inadequacy, isolation, and nothingness for those who do not experience such attraction (with the implication that such an experience does not exist) are pervasive. Subsequently, the posts analyzed in this chapter powerfully encapsulate the best of what Todd Chavez has offered the AVEN community: the dissemination of his asexual identity when many members did not know that such identities existed or were even a possibility, and a solidaric validation and reaffirmation of asexual identities for those who did. Furthermore, just as the author of Post 5's words, "when that 'nothing' changed into something, it was a huge relief for me" describe the feeling of solace that overcame many AVEN aces when they discovered their asexuality, it is also a fitting description of Todd's contribution to asexual representation: where there once was little to no representation—nothing—now there is something.

The author of Post 5 ends with a description of her peaceful state of mind even as she floats through "uncharted waters, trying to find my course, but enjoying the slow drift for now," further reflecting on the feeling of discovering an asexual identity. Likewise, asexual representation and research on asexual folks is largely uncharted waters. But for those who endeavor to explore these waters, we are hopeful that they will begin to chart new courses with care and commitment to asexual communities.

Limitations and Future Directions

While AVEN is the largest asexual online community and a valuable resource, it is one site of investigation and may not represent all instances of GRC/S among asexual viewers of *BoJack Horseman*. Another notable limitation of the AVEN website is that it is not conducive to an intersectional analysis since it does not provide user demographic information such as race, ethnicity, age, religious affiliation, gender identity, and so on. Although the site does provide a space for members to provide some of this information if they so desire, not all of them choose to do so. We sought to minimize further data-related limitations by analyzing all data relating to the topic, without filters or other exclusionary criteria.

In addition, future studies would benefit from gathering longitudinal data that would provide insights into how experiences of GRC/S may evolve over time for asexual folks along intersectional lines. Whatever directions future studies may take, it is our sincere hope that scholars and practitioners will continue their inquiries into the importance of representation for aces and develop strategies for solidarity and community.

REFERENCES

Bob-Waksberg, R. (Writer), & Winfrey, A. (Director). That went well (Season 3, Episode 12) [Netflix series episode]. In R. Bob-Waksberg (Executive Producer), *BoJack Horseman.*

Brake, E. (2012). *Minimizing marriage: Marriage, morality and the law.* Oxford University Press.

Braun, V., & Clarke, V. (2006). Using thematic analysis in psychology. *Qualitative Research In Psychology, 3*(2), 77–101. doi:10.1191/1478088706qp063oa.

Cerankowski, K. J., & Milks, M. (2014). *Asexualities: Feminist and queer perspectives.* Routledge.

Clark-Florey, T. (February 1, 2012). "House" gets asexuality wrong. *Salon.* www .salon.com/2012/01/31/house_gets_asexuality_wrong/.

Connell, R., & Pearse, R. (2015). *Gender in world perspectives* (3rd ed.). Cambridge and Malden.

Dyer, R. (1993). *The matter of images: Essays on representations.* Routledge.

Eguchi, S., & Kimura, K. (2020). Racialized im/possibilities: Intersectional queer-of-color critique on Japaneseness in Netflix's Queer Eye: We're in Japan! *Journal of International and Intercultural Communication.* DOI: 10.1080/17513057.2020.1829675.

Elgie, E. (2020). *Being and doing: Interrogating dominant narratives of asexual kinship in an amatonormative culture* [master's thesis]. Retrieved from https://open .library.ubc.ca/cIRcle/collections/ubctheses/24/items/1.0390049.

Gupta, K. (2017). "And now I'm different, but there's nothing actually wrong with me": Asexual marginalization and resistance. *Journal of Homosexuality, 64*(8), 991-1013. DOI: 10.1080/00918369.2016.1236590.

Jackman, J. (September 11, 2017). BoJack Horseman's Todd just came out as asexual, and fans are in tears. *Pink News.* www.pinknews.co.uk/2017/09/11/bojack-horsemans-todd-just-came-out-as-asexual-and-fans-are-in-tears/.

Johnson, A. L. (2020). The dark matter(s) of Wakanda: A poetic performative. *Review of Communication, 20*(3), 244-249. DOI: 10.1080/15358593.2020.1778066.

Kelemen, E. (2007). Asexuality. In Fedwa Malti-Douglas (Ed.), *Encyclopedia of Sex and Gender* (vol. 1). Macmillan.

Kelly, C. R. (2018). Emasculating Trump: The incredulous gaze, homophobia, and the spectacle of White masculinity. *QED: A Journal of GLBTQ Worldmaking 5*(3), 1–27.

Kliegman, J. (September 26, 2018). Todd's asexuality on 'BoJack' isn't a perfect depiction, but it's made me feel understood. *Bustle.* www.bustle.com/p/todds

-asexuality-on-bojack-horseman-isnt-a-perfect-depiction-but-its-made-me-feel
-understood-12057178.

Lawless, B., & Chen, Y. (2019). Developing a method of critical thematic analysis for Qualitative communication inquiry. *Howard Journal of Communications, 30,* 92–106. doi: 10.1080/10646175.2018.1439423.

McDonald, J., Harris, K., & Ramirez, J. (2020). Revealing and concealing difference: A critical approach to disclosure and an intersectional theory of "closeting." *Communication Theory, 30*(1), 84–104. https://doi.org/10.1093/ct/qtz017.

Miller, L. S., Travers, B., Schneider, M., Nguyen, H., Greene, S., Stone, J., & Lopez, K. (2020). The best animated series of all time. *Indiewire.* www.indiewire.com/feature/best-animated-series-all-time-cartoons-anime-tv-1202021835/5/.

Mollet, A. L. (2020). "I have a lot of feelings, just none in the genitalia region": A grounded theory of asexual college students' identity journeys. *Journal of College Student Development 61*(2), 189–206. doi:10.1353/csd.2020.0017.

Nakayama, T. K., & Krizek, R. L. (1995). Whiteness: A strategic rhetoric. *Quarterly Journal of Speech, 81,* 291–309.

Nickalls, S. (September 8, 2017). 'BoJack Horseman' gives us TV's first out-and-proud asexual icon. *Dot and Line.* https://dotandline.net/todd-chavez-asexual-bojack
-horseman-season-4/.

O'Neil, J. M. (1981). Patterns of gender role conflict and strain: Sexism and fear of femininity in men's lives. *Journal of Counseling and Development, 60*(4), 203–210.

———. (2008). Summarizing 25 years of research on men's gender role conflict using the gender role conflict scale: New research paradigms and clinical implications. *The Counseling Psychologist, 36*(3), 358–445. DOI: 10.1177/0011000008317057.

O'Neil, J. M., Fishman, D. M., & Kinsella-Shaw, M. (1987). Dual-career couples' career transitions and normative dilemmas: A preliminary assessment model. *The Counseling Psychologist, 15,* 50–96.

O'Neil, J. M., Helms, B. J., Gable, R. K. *et al.* (1986). Gender-role conflict scale: College men's fear of femininity. *Sex Roles, 14,* 335–350. https://doi.org/10.1007/BF00287583.

Orbe, M., & Allen, B. (2008). "Race matters" in the Journal of Applied Communication Research. *Howard Journal of Communications, 19*(3), 201–220. https://doi.org/10.1080/10646170802218115.

Ott, B. L., & Mack, M. L. (2020). *Critical media studies: An introduction* (3rd ed.). Wiley and Sons.

Pompper, D. (2017). *Rhetoric of femininity: Female body image, media, and gender role stress/conflict.* Lexington Books.

Przybylo, E. (2014). Masculine doubt and sexual wonder: Asexually-identified men talk about their (a)sexualities. In K. J. Cerankow and M. Milks (Eds.), *Asexualities: Feminist and queer perspectives* (pp. 225–246). Routledge.

Renninger, B. J. (2015). "Where I can be myself . . . where I can speak my mind": Networked counterpublics in a polymedia environment. *New Media and Society, 17*(9), 1513–1529.

Simpson, E. (2017). An ace in the crowd: Asexual representations and signifying practices in television sitcom [bachelor's thesis]. Retrieved from https://www .academia.edu/44743483/An_Ace_in_the_Crowd_Asexual_representation s_and _signifying_practices_in_television_sitcom.

Soriano, C. R. R. (2014). Constructing collectivity in diversity: Online political mobilization of a national LGBT political party. *Media, Culture & Society, 36*(1), 20–36. https://doi.org/10.1177/0163443713507812.

Trevor Project. (2017). *Asexual* [webpage]. Retrieved from www.thetrevorproject .org/asexual/.

Chapter Four

Pulling Back the Curtain on Advertisers' Perceptions of Male Images in U. S. Ads

Juan Mundel and Maria De Moya

INTRODUCTION

Ads are impersonal messages from an identifiable source delivered through mass-media channels to persuade consumers to purchase products and services (Sheehan, 2013). They also are powerful socialization agents that motivate individuals to compare themselves to the imagery and ideals portrayed (Morrison, et al., 2004), as social learning theorists have posited (e.g., Bandura, 1994). Advertising scholarship has explored the messaging medium's impact on people's perceptions of others and of themselves, especially in terms of beauty standards and body image. Findings suggest consistency in perceptions of male beauty standards across cultures, ages, and media (Chapa et al., 2020).

Ads' use of endorsers conveying messages about the use and appeal of a product offers a powerful source of information for consumers. Additionally, extrinsic attributes of the endorser, such as age and body type, elicit among consumers a self-categorization process which communicates to them whether a product or service is for them or not (Alhabash et al., 2020). Although masculinity is a multidimensional construct with a continuum of meanings (e.g., Zayer, et al., 2019), ads tend to favor a stereotypical representation of how a man is supposed to look and act (Pompper et al., 2007)—i.e., like the Marlboro man, a rugged cowboy image strategically used to make filter cigarettes seem less feminine (Baglia, 2005). Ads are a ubiquitous component of our social landscape, but researchers have revealed problematic impacts. Ads can have negative consequences by amplifying a certain variety of masculine ideal that not all bodies or expressions of masculinity can conform to (Fildes et al., 2014).

There remains a dearth of understanding about male gender role conflict/ stress (GRC/S) (O'Neil, 1981; 1990) as it relates to masculinity ideals represented in advertisements. Our attention is focused on interrogating processes that go on behind advertising's creative desk—in the ways actors are cast for ads—since this, ultimately, is linked to setting the stage for GRC/S some male audiences may experience. This chapter provides a contextualized exploration of advertisers' views of the archetypal male model in the current media landscape, what they want to see in mediated male images, and the role of consumer perceptions of men.

REVIEW OF LITERATURE

As foundation for our inquiry into the behind-the-scenes view of ways advertising producers consider male bodies, we examined sets of research findings that lead us to posit a formal research question. The literature undergirding our study is: 1) gender roles and advertising, 2) masculinity and stereotyping, 3) using masculinity to sell, 4) masculinity across cultures, and 5) male gender role conflict/stress (GRC/S) theory.

Gender Roles and Advertising

Research findings about interplay of male gender and masculinity often reveal important details about roles men play in society, as impacted by family, peers, and media representations like ads—with a variety of effects. As a social identity dimension, gender consists of a set of norms and traits ascribed to men and women in social groups and systems (Connell, 1987). Overall, male gender standards can be physical or exhibited in personality, behaviors, and professional occupations (e.g., Ashmore & Del Boca, 1981). Hence, masculinity and male gender and body ideals are intertwined as they play out across sociocultural milieu. Men end up internalizing these images by comparing themselves to the ideals and to other men (Shroff & Thompson, 2006). An important means for exploring representations of maleness has been to study media; advertising, in particular, given its salience across worldwide audiences (e.g., Eisend & Langner 2010; Eisend, 2019; Wang & Sun, 2010).

In the U. S., men in ads typically are represented as muscular and strong—or, the opposite of women who are represented as gentle and fragile (Parent, et al., 2020). Since the 1980s, men's *and* women's bodies have been idealized and represented as sex objects in ads (Elliott & Elliott, 2005). In fact, the "Adonis" figure associated with potency, dominance, and power is a key component of masculinity in media representations of men (Bordo,

2000)—with masculine images amplifying aggression (Tan, et al., 2013), assertiveness, toughness, strength, and a focus on material success (Pompper, 2010).

Masculinity and Stereotyping

Advertising researchers investigate gender stereotypes to gain deeper understanding of attributes differentiating men and women (Ashmore & Del Boca, 1981), such as physical characteristics (e.g., muscularity, weight, height), role behaviors (e.g., responsible for children's well-being or serving as breadwinner), and trait descriptors (e.g., assertiveness) (Deaux & Lewis, 1984). Findings suggest that there is a fairly consistent media representation of male gender (e.g., De Meulenaer, et. al, 2018; Diedrichs & Lee, 2010; Pounders, 2018) that become standardized, amplifying ideals and contributing to stereotyping (Eisend, 2019), or mental shortcuts used to help the human brain sift through large amounts of information to arrive at quick images and ideas (Fiske et al., 2002).

Outcomes of stereotyping social identity dimensions along gender lines often are grounded in limiting binary dualisms (Pompper, 2014) and can have negative individual and social outcomes. Evidence shows that stereotypical gender portrayal effectiveness is determined in part by consumers' existing social and cognitive schemata about gender-role expectations (Diedrichs & Lee, 2010). When consumers hold more stereotypical views about gender portrayals as realized by certain attributes, consumers respond more positively to ads that conform with idealized representations of female and male gender bodies (Eisend, 2019). However, nontraditional or non-stereotypical representations are evaluated more positively by consumers with a nontraditional gender-role ideology (Baxter, Kulczynski, & Ilicic, 2016), suggesting that changes may be underway in terms of ways masculinity and male gender roles are considered.

Using Masculinity to Sell

Expanding our knowledge about male stereotyping, ideals, and roles—in order to sell products and services to consumers—is timely since stereotypical representations of masculinities are being challenged across cultures (Zayer, et al., 2019), as evidenced in the increasing popularity of K-pop bands featuring "effeminate" men (Baculinao, 2017) and recent ads challenging conceptions of masculinity (Ceron, 2019; Crouch, 2016). For example, Axe Body Spray's Superbowl ad in 2016 showed men of varying body shapes, skin tones, and styles celebrating "a wider, more realistic definition of manhood" (Crouch, 2016, para. 5). Three years later, Gillette's Superbowl ad titled "We

Believe: The Best Men Can Be" called attention to harmful behaviors associated with toxic masculinity, such as bullying and sexual harassment (Ceron,
2019). Both ads suggest that representations of masculinity may be shifting to
become less rigid and idealistic by accommodating greater social acceptance
of diversity. Advertisers in the United States are introducing a new masculine ideal that embraces diverse masculinities according to body type, or a
new American man—currently portrayed as tall men with flat stomachs and
inflated shoulders and pecs (Baglia, 2005)—realizing the potential to sell new
images to male consumers (McCartan & McMahon, 2020). This shift suggests that traditional representation of body type ideals is being challenged,
as society embraces a more fluid gender discourse (Zayer et al., 2019).

For decades, United States advertisers have capitalized on male muscularity to attract consumer attention and elicit positive purchase intention (Bordo,
2000; Kalb, 2013; Pounders, 2018; Windels, 2016). The western ideal of
male beauty long has been muscular, tall, and well-groomed (Diedrichs, et
al., 2011). Although the body composition of the average American male is
endomorphic (Hamblin, 2013; Gerrard et al., 2020), such models rarely have
been featured in U. S. ads regardless of product category (Slater & Tiggemann, 2006)—unless being featured as the object of humor (Patterson &
England, 2000). Instead, mesomorphic models have dominated ads (Patterson
& England, 2000), idealizing fit men who are aggressive, highly muscular,
and tough (Connell & Messerschmidt, 2005; Kolbe & Albanese, 1996). Casting attractive models who fit these ideals to grab consumers' attention is a
common practice in advertising, so that most ads feature models with "wash-
board abdominal muscles, massive chests, and inflated shoulders" (Pope et
al., 2000, p. 34).

This combination of muscularity and leanness among men is difficult to
accomplish with any regular exercising routine. Overexposure of these ideal
male body images can lead to the development of an "Adonis complex" and
eating disorders (Elliott & Elliott, 2005). Yet, advertisers have entrenched
an idealized narrow conception of male attractiveness, which research has
shown can lead to negative and unintended effects that may contribute to
male GRC/S (Pompper, 2010) because the combination of muscularity and
leanness among men is difficult to attain.

Masculinity Across Cultures

Masculinity is expressed uniquely across and among social identity dimension intersectionalities, with men choosing various personal traits to express
their unique brand of masculinity (Orehek & Human, 2017). In terms of
ethnicity, White men are expected to be aggressive, highly muscular, and
tough (Connell & Messerschmidt, 2005). Asian men, tend to have a smaller

build and are less muscular, and have been discriminated against as asexual, effeminate, and undesirable romantic partners) (Lu & Wong, 2013; Liang et al., 2010). Similarly, Latino and African American men showcase unique attitudes when asserting their gender (Pompper, 2010). Hence, culture dimensions often play out in demonstrations of masculine behavior, such as: the more traditional *tough and macho* persona "with a traditional cowboy look and temperament" and muscular body; the *refined and gentle* "intellectual" persona that appears "cultured, polite, graceful and good-mannered;" the *trendy and cool* persona; and the *androgynous* persona signaled by "more feminine" dress and behavior (Tan et al. 2013; p. 239).

Men across age groups point to the significant role of mass media in shaping perceptions of masculinity. For example, Pompper (2010) found men "were quick to blame mass media producers for depicting masculinity in terms of some physical ideal in advertising, infomercial, feature films" and other media (p. 689). This, in turn, affects men's perceptions, attitudes, and beliefs about their own sense of masculinity.

Gender Role Conflict/Stress Theory

Research findings suggest that exposure to ads featuring body stereotypes and models with idealized bodies can lead to negative self-evaluations, eating disorders, depression, and other negative outcomes (Fildes et al., 2014; Levine & Murren, 2009). Specifically, people can be negatively impacted by feeling they cannot meet the expectations of gender role as represented in popular media and advertising. O'Neil (1990) described this phenomenon as GRC/S, "a psychological state in which gender roles have negative consequences or impact on the individual or others" (p. 25). Theorizing the phenomenon, it is possible to measure men's responses to gender conflict according to four factors: (1) success, power, and competition; (2) restrictive emotionality; (3) restrictive affectionate behavior (toward other men); and (4) conflicts in work and family relationships (O'Neil et al., 1986). GRC/S can help explain the effect of mediated gender representations and raises questions about advertisers' complicity in designing images that may end up causing harm.

To summarize this review of literature as foundation for our inquiry about advertisers' behind-the-scenes deliberations about men and masculinity, we explored the role of media and male body ideals in influencing men's self-perceptions of their body image and sense of masculinity. Because too little is known about advertisers' perspectives on this set of connected issues, we set out to examine what practitioners in the advertising industry think about idealized images of men, as well as to shed light on these communication professionals' model casting processes. Hence, we pose this research question:

RQ: What are advertising professionals' perceptions of male images based on what they think brands and consumers want to see in ads?

METHOD

Data Collection

First, we conducted semi-structured interviews with advertising professionals to understand the practices, beliefs, and choices that lead to selecting models, and thus portraying masculinity, in advertising. The first author and a research assistant conducted the interviews.

Participants were recruited during the 2018 *Cannes Lions International Festival of Creativity.* First organized in 1954, this event brings together creative communication industry workers for networking (Our mission, n.d.) Through convenient intercept and snowball sampling techniques at the event, we interviewed advertising professionals who are in a privileged position in their practice arena (Huggins, 2014), and/or serve as "key decision makers who have extensive and exclusive information and the ability to influence important firm outcomes" (Aguinis & Solarino, 2019, p. 1293). After selecting only experts actively involved in producing ads and making choices regarding male representation in advertising, we developed an initial sample for 10 interviews.

Second, five additional phone interviews were conducted with mid-to-senior-level professionals in advertising agencies in the Midwest. In all, a total of (N=15) respondents were interviewed. No incentives for participation were offered.

A semi-structured interview protocol was used to guide the conversation among all research participants, while giving them the opportunity to express their thoughts and allowing the interviewer to ask follow-up questions for deeper understanding (Ravitch & Carl, 2015). This process was consistent with procedures used for interviewing elite informants and accommodating a natural and insightful conversation flow (Aguinis & Solarino, 2019). Each Interview was recorded and transcribed verbatim. Interviews ranged from 27 to 40 minutes. Participants' names were replaced with numbers during the transcription process, from P-1-P-15, to assure anonymity.

Data Analysis

First, both authors conducted a thematic analysis of the interviews by analyzing the complete text to identify both implicit and explicit ideas in the data, or themes that represent or describe the phenomenon being investigated (Guest, et al., 2012). Our thematic analysis followed the process described by Hsieh and Shannon (2005), which involves analyzing every sentence to discover themes and ensure these are derived from the data without imposing existing ideas or theoretical perspectives.

Second, to ensure the quality of the findings, the authors first worked independently, then came together to compare and discuss the findings, and refine the themes, following approaches recommended in the literature (Ravitch & Carl, 2015).

FINDINGS

Among the 15 advertising professionals interviewed as research participants (N=15), eight were male and seven were female. Job titles ranged from assistant account executive through executive vice president and director. One research participant was no longer working in advertising at the time of the interview. (See Table 4.1).

Table 4.1. Research Participant Profiles

Participant #	Gender	Job Title
P-1	F	VP of Marketing for a consumer brand
P-2	F	Assistant Account Director at an advertising agency
P-3	M	Executive Vice President for an advertising agency
P-4	M	Designer at a marketing agency
P-5	M	Director at a marketing agency
P-6	M	Copywriter at an advertising agency
P-7	F	Senior Vice President and Executive Creative Director at a marketing agency
P-8	M	Creative Director at an advertising agency
P-9	M	Director at a marketing agency
P-10	F	Assistant Account Executive at an advertising agency
P-11	F	Senior Account Executive at an advertising agency
P-12	M	Account Manager at an advertising agency
P-13	M	Chief Client Officer at an advertising agency
P-14	F	former Client Officer at an advertising agency
P-15	F	Senior Strategist at a media research company

When characterizing rationales for their selection of male images for ad campaigns, research participants explained that the main drivers are brand needs, client's wishes, and to a lesser extent, the potential for making a positive impact on society. Two overall themes emerged among the interview data of *94* single-spaced pages: 1) *Theme One: Men's Appearance*, and 2) *Theme Two: Men's Character*. Both themes captured research participants' responses to interview probes and were collected and thematically organized to respond to our research question:

RQ: What are advertising professionals' perceptions of male images based on what they think brands and consumers want to see in ads?

1) *Theme One: Men's Appearance*

For *Theme One: Men's Appearance*, we created a visual representation in the form of a Male Body Archetypes in Advertising Continuum, ranging from "most desirable" to "least desirable." Research participants frequently referred to perceptions of men's size, shape, and overall appearance when characterizing men and masculinities desired by brands, clients, and consumers. (See Figure 4.1).

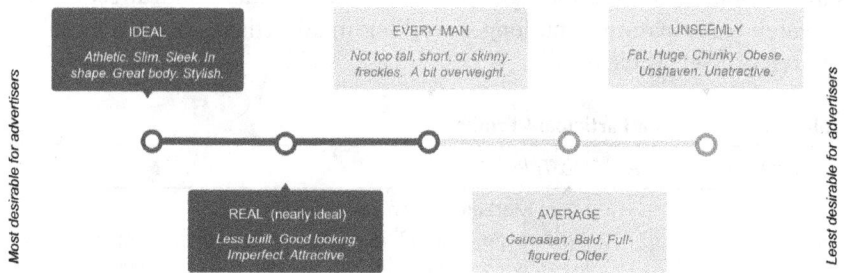

Figure 4.1.   Model
Created by Authors.

At the "most desirable" end of the continuum is the mesomorph body type "ideal athletic build" which is aspirational and used by brands that want this representation to be associated with their products and services. In other words, the *Ideal Man* is one who consumers can relate to and aspire to be, as P-7 explained: "I do believe that consumers want to see a true reflection of themselves or what they aspire to . . . If I am Nike and I wanna advertise running shoes, I better show a runner because I aspire to be a great runner." Also, P-7 added that products like trucks which are aspirational in that consumers want to see someone they can look up to or who reflects how they see themselves. Similarly, P-11 explained that when advertising beauty products, showing attractive models sells more "because that's what people want to see." When casting men for ads, overall, advertising creative professionals are guided by what's considered best for the brand. As P-15 explained: "I think it depends on the industry . . . when the product or service is more geared towards appearance or aesthetics, I think they're very conscious about that person's appearance . . . these clothes are not made for every man." Yet, P-15 added that for healthcare brands, ads "tend to be a little bit more diverse in their casting and who they're featuring." Also, advertising of non-fashion products may demand including diverse images of men because "an ad with only beautiful people really wouldn't show the breadth of [the city]."

Research participants noted several concerns about the *Ideal Man* image as they cautioned that any ideal-but-too-unreal version of a man can be unacceptable to certain consumers. For example, P-12 explained that a model who is "chiseled muscular" quickly can be considered a "very fake looking man" and "overly groomed." Respondent P-7 tended to agree that sometimes this ideal is so unreal "that [he] seems more like a character."

At the opposite end of the continuum is a man who appears physically unfit and is considered "least desirable," or someone advertisers do not want representing their clients' products and services because they believe consumers don't want to see such men in ads. This perception among research participants focused on men who are considered *Unseemly*, a term used by P-9 who also described these men "unshaven" "overweight" and overall "unattractive." P-10 characterized them as men who look "like a slob," are "unkempt," or have "sloppy presentation." Along the same lines, P-14 explained that this type of man tends to be overweight, or "huge," "chunky," and "funny;" perhaps bald and maybe portray a sidekick role in an ad's story.

Hence, professionals working in advertising said they must carefully consider both extremes represented on our Desirable Male Body Archetypes in Advertising Continuum since each extreme look may be perceived as unappealing and, as P-9 explained, likely to "turn a lot of people off" and thereby render an ad ineffective.

In between the "most desirable" and "least desirable" ends of the continuum are men respondents characterized as *Real Man, Every Man,* and *Average Man* which research participants may prefer to select for ads to "get away from being superficial," according to P-7. Often, these types move away from perfect mesomorphic male body types or "fake-looking men" according to P-12, because "people have seen through that bs and know that it's not real." Instead, research participants like P-9 noted that consumers want to see a man who "clearly doesn't hit the gym every day or has a perfectly coiffed head of hair." P-12 added that selecting or casting men for ads really depends on the brand: "Because what we have now [is that] the people that are buying those products are probably not the picture-perfect image . . . I think people are okay with seeing people they see in their everyday lives." What follows is greater detail shared by research participants on each of the three male types that fall between the "most desirable" and "least desirable" ends of the Desirable Male Body Archetypes in Advertising Continuum.

Real Man

Research participants equated the *real* man who is a normal manly guy, although closer to that idealized image. In other words, these are men who "look like everyone else . . . don't look like models because they aren't your typical models," according to P-5. Another research participant, P-7 summarized this perspective, explaining that selecting men to feature in ads is "more about trying to get away from being superficial and showing that they're more inclusive, more real." Thus, "real" men likely have some imperfections that make consumers relate more to them. A "real" man type is one who is appealing but not "classically perfect," according to P-8. The *Real Man* category could include "comedians, funny people, musicians, artists...the interesting people of the world" but P-5 qualified these men as residing closer to the idealized end of the Desirable Male Body Archetypes in Advertising Continuum, as they are desirable "so long as they are attractive." These are still the men women want to have as boyfriend or husbands, and men can relate to (P-9). Research participant P-7 added that the real man type also must be manly: "I don't want to see men emasculated in the media."

Every Man

At the center of the spectrum is the "every man," who P-7 described as someone you know and likely respect, adding: "he looks like a good guy, like someone you'd want to hang out with." Along those same lines, P-4 described this every man as someone who is approachable-looking, which might be a man "with freckles and a little overweight," as described by P-8.

This man is at the center of the spectrum of those most and least desired types for advertisers, being more relatable than the idealized version of the "real man" they described, but still not as imperfect as the average man. The physical appearance of the "every man" is less precise, and more varied than that of other categories. He could be "not too tall, not too short, not too fat, not too skinny; very . . . middle of the road" (P-7).

Average Man

In terms of race and ethnicity, respondents overwhelmingly considered the "average" man to be White, as P-15 explained: "[T]he Caucasian male is still very much the most frequently seen in advertisements." Although closer to the "least desirable" end of the continuum, the "average" man is one consumers want to see more of in ads, according to P-10. This man is, as P-11 said, "a very normal overweight" guy, who might be "older men," look like "dad type[s]" are "not really popular, might wear glasses and don't have cool hair," according to P-7.

Notably, research participants perceive this effort to lean toward the *Real Man, Every Man,* and *Average Man* in advertising is a shift that lends greater credibility to brands—yet a paradoxical one since many also referenced ideal desirable types of male bodies. In fact, only P-14 opined that if a man's build is not directly related to the product or service being advertised, then it should not be a factor in determining specific men's appropriateness for the ad. P-5 offered this explanation: "For most of my career, the men were always an iteration of James Bond—successful, good looking, suave. But actually, [in] the last 10 years, there has been a shift for *the odd, the strange, a bit weird.* The eclectic guys have become heroes, which I think is a good thing, because not everyone can look like [an actor] and not everyone can be successful." Moreover, advertisers that only represent *Ideal Man* images risk alienating consumers who would perceive the strategy "as a scam," as P-12 explained in the context of fast food, for example. By contrast, featuring a *Real Man, Every Man,* or *Average Man* can lead to better opinions about the brand. According to P-15, this strategy can make consumers think "Oh cool! That brand actually cares and they're trying to be more respectful with how they show who the product is for."

2) *Theme Two: Men's Character*

For this second theme, we created Table 4.2 to visually capture research participants' descriptions of idealized images of men for ads that goes beyond just appearance to capture the character of a man. Much like the Marlboro Man, the ideal image of men in advertising celebrates those who display individualism, autonomy, attractiveness, charisma, and virility without vulgarity (White, Oliffe, & Bottorff, 2012). Just as the Marlboro man was an escape from the American boredom with white goods and the suburban life (White, Oliffe, & Bottorff, 2012), men in today's ads depict "heroes" that allow individuals to dare to escape the routine of everyday life in America. The real man, similarly, is described as having room for imperfections. Although real men look good and are likeable, they are not obsessed with their image. On the other hand, the average and every men, are often described in humorous attributes.

When considering men for ads, research participants also look for certain non-physical attributes such as men who are articulate and possess charisma. These are men who might appear on a magazine cover, who are interesting and have many achievements. The archetype also is highly idealized and difficult to achieve. For example, P-5 said the ideal is British soccer superstar and model David Beckham: "[P]robably the all-around good-looking sports guy" whom both men and women like and is "not offensive, doesn't irritate you, not arrogant," given his sports achievements and his charisma fueling celebrity status.

Table 4.2. Male Character Attributes

Ideal Man	Real Man	Every Man	Average Man	Plus Size Man
Interesting, Achiever. Guy attitude. Not intellectual. Articulate. Charismatic. Respected. Passionate. Beautiful. Sophisticated. Great body. Driven.	More masculine. Boy next door. Sports guy. Women like them. Relatable. Imperfect. "Looks like a good guy" and "someone you'd want to hang out with"	Not popular. Middle of the road. Not overpowering Dad type. Relatable. "Just not that classically perfect" A man "who clearly doesn't hit the gym every day, or has a perfectly coiffed head of hair"	Funny. Goofy. Sidekick. Acceptable.	"The butt of the joke"
"Do nothing but watch what they eat and work out"	"Not obsessed with your body, but show you take care of yourself"			

Another non-physical quality that advertising professionals look for is a "boy next door" who exudes a wholesome quality. For example, P-4 explained that American actor Chris Evans "makes people feel comfortable." Perhaps this is why Evans was cast as "Captain America" in the 2011 film.

P-1 described a recent round of creative work where actors and models were not included: "Most people were dancers or musicians or artists . . . We weren't necessarily checking for body type." In sum, the insights show that when advertisers seek for talent to feature in ads, professionals prefer those who are likeable or admired, which coincide with perfect or almost perfect physical characteristics. On the contrary, when professionals seek for alternative attributes to physical appearance to appeal to audiences, men with less desirable body types are cast for humorous appeals.

DISCUSSION

Insights from Advertising Creatives

Our interviews with 15 advertising creative professionals offered a contextualized exploration of processes associated with selecting male images for ads for greater depth in our understanding what goes on behind the curtain.

Overall, these professionals still conform to a Western standard of *Ideal Man* attractiveness, which mostly is defined as attractive, lean, and muscular. Images of male celebrities such as Chris Evans and David Beckham were offered, suggesting that an idealistic representation of male beauty remains deeply entrenched in the advertising creative process. The rationale they offered is one of consumers exhibiting more positive evaluations of attractive individuals. Collectively, this dynamic results in an overrepresentation of idealized male models in advertisements. Ongoing proliferation of these images exacerbates decades-long contribution to male GRC/S that may play out across four factors of men's perceptions of their (1) success, power, and competition; (2) restrictive emotionality; (3) restrictive affectionate behavior (toward other men); and (4) conflicts in work and family relationships—when they feel that they cannot measure up to such idealized imagery (O'Neil et al., 1986).

GRC/S, as a theoretical lens, enables us to further caution advertising creative professionals to instead pursue this emerging trend of embracing images of *Real Man, Every Man,* and *Average Man* to avoid complicity in creating media representations that cause harm among men and across social spheres. Ethnicity/race, culture, and media intersect to shape preferences for *Ideal Man* (mesomorph), while research participants acknowledge that consumers may prefer slightly less muscular bodies (ectomorph and endomorph) for greater believability of advertising messages. Our findings reported in this chapter build upon and support Diedrichs and colleagues' (2011) conclusions that there seems to be a barrier to accepting non-idealized models in media. Stigmatization of obesity has been well documented (e.g., Strings, 2019) and casting a majority of idealized male models in ads can communicate to consumers that other types of bodies are deemed to be of lesser value and importance and negatively impact self-esteem and interpersonal relationships for consumers who do not conform to the ideal (Greenberg et al., 2002; 2003). Clearly, some advertising creative professionals would like to see greater diversity among men represented in ads—in terms of appearance and inner qualities—but most seem conditioned to cast *Real Man, Every Man,* and *Average Man* types only for certain product categories (e.g., alcohol, insurance, cleaning products) or characters (e.g., funny guy, goofy). Having real, believable men who appeal to the consumers was one of the most important factors in advertisers' descriptions of desirable male archetypes.

The finding we consider most troubling is research participants' characterization of Whiteness as part of *Ideal Man* and *Average Man* male images even though they perceive that consumers might prefer greater diversity by increasing representation of men featuring multiple skin tones. Clearly, masculinity is a multifaceted construct predominantly considered in terms of

Whiteness as the acceptable masculinity standard—to the detriment of self-perception among Black and multiracial boys (Newman, 2019) —and given that ideal male images tend to vary by culture (De Meulenaer, et al., 2018). Moreover, even advertising professionals' understanding of who men are seems to be indexed by idealized types of actors, superheroes, sports figures, and dancers so that our results point to the pervasiveness of the White ideal in casting endorsers for ads. Besides being White, both Beckham and Evans are tall, fit, fair haired, and heterosexual. Only P-15 noted that a more diverse cast can add a "cool factor" to an ad or brand by appealing to a "wider audience and show that, for America, it's not all the same color or the same look, that only makes your brand more widely appealing." From an economics perspective, surely advertising creatives can see the value in diversifying images that appeal to a wider consumer base. Although several advertisers spoke of their efforts to diversify their casting, the ideal of an attractive, thin, muscular White man was the benchmark for their description.

The focus of this chapter has been on contributing to understanding of how men are represented in ads by creative professionals based on limitations of their client and brand demands and perceptions of consumers. GRC/S effects that result from men comparing themselves to male body image ideals leads to negative self-image, depression, and more (O'Neil, 1990; Pompper, 2010)—so it is important to acknowledge that advertising professionals may take an active role in reversing negative trends.

Limitations and Future Research

There are some limitations worth noting. First, our findings cannot be generalized but may serve as a point of departure for future hypothesis testing. Second, because the number of interviews was relatively small, future studies should consider increasing the number of respondents—as well as illuminating their demographic profile beyond simply gender identification. Third, we also wonder if conducting interviews at the 2018 *Cannes Lions International Festival of Creativity*, while convenient for us, may have primed research participants' responses since the event included several talks about gender representation in ads.

Moving forward, we offer these recommendations to build upon our findings.

1. Expand upon research of male representations in ads by exploring advertising creatives' and consumers' perceptions of relationships among body image, body fitness, and healthfulness.

2. Consider including photo or video stimulus materials to probe research participants' reactions and degrees of acceptance of diverse male model body types.
3. Examine social identity dimension intersectionalities among both male images and among perceptions of advertising producers.
4. Build upon our *Men's Character* theme to discover nuances among male qualities useful for advertising messages and discover more about why advertisers still revert to predominantly considering male attractiveness.

Summary

In sum, research participants undoubtedly cling to old male body image ideals that they believe have been left behind. Ubiquity of a particular masculinity standard—Whiteness—persists. Advertising creatives and their clients do not seem to be as flexible as they believe they are when considering images of men to tell their brand story and appeal to consumers. Indeed, more research is needed to examine these dynamics because GRC/S is a serious issue playing out in toxic masculinity effects that are plaguing many nations globally. Advertising creatives manifest the potential to serve as advocates for DEI; a socially responsible goal in the wake of social movements demanding BIPOC justice.

REFERENCES

Aguinis, H. & Solarino, A. M. (2019). Transparency and replicability in qualitative research: The case of interviews with elite informants. *Strategic Management Journal, 40*, 1291–315. https://doi.org/10.1002/smj.3015.

Alhabash, S., Mundel, J., Deng, T., McAlister, A., Quilliam, E. T., Richards, J. I., & Lynch, K. (2020). Social media alcohol advertising among underage minors: effects of models' age. *International Journal of Advertising*, 1–30. https://doi.org/10.1080/02650487.2020.1852807.

Ashmore, R. D., & Del Boca, F. K. (1981). Conceptual approaches to stereotypes and stereotyping. In D. Hamilton (Ed.), *Cognitive Processes in Stereotyping and Intergroup Behavior,* (pp. 1–35). Psychology Press.

Baculinao, E. (2017), "China tackles 'masculinity crisis,' tries to stop 'effeminate' boys", available at: https://nbcnews.to/3tfcvJJ (accessed January 9, 2019).

Baglia, J. (2005). *The Viagra ad venture: Masculinity, marketing, and the performance of sexual health.* Peter Lang.

Bandura, A. (1994). Social cognitive theory of mass communication. In J. Bryant and D. Zillmann (Eds.), *Media effects: Advances in theory and research* (pp. 61–90). Erlbaum.

Baxter, S. M., Kulczynski, A., & Ilicic, J. (2016). Ads aimed at dads: Exploring consumers' reactions towards advertising that conforms and challenges traditional gender role ideologies. *International Journal of Advertising, 35*(6), 970–982. https://doi.org/10.1080/02650487.2015.1077605.

Bordo, S. (2000). *The male body: A new look at men in public and in private*. Farrar, Straus and Giroux.

Ceron, E. (January 15, 2019). MRAs outraged after razor company asks men to show common decency. *New York Magazine*. Retrieved from: http://bit.ly/cut190115.

Chapa, S., Jackson, J., F. F., & Lee, J. (2020). Antecedents of ideal body image and body dissatisfaction: The role of ethnicity, gender and age among the consumers in the USA. *Journal of Global Fashion Marketing, 11*(2), 190–206. https://doi.org/10.1080/20932685.2019.1703780.

Connell, R. W. (1987). *Gender and Power: Society, the Person and Sexual politics*. Polity.

Connell, R. W., & Messerschmidt, J. W. (2005). Hegemonic masculinity. *Gender and Society, 19,* 829–859. http://dx.doi.org/10.1177/0891 243205278639.

Crouch, I. (2016, February 7). Super Bowl commercials: The best and worst of 2016. *The New Yorker*. Retrieved from: https://bit.ly/3ynxCNz.

Deaux, K., & Lewis, L. L. (1984). Structure of gender stereotypes: Interrelationships among components and gender label. *Journal of Personality and Social Psychology, 46*(5), 991. https://doi.org/10.1037/0022-3514.46.5.991

De Meulenaer, S., Dens, N., De Pelsmacker, P., & Eisend, M. (2018). How consumers' values influence responses to male and female gender role stereotyping in advertising. *International Journal of Advertising, 37*(6), 893–913. https://doi.org/10.1080/02650487.2017.1354657.

Diedrichs, P. C. & Lee, C. (2010). GI Joe or Average Joe? The impact of average-size and muscular male fashion models on men's and women's body image and advertisement effectiveness. *Body Image, 7*(3), 218–226. https://doi.org/10.1016/j.bodyim.2010.03.004.

Diedrichs, P. C., Lee, C., & Kelly, M. (2011). Seeing the beauty in everyday people: A qualitative study of young Australians' opinions on body image, the mass media and models. *Body Image, 8*(3), 259–266. https://doi.org/10.1016/j.bodyim.2011.03.003.

Eisend, M. (2019). Gender roles. *Journal of Advertising, 48*(1), 72–80. https://doi.org/10.1080/00913367.2019.1566103.

Eisend, M., & Langner, T. (2010). Immediate and delayed advertising effects of celebrity endorsers' attractiveness and expertise. *International Journal of Advertising, 29*(4), 527–546. https://doi.org/10.2501/S0265048710201336.

Elliott, R. & Elliott, C. (2005). Idealized images of the male body in advertising: a reader-response exploration. *Journal of Marketing Communications, 11*(1), 3–19. https://doi.org/10.1080/1352726042000263566.

Fildes, J., Robbins, A., Cave, L., Perrens, B., & Wearring, A. (2014). *Mission Australia's 2014 Youth Survey Report* [Data Set]. Mission Australia. Retrieved from: https://bit.ly/3nK8ifT.

Fiske, S. T., Cuddy, A. J. C., Glick, P., & Xu, J. (2002). A model of (often mixed) stereotype content: Competence and warmth respectively flow from perceived status and competition. *Journal of Personality and Social Psychology*, 82(6), 878–902.

Gerrard, O., Galli, N., Santurri, L., & Franklin, J. (2020). Examining body dissatisfaction in college men through the exploration of appearance anxiety and internalization of the mesomorphic ideal. *Journal of American College Health*, 1–7. https://doi.org/10.1080/07448481.2019.1704412.

Greenberg, B. S., Mastro, D., & Brand, J. E. (2002). Minorities and the mass media: Television into the 21st century. In J. Bryant and M. B. Oliver (Eds.), *Media effects: Advances in theory and research*, pp. 333–351.

Greenberg, B. S., Eastin, M., Hofschire, L., Lachlan, K., & Brownell, K. D. (2003). Portrayals of overweight and obese individuals on commercial television. *American Journal of Public Health*, 93(8), 1342–1348. https://doi.org/10.2105/AJPH.93.8.1342.

Guest, G., MacQueen, K. M., & Namey, E. E. (2012). *Applied Thematic Analysis*. Thousand Oaks, CA: Sage.

Hsieh, H. F., & Shannon, S. E. (2005). Three approaches to qualitative content analysis. *Qualitative Health Research*, 15(9), 1277–1288. https://doi.org/10.1177/1049732305276687.

Huggins, C. (2014). Arranging and Conducting Elite Interviews: Practical Considerations. SAGE Research Methods Cases. London: SAGE Publications. http://dx.doi.org/10.4135/978144627305013514687.

Kalb, I. (2013). Why Kraft's Sexy Ad For Italian Dressing Totally Backfired. *Business Insider*. Retrieved from https://bit.ly/3xMKj4y.

Kolbe, R. H., & Albanese, P. J. (1996). Man to man: A content analysis of sole-male images in male-audience magazines. *Journal of Advertising*, 25(4), 1–20. https://doi.org/10.1080/00913367.1996.10673509.

Levine, M. P., & Murnen, S. K. (2009). "Everybody knows that mass media are/are not [pick one] a cause of eating disorders": A critical review of evidence for a causal link between media, negative body image, and disordered eating in females. *Journal of Social and Clinical Psychology*, 28(1), 9–42. https://doi.org/10.1521/jscp.2009.28.1.9.

Liang, C. T. H., Rivera, A. L. Y., Nathwani, A., Dang, P., & Douroux, A. N. (2010). Dealing with gendered racism and racial identity among Asian American men. In W. M. Liu, D. K. Iwamoto, and M. H. Chae (Eds.), *Culturally responsive counseling with Asian American men* (pp. 63–81). New York: Routledge/Taylor and Francis Group.

Lu, A., & Wong, Y. J. (2013). Stressful experiences of masculinity among U. S.-born and immigrant Asian American men. *Gender and Society, 27*, 345–371. http://dx.doi.org/10.1177/0891243213479446.

Magkos, F. (2019). Metabolically healthy obesity: what's in a name? *The American Journal of Clinical Nutrition, 110*(3), 533–539. https://doi.org/10.1093/ajcn/nqz133.

McCartan, A., & McMahon, F. (2020). Gender and Advertising. *The International Encyclopedia of Gender, Media, and Communication*, 1–17.

Morrison, T. G., Kalin, R., & Morrison, M. A. (2004). Body-image evaluation and body-image investment among adolescents: A test of sociocultural and social comparison theories. *Adolescence, 39*(155), 571.

Newman, A. M. (2019). Desiring the standard light skin: black multiracial boys, masculinity and exotification. *Identities, 26*(1), 107-125. https://doi.org/10.1080/1070289X.2017.1377420.

O'Neil, J. (1981). Male sex-role conflict, sexism and masculinity. *The Counseling Psychologist, 9*, 61-80. https://doi.org/10.1177/001100008100900213.

O'Neil, J. M., Helms, B. J., Gable, R. K., David, L., & Wrightsman, L. S. (1986). Gender-Role Conflict Scale: College men's fear of femininity. *Sex Roles, 14*(5), 335–350. https://doi.org/10.1007/BF00287583.

O'Neil, J. M. (1990). Assessing men's gender role conflict. In D. Moore and F. Leafgren (Eds.), *Problem Solving Strategies and Interventions for Men in Conflict*, (pp. 23–38). American Association for Counseling and Development.

Orehek, E., & Human, L. J. (2017). Self-expression on social media: Do tweets present accurate and positive portraits of impulsivity, self-esteem, and attachment style? *Personality and Social Psychology Bulletin, 43*(1), 60–70. https://doi.org/10.1177/0146167216675332.

Our mission (n.d.) Cannes Lions International Festival of Creativity. Accessed May 28, 2021, from https://www.canneslions.com/about.

Parent, M. C., Davis-Delano, L. R., Morgan, E. M., Woznicki, N. W., & Denson, A. (2020). An inductive analysis of young adults' conceptions of femininity and masculinity and comparison to established gender inventories. *Gender Issues, 37*(1), 1–24. https://doi.org/10.1007/s12147-019-09246-y.

Patterson, M. & England, G. (2000). Body work: depicting the male body in magazines, in Proceedings of the Academy of Marketing Annual Conference, University of Derby.

Pompper, D. (2014). *Practical and theoretical implications of successfully doing difference in organizations.* Emerald Group Publishing Limited.

Pompper, D. (2010). Masculinities, the metrosexual, and media images: Across dimensions of age and ethnicity. *Sex Roles, 63*(9-10), 682–696. https://doi.org/10.1007/s11199-010-9870-7.

Pompper, D., Soto, J., & Piel, L. (2007). Male body image and magazine standards: Considering dimensions of age and ethnicity. *Journalism and Mass Communication Quarterly, 84*(3), 525–545. https://doi.org/10.1177/107769900708400308.

Pope, H., Phillips, K. A., & Olivardia, R. (2000). *The Adonis Complex: The Secret Crisis of Male Body Obsession.* Simon and Schuster.

Pounders, K. (2018). Are portrayals of female beauty in advertising finally changing? *Journal of Advertising Research, 58*(2), 133–137. https://doi.org/DOI: 10.2501/JAR-2018-021.

Ravitch, S. M., & Carl, N.M. (2015). Qualitative research. SAGE Publications.

Sheehan, K. B. (2013). *Controversies in contemporary advertising.* Sage Publications.

Shroff, H., & Thompson, J. K. (2006). The tripartite influence model of body image and eating disturbance: A replication with adolescent girls. *Body Image, 3,* 17–23. http://dx.doi.org/10.1016/j.bodyim.2005.10 .004.

Slater, A., & Tiggemann, M. (2006). The contribution of physical activity and media use during childhood and adolescence to adult women's body image. *Journal of Health Psychology, 11*(4), 553–565. https://doi.org/10.1177/1359105306065016.

Strings, S. (2019). *Feating the Black body: The racial origins of fat phobia.* NYU Press.

Tan, Y., Shaw, P., Cheng, H., & Kim, K. K. (2013). The construction of masculinity: A cross-cultural analysis of men's lifestyle magazine advertisements. *Sex Roles, 69*(5-6), 237–249. https://doi.org/10.1007/s11199-013-0300-5.

Wang, Y., & Sun, S. (2010). Assessing beliefs, attitudes, and behavioral responses toward online advertising in three countries. *International Business Review, 19*(4), 333–344. https://doi.org/10.1016/j.ibusrev.2010.01.004.

White, C., Oliffe, J. L., & Bottorff, J. L. (2012). From the physician to the Marlboro Man: Masculinity, health, and cigarette advertising in America, 1946–1964. *Men and Masculinities, 15*(5), 526–547.

Windels, K. (2016). Stereotypical or just typical: how do US practitioners view the role and function of gender stereotypes in advertisements? *International Journal of Advertising, 35*(5), 864–887. https://doi.org/10.1080/02650487.2016.1160855.

Zayer, L. T., McGrath, M. A., & Castro-González, P. (2019). Men and masculinities in a changing world:(de) legitimizing gender ideals in advertising. *European Journal of Marketing, 54*(1), 238–260. https://doi.org/10.1108/EJM-07-2018-0502.

Chapter Five

Dirty Work Masculinity and Coping Strategies among Garbage Collectors

Akira Sai and Taro Yamauchi

INTRODUCTION

Masculinity, more suitably recognized in its plural form of *masculinities* (Kimmel, 2001), has been an important and complex concept for helping sociologists and other social science researchers to understand social identity, gender roles, body image, and intersectionality of social identity dimensions across multiple ages, cultures, ethnicities, sexual orientations, and more. *Masculinity* is what a culture expects of men (Craig, 1992); a human construct, variable, slippery concept. Being masculine means having "a particular psychological identity, social role, cultural script, place in the labor force" (Stimpson, 1987, p. xi). While much recent research among males has emphasized that masculinity is something that takes place internally, we also must recognize that one's self-conception of it is embedded within a social milieu and is shaped by media representations (Bordo, 2000). For example, mental, nonphysical inner qualities of character, attitude, responsibility, and confidence/assertiveness represent a core meaning of masculinity for men across ethnic groups in the United States (Pompper, 2010), yet advertising and media images impress external physical ideals for which many men strive to emulate (Pompper, et al., 2007). Overall, masculinity embodies power and dominance over femininity (e.g., Connell, 2005; O'Neil, 1981) and is equated with muscularity (McCreary & Saucier, 2005; Swami, 2016). This phenomenon places some males at greater risk for negative body image when they feel that their own muscles fail to measure up to an ideal, resulting in body dissatisfaction, low self-esteem, low confidence, social dysfunction, supplement use, and muscle dysmorphic disorder (e.g, Hobza & Rochlen, 2009).

We know too little about how masculinity plays out in the context of low occupational prestige. Hughes (1951, 1958, 1962) introduced the *dirty work* concept to refer to occupations and tasks considered distasteful, disgusting, or demeaning. More specifically, dirty work is deemed physically, mentally, and socially degrading to the degree that it can wound one's dignity (Zock, 2005). In the West, significant value is placed on work that yields reasonable pay, safe work conditions, equality, esteem, autonomy, and respect (Lucas et al., 2013). Yet, unlike high-status, white-collar occupations such as business and management which take place primarily in office buildings and are socially considered to be prestigious, much manual labor conducted outdoors is considered to be low-status blue collar labor for uneducated men. Despite efforts to keep people safe at the cost of their own safety, health, and dignity, workers who engaged in physically, mentally and socially distasteful work environments during the COVID-19 pandemic faced social stigmatization even though they are considered *essential workers*—especially healthcare workers who directly or indirectly deliver health services.

The physical manual labor required, combined with the sights and smells associated with garbage collection make it an "exemplar dirty work job" (Hamilton et al., 2019, p. 899). In some areas, *sanitation worker* has replaced the term *garbage collector*, but there are many labels attached to this industry and its employees regardless of gender: trash man, garbage man, dustman, binman. Perhaps the first people to do this job, officially, were in Britain in the 1350s as "rakers" cleaned up throughout the Black Plague (History, n.d.) Earlier, people simply burned it, fed it to animals, buried it, dumped it in

Figure 5.1.   The dirty work of being a garbage collector is socially stigmatized globally.
Courtesy of Depositphotos Inc.

the ocean, or let it lay where it dropped and by 2000 B.C., China developed composting/recycling techniques (History, n.d.) By the 1920s in the United States, a mechanized arm improved efficiency by lifting garbage cans and dumping them into trucks and today, dumpster bins are mechanically loaded into metal boxes that travel by rail to their final destination (History, n.d.) Despite the critical role they play in keeping everyone healthy and safe, garbage collectors who "have a markedly higher risk of becoming infected" during a pandemic (Schmerling, 2020) face social stigmatization in forms of suspicion and avoidance. During the COVID-19 pandemic, some sanitation workers fought back, demanding better working conditions because their health and well-being consistently is at risk (Monroe, 2020).

The stigmatization of men who do dirty work is an important issue to study as we expand our understanding of masculinities. So, examining ways that men who may be considered less masculine because of the way they earn their living amidst garbage, deal with lack of social appreciation, and being invalidated as they negotiate their own sense of self-worth and masculinity is the focus of the essay reported in this chapter.

REVIEW OF LITERATURE

This chapter explores men's lived experiences in the face of social stigmatization. We combine social identity theory and male gender role conflict/stress theory to examine the dirty work phenomenon and to inspire future study with expanded theory building and data collection for hypothesis testing.

The foundation for this essay is built upon our exploration of: 1) Masculinities in review, 2) Dirty work in review, 3) Necessary but stigmatized, and 4) Theoretical underpinnings for examining blue collar occupations. Central to our inquiry is an examination of the harm men experience as essential workers as they are socially stigmatized and dehumanized, and ways this plays out amidst their self-assessment as masculine men.

Masculinities in Review

Just what constitutes a *man* is not a universal idea, but rather a deeply contextualized social construction (Pleck, 2006). Some scholars have noted that masculine inner qualities include power, dominance, achievement, independence, and self-confidence—as well as anti-feminine qualities such as calm and showing little emotion and aggression (Thompson & Pleck, 1986; O'Neil, 1981; Pompper, 2010). Males who fail to live up to masculine norms are regarded negatively, which can result in male gender role conflict and stress (GRC/S) which negatively affects males' perceptions of success, power, and competition, restricts emotionality, confines affectionate behaviors between men which can lead to homophobia, and fosters conflict between work and family relations (O'Neil 1981; O'Neil et al., 1986).

Examining relationships among media representations of ideal masculinity and a man's self-image is well traveled territory in the social science literature. In particular, high degrees of muscularity are equated with masculinity and the drive to develop an inverted triangle body shape of upper torso with broad shoulders, thick pectoral regions, well-developed arms and narrowed waist (Grogan & Richards, 2002; Swami & Tovee, 2005; Pompper et al., 2007) runs counter to a thinness ideal equated with the feminine ideal (Pompper, 2017; Ricciardelli & McCabe, 2001). Research findings suggest that males who conform to a hyper-muscular ideal claim that the more muscular they are, the more masculine they are (Griffiths et al., 2015; McCreary et al., 2005).

Examining masculinity according to cultural and ethnic dimensions as they intersect with male gender is fertile research territory since we know very little about these dynamics across lived experiences of Asian men. A small subset of research findings suggests that the drive for muscularity is a Western-hegemonic phenomenon that increasingly is impacting sociocultural groups globally (Leit et al., 2001; Pope et al., 1999; Ricciardelli & McCabe, 2001). The "Orient," according to Said (1978), is a feminized region because it is "penetrated, silenced, and possessed" (p. 207). According to Dutch social psychologist Geert Hofstede (2010), cultures have six dimensions such as being either feminine or masculine—as determined by gender role distributions. In masculine societies, women's and men's roles overlap less and males are expected to exhibit assertive behaviors and be strong and fast.

In the East, China and Japan are considered masculine cultures, while Taiwan and Korea are considered to be feminine cultures (Hofstede, 2010). Masculinities in China are explained by a wen-wu model, with wen referring to cultural attainment (literary and artistic) and wu referring to martial valor (physical strength and military prowess (Song, 2004). Among college students in Malaysia, Chinese men (as compared to Malay and Indian men) have an accelerated drive for muscularity so that they may measure up to other men; a desire that may be inspired by media use and puts men at risk for "excess muscularity-oriented thoughts and behaviors" (Sai et al., 2020a, p. 3). In Japan, salary man masculinity is used to describe a loyal white-collar male employee (Dasgupta, 2003). In Taiwan, a lower drive (as compared to the West) for muscularity reflects a conception of masculinity as stemming from internal, or cerebral, qualities linked to competence and success (Yang, et al., 2005). In the United States, Chinese and South Korean college men stressed that they do not consider masculinity in terms of physical attributes and criticize U.S. culture for emphasizing male muscularity (Pompper, 2010). Being an ethnic minority in Britain can negatively impact Asian men's self-esteem and body image, which negatively fosters a sense of subordinate masculinity—so men compensate for low degrees of muscularity by working to build their body muscles to satisfy their greater need for power (Swami, 2016).

Dirty Work in Review

What exactly is *dirty work*? In the United States, a television host now worth $35 million (Nihalani, 2020) hit a career high by hosting a syndicated show called "Dirty Jobs" through 2003–2012 wherein he entertainingly interviewed and worked alongside men with occupations like sewage cleaner, coal miner, farmhand, and garbage collector. It is this last occupation that we examine more closely in the following subsections: 1) Necessary but stigmatized, and 2) Why work at a dirty job?

Necessary but Stigmatized

Garbage workers play a significant role in society—at 60,828 strong in the United States in 2020, with 87.1 percent men and 8.3 percent women of which 67 percent are White, 13.6 percent are Hispanic/Latino, and 12.5 percent are Black/African American who are more likely to work at private companies than municipalities (Garbage, n.d.) Demographic profiles vary according to nation, and in the United States, 42 percent have a high school diploma.

Although their work importantly supports sanitation infrastructures, garbage collectors often risk their dignity, safety, and health. Situations are worse in developing nations characterized by a lack of sanitation infrastructure, largely relying on an informal sector of garbage workers (Sharma et al., 2020). Two problematic outcomes make the direct handling of waste risky—when workers lack proper personal protective equipment (PPE) and when they come into contact with infected or hazardous materials (e.g., biomedical waste). Both scenarios predispose these workers to a range of health risks daily, including respiratory and infectious diseases (Kuijer & Frings-Dressen, 2004; Sai et al., 2020b; Sharma et al., 2020). In a pandemic, conditions are exacerbated by massive amounts of biomedical and household waste that may be improperly collected, handled, and sorted. Such practices put garbage workers in danger of infection.

Dirty work like garbage collection is socially necessary, but that doesn't mean it's an esteemed, respected, or well-regarded occupation. According to the World Health Organization, garbage collection is an occupation that is "far too often invisible, unquantified, and ostracized" (WHO, 2019, p. ix).

Even calling garbage collectors *sanitation workers* has done little to elevate the social status of the job. On the contrary, dirt and odor basically make garbage collection a thankless job. *Dirtiness* is not an intrinsic quality but rather is socially constructed based on our subjective standard of cleanliness and purity (Ashforth & Kreiner, 1999). Because most cultures consider cleanliness to be good and dirtiness to be bad, people try to distance themselves from that which is associated with dirt (Douglas, 1966). Hence, garbage collectors are dirty by association with the garbage they collect and have become socially stigmatized and dehumanized (Valtorta et al., 2019).

The paradox is that dirty work has to be done by someone—and this leads to rationalizing that the doer must be deserving of physical, social, and moral taints—and often those doing it already are considered marginalized others due to their ethnicity, socioeconomic status, or low education levels (Walzer 1984). Ashforth and Kreiner (2014) characterized a "monolithic construct" of dirty work (p. 81) and developed propositions suggesting that globally, physically stigmatized work is more universally agreed upon than social and moral dirty work. Dirty work with physical taint refers to jobs that require constant contact with dirt and death (e.g., garbage workers, funeral directors, domestic workers, plumbers, janitors) and/or a noxious and dangerous work environment (e.g., firefighters, miners, soldiers). Social taint refers to jobs characterized by serving others (e.g., cab drivers, shoe shiners, flight attendants, sales assistants) or regularly coming into contact with stigmatized persons (e.g., public defenders, some healthcare workers). Lastly, moral taint describes work of dubious virtue (e.g., exotic and go-go dancers at nightclubs, prostitutes), as well as work that involves deceptive, intrusive and antagonistic features (e.g., bill collectors, tabloid reporters, door-to-door salespersons). For garbage collectors, the physical taint comes more from their association with physical dirt "as if dirt were contagious" more so than actually getting physically dirty (Ashforth & Kreiner, 2014, p. 83).

Low-status jobs like garbage collection could serve as one end of a continuum used to categorize occupational prestige. *Prestige* refers to the social standing of a job and the employee, which is a composite of socioeconomic status and education (Treiman, 1977). Opposite the garbage collector are higher occupational prestige workers with greater job stability, respect, and social acceptance (Ashforth & Kreiner, 1999). Since waste, garbage, and dirt are disdained and avoided in just about every human society (Ashforth and Kreiner, 1999), this means garbage collectors have very little power over how they are perceived by others and this results in internalizing disdain (Jost & Elsbach, 2011). For example, cleaning garbage off city streets often includes dog feces and dead animals; work called "not exactly glamorous" (Hamilton et al., 2019, p. 893). It's not unusual for garbage collectors to encounter people who hold their nose and hurl verbal abuse insults when passing garbage collectors doing their job (Hamilton et al., 2019). Indeed, garbage collection is an occupation rife with male GRC/S.

Why Work at a Dirty Job?

So, what do garbage collectors get out of working a dirty job that requires physical and mental endurance and is socially stigmatized? The question here is how members of this tainted occupation seek to attain some semblance of a positive identity in the face of low social status. A quest for meaningfulness of work is subjective and socially constructed (Rosso et al., 2020) and among studies of work dignity, which can be easily eroded and undermined among stigmatized workers, scholars have discovered that incentives such as good pay, autonomy, and feelings of self-worth can overcome the negatives (Bolton, 2007). Also, dignity associated with strong occupational and work-group cultures shaped by strong fellowship can negate other negative qualities of dirty jobs (Deery et al., 2019). Workers in low occupational prestige are known to coalesce into a group to confront the negative qualities attached to them and assert their social significance through occupational ideologies and selective social comparisons (Ashforth & Kreiner, 1999). In other words, when working at a dirty job and experiencing others' disdain, garbage collectors form their own collective norm.

This closer look at the dynamics of garbage collection work offers a clearer view for understanding stigmatized workers' identities and theorizing about how this dynamic plays out in the shaping of their masculine identities.

Theoretical Underpinnings for Examining Blue Collar Occupations

Two important theory streams are useful for examining the context of manual labor considered to be *dirty work*—and the social stigma attached to it that may negatively impact men's self-esteem and sense of masculinity.

Social Identity Theory

Social psychologists have theorized that one's identity is a sense of who they are based on their membership among groups defined by gender, ethnicity, occupation, and more (Tajfel & Turner, 1986), making one's identity a social construction. Having a masculine identity means having a particular "social role, cultural script, place in the labor force" (Stimpson, 1987, p. xi). Overall, identity is intersectional in that it relates also to forms of privilege/discrimination rooted in power relation hierarchies (Edwards, 2015; Vernon & Swain, 2002). Social identity theory explains how in-groups and out-groups form (Tajfel & Turner, 1986; Turner, 1985) in organizations; a cauldron for

negative perceptions about *the other* which contribute to systemic discrimination and can become embedded in informal relations which follow people
across their life course.

A significant component of social identity theory is the process of social
comparison. Once we identify ourselves as part of a gender or ethnic group,
for example, we begin comparing ourselves to others in the group—as well
as those outside of the group. Our sense of self-esteem is linked to in-group
membership, how we measure up, and sometimes how we discriminate
against out-group members (Jost & Elsbach, 2011; Tajfel et al., 1979). These
processes are "woven into the very structure and fabric of society" (Vernon &
Swain, 2002, p. 78). Thus, social identity theory is used to predict intergroup
behaviors based on perceived group status differences, as well as perceptions
of legitimacy and stability of those differences (Tajfel & Turner, 1979).

Gender Role Conflict/Stress

Whereas social identity theory explains how conflict can arise within and
between groups, male gender role conflict/stress (GRC/S) explains how
men, as individuals, internalize and act upon the outcomes. When men feel
they fail to live up to society's expectations of them, then the inner conflict
and stress can have adverse physical and psychological effects such as feeling effeminate, incapable of meeting society's traditional male breadwinner
role, or sexual objectified in mass media images (O'Neil, 1981; Pompper,
2010) that can lead to muscle dysmorphia (McCreary et al., 2005; Olivardia
et al., 2004). Moreover, the paid workplace has accommodated more and
more women post-World War II, causing a shift in the breadwinner role as
a basis for male identity (Tolson, 1977; Sherman, 2009) that continues to
evolve as even women move into occupations considered to be dirty work
(Garbage, n.d.).

Occupation or place in the labor force—in conjunction with perceptions
of degrees of dignity associated with the work—contribute to men's sense
of self-worth. For example, physically and economically unsatisfying occupations are associated with lower dignity (Berg & Frost, 2005). Degrading
work that is underestimated by others can erode dignity (Sayer, 2007), and
having one's work labeled by derogatory language also negatively impacts
a man's sense of self worth. For male workers with limited job options who
are simply trying to make ends meet, doing dirty work can prove exceptionally stressful.

Examining relationships between masculinity and dirty work opens a portal to understanding a specific kind of male GRC/S that can build up or break
down a man's perceptions of social identity and masculinity. The physical
and mental rigor required for dirty work like garbage collection enables us

to examine how the dynamics interplay and to begin processes of building theory about lived experiences of men who perform dirty work. A study of garbage collection in Britain labeled the occupation as low-status and while theory was not used to undergird the study, researchers used the interview method to discover how workers discursively construct paternalism in terms of caring for their community and those who live there despite others' negative perceptions of garbage collection (Hamilton et al., 2019)—not unlike firefighters who walk into burning buildings occupy a masculine identity as "strong, courageous and daring," (Tracy & Scott, 2006). Findings of a study of Belgian domestic workers who perform dirty work in a context of servile relationships with clients/employers suggested that workers develop coping mechanisms to avoid or minimalize external insults that yield internal discomfort (Bosmans et al., 2016).

So, upon a joined social identity theory and GRC/S theory platform, we interrogate the dirty work phenomenon as it intersects with male garbage collectors' lived experiences.

IDENTITY-ENHANCING STRATEGIES AND COPING MECHANISMS

To begin, we introduce the concept of *dirty work masculinity* as a stigma-coping, identity-enhancing, and conflict/stress-reducing strategy to better understand the lived experiences of men who work in jobs like garbage collection who may struggle to construct a satisfying masculine identity. We posit that dirty work forces men to come up with at least three coping mechanisms to discursively deal with factors that threaten to diminish their sense of masculinity.

First, masculinities shape relationships among people (Connell, 2005). For men who perform dirty work, social identity theory's in-group membership may develop into *Camaraderie* for male garbage collectors, or a sense of being "in the same boat" (Ashforth & Kreiner, 1999, p. 421; Deery et al., 2019), or same social context, with co-workers. Emphasizing their masculinity together can offer expressive resistance and opposition to social stigmatization of garbage collection. Moreover, by comparing themselves to workers in other groups, or downward social comparison, dirty work employees may find "protection for a vulnerable ego" (Ashforth & Kreiner, 1999, p. 425). This outcome can offer dirty work employees support that translates to social validation, value, justification, and paternalistic community service. Instead of focusing on the unsanitary conditions within which they work and the disrespect and negative perceptions of others, male garbage collectors can avoid GRC/S by reframing *how they think about* what they do for a living. Recalibrating is a technique that adjusts the implicit standards to assess an occupation by magnifying the small-but-significant aspects, whilst minimalizing the large, stigmatized ones.

Second, social identity's in-group membership also may involve perceptions of *Self-Sacrificing Hero*. Some men who perform dirty work respond to others' negativity by thinking in paternalistic terms of keeping their community safe and clean (Hamilton et al., 2019). Paternalism traditionally is linked to dominance and power in masculinity (Connell, 2005), and this can play out as the traditional male gendered family-caregiving-in-terms-of-breadwinning role (Kimmel, 1996). Men's perceptions of *somebody's gotta do it* become undergirded by physical and mental acuity traditionally associated with "heroic masculinity" as tough, virile, breadwinners (Korobov, 2008, p. 99). For example, hospital cleaning workers explained that their job contributes to overall patient healing and caring services; a meaningful occupational endeavor (Wrzesniewski et al., 2003). Through their labor at dirty work, garbage collectors manage communities to prevent residents from complaining and to promote sanitary conditions (Sai et al., 2020b). Garbage collection work also means looking out for their neighbors and this kind of service restores a certain kind of dignity to stigmatized dirty work (Hamilton et al., 2019) among out-groups. So, internalized GRC/S traditionally associated with dirty work can be replaced by feeling valued as essential community service providers.

Finally, dirty work such as performed by garbage collectors may play into an affirmation movement known as the cult of the outdoorsman (Kimmel, 1996). Perry (1998) found that garbage handlers reported enjoying work in the outdoors where they find a general variety in tasks. Perhaps garbage-lined city streets—as a new millennial frontier—offer garbage collectors visions of being an *Outdoorsman* returning to authentic masculinity tested and honed by strenuous virtuous labor. Among men who may lack opportunities to venture into wilderness areas where they may experience masculine freedoms beyond feminized, domesticated cities (Kimmel, 1996), the best they can do at the moment is to engage with dirty work that requires strength inherent in frontier masculinity. Benefits include degrees of autonomy, flexible work hours (Sai et al., 2020b), and simply being outdoors rather than working indoors in a factory (Boulton & Houlihan, 2009). Combatting GRC/S by working outdoors in the open air, dirty work masculinity means enhancing feelings of self-respect by recalibrating work context as active agents rather than passive recipients.

DISCUSSION

Ways garbage collectors construct a positive identity in conjunction with *dirty work masculinity*—in the face of unjust social evaluations—is a phenomenon that deserves global attention. Active players in their work environments, male dirty work employees reframe their context to yield greater satisfaction from their work (Deery et al., 2019). In this chapter, we have identified stigma-coping, identity-enhancing, and conflict/stress-reducing strategies to raise awareness about better understanding the lived experiences of garbage collectors. Social identity theory combined with GRC/S promotes introducing to the masculinities literature three coping mechanisms of garbage collectors in the form of 1) *Camaraderie,* 2) *Self-Sacrificing Hero,* and 3) *Outdoorsman* that positively characterize masculinity in a context of dirty work. We posit that these coping mechanisms support men dealing with internalized GRC/S due to a socially stigmatized occupation wherein out-group members dehumanize garbage collectors.

Moving forward, we encourage further research that involves hypothesis testing to discover degrees to which the 1) *Camaraderie,* 2) *Self-Sacrificing Hero,* and 3) *Outdoorsman* coping mechanisms enable male garbage collectors to combat GRC/S. We also invite researchers to consider two other conditions of their occupational field that may interplay with male garbage collectors' lived experiences: 1) Labor automation threats, and 2) female labor threats.

Labor Automation Threats

As agriculture and mining industries increasingly turn to automation technology, or artificial intelligence (AI), to perform dirty and dangerous work (McCausland, 2020), we worry that garbage collector's jobs increasingly may disappear. Historically, mechanized tools have altered the garbage collection field for lifting waste containers and dumping them into trucks (History, n.d.) Findings of a study of 2,000+ work activities in more than 800 occupations, based on U.S. Bureau of Labor statics, suggest that automation will not replace any occupation entirely in the next decade—but automation will impact nearly every industry in some way (Chui et al., 2016).

Female Labor Threats

While there are only 8.3 percent women now working as garbage collectors in the U.S. (Garbage, n.d.), that number could change. Findings of a recent study of women in the Israeli military suggest that working in a masculinized field while female finds women complying with and resisting a dichotomized gender order by distancing themselves from traditional femininity norms and by trivializing sexual harassment (Sasson-Levy, 2003). How such a dynamic plays out amidst the dirty work of garbage collection is a worthy investigation. In terms of men's potential GRC/S, competing with women as breadwinners could have implications for men's masculine identities. Future studies should explore and expand investigations of masculinity and the dirty work concept by examining male workers' views of women as potential threats and women's lived experiences with equitable treatment in a masculinized occupational field.

Other Recommendations Moving Forward

In addition, we suggest a number of opportunities to expand gendered GRC/S research.

1. New research is needed to expand upon our essay about ways men search for dignity while performing dirty work. Similarly, new research is needed to explore the added dimension of competition forthcoming from an inevitable introduction of AI to garbage collection work and implications for men's GRC/S.
2. Hypothesis testing by using survey, interview, and focus group methods will provide for deeper understanding of the *dirty work masculinity* concept. Collectively, such a research stream should enable us to visualize and interrogate challenges of maintaining and constructing positive self-identity across stigmatized occupational fields.
3. Exploring relationships among dirty work and paternalistic mindsets offers fertile territory for further examining ways traditional masculinity is morphing in this new century. The paradox that patriarchy demands when men exert dominance over children, women, and the elderly while simultaneously providing care and protection is one that deserves greater scrutiny to investigate GRC/S dimensions.
4. The concept of *dirty work masculinity* must be examined among multiple cultures, especially those in the East where muscularity is less valued and men tend to have smaller hands in comparison to men in the West.
5. The role of media in representing dirty work muscularity must be investigated in terms of male gender role socialization, as well as how audiences interpret and making meaning about it.
6. Deeper understanding of social comparison within in-group dynamics among dirty work employees is needed to investigate degrees to which men who are considered lacking in masculinity may be labeled as feminine or gay and expelled from the in-group to experience psychological distress.

ACKNOWLEDGMENT

Firstly, we would like to show our heartfelt appreciation to Editor Donnalyn Pompper for the opportunity to contribute and valuable comments in elaborating our chapter. Deep gratitude is also extended towards the great support offered by the project members of the Sanitation Value Chain at the Research Institute of Humanity and Nature and its research counterpart, and the Laboratory of Human Ecology at Hokkaido University and to Dr. S. Nyambe, in particular, for helping us to elaborate this chapter. Finally, we thank everyone that has been a light on this incredible journey.

REFERENCES

Ashforth B. E., & Kreiner, G. E. (2014). Dirty work and dirtier work: Differences in countering physical, social, and moral stigma. *Management and Organization Review, 10*(1), 81–108. doi: https://doi.org/10.1111/more.12044.

———. (1999). "How can you do it?": Dirty work and the challenge of constructing a positive identity. *Academy of Management Review, 24*(3) 413–434. doi: https://doi.org/10.5465/amr.1999.2202129.

Berg, P., & Frost, A. (2005). Dignity at work for low wage, low skill service workers. *Industrial Relations, 60*(4), 657–682. doi: https://www.jstor.org/stable/23077680.

Bolton, S. (2007). Dignity in and at work. In S. Bolton (Ed.), *Dimensions of dignity at work* (pp. 3–16). Butterworth-Heinnemann.

Bordo, S. (2000). *The male body: A new look at men in public and in private*. Farrar, Straus and Giroux.

Bosmans, K., Mousaid, S., De Cuyper, N., Hardonk, S., Louckx, F., & Vanroelen, C. (2016). Dirty work, dirty worker? Stigmatization and coping strategies among domestic workers. *Journal of Vocational Behavior, 92*, 54–67. doi: https://doi.org/10.1016/j.jvb.2015.11.008.

Chui, M., Manyika, J., & Miremadi, M. (2016). Where machines could replace humans—and where they can't (yet). *McKinsey Quarterly*. Downloaded May 11, 2021, from https://rb.gy/orfj1m.

Connell, R. W. (2005). *Masculinities*. Cambridge: Polity.

Dasgupta, R. (2003). Creating corporate warriors: The "salaryman" and masculinity in Japan. In K. Louie and M. Low (Eds.), *Asian masculinities: The meaning and practice of manhood in China and Japan* (pp. 118–135). Routledge.

Deery, S., Kolar, D., & Walsh, J. (2019). Can dirty work be satisfying? A mixed method study of workers doing dirty jobs. *Work, Employment and Society, 33*(4), 631–647. doi: 10.1177/10950017018817307.

Douglas, M. (1966). *Purity and danger: An analysis of concepts of pollution and taboo*. Routledge and Kegan Paul.

Edwards, L. (2015). *Power, diversity and public relations*. Routledge.

Eisler, R. M., & Skidmore, J. R. (1987). Masculine gender role stress: Scale development and component factors in the appraisal of stressful situations. *Behavior Modification, 11*(2), 123–136. doi: https://doi.org/10.1177%2F01454455870112001.

Garbage collector demographics in the U.S. (n.d.) Zippia Careers. Downloaded May 11, 2021, from https://rb.gy/qdatla.

Griffiths, S., Murray, S. B., & Touyz, S. (2015). Extending the masculinity hypothesis: An investigation of gender role conformity, body dissatisfaction, and disordered eating in young heterosexual men. *Psychology of Men and Masculinity, 16*(1), 108–114. doi: https://psycnet.apa.org/doi/10.1037/a0035958.

Grogan, S., & Richards, H. (2002). Body image: Focus groups with boys and men. *Men and Masculinities, 4*(3), 219–232. doi: https://doi.org/10.1177%2F1097184X02004003001.

Hamilton, P., Redman, T., & McMurray, R. (2019). 'Lower than a snake's belly': Discursive constructions of dignity and heroism in low-status garbage work. *Journal of Business Ethics, 156*(4), 889–901. doi: https://doi.org/10.1007/s10551-017-3618-z.

History of the garbage man (n.d.) Waste and Recycling Workers Week. Downloaded May 11, 2021, from https://rb.gy/q1zpwz.

Hobza, C. L., & Rochlen, A. B. (2009). Gender role conflict, drive for muscularity, and the impact of ideal media portrayals on men. *Psychology of Men and Masculinity, 10*, 120–130. doi: https://psycnet.apa.org/doi/10.1037/a0015040.

Hofstede, G. (2010). *Cultures and organizations: Software of the mind*, 3rd ed. McGraw-Hill.

Hughes, E. (1951) Work and the self. In J. H. Rohrer and S. Muzafer (Eds.), *Social psychology at the crossroads* (pp. 313–323). Oxford Harper.

———. (1958). *Men and their work*. Free Press.

———. (1962). Good people and dirty work. *Social Problems, 10*, 3–11. doi: https://doi.org/10.2307/799402.

Jost, J., & Elsbach, K. (2001). How status and power differences erode personal and social identities at work: A system justification critique of organizational applications of social identity theory. In M. A. Hogg and D. J. Terry (Eds.), *Social identity processes in organizational contexts* (pp. 181–196). Psychology Press.

Kimmel, M. S. (2001). Global masculinities: Restoration and resistance. In B. Pease and K. Pringle (Eds.), *A man's world: Changing men's practices in a globalized world* (pp. 21–37). Zed Books.

———. (1996). *Manhood in America: A cultural history*. Free Press.

Korobov, N. (2008). 'He's got no game': Young men's stories about failed romantic and sexual experiences. *Journal of Gender Studies, 18*(2), 99–114. doi: https://doi.org/10.1080/09589230902812406.

Leit, R. A., Pope Jr, H. G., & Gray, J. J. (2001). Cultural expectations of muscularity in men: The evolution of *Playgirl* centerfolds. *International Journal of Eating Disorders, 29*(1), 90–93. doi: https://doi.org/10.1002/1098-108X(200101)29:1%3C90::AID-EAT15%3E3.0.CO;2-F.

Lucas, K., Kang, D., & Li, Z. (2013). Workplace dignity in a total institution: Examining the experiences of Foxconn's migrant workforce. *Journal of Business Ethics*, *114*(1), 91–106. doi: 10.1007/s10551-012-1328-0.

McCausland, T. (2020). News and analysis of the global innovation scene: Robots an AI take on dirty jobs. *Research-Technology Management*, *63*(2), 203. doi: 10 .1080/08956308.2020.1706992.

McCreary, D. R., Saucier, D. M., & Courtenay, W. H. (2005). The drive for muscularity and masculinity: Testing the associations among gender-role traits, behaviors, attitudes, and conflict. *Psychology of Men and Masculinity*, *6*(2), 83. doi: https:// psycnet.apa.org/doi/10.1037/1524-9220.6.2.83.

Monroe, H. (June 9, 2020). Philadelphia sanitation workers rallying for better working conditions after consistently putting health at risk during COVID-19 pandemic. 3CBSPhilly. Downloaded May 9, 2020, from https://rb.gy/raouna.

Nihalani, B. (December 13, 2020). Mike Rowe net worth in 2021. Browsed. Downloaded May 9, 2021, from https://browsed.org/mike-rowe-net-worth/.

Olivardia, R., Pope Jr, H. G., Borowiecki III, J. J., & Cohane, G. H. (2004). Biceps and body image: the relationship between muscularity and self-esteem, depression, and eating disorder symptoms. *Psychology of Men and Masculinity*, *5*(2), 112–120. doi: https://doi.org/10.1037/1524-9220.5.2.112.

O'Neil, J. M. (1981). Patterns of Gender Role Conflict and Strain: Sexism and Fear of Femininity Men's Lives. *Journal of Counseling and Development*, *60*(4), 203–210. doi: https://doi.org/10.1002/j.2164-4918.1981.tb00282.x.

O'Neil, J. M., Helms, B. J., Gable, R. K., David, L., & Wrightsman, L. S. (1986). Gender-Role Conflict Scale: College men's fear of femininity. *Sex Roles*, *14*(5), 335–350. doi: https://doi.org/10.1007/BF00287583.

Perry, S. (1998). *Collecting garbage*. Transaction Publishers.

Pleck, J. H. (2006). The gender role strain paradigm: un update. In S. M. Whitehead (Ed.), Men and *Masculinities: Identity, association and embodiment* (pp. 27–48). Routledge.

Pompper, D. (2010). Masculinities, the metrosexual, and media images: Across dimensions of age and ethnicity. *Sex Roles*, *63*(9–10), 682–696. doi: https://doi .org/10.1007/s11199-010-9870–7.

———. (2017). *Rhetoric of femininity: Female body image, media, and gender role stress/conflict*. Lexington Books.

Pompper, D., Soto, J., & Piel, L. (2007). Male body image and magazine standards: Considering dimensions of age and ethnicity. *Journalism and Mass Communication Quarterly*, *84*(3), 525–545. doi: https://doi.org/10.1177%2F107769900708400308.

Pope Jr., H. G., Olivardia, R., Gruber, A., & Borowiecki, J. (1999). Evolving ideals of male body image as seen through action toys. *International Journal of Eating Disorders*, *26*(1), 65–72. doi: https://doi.org/10.1002/(sici) 1098-108x(199907)26:1%3C65::aid-eat8%3E3.0.co;2-d.

Ricciardelli, L. A., & McCabe, M. P. (2001). Self-esteem and negative affect as moderators of sociocultural influences on body dissatisfaction, strategies to decrease weight, and strategies to increase muscles among adolescent boys and girls. *Sex Roles*, *44*(3), 189–207. doi: https://doi.org/10.1023/A:1010955120359.

Sai, A., Furusawa, T., Othman, M. Y., Tomojiri, D., Zaini, W. F. Z. W., Tan, C. S. Y., & Norzilan, N. I. B. M. (2020a). Sociocultural factors affecting drive for muscularity among male college students in Malaysia. *Heliyon, 6*(7), 1–3. doi: https://doi.org/10.1016/j.heliyon.2020.e04414.

Sai, A., Al Furqan, R., Ushijima, K., Hamidah, U., Ikemi, M., Sintawadani, N., & Yamauchi, T. (2020b). Personal Hygiene, Dignity, and Economic Diversity among Garbage Workers in an Urban Slum of Indonesia. *Sanitation Value Chain, 4*(2), 51–66. doi: https://doi.org/10.34416/svc.00019.

Said, E. (1978). *Orientalism*. Random House.

Sasson-Levy, O. (2003). Feminism and military gender practices: Israeli women soldiers in "masculine" roles. *Sociological Inquiry, 73*(3), 440–465. doi: https://doi.org/10.1111/1475-682X.00064.

Sayer, A. (2007). What dignity at work means. In S. Bolton (Ed.), *Dimensions of dignity at work* (pp. 17–29). Butterworth-Heinemann.

Schmerling, R. H. (2020, April 8). What's it like to be a healthcare worker in a pandemic. Downloaded May 9, 2021, from https://rb.gy/inthbr.

Sharma, H. B., Vanapalli, K. R., Cheela, V. S., Ranjan, V. P., Jaglan, A. K., Dubey, B., & Bhattacharya, J. (2020). Challenges, opportunities, and innovations for effective solid waste management during and post COVID-19 pandemic. *Resources, Conservation and Recycling, 162*, 105052. doi: https://doi.org/10.1016/j.resconrec.2020.105052.

Sherman, J. (2009). Bend to avoid breaking: Job loss, gender norms, and family stability in rural America. *Social Problems, 56*, 599–620. doi: https://doi.org/10.1525/sp.2009.56.4.599.

Stimpson, C. R. (1987). Forward. In H. Brod (Ed.), *The making of masculinities: The new men's studies* (pp. xi–xiii). Allen and Unwin.

Swami, V. (2016). Masculinities and ethnicities: Ethnic differences in drive for muscularity in British men and the negotiation of masculinity hierarchies. *British Journal of Psychology, 107*(3), 577–592. doi: https://doi.org/10.1111/bjop.12162.

Swami, V., & Tovee, M. J. (2005), Male physical attractiveness in Britain and Malaysia: A cross-cultural study. *Body Image, 2*, 383–393. doi: https://doi.org/10.1016/j.bodyim.2005.08.001.

Tajfel, H., & Turner, J. C. (1986). The social identity theory of intergroup behavior. In S. Worchel and W. G. Austin (Eds.), *Psychology of intergroup relations* (2nd ed.), pp. 7–24. Nelson.

Tajfel, H., Turner, J. C., Austin, W. G., & Worchel, S. (1979). An integrative theory of intergroup conflict. In M. J. Hatch and M. Schultz (Eds.), Organizational identity: A reader, 56–65. Oxford.

Thompson, E. H., & Pleck, J. H. (1986). The structure of male role norms. *American Behavioral Scientist, 29*(5), 531–543. doi: https://doi.org/10.1177%2F000276486029005003.

Tolson, A. (1977). *The limits of masculinity*. Harper and Row.

Tracy, S. J., & Scott, C. (2006). Sexuality, masculinity, and taint management among firefighters and correctional officers: Getting down and dirty with "America's heroes" and the "scum of law enforcement." *Management Communication Quarterly, 20*(1), 6–38. doi: https://doi.org/10.1177%2F0893318906287898.

Treiman, D. J. (1977). *Occupational prestige in comparative perspective*. Academic Press.

Vernon, A., & Swain, J. (2002). Theorizing divisions and hierarchies: Towards a commonality or diversity? In C. Barnes, M. Oliver, and L. Barton (Eds.), *Disability studies today* (pp. 77–97). Polity.

Walzer, M. (1984). *Spheres of justice: A defense of pluralism and equality*. Basic Books.

World Health Organization. (2019). *Health, safety and dignity of sanitation workers*. Downloaded May 10, 2021, from https://rb.gy/vufwfx.

Wrzesniewski, A., Dutton, J. E., & Debebe, G. (2003). Interpersonal sensemaking and the meaning of work. *Research in Organizational Behavior, 25*, 93–135. doi: https://doi.org/10.1016/S0191-3085(03)25003-6.

Yang, C. F. J., Gray, P., & Pope Jr, H. G. (2005). Male body image in Taiwan versus the West: Yanggang Zhiqi meets the Adonis complex. *American Journal of Psychiatry, 162*(2), 263–269. doi: https://doi.org/10.1176/appi.ajp.162.2.263.

Zock, J. P. (2005). World at work: Cleaners. *Occupational and Environmental Medicine, 62*, 581–584. doi: http://dx.doi.org/10.1136/oem.2004.015032.

Unit II

MASCULINITY & SOCIAL IDENTITY INTERSECTIONALITIES

Chapter Six

Exploring Masculinities in Ancient and Up-and-Coming Sports in South East Asia

Mark Brooke

INTRODUCTION

Dominant sport forms of the West continue to construct normative values of ideal masculine traits that lead to an internalized jock habitus for a "dominant, heterosexual, masculine orientation to the world" (Sparkes et al., 2007, p. 295). Often, these forms play out negatively and become rooted in physical education pedagogy. Hence, sports like football, soccer, and rugby end up celebrating and normalizing "anti-intellectualism, sexism, homophobia, competitiveness, and binge drinking" (MacDonald & Kirk, 1999, p. 132). Sports media also play a significant role in perpetuating such understandings through their representations. Yet, masculinity is a much more complex concept (Hearn, 2004) than what might appear in Western dominant sport forms and their media representations. As Gender Role Conflict and Stress theory researchers posit, gender role definitions are individualized, generational, and contextual (O'Neil, 2008). This chapter offers findings of my investigation of the South East Asia context for masculinity representations and perceptions of the ancient sporting culture of wushu as well as new developing sports like e-sports, skateboarding, tchoukball, and ultimate frisbee.

LITERATURE REVIEW

To answer a fundamental curiosity about how masculinity is defined in South East Asia, I build a foundation of: 1) Masculine Gender Role Conflict (MGRS/C) theory, 2) Media representations of masculinity in sports, and 3) Sports and masculinity in South East Asia.

119

Masculine Gender Role Conflict (MGRS/C) Theory

Masculinity is a complex intersectional phenomenon composed of social identity dimensions according to sexuality, age, ethnicity, ability, socio-cultural values, and more—all subject to change over time. Hence, the plural form, masculinities, is widely accepted (Kimmel, 2001). The masculinity concept becomes internalized based on perceptions of one's outer physical appearance and behaviors (Thompson et al., 1999). A normative hegemonic version of masculinity in some Western patriarchal societies tends to relate to heterosexuality, machismo, and subordination of women (e.g., Connell, 2005). Consequently, a MGRS/C theory lens is useful for exploring effects of men being socialized into restrictive gender roles and how they sometimes deviate from or actively resist or counter hegemonic masculinity norms (O'Neil, 2008).

Masculine gender role stress (MGRS/C) may develop when men feel that they are not fulfilling their masculine roles consistently with society's expec-tations. For example, when men act in what society deems to be feminized ways, they are considered deviant and may be marginalized, oppressed, stig-matized, and/or physically harmed (Maida & Armstrong, 2005). This reaction fuels stress in men that can lead to negative psychological outcomes, includ-ing anxiety, depression (McCreary, et al., 1996), confusion, and frustration (Pompper, 2010). Yet, Anderson (2005) suggested that the masculinity concept is evolving with more inclusive forms that could contribute to male athletes' reduced experiences of conflict and stress. Pompper (2010) found that age, ethnicity and culture demographics, in particular, reveal additional dimensions of the masculinities concept such as positive mental qualities of character, attitude, responsibility, and confidence/assertiveness. Globally, masculinity is understudied—especially in non-Western contexts—so it is about time we investigate ways masculinity plays out in non-traditional sports beyond U.S. borders.

Media Representations of Masculinity in Sports

Globally, sports media continue to grow with increasingly wider distribution of messages about hegemonic masculinity and its representations (Kim et al., 2020). Media coverage of sports proffers up an ideal hyper-masculine male athlete, fostering what has come to be known in the West as jock culture (Sparkes et al., 2010). A jock habitus has become socially accepted, idealized, and normalized—a "practical and symbolic manifestation of a dominant, heterosexual, masculine orientation" (Sparkes et al., 2007, p. 295), which personifies "mesomorphy, anti-intellectualism, sexism, homophobia, competitiveness and binge drinking" (MacDonald & Kirk, 1999, p. 2). Sports media capitalize on and amplify these masculinity representations around the globe (Anderson, 2005, 2010, 2014). For example, a win-at-all-cost attitude legitimates aggressive behavior and violence in team sport competition (Hughes & Coakley, 1991; McCormack and Anderson, 2014), as well as normalized attitudes of accepting off-the-athletic-field boys-will-be-boys violence (Clark, 2017), unprotected sex and cheating at school (Miller, et al., 2003; Pascoe, 2003), as well as celebration of a hyper-muscular ideal (Pompper, 2010).

Such representations are important for academic study because a hegemonic jock culture breeds toxicity (Flintoff, 1994; Miller, 2009; Sparkes et al., 2007) and has become normalized across popular entertainment like video games (Conway, 2020), television programming like HBO's *True Detective* (Albrecht, 2020), and popular fictional films where jocks are the masculinity standard bearers against which physically weaker, nerdy characters are assessed (Kendall, 1999). Among sports and other news media coverage, attention to athletes' bad behavior linked to alcohol and drug addiction that sometimes includes gendered violence receives significant attention. Outcomes seem to include special treatment of professional athletes like boxers, football players, and basketball players (e.g., Lule, 1995). These incidents serve as windows for observing cultural assumptions through which athletics operate (Miller, 2010).

Also, effects of jock culture embracing hegemonic masculinity finds its way into athletes' self-perceptions which can lead to masculine gender role conflict and stress. For example, athletes who see themselves as different from the ideal work at hiding any hints of counter-hegemonic social identity dimensions. Regarding sexual orientation among male athletes, those labeled as *gay* undergo verbal harassment, physical assault, and social exclusion (Anderson, 2002; McCormack & Anderson, 2014). As a consequence, gay athletes like American football player Phil Cloudy mask their homosexuality by presenting a hyper-masculinized outward jock image—a dynamic that may contribute to gender role stress (McCreary et al., 1996). Overall, these situations undergird homohysteric culture wherein dislike of homosexuals becomes normalized (McCormack & Anderson, 2014).

Racial stereotypes about Asians may find their way into representations of Asian athletes and coverage of Asian sports by defaulting to Western ideas about masculinity. Findings of a study of racial stereotypes suggested that Asians are less likely to be considered as ideal for masculine leadership positions or masculine athletics, compared to White or Black people (Galinsky et al., 2013). Western-oriented masculinity images consistent with jock culture feature highly muscular male athletic bodies that also are perpetuated by sports media covering professional sports in South East Asia (Brooke, 2017;

Karan & Khoo, 2007) with school curricula amplifying them, too (Goh, 2015).

Despite continual exposure to sports media with overly-muscular representations of the jock archetypal identity, learned male-ness in terms of representations of masculinity must be problematized and individuated across contexts (e.g., Dewar, 1990; Pascoe, 2003). Anderson (2014) argued that traditional forms of jock culture increasingly are being displaced by inclusive masculinity forms. Alternately, some media root sports coverage in spiritual Confucianism and state/market collectivism, which promotes social solidarity and harmony (Giulianotti, 1999; Rowe & Gilmour, 2010) in contrast to a hyper-masculinized heterosexual construct. For example, increasing are the number of straight men who reject homophobia and who are physically tactile with other men, embracing once-coded feminine behaviors and activities (Anderson & McCormack, 2014). Brooke (2017) concluded that Chinese martial arts in Singapore position masculinity in terms of a holistic physical development consistent with psychosocial attributes. Overall, masculinity is more than a Western concept, and we stand to learn much about interplay of sports and masculinities in the East.

Sports and Masculinity in South East Asia

Masculinity among men of Asian descent remains under-theorized. Yet, we do know that the legacy of internationally recognized martial artist and Hong Kong-American film star, Bruce Lee, is one of shifting from icon-to-stereotype play—as on the popular Angry Asian Man website and among Giant Robot t-shirt enthusiasts which offers space to speak back to dominant media representations of Asian males as nerds, computer geeks, and romance failures (Nishime, 2017). Moreover, we know that countries celebrate their athletes as manifestations of national values and citizenship—and that the world of sports is where masculinity is created and expressed. For example, Olympic Games' Parade of Athletes opening ceremony offers a source of nationalistic pride. Countries inscribe the nation "onto the bodies of athletes" and even at non-elite levels, sporting activities inject nationalistic meaning and purpose for young men (Guinness & Besnier, 2016, p. 1110). Yet, nation-sport interplay can inspire unease and stress for athletes. For example, young men who play rugby in Fiji strive to measure up to a warrior image (Guinness & Besnier, 2016), only "real boys" in Indonesia play sports (Lowe, et al., 2016, p. 614), and young men of Philippine fishing villages feel compelled to reaffirm their "masculine selves" through talk about celebrity athletes like boxer Manny Pacquiao (Turgo, 2014). In China to the north, masculinity is characterized by a wen-wu model wherein men refer to literary and artistic cultural attainment (Song, 2004).

Sports teams across South East Asia are extremely popular and highly diverse in form, such as baseball, football, cricket, hockey, table tennis, golf, rugby and basketball. There is an intensive fan base for football's English Premier League and the men's National Basketball Association (Rowe & Gilmour, 2010). Yet, Western sports imports of football and basketball have tended to crowd out domestic Asian professional sport and prevent the further development of indigenous Asian sport and media coverage of it (Rowe & Gilmour, 2010). Consequently, spectators consistently are exposed to the traditional forms of masculinity related to what's come to be known as a hegemonic heterosexual and aggressive *jock culture* of the West (Pascoe, 2011). Outcomes are often negative, such as when high school and college video gamers are considered to be lacking a "true sense of competition" (Ritter & Ueno, 2017, p. 545).

Despite such negative trends, unique traditional sports across South East Asia attract significant local interest, such as the South East Asian Games held every two years. Several of the most popular regional sports are martial arts such as wushu, muay thai, silat, and kurash. Other considerably popular sports are ball-based such as sepak takraw, similar to volleyball but for which players use their feet, head, knees, and chest to send an intricately woven ball across the net. Also, chinlone, is part sport and part dance. Additional popular

Figure 6.1. **Flow, grace, creativity, agility, intensity of focus, determination, modesty, and self-control characterize South East Asia's ancient sport of wushu.**
Courtesy of Depositphotos Inc.

up-and-coming non-contact sport forms include e-sports, skateboarding, tchoukball, and ultimate frisbee. In Singapore, there are over 10 custom-built skate parks and skateboarding is an official sport of the South East Asian Games. E-sport is highly competitive at school and varsity intercollege levels and wushu, a traditional Chinese martial art, is very popular and part of school curricula in Singapore. Professional sports teams win awards, such as the 2021 ONE Esports Dota 2 Singapore Major involved teams competing for a US $500,000 prize pool. Singapore won bronze at the mixed gender competition of the tchoukball World Championships and another bronze at the world U-24 mixed gender ultimate frisbee meet in 2019. The Singapore national wushu team frequently wins medals at the South East Asian Games and the team took several gold, silver, and bronze medals in the games held in Singapore.

Comparatively, there is significantly less research on masculinity in the context of e-sports, skateboarding, tchoukball, ultimate frisbee, and wushu—than on masculinity in sports contexts of football, soccer, baseball, or basketball. Briefly, e-sports, or electronic sports, is a form of sport competition using video games. Skateboarding is an action sport performed by standing on a board with wheels, riding and performing tricks. Tchoukball is a co-ed indoor team sport of non-aggressive play wherein players earn points when they run, bounce a ball off a trampoline, throw, and catch it. Ultimate frisbee is a low-contact team sport played with a flying plastic disc and players earn points by passing the disc to a teammate in the opposing end zone. Competitive wushu is a martial art that can take several forms and includes being judged on acrobatic techniques and movements (taolu) or as a fighting contact sport that involves boxing, kicking, and wrestling (sanda). Given the paucity of research about masculinity and these five popular sports in South East Asia, I pose this research question:

RQ: How is masculinity defined in the context of five South East Asian sports of e-sports, skateboarding, tchoukball, ultimate frisbee, and wushu?

METHOD

The study takes a critical, interpretivist approach in order to reveal underlying belief systems and practices associated with understandings of masculinity in South East Asian sports that might circumscribe the hegemonic jock image and culture. I concur that a given social context has unique characteristics and that knowledge is subjectively constructed through people's perceptions and interactions in the cultures in which they live (Gubrium & Holstein, 1997).

This research approach enables an in-depth view of masculinities and sports in a geographic region rarely examined.

Human subjects approval from the my university's internal review board was given to conduct the survey and focus group discussions for the study. An email message explaining research and data security procedures was sent to potential participants. No identifying features are disclosed.

Data Collection

To collect a rich pool of data, multiple methods were used (Hastings, 2010; Vivar et al., 2007).

Content Analysis of Official Sports Federation Sites and Magazine Articles

To examine representations of these non-traditional sports and to provide stimulus materials for focus groups and interviews, I visited official websites in 2020, such as the wushu website and Facebook page of the International Wushu Federation. Both provided a rich data source describing the sport's history as well as the culture of the non-contact form taolu (performing set routines). The International Federation governs wushu in all its forms worldwide. Also, data were selected from the Tchoukball Association of Singapore's Facebook page as well as articles from a set of news sources posted on the Association's official website. A non-random sample of 30 news articles from the most popular (based on circulation and website visits) online niche magazines in up-and-coming non-traditional sports (e-sports, skateboarding, and ultimate frisbee) also was constructed. Selection criteria for these data sources were twofold: 1) published within the last three years, and 2) offered narratives of active athletes in the targeted sports. For skateboarding, ultimate frisbee and e-sports, the most popular online magazines are *Thrasher, Skateboarder* and *SHIT* (skateboarding); *Ultiworld* (ultimate frisbee); and *E-sports Insider*.

First, I conducted conventional content analysis (Hsieh & Shannon, 2005) of web articles from official sports association sites as well as the Facebook pages of the ancient sporting culture of wushu and tchoukball. I also explored web articles from online niche magazines of new developing sports such as e-sports, skateboarding, and ultimate frisbee (n=30 articles).

Survey

Second, 31 South East Asian male and 17 female undergraduate student respondents (all aged 18-25) from a university in Singapore were asked in 2020 to complete a questionnaire containing four open-ended questions about their characterization of masculinity in wushu (observed in film or in practice/competition). Participants were first- and second-year undergraduates from Singaporean Chinese, Malay, and Tamil backgrounds. Open-ended survey questions invited thick descriptions of 30 words or more (Smith & Caddick, 2012) to offer views on masculinity in wushu.

Focus Groups

Finally, I facilitated four 30-minute focus group discussions with 24 (12 male, 12 female) South East Asian undergraduate students (all aged 18–25) at the same university in Singapore, using a topic guide instrument of five prompts. Focus group participants each had 1-10 years of experience in recreational and varsity competition in e-sports, skateboarding, tchoukball, ultimate frisbee, or wushu. Following comparable procedures used by Smith and Caddick (2012), I used stimulus materials of photographed South East Asian athletes (ages 18-25) in active and inactive poses. Typically, an athlete in *action* would be involved in a taolu routine, gaming competitively, performing a skateboarding trick, or catching a disc or ball in frisbee or tchoukball. Athletes in the same sports in *inactive* poses stood with teammates facing the camera. After viewing the images, respondents offered thick descriptions about their perceptions of masculinity in these sports.

Data Analysis

Once data from these three sources were gathered, the texts were read as an ensemble and common meanings identified through an inductive process of conventional content analysis (Hsieh & Shannon, 2005), moving inductively from open coding to derive meanings, and then to selective coding, to interpret the open codes as meaning units or themes. To facilitate transferability (Houghton et al., 2013; Silverman, 2000), I compared data to other research conducted on the five sports in this study to ground properly findings in MGRS/C research.

FINDINGS

RQ: How is masculinity defined in the context of five South East Asian sports of e-sports, skateboarding, tchoukball, ultimate frisbee, and wushu?

Seven main themes regarding characteristics of masculinity in South East Asian sports (e-sports, skateboarding, tchoukball, ultimate frisbee, and wushu) emerged among data sets, enabling me to answer this question. Each theme represents a pattern of meaning and they are presented alphabetically, rather than according to frequency due to the qualitative, exploratory nature of the study: 1) *Flow, Grace, Creativity and Agility through Physical Movement*, 2) *Inclusivity*, 3) *Intensity of Focus and Determination;* 4) *Modesty*, 5) *Risk Taking*, 6) *Self-Control*, and 7) *Toxicity.*

Theme One: Agility, Flow, Grace, and Creativity through Physical Movement

Considering masculinity in the context of e-sports, skateboarding, tchoukball, ultimate frisbee, and wushu, focus group respondents expressed appreciation for the skilful precision and creativity displayed by male athletes in all five sports—except e-sports. Masculinity in tchoukball and ultimate frisbee were linked to "agility" in physical displacement. Wushu was juxtaposed with bodybuilding in the survey results because the sport involves bodily display. Muscular strength is needed for functionality to create what one focus group respondent characterized as "aesthetics in motion, or movements and agility rather than appearance." Also, in the focus groups, a wushu practitioner reported that "flowing in motion" is an essential characteristic of performances. Additionally, in the focus groups, male skateboarders were described as "needing balance" and "flow" and the adjective "graceful" also was associated several times with the photographs of male players catching the frisbee in ultimate and jumping to throw the ball onto the rebound in tchoukball. Finally, a focus group respondent described masculinity as possessing a sense of "creativity in movement" in skateboarding: "Skateboarding is something you can do when you don't have to follow any set guidelines, you can just do whatever you want, and I think that's the kind of freedom everyone needs but nobody realizes they need."

In contrast to these four sports, focus group participants considered e-sports participants as comparatively lacking in masculinity because playing games using tech devices does not require much physical movement. According to focus group respondents, e-sports athletes lacked agility and physical movement. They were described as "inactive," "sedentary," and "lacking masculinity." Focus group respondents who are e-sports athletes confirmed that e-sports is stereotyped as "a bad and addictive habit" which is "purely wasting time" because "e-sports isn't as physically strenuous as [traditional] sports."

Theme Two: Intensity of Focus and Determination

"Intense focus" and "determination" in order to perform a task to the highest level were linked to masculinity as focus group respondents examined photographs of athletes in action such as a skateboarder concentrating before performing a stunt. One focus group respondent who identifies as an e-sports athlete also described an athlete in the stimulus materials as "intensely focused." Focus group participants who are e-sports athletes explained that one must "think quickly" and "persevere"—so that "intensity of focus" is essential. Another focus group participant commented on a "determined" male tchoukball player throwing a ball into a "D" or "forbidden zone" rebound frame so that the ball might rebound off the frame and land outside the "D" to score a point.

Theme Three: Risk Taking

"Tenacity," "commitment," "being daring," and "being adventurous" also were positive characteristics of masculinity shared by focus groups when describing masculinity in contexts of skateboarding, tchoukball, and ultimate frisbee. Collectively, these characteristics constitute risk taking since athletes need to catch a ball or disc as they travel toward one's face in tchoukball and ultimate frisbee and risk falling injuries when skateboarding. Gender differences emerged in focus group discussions about risk-taking aspects of masculinity in skateboarding when female participants said such behaviours and displays among men tend to discourage women from wanting to skate with men. A woman explained in her focus group: "I just feel like all the guys will stick to each other and attempt crazy tricks." She said that risk taking translates to male skateboarders sticking together and alienating the female skateboarders.

Theme Four: Self-Control

One important characteristic of being masculine when participating in wushu is restraint and self-control, which may be interpreted as keeping emotions in check. This links with the masculinity concept since men are expected to avoid showing emotions beyond anger (e.g., Connell, 2005; Kimell, 2001). Wushu involves avoiding impulsive and aggressive behaviour in order to perform taolu movements. One focus group respondent who practices wushu commented: "A lot of control is needed in the execution of the movement in Chinese martial arts." Moreover, focus group respondents noted how it is common in wushu films to witness a Chinese male who exhibits calm and emotional control—such as well-known wushu-trained film actors such as Ronny Yu and Jet Li who often refer to the non-physical aspects of their martial arts teaching.

Self-control was also reported to be an important element of masculinity in e-sports. One focus group participant who also identifies as an e-sports athlete said he "keeps calm" when playing because losing self-control can upset his play and negatively impact performance: "It really takes a lot of discipline to not rage quit and continue thinking properly and try to comeback in the game. A lot of times, I get tilted whenever I play badly, and it just snowballs." This respondent explained how losing his concentration if he plays badly can lead to anger, decreased concentration, and poor performance. Functioning at competitive levels in e-sports like *Counter Strike* requires a player to be aware of what his other four teammates are doing at all times while simultaneously focusing on his own play.

Theme Five: Modesty

Focus group participants also discussed their perceptions of degrees of acceptability when men show off their body. Participants seemed disapproving of those who show off their muscles, mentioning how Jean Claude van Damme, also known as "The Muscles from Brussels," is an example of a martial artist who puts his masculinity on display and is considered "showy," "vain," and "ostentatious" in order to exhibit his sex appeal. Focus group participants also noted that wushu practitioners, like bodybuilders, "often chart their gym progress on social media" and post photographs presenting their achievements for "looking toned and bulking up." Focus group participants seemed more approving of wushu practitioners as demonstrating "modesty" with their body as they compete or perform in a full body uniform.

Theme Six: Inclusivity

Focus group participants who participate in skateboarding, tchoukball, and ultimate frisbee suggested that their sports define masculinity more progressively because the sports are gender-integrated and diverse. Research participants who engage in skateboarding noted that "competition shouldn't be the main thing." Rather, masculinity is positively embracing a healthy collaborative environment wherein athletes can share and comment on their activities with one another. With tchoukball and ultimate frisbee, there is a requirement to have at least two females out of the seven in play on the terrain at all times. Moreover, an ultimate athlete focus group participant stated that the sport is one in which "players truly feel empowered to push for gender equity." Males tended to act less aggressively because they interact with females on the field. Skateboarding niche magazines also appear to support diversity in sexual orientation, too. Jeffrey Cheung, an Asian-American queer artist, hand crafts skateboards with a painted statement on the bottom of the board: "Unity: Queer skateboarding like it or not." Moreover, *Thrasher*, a popular skateboarder magazine qualified male skateboarder, Andy Anderson's "long hair" as an "attribute," which might be construed as a feminine characteristic in jock culture in traditional sports.

Theme Seven: Toxicity

Although focus group participants qualified e-sports as "not masculine" and criticized e-sports athletes for a lack of physical movement as "sedentary," "physically weak," and "non-assertive," they shared incidences of a toxic masculinity in the form of sexist behaviors exhibited. Some women among focus group participants explained how they play video games online without revealing their true gender to avoid harassment by male players. One female focus group participant explained: "Once they found out I was a female, the chat was spontaneously filled with sexual comments and harassments which made me feel inferior." Also, gaming culture is characterized by women assuming support rather than lead roles so that they follow male players and remain at the periphery. Focus group participants suggested that this is a defensive measure to avoid exposure to sexualized toxicity from male gamers.

DISCUSSION AND CONCLUSION

The seven themes that emerged among data sets collected using content analysis, survey, and focus group research methods suggest there are nuanced dimensions to the masculinities concept associated with ancient and up-and-coming sports South East Asia.

The *Risk Taking* theme and the *Toxicity* theme are consistent with current understanding of hegemonic masculinity, or the jock habitus in Western societies as earmarked by displays of strength and power through risk-taking that may create male gender role conflict or stress—and negative experiences for women. In particular, the *Toxicity* theme characterized lived experiences among female e-sports gamers who avoid harassment by playing online without revealing their gender or assume support roles rather than lead roles in team games. It is well documented that e-sports can be plagued by rampant racism, misogyny, and homophobia (Cote, 2020; Funk et al., 2018). Well documented outcomes of this dynamic also include male gender role stress and conflict. For example, the win-at-all-cost attitude and intense competitive rivalry (Hughes and Coakley, 1991) forces men to alter their outward behaviors at the risk of creating inner turmoil (Pompper, 2010). On the other hand, these sports in South East Asia may support what Salter and Blodgett (2012) characterized as "geek masculinity" (Salter & Blodgett, 2012, p. 401), enabling a wide variety of men to participate. Yet, this dynamic also can produce toxic effects.

Reversing Gender Role Conflict and Stress

More telling are the next three conclusions that may be used to support a more complete conception of bricolage masculinity and may be used to dismantle harmful behaviors contributing to gender role conflict and stress.

First, a rupture to hegemonic masculinity is evident among South East Asian male sports representations and fans' perceptions of qualities more often linked with the concept of femininity. The *Flow, Grace, Creativity and Agility through Physical Movement* theme emerged among online magazine images and focus group and survey participants' celebration of muscular strength used to produce agile movements rather than brutish displays of toughness created by using one's muscles. Namely, wushu requires power to produce a flow of positive energy through seamless motion (Kuan and Roy, 2007). Masculine attributes in the form of flow, grace, creativity, and agility—rather than aggressive contact—are exhibited by South East Asian male athletes and are perceived positively among fans and wushu participants.

Even though e-sports were critiqued among focus group participants as being less of a sport as compared to others examined in this study—and for producing toxicity—some researchers have found benefits for men who engage with e-sports as a source of physical exercise. Considering that elite e-athletes engage in in at least one hour of physical training each day, more than three times the daily twenty-one-minute activity recommendation given by World Health Organization, researchers emphasize e-sports' value for male players (Kari & Karhulahti, 2016). These elite e-athlete respondents consider physical exercise has a positive effect on their e-sport performance, helping them to concentrate effectively when gaming. Further research is needed to examine perceptions that players appear to be sedentary while playing e-sports against players' self-perceptions about athleticism and masculinity.

Second, the *Intensity of Focus and Determination* theme and the *Self-Control* theme stand in stark contrast to hegemonic masculinities and brute strength associated with highly muscular athleticism. In the South East Asian context of these five sports, masculinity is expressed and embraced in terms of intense focus and determination. In Western sport cultures, overt and passionate displays of anger and frustration in public areas are socially accepted (Pascoe, 2003). However, Confucian values have influenced South East Asian nations (Goh, 2015) and this is expressed in martial arts like wushu which values control of the mind (Hiramoto, 2012; Weiser et al.,1995) and extols virtues of mind strength over physical might or brute force. For wushu, the origins of this self-control are most likely linked to the Shaolin Moral Code, which values insight and awareness (Wong, 1981). This awareness is required for the development of the interior, the "power within" or Chi (Qi) —an essential part of wushu training (Jou, 1981). Thus, mental equilibrium tends to take precedence over physical activity in wushu. Moreover, in relation to the other sports studied, when performing a skateboard trick, shooting in tchoukball, catching in ultimate frisbee, or playing e-sports, both the *Intensity of Focus and Determination* theme and the *Self-Control* theme emerged among descriptions and representations of the masculinity concept.

Third, the *Inclusivity* theme and the *Modesty* theme offer men permission to enjoy sports with women as equal participants in social solidarity and harmony by exhibiting virtues linked to humility and equity. Male athletes who engage with these five sports in South East Asian sports need not flamboyantly flex their biceps to prove their sex appeal or value. Rather, Confucianist societies like Singapore (Giulianotti, 1999; Rowe & Gilmour, 2010) embrace mixed-gender sports. This dynamic is consistent with the Confucian Analects (551 BC–479 BC), which explain: "The firm, the enduring, the simple, and the modest are near to virtue" (Gao, 2015, p. 26). Non-violent sports and gender equity are developing as more women are playing important roles in mixed teams in South East Asia, as Robbins (2004) found among players in non-contact sports like ultimate frisbee and tchoukball that employ "welfare-maximizing norms to facilitate and maximize game interaction, quality and fluidity" (p. 316). Sports like ultimate frisbee and skateboarding also accept diversity in sexual orientation and gender expression. This informal ethos recently has been confirmed in the production of a new Gender Inclusion Policy, allowing players at all levels of competition to play "regardless of sex assigned at birth, identification within a gender binary, or any other form of gender identity or expression" (New, n.d.). Moreover, gender binary boundaries increasingly blur in skateboarding as female skateboarders "have the potential to transform the hierarchical gender order between and among masculinities and femininities" (Bäckström, 2013, p. 29). Thus, I argue that the inclusivity of non-reliance on a gender binary in ultimate frisbee has the potential to rupture hegemonic masculinity in sports and reduce gender role stress and conflict among male athletes. This brand of inclusiveness also plays out among male cheerleaders as these athletes are re-socialized to display their power and acceptance of feminine performativity on par with their own without a need to display dominance (Anderson, 2005). Sports infused with inclusivity and modesty values embrace all ages, genders, and sexual orientations (Karsten & Pel, 2000), in stark contrast to Westernized jock culture.

All but two themes (*Risk Taking* and *Toxicity*) that emerged among data collected and analyzed for this study value good sportspersonship wherein masculinity is connected to an athlete's ability to compete cooperatively, to embody virtue, and to display mutual respect. This finding mirrors a core component of the *spirit of the game* concept wherein there is an accepted level of moral obligation to play by the agreed rules for the sport to be enjoyed (Griggs, 2011). In lifestyle sports like skateboarding, this plays out in urban sites where ideals of creativity, freedom, and do-it-yourself ethos underpin play (O'Connor, 2018; Wheaton & Beale, 2003).

Collectively, the themes that emerged in this study of masculinity across five sports in the South East Asian context offer a portal for examining a facet of bricolage masculinity with greater nuance in our journey to better understand male Gender Role Conflict and Stress. We already know that when males are socialized into less restrictive gender roles, they generally are more comfortable deviating from or actively resisting toxic hegemonic masculinity norms (O'Neil, 2008) such as machismo and related forms that subordinate women (e.g., Connell, 2005). More accepting forms of the masculinity concept—in terms of accommodating flexibility and fluidity in context—must be developed and nurtured. Like Anderson (2005, 2010, 2014), I argue that the masculinity concept is evolving and that it must be more inclusive to reduce male athletes' experiences with conflict and stress. Therefore, both athletes and consumers of sports media must resist proliferation of overly muscular representations of the jock archetypal identity. Among researchers, we must continue to problematize representations of masculinity that contribute to MGRS/C. Consistent with Pompper (2010), I concur that age, ethnicity and culture social identity dimensions do reveal additional facets of the masculinities'-as-bricolage concept. The context for research findings revealed in the study reported in this chapter are partly steeped in opinions of undergraduate at a Southeast Asian university; voices central to forging new understandings of the masculinity concept related to psychosocial attributes. These include positive mental character qualities like focus and determination, as well as respect and responsibility toward others regardless of (or in spite of) gender binary dualisms and comparable labelling of *masculine or feminine*. A key and useful finding is that masculinity, as a concept, extends beyond a Western concept. We stand to learn much more about bricolage masculinities and MGRS/C amidst interplay with sports in Southeast Asia.

Limitations and Future Study

The main limitation to this study is the survey's small sample size and the convenience sample used to solicit for focus group participants. Future larger scale survey research might be conducted with undergraduate students aged 18 to 25 to help to consolidate and make findings more generalizable. Additionally, despite its popularity in Singapore, very little information exists about tchoukball in the media. This made it a difficult sport to critically analyze. As participation in the sport continues to increase, I hope that social media sites also might develop for tchoukball, such as those for ultimate frisbee. This could lead to better understanding of the masculinity concept and gender dynamics across tchoukball play.

CONCLUSION

Years ago, O'Neil (2008) recommended greater use of qualitative research methods for identifying situations wherein men violate or conform to masculine norms. This study's findings offer a South East Asian sports context for greater understanding of masculinity in terms of internal elements rather than only physical attributes. Findings also call for expanding masculine Gender Role Conflict and Stress theory. Masculinity is a broad, contextual concept that is difficult to define. Yet, we must continue studying it in order to reduce masculine gender role stress and conflict for men—and the symptoms that also negatively impact women, gay men, and have broader social implications.

Also, there are lessons for sports media that perpetuate limited representations of male athletes and the sports they play. New space must be carved out for e-sports, tchoukball, skateboarding, ultimate frisbee, wushu, and other sports—especially those that may not rely on human contact. Such sport cultures tend to advocate for gender equity and sexual orientation diversity, and thus sharply depart from the jock culture of traditional sports with their hegemonic masculinity and negative toxicity. Notwithstanding that several of the sports investigated in this study still exist at the periphery in South East Asia—compared to sports like soccer and basketball—they are sports with deep cultural roots and bridge professional arenas with regional-local identities for important recreation that need not rely on media. Indeed, these lesser-known sports might be key to spread of a new bricolage masculinity concept from the South East Asian region where values are experienced and felt through the lived experiences of harmonious insider participation rather than violent external outsider observation.

REFERENCES

Albrecht, M. M. (2020). You wonder ever if you're a bad man? Toxic masculinity, paratexts and think pieces circulating around season one of HBO's True Detective. *Critical Studies in Television*, 15(1), 7-24. doi: https://doi.org/10.1177%2F1749602019893575.

Anderson, E. (2005). Orthodox and inclusive masculinity: Competing masculinities among heterosexual men in a feminized terrain. *Sociological Perspectives*, *48*(3), 337–355. doi: https://doi.org/10.1525/sop.2005.48.3.337.

————. (2010). *In the game: Gay athletes and the cult of masculinity.* SUNY press.

————. (2014). *21st century jocks: Sporting men and contemporary heterosexuality.* Palgrave-Macmillan.

Anderson, E. & McCormack, M. (2018). Inclusive masculinity theory: overview, reflection and refinement. *Journal of Gender Studies, 27(5),* 547–561. doi: https://doi.org/10.1080/09589236.2016.1245605.

Atencio, M., Beal, B., & Wilson, C. (2009). The distinction of risk: Urban skateboarding, street habitus and the construction of hierarchical gender relations. *Qualitative Research in Sport and Exercise,* 1(1), 3–20. doi: https://doi.org/10.1080/19398440802567907.

Bäckström, Å. (2013). Gender manoeuvring in Swedish skateboarding: Negotiations of femininities and the hierarchical gender structure. *Young,* 21(1), 29–53. doi: https://doi.org/10.1177/1103308812467670.

Bányai, F., Griffiths, M. D., Király, O., & Demetrovics, Z. (2019). The psychology of esports: A systematic literature review. *Journal of Gambling Studies,* 35(2), 351–365. doi: https://doi.org/10.1007/s10899-018-9763-1.

Beasley, C. (2008). Rethinking Hegemonic Masculinity in a globalizing world. *Men and masculinities,* 11(1), 86–103. doi: https://doi.org/10.1007/s10899-018-9763-1.

Beynon, J. (2002). *Issues in cultural and media studies, masculinities and culture.* Open University Press.

Brayton, S. (2005). Black-lash: Revisiting the 'White Negro' through skateboarding. *Sociology of Sport Journal,* 22, 356–372. doi: https://doi.org/10.1123/ssj.22.3.356.

Brooke, M. (2017). Masculinity in Singapore: the residual culture of the Chinese martial artist. *Sport in Society, 20(9),* 1297–1309. doi: https://doi.org/10.1080/17430437.2017.1284799.

Buchbinder, D. (1998). *Performance anxieties: Re-producing masculinity.* Allen and Unwin.

Clark, D. (2017). Boys will be boys: Assessing attitudes of athletic officials on sexism and violence against women. *The International Journal of Sport and Society,* 8(1), 31–50. doi:10.18848/2152-7857/CGP/v08i01/31-50.

Connell, R. W. (2005). *Masculinities,* 2nd ed. University of California Press.

Conway, S. (2020). Poisonous pantheons: God of War and toxic masculinity. *Games and Culture,* 15(8), 943–961. doi: 10.1177/1555412019858898.

Cote, A. (2020). *Gaming sexism.* NYU Press.

Dasgupta, R. (2003). Creating corporate warriors: The "salaryman" and masculinity in Japan. In K. Louie and M. Low (Eds.), *Asian masculinities: The meaning and practice of manhood in China and Japan* (pp. 118–135). Routledge Curzon.

Dewar, A. (1990). Oppression and privilege in physical education: Struggles in the negotiation of gender in a university programme. In D. Kirk and R. Tinning (Eds.), *Physical education, curriculum and culture: Critical issues in the contemporary crisis* (pp. 67–100). Falmer Press.

Eng, D. L. (2001). *Racial castration: Managing masculinity in Asian America.* Duke University Press.

Flintoff, A. (1994). Sexism and homophobia in physical education: the challenge for teacher educators. *Physical Education Review*, *17*(2), 97–105. doi: https://www.cabdirect.org/cabdirect/abstract/19951800274.

Funk, D. C., Pizzo, A. D., & Baker, B. J. (2018). Esport management: Embracing eSport education and research opportunities. *Sport Management Review*, 21(1), 7–13. doi: https://doi.org/10.1016/j.smr.2017.07.008.

Galinsky, A. D., Hall, E. V., & Cuddy, A. J. C. (2013). Gendered races: Implications for interracial marriage, leadership selection, and athletic participation. *Psychological Science*, 24(4), 498–506. doi: https://www.jstor.org/stable/23409253.

Goh, D. P. (2015). Elite schools, postcolonial Chineseness and hegemonic masculinities in Singapore. *British Journal of Sociology of Education*, *36*(1), 137–155. doi: https://doi.org/10.1080/01425692.2014.971944.

Griggs, G. (2011). 'This must be the only sport in the world where most of the players don't know the rules': operationalizing self-refereeing and the spirit of the game in UK Ultimate Frisbee. *Sport in Society*, *14*(1), 97–110. doi: https://doi.org/10.1080/17430437.2011.530013.

Gubrium, J. F., & Holstein, J. A. (1997). *The new language of qualitative method*. Oxford University Press on Demand.

Guinness, D., & Besnier, N. (2016). Nation, nationalism, and sport: Fijian rugby in the local-global nexus. *Anthropological Quarterly*, 89(4), 1109–1141. doi: https://www.jstor.org/stable/44245441.

Hastings, S.L. (2010). Triangulation. In N. J. Salkind (Ed.). *Encyclopedia of research design* (pp. 1538–1541). Sage.

Hearn, J. (2004). From hegemonic masculinity to the hegemony of men. *Feminist Theory*, 5, 49–72. doi: https://doi.org/10.1177/1464700104040813.

Houghton, C., Casey, D., Shaw, D., & Murphy, K. (2013). Rigour in qualitative case-study research. *Nurse Researcher*, *20*(4), 12–17. doi: 10.7748/nr2013.03.20.4.12.e326.

Hsieh, H. F., & Shannon, S. E. (2005). Three approaches to qualitative content analysis. *Qualitative Health Research*, *15*(9), 1277–1288. doi: https://doi.org/10.1177/1049732305276687.

Hsiung, P. C. (2008). Teaching reflexivity in qualitative interviewing. *Teaching Sociology*, *36*(3), 211–226. doi: https://doi.org/10.1177/0092055X0803600302

Hughes, R., & Coakley, J. (1991). Positive deviance among athletes: The implications of over-conformity to the sport ethic. *Sociology of Sport Journal*, *8*(4), 307–325. doi: https://doi.org/10.1123/ssj.8.4.307.

Jou, T. H. 1981. *The tao of tai-chi chuan*. Warwick, NY: Tai Chi Foundation.

Karan, K., & M. C. Khoo. (2007). "The power of gaze in the media: Visual representations in For Him Magazine (FHM) Singapore." Paper presented at the annual meeting of the International Communication Association, TBA, San Francisco, CA. April 10, 2016. Retrieved December 2020 from http://www.allacademic.com/meta/p170513_index.html.

Kari, T., & Karhulahti, V. M. (2016). Do E-athletes move? A study on training and physical exercise in elite E-Sports. *International Journal of Gaming and Computer-Mediated Simulations*, 8(4), 53–66. doi: 10.4018/IJGCMS.2016100104.

Karsten, L., & Pel, E. (2000). Skateboarders exploring urban public space: Ollies, obstacles and conflicts. *Journal of Housing and the Built Environment, 15*(4), 327–340. doi: https://doi.org/10.1023/A:1010166007804.

Kendall, L. (1999). Nerd nation: Images of nerds in U.S. popular culture. *International Journal of Cultural Studies, 2*(2), 260–283. doi: https://doi.org/10.1177%2F136787799900200206.

Kim, A., Qian, Y., Lee, H-W, & Mastromartino, B. (2020). Growth in sport media and rise of new sport fandom. In R. A. Dunn (Ed.), *Multidisciplinary perspectives on media fandom* (pp. 150–171). IGI Global.

Kimmel, M. S. (2001). Global masculinities: Restoration and resistance. In B. Pease and K. Pringle (Eds.), *A man's world: Changing men's practices in a globalized world* (pp. 21–37). Zed Books.

Kuan, G., & Roy, J. (2007). Goal profiles, mental toughness and its influence on performance outcomes among Wushu athletes. *Journal of Sports Science and Medicine, 6* (CSSI-2), 28–33. doi: https://www.ncbi.nlm.nih.gov/pmc/articles/PMC3809050/.

Lowe, J., Ghaill, M., & Haywood, C. P. (2016). The cultural (re)production of masculinities: Class, Chinese ethnicity and elite schooling in Indonesia. *Asia Journal of Social Science, 44*(4/5), 600–625. doi: https://www.jstor.org/stable/43954183.

Lule, J. (1995). The rape of Mike Tyson: Race, the press and symbolic types. *Critical Studies in Mass Communication, 12*(2), 176–195. doi: https://doi.org/10.1080/15295039509366930.

MacDonald, D., & Kirk, D. (1999). Pedagogy, the body and Christian identity. *Sport, Education and Society, 4*(2), 131–142. doi: https://doi.org/10.1080/1357332990040202.

McCormack, M., & Anderson, E. (2014). The influence of declining homophobia on men's gender in the United States: An argument for the study of homohysteria. *Sex Roles, 71*(3–4), 109–120. doi: https://doi.org/10.1007/s11199-014-0358-8.

McCreary, D. R., Wong, F. Y., Wiener, W., Carpenter, K. M., Engle, A., & Nelson, P. (1996). The relationship between masculine gender role stress and psychological adjustment: A question of construct validity? *Sex Roles, 34*(7), 507–516. doi: https://doi.org/10.1007/BF01545029.

Miller, K. E. (2009). Sport-related identities and the "toxic jock." *Journal of Sport Behavior, 32*(1), 69–91. doi: https://www.ncbi.nlm.nih.gov/pmc/articles/PMC3107047/.

Miller, K. E., Melnick, M. J., Farrell, M. P., Sabo, D. F., & Burns, G. M. (2006). Jocks, gender, binge drinking, and adolescent violence. *Journal of Interpersonal Violence, 21*, 105–120. doi: https://doi.org/10.1177/0886260505281662.

Miller, K. E., Sabo, D. F., Farrell, M. P., Barnes, G. M., & Melnick, M. J. (1998). Athletic participation and sexual behavior in adolescents: The different worlds of boys and girls. *Journal of Health and Social Behavior, 39*: 108–123. doi: https://doi.org/10.2307/2676394.

Miller, P. S, & Kerr, G. A. (2003). The role experimentation of intercollegiate student athletes. *Sport Psychologist, 17*: 196–219. doi : https://doi.org/10.1123/tsp.17.2.196.

Miller, S. A. (2010). Making the boys cry: The performative dimensions of fluid gender. *Text and Performance Quarterly*, 30(2), p. 163–182. doi: https://doi.org/10.1080/10462931003658099.

Nicholls, J. G. (1989). *The competitive ethos and democratic education*. Harvard University Press. New USAU gender inclusion policy allows division self-selection for all (n.d.) Downloaded March 28, 2021, from https://rb.gy/hmkyoh.

Nishime, L. (2017). Reviving Bruce: Negotiating Asian masculinity through Bruce Lee paratexts in Giant Robot and Angry Asian Man. *Critical Studies in Media Communication*, 34(2), 120–129. doi: http://dx.doi.org/10.1080/15295036.2017.1285420.

O'Connor, P. (2018). Handrails, steps and curbs: Sacred places and secular pilgrimage in skateboarding. *Sport in Society*, *21*(11), 1651–1668. doi: https://doi.org/10.1080/17430437.2017.1390567.

———. (2018). Hong Kong skateboarding and network capital. *Journal of Sport and Social Issues*, *42*(6), 419–436. doi: https://doi.org/10.1177/0193723518797040.

O'Neil, J.M. (2008). Summarizing 25 years of research on men's gender role conflict using the Gender Role Conflict Scale: New research paradigms and clinical implications. *Counseling Psychologist*, 36, 358–445.doi : https://doi.org/10.1177/0011000008317057.

Pascoe, C. J. (2003). Multiple masculinities? Teenage boys talk about jocks and gender. *American Behavioral Scientist*, 46, 1423–1438. doi: https://doi.org/10.1177%2F000276420304610009.

Petrone, R. (2010). "You have to get hit a couple of times": The role of conflict in learning how to "be" a skateboarder. *Teaching and Teacher Education*, *26*(1), 119–127. doi: https://doi.org/10.1016/j.tate.2009.05.005.

Pompper, D. (2010). Masculinities, the metrosexual, and media images: Across dimensions of age and ethnicity. *Sex Roles*, *63*(9–10), 682–696. doi: https://doi.org/10.1007/s11199-010-9870-7.

Pronger, B. (1990). Gay jocks: A phenomenology of gay men in athletics. In M. A. Messner and D. F. Sabo (Eds.), *Sport, men and the gender order: Critical feminist perspectives* (pp.19–30). Human Kinetics Press.

Ritter, L. J., & Ueno, K. (2017). Construction and management of stigma based on a voluntary-achieved status. *Symbolic Interaction*, 40(4), 541–560. doi: https://www.jstor.org/stable/10.2307/90015656.

Robbins, B. (2004). "That's cheap." The rational invocation of norms, practices, and an ethos in ultimate Frisbee. *Journal of Sport and Social Issues*, *28*(3), 314–337. doi: https://doi.org/10.1177/0193723504266992.

Rowe, D., & Gilmour, C. (2010). Sport, media, and consumption in Asia: A merchandised milieu. *American Behavioral Scientist*, *53*(10), 1530–1548. doi: https://doi.org/10.1177/0002764210368083.

Salter, A., & Blodgett, B. (2012). Hypermasculinity and dickwolves: The contentious role of women in the new gaming public. *Journal of Broadcasting and Electronic Media*, *56*(3), 401–416. doi: https://doi.org/10.1080/08838151.2012.705199.

Silverman, D. (2000). *Doing qualitative research: A practical handbook*. London: Sage.

Singh, S. (2017). Gender, Conflict and Security: Perspectives from South Asia. *Journal of Asian Security and International Affairs* 4(2) 149–157. doi: 10.1177/2347797017710560.

Smith, B., & Caddick, N. (2012). Qualitative methods in sport: A concise overview for guiding social scientific sport research. *Asia Pacific journal of Sport and Social Science*, *1*(1), 60–73. doi: https://doi.org/10.1080/21640599.2012.701373.

Song, G. (2004). *The fragile scholar: Power and masculinity in Chinese culture*. Hong Kong University Press.

Sparkes, A. C., Brown, D. H., & Partington, E. (2010). The "jock body" and the social construction of space: The performance and positioning of cultural identity. *Space and Culture*, 13(3), 333–347. doi: https://doi.org/10.1177%2F1206331210365288.

Sparkes, A, Partington, E & Brown, D. H. K. (2007) Bodies as bearers of value: the transmission of jock culture via the 'Twelve Commandments'. *Sport, Education and Society*, *12*(3), 295–316. doi: https://doi.org/10.1080/13573320701464150.

Thompson, J. K., Heinberg, L., Altabe, M., & Tantleff-Dunn, S. (1999). *Exacting beauty: Theory, assessment, and treatment of body image disturbance*. American Psychological Association.

Turgo, N. V. (2014). Redefining and experiencing masculinity in a Philippine fishing community. *Philippine Sociological Review*, 62, 7–38. doi: https://www.jstor.org/stable/43486386.

Vivar, C. G., McQueen, A., Whyte, D. A., & Armayor, N. C. (2007). Getting started with qualitative research: Developing a research proposal. *Nurse Researcher*, 14(3), 60–73. doi: 10.7748/nr2007.04.14.3.60.c6033.

Weiser, M., Kutz, I., Jacobson, S., & Weiser, D. (1995). Psychotherapeutic aspects of the martial arts. *American Journal of Psychotherapy*, 49(1), 118–127. doi: https://doi.org/10.1176/appi.psychotherapy.1995.49.1.118.

Wheaton, B., & Beal, B. (2003). Keeping it real: Sub-cultural media and the discourses of authenticity in alternative sports'. *International Review for the Sociology of Sport*, 38(2):155–176. doi: https://doi.org/10.1177/1012690203038002002.

White, A. J., Magrath, R., & Emilio Morales, L. (2020). Gay male athletes' coming-out stories on Outsports. com. *International Review for the Sociology of Sport*, doi: https://doi.org/10.1177/1012690220969355.

Wong, K. K. 1981. *Introduction to Shaolin Kung Fu*. Caric Press.

Xiaopan, T. J. Z. (2013). On the application of the decomposition method in wushu teaching. *Wushu Science* 7: 1–12. doi: https://en.cnki.com.cn/Article_en/CJFDTotal-WSKX201307025.htm.

Chapter Seven

Masculinity, Identity, and Disabled Veterans

How British Audiences Respond to Representations of Military Veterans on Prime-Time BBC Programmes

Jenna Pitchford-Hyde

INTRODUCTION

In recent years, media coverage of the London Paralympics (2012) and Invictus Games (2014) significantly increased the visibility of disabled people, specifically veterans, on British television. In contrast to NBC's five and a half hours of coverage in the United States, Channel 4 provided over 150 hours of coverage of the games to UK audiences and foregrounded well-known disabled presenters. Through coverage of these events, media producers highlighted veterans' journeys of recovery and overcoming disability and injury (Kelly, 2016), giving them the opportunity to shape public perceptions of veterans.

As awareness of the issues facing veterans increased, the House of Lords' report on the government's veterans' strategy cited the "media portrayal of veterans as one of the key drivers of the public's perception" (Attlee, 2018, p.7). The report claimed that "television documentaries and news are the most important basis for people's impressions about service leavers and veterans," and it called for a more proactive approach from government media departments and from ministers (Attlee, 2018, p.7). In April 2018 the Defence Secretary Gavin Williamson created a new veterans' strategy and cross-government Veterans Unit, identifying how veterans are perceived by the wider public as a key priority: "perceptions are often inaccurate, outdated or clichéd and do not recognise that most veterans are proud members of our society with a huge amount to offer" (Ministry of Defence press release,

2018). Lord Ashcroft's Veterans' Transition Review (2017) highlights an important point which has been taken forward in the new government strategy for veterans: it is crucial to focus research on how public perceptions are shaped by media representations (Ashcroft, 2017, p. 11). As such, the study reported in this chapter provides an important intervention in the way that we approach the representation of veterans in the media—with implications for media producers in the U.K. and elsewhere.

Where previous studies have analysed media representation of disabled people (Mitchell & Snyder, 1997), veterans (Phillips, 2020), and disabled veterans (Cree & Caddick, 2019), this chapter focuses specifically on audience responses to the representation of disabled veterans in two prime-time BBC shows: *The People's Strictly* (2015) and *Without Limits: Australia* (2018). Crucially, by applying ideas from GRC, disability, and media studies, this chapter offers new perspectives on the complexities of representing veterans on British television, and the impact of these on public perceptions.

LITERATURE REVIEW

There have been a significant number of studies addressing gender role conflict (O'Neil et al., 1995) and representations of disability on television (Ofcom, 2018), how disability is presented in print media (Haller, 2000), the portrayal of disability on social media (Hill, 2017), and how audiences use social media to react to television programmes (Guo, 2018). There also have been studies on perceptions of veterans in UK society using opinion polls (Phillips, 2020). However, the study outlined in this chapter is the first to analyse social media audience perceptions of veterans in highly influential prime-time television programmes on the public-funded BBC. The following sections provide an overview of the focal television shows and identify the existing research which led me to develop my research questions: 1) *Strictly Come Dancing* and *Without Limits: Australia*; 2) Gender role conflict theory, emotionality, and performing masculinity; 3) Genre and representation; 3) Social significance of Twitter, and 4) Disability, media, and masculinities.

Strictly Come Dancing and Without Limits: Australia

Both television shows offer a documentary feel. *The People's Strictly* can be seen as belonging to what Bonner (2011) identifies as the "reality talent" genre, and more specifically as a reality competition show. *Without Limits: Australia* also includes elements of the factual travel genre. In 2015, Royal

Marines medic Lance Corporal Cassidy Little competed against able-bodied civilian contestants in *The People's Strictly*. This was a special edition of *Strictly Come Dancing* that rewarded "deserving" members of the British public who had made an outstanding contribution to their community. Little had lost his right leg below the knee when an Improvised Explosive Device (IED) was triggered during a tour of Afghanistan in the summer of 2011. He was selected on the basis of his service and sacrifice for the country. Subsequently, Little also took part in the *Strictly Come Dancing Christmas Special* alongside celebrity past champions of the main *Strictly* show.

In 2018, the BBC broadcast the documentary *Without Limits: Australia* as a precursor to the Invictus Games in Sydney. The documentary followed a small group of British and Australian veterans with a wide range of physical disabilities and mental health issues (Parachute Regiment officer Martin Hewitt, Fusilier Shaun Stocker, Army aircraft technician Keanie Trick, Private Matt Tolson and Corporal Dean West) as they embarked on a 1,000-mile expedition across Western Australia's remote Kimberley region.

Gender Role Conflict Theory, Emotionality, and Performing Masculinity

Much of the theoretical underpinning for this chapter is based in O'Neil's suggestion that gender role conflict (GRC) occurs when "rigid, sexist, or restrictive gender roles result in restriction, devaluation, or violation of others or self" (O'Neil et al., 1995). I use this framework to examine societal expectations of the masculinised military figure. O'Neil, et al. (1995) identify four key patterns of male gender role conflict: first, "success, power, and competition" (SPC); second, "restricted emotionality" (RE); third, "restricted affectionate behaviour between men" (RABBM); and fourth, "conflict between work and family relationships" (CBWFR). By 2012, more than 230 separate studies had been conducted exploring the nature of GRC as it is experienced by men, as well as the variables associated with that experience (O'Neil, 2008; Wester & Vogel, 2012).

Using a GRC lens to examine military culture is useful for examining this male dominated, competitive, disciplined, and hierarchal arena (Higate, 2003). However, McAllister et al. (2018) argue that the construct of military masculinity in the UK is more complex than a simple exclusion of the "feminine" and the "emotional" when characterizing masculinities. These and other findings suggest a more nuanced analysis of how masculinity is constructed across military culture (Lorber & Garcia, 2010; Green et al., 2010). There seems to be a dichotomy at work within which military masculinity simultaneously has the capacity to limit emotional expression, but also can create safe masculine spaces based on solidarity and brotherhood—which encourage and support the expression of emotion. Rather, "it is not the case

Figure 7.1.   The Iraq War Veteran
Photo by Stuart Griffiths.

that emotion is simply *suppressed* in military culture; rather it is expressed *differently*" (McAllister et al., 2018, p. 2).

Genre and Representation

Both *Strictly* and *Without Limits* make use of short introductory films produced to construct the veterans' identities in specific ways. Although the two programmes belong to different genres, they both carry elements of documentary and both rely on the intensity of their "speech events" (Corner, 2006) to construct veterans' identities through narrative segments. Bonner (2013) suggests that such films are essential to building engagement with the audience in the reality-talent format. Whilst Bonner describes *Strictly* as an example of what Mills refers to as "invisible television" (Mills, 2010, p. 2), *Without Limits* has a more documentary feel. Whilst Corner (2006) focuses on how such speech events can build a sense of drama, I am interested in how constructing narratives in this way influences audience perceptions of veterans.

Social Significance of Twitter

In recent years social media has played an increasingly influential role in shaping public opinion, with 330 million registered users around the world and 16.45 million UK users (as of January 2021). Recent studies have examined how Twitter plays an important part in our lives, from social media checks in the job recruitment process (Melton et al., 2017), to Twitter being utilised in political campaigns (Parmelee & Bichard, 2012). Whilst it is important to remember that it is difficult to ascertain the demographic of any sample when using Twitter (Sloan, 2017), the platform was at the height of its popularity at the time that these shows were broadcast (2015-2018) (Statista, 2019), making it an invaluable tool for obtaining contributors' immediate reactions to media events.

Disability, Media, and Masculinities

Several studies have emerged at the intersection of disability studies, media studies, and masculinity studies in recent years, with foci including masculinity and effeminophobia in dancing (Richardson, 2016), disability and dancing (Quinlan & Bates, 2008), and disability in sport (Silva & Howe, 2017). Also, there have been studies examining media narratives and the positioning of military and veteran identities (Caso, 2016) and disabled veterans and the Invictus games (Cree & Caddick, 2019). In terms of audience perceptions of disability, Mitchell and Snyder's research (1997) suggests that able-bodied audiences are caught in a dichotomous relationship with the image of the disabled body which they refer to as the "double bind of our fascination/repulsion with physical difference" (p. 15).

Crucial to this chapter is its exploration of how discourses of disability are represented in the media. Quinlan and Bate's (2008) analysis of discourses of disability on *Dancing with the Stars*, is based on the premise that it is essential to acknowledge difference in disability in order to achieve a fair representation. Drawing on the previous work of Haller (2000) and Nelson (2000), they suggest that media producers, and society more broadly, must move away from the idea that "difference" equals "deficit" (Quinlan & Bates, 2008, p. 76).

Another key focus in this chapter is interplay of cultural narratives and political factors. Cree and Caddick (2019) examine the political implications of the cultural narratives constructed for veterans in the Invictus Games, arguing that although the Invictus Games works to redeem the violence of the state, the way that it is done is "symbolically violent" (p. 4). Claiming that the "warrior body" is created through sporting achievements, in which veterans push their bodies to the limits and show their "more-than-human capacity to 'overcome,'" Cree and Caddick (2019, pp. 2, 11) focus on what cultural nar-ratives constructed around disabled veterans do politically, while I suggest that it is critical to examine how programmes represent disabled veterans because they have a direct impact on public perceptions, and consequently, veterans' mental health, treatment by society, and prospects of post-service employment.

Summary and Research Questions

This chapter uses the key concepts of masculine GRC (O'Neil et al., 1986) to analyse how representations of veterans that imply they have either succeeded or failed in meeting societal gendered expectations impact on audience perceptions. At the heart of this analysis and discussion are the well-established concepts in disability studies of "the overcoming narrative" (Achter, 2010; Quinlan & Bates, 2008) and the "supercrip" (McGillivray et al., 2021; Silva & Howe, 2017). Crucially, the analysis of this data is framed by two of the four patterns identified by O'Neil, et al. (1995) as forming the cornerstones of gender role conflict theory: success, power, and competition (SPC), and restricted emotionality (RE). I analyse the responses in the context of these categories, paying particular attention to the construction of military masculinity and notions of heroism. Specific focal research questions for this chapter are:

RQ1: To what extent are media producers influenced by societal ideas about militarised masculinity?

RQ2: How do narratives constructed by media producers impact public per-ceptions of disabled veterans' gendered identities?

RQ3: To what extent does military status influence audience perceptions of masculinity?

METHOD

Data Collection

In order to analyse public perceptions of disabled veterans in mainstream media I collated audience responses from Twitter to two recent British televi-sion programmes within a two-week time period from when they aired. *The People's Strictly* aired from 25 February to 13 March 2015, and *Without Lim-its: Australia* aired between 2 and 8 November 2018. The two programmes were broadcast in similar prime-time slots on Wednesday evenings at 21.00 and 20.00 respectively, with *Strictly Come Dancing* averaging a viewership of 11 million in 2015. Both shows had significant scope to influence public opinion and create the positive changes that the government reports (outlined in the introduction) suggest is necessary.

My rationale for focusing on these programmes is that they both contain strong elements of the documentary genre by drawing on documentary techniques in order to construct overcoming narratives for the disabled veterans featured. Bignell (2008) claims that "there is a tension between producing a documentary which is representative and 'accurate' and providing the audience with a programme which conforms to the conventions of argument and storytelling" (pp. 201–202). Public demand for more inclusive programming is increasing and producers are therefore required to create programmes that will be entertaining enough to attract viewers whilst maintaining a fair representation of the disabled veterans they feature.

I chose to focus on Twitter responses to the narrative constructions of the shows for two reasons. First, these responses provide an insight into the immediate reactions of audiences and are therefore less likely to be influenced by the opinions of family, friends, or other media reactions to the programmes. Second, Twitter provides access to responses from a range of demographic groups which I may not otherwise be able to analyse. I collected the data as follows:

1. I obtained ethical approval for the research in May 2019.
2. All of the data was collected in June and July 2019.
3. Given ethical guidelines on social media research, I have collected my data by searching for the hashtags: #cassidylittle strictly, #cassidy strictly, #peoplesstrictly Cassidy, #withoutlimits #bbc, #without limits bbc, and #withoutlimits Invictus (data was collected as screen grabs of whole tweets).
4. All usernames and Twitter handles were anonymised and URLS have been removed. The users were strategically using hashtags to bring their comments into the public domain, so it was not necessary to paraphrase quotations or obtain informed consent.
5. I participated in the Twitter conversations only as a reader, not a contributor.
6. To avoid any confusion with other series of these shows, I only included tweets from 2015 for *The People's Strictly* and 2018 for *Without Limits* which referred directly to these focal veterans. I also included tweets and retweets which were linked to the results of my original hashtag search (for example, Instagram posts where they are necessary for context).

7. I discounted tweets by the programme makers unless they were referencing a tweet from an audience member. The sample includes responses predominantly from members of the public, but also from military bodies and charities (which may impact on the kinds of language used).

Data Analysis

Due to the potential differences in convention between the two focal television programmes *The People's Strictly* (2015) and *Without Limits: Australia* (2018), I conducted a thematic discourse analysis involving three stages:

1. First, I read all of the tweets to identify initially emerging themes. Then I analysed each tweet to establish which category it should be placed into (in terms of its text, key words, images, implied meanings, hashtags used, and Twitter user). Given the kind of data being analysed, I found it most effective to capture the complete tweets in separate thematic PowerPoint pages.
2. Next, I read tweets for a second time to identify more subtle themes, bringing the total number of categories to 12.
3. Then I identified the three most dominant themes as (1) *Overcoming Narrative*, (2) *Inspirational*, and (3) *Heroism/Deservingness*.
4. Finally, I conducted a detailed qualitative analysis of the tweets in the three most dominant categories to reveal how media representations interact with societal expectations about military identity and masculinity.

FINDINGS AND DISCUSSION

In total, I collected (N=116) responses to Little's appearance on *Strictly* and (N=74) responses to the disabled veterans' appearances on *Without Limits*. In the course of my initial textual analysis of the tweets, two things became obvious. First, the responses to *Strictly* were relatively evenly spread across a wide range of categories. The responses to *Without Limits* were tightly grouped under just three themes: (1) *Overcoming Narrative*, (2) *Inspirational*, (3) *Heroism/Deservingness*. Second, the majority of *Strictly* responses fit quite comfortably under a single theme. Responses to *Without Limits* were much harder to categorise, with most fitting into multiple categories. Here are the results of my secondary, more detailed analysis that grouped tweets according to which category they most strongly belonged:

Table 7.1. Dominant Themes of Tweets

Category	People's Strictly	Without Limits
Inspiration	11	28
Heroism/Deserving	4	10
Overcoming Narrative	9	13
Pride	4	1
Military Identity	24	3 (in addition, 32 mention Invictus and 8 mention the military in other forms)
Provoking Emotion	4	6
Masculinity	1	0
Sexualisation/Attractiveness	8	0
Quality/judgement	26	2
Expressing Support/Admiration	15	0
Achievement	8	0
Promoting the Show	2	14
Total Tweets Analysed	116	74

Without Limits was harder to categorise, with the majority of the responses falling under the themes of (1) *Overcoming Narrative,* (2) *Inspirational,* and (3) *Heroism/Deservingness,* and many responses applying to all three categories. Whilst the responses to *Strictly* were distributed over a wider range of areas, the same three categories also emerged as dominant. Whilst fewer tweets were designated in the remaining categories, they all inform my analysis of the three dominant themes, especially when we think about them in terms of the GRC components success, power, competition (SPC) and restricted emotionality (RE).

The three categories of (1) *Overcoming Narrative,* (2) *Inspirational,* (3) *Heroism/Deservingness* emerged as the most dominant themes, and speak to RQ1, RQ2, and RQ3, respectively. However, it is important to note is that the tweets in all three of the categories (1) *Overcoming Narrative,* (2) *Inspirational,* (3) *Heroism/Deservingness* are shaped and influenced by the strong overcoming narratives constructed by the programmes' producers. As such, theoretical ideas about overcoming narratives are not limited to RQ1, but rather, provide a framework to address all three RQs.

RQ1: To what extent are media producers influenced by societal ideas about militarised masculinity?

With nine responses to *Strictly* and 13 responses to *Without Limits* predominantly focused on the theme of "*overcoming,*" the audience responses confirm the conclusions of my preliminary textual analysis of the shows that both programmes construct strong *"overcoming"* narratives for the disabled veterans. This is highly problematic in terms of the impact that it has on societal expectations of disabled veterans. Such discourses can be damaging for disabled veterans if they struggle to reconcile the media image of veterans overcoming disability with their own experiences and identities. O'Neil describes gender role conflict (GRC) as "a complex, multidimensional construct describing an unconscious phenomenon produced when perceptions of masculine gender roles deviate from, restrict, devalue, or violate norms" (O'Neil, 2008). The *overcoming* narratives constructed by these shows are heavily dependent on the GRC components "success, power, and competition" (SPC) and "restricted emotionality" (RE). In the responses to both programmes, the veterans are praised for adhering to society's expectations of military masculinity. By *"overcoming"* their disabilities in order to participate in the shows, they prove themselves to be successful, physically and mentally powerful, and capable of thriving when in competition with others.

The societal expectation is that disabled veterans' masculinised military identity will enable them to overcome their injuries and to reclaim able-bodiedness, thus adhering to some expected norm. However, O'Neil and colleagues (1995) suggests that such "rigid, sexist, or restrictive gender roles result in restriction, devaluation, or violation of others or self" (p. 362). Despite so many veterans returning from contemporary wars with a wide variety of life changing disabilities, few would be able to achieve the same level of physical strength that they see depicted in these programmes.

Cassidy Little and the veterans on *Without Limits* are depicted as reclaiming their military status and masculinised identities through their successful participation in the programmes. Little's below-the-knee amputation means that he is better able to pass as able-bodied in his performance than many others would. In line with the restricted emotionality (RE) component of GRC, more emphasis was put on his *overcoming* narrative in terms of achievement than on showing him struggling both physically and emotionally in training. The audience responses reinforce this, with one contributor highlighting Little's disability and emphasising how impressive his dancing is in spite of it: "@bbc strictly just because you are #disabled doesn't mean you don't keep marching on [heart emoji] #cassidy little" (Anonymised contributor A, 2015).

The importance of *overcoming* his disability and reclaiming able-bodiedness in order to avoid gender role conflict is epitomised by Little's decision to perform the Jive in the *Strictly* Christmas Special competition. Little's performance had a significant impact on viewers' reactions: "#Cassidy dancing the jive on #scd was amazing inspirational fabulous awesome . . . should I go on?" (Anonymised contributor B, 2015). The very fact that

Little had attempted the high impact Jive whilst wearing a prosthetic leg earned him the respect of the audience. The link between *overcoming* and his military identity is crucial to recognise here. Little has performed able-bodiedness to the extent that he has reclaimed his masculinised military identity through success, power, and competing effectively (SPC). Since the Jive is a usual component of the show for able-bodied competitors, this is an example of disabled veterans being regarded as "super" for achieving things that able-bodied people regard as ordinary.

The positioning of the veterans and other athletes as superhuman is highly problematic. Hardin and Hardin (2004) suggest that the "supercrip" stereotype situates the disabled person as heroic by virtue of his or her ability to perform feats normally considered not possible for people with disabilities or by virtue of the person living a regular life in spite of a disability. In this case, disabled veterans are deemed super for adhering to societal gender norms in SPC and RE terms: Little achieves success, power, and holds his own in the competition by performing able-bodiedness, therefore reclaiming his masculinised military identity and avoiding GRC.

Little's narrative focuses on his ability to perform able-bodiedness through the use of prosthetics. Howe (2011) argues that "bodies that are the product of cyborgification . . . are the vanguard of the sport for the disabled and as such they are celebrated far more than those competitors that do not use mobility technologies" (p. 869). He warns that such celebrations of supercrip athletes wearing prostheses or using wheelchairs can be detrimental to other athletes who are unable to take advantage of these technologies, leaving their statuses "at best unaltered and at worst increasingly their liminality" (Howe, 2011, p. 880). With his sports blade prosthetic, Little is able to perform the bounce of the Jive effectively, perhaps even more effectively than he would have done as an able-bodied competitor. Whilst this might enable Little to embrace a technomasculine cyborg identity and become "super," this is not achievable for all amputee veterans.

The narratives constructed for the veterans in *Without Limits* represent a divergence of the cyborgification of disability sports and military technomasculinity. The nature of the challenge and the roots of the programme in the Invictus Games makes it an ideal vehicle through which to showcase the capabilities of disabled veterans with prosthetics. There is the potential for *Without Limits*, and by extension the Invictus Games, to embrace what James Der Derian (2001) defines as technomasculinity, and showcase the cyborg nature of disabled veterans competing in sports. Instead, however, both opt to reinforce a grittier, more traditionally masculinised image of veterans, constructing an image of a physical, masculinised military rather than a progressive technological military.

The legacy of the First World War and the importance placed on recuperation for veterans returning as amputees is, perhaps, at the root of the UK media producers' approach to representing veterans. As Cree and Caddick (2019) summarise, in the cultural narratives and imaginations of the nation, "the absence of a limb can represent patriotism and sacrifice, as well as state power, rather than vulnerability and femininity, while the presence of prosthetic limbs points to a new kind of post-human techno-masculinity" (p. 8). This is evident in the responses to *Strictly* and *Without Limits* which celebrate the veterans' ability to compete despite their disabilities: "#cassidylittle on the people's @bbcstrictly was mind blowing and with 1 leg #winner" (Anonymised contributor C, 2015). Caso (2016) suggests that "prostheses function to techno-masculinize amputee veterans by rehabilitating them, and buttress the power of the state as the producer of war heroes" (p. 223). In other words, by embracing sports prosthetics, the veterans on *Strictly* and *Without Limits* are able to achieve success, power, and compete by performing technomasculinity effectively, thus reinforcing the masculinised image of the military and the state.

RQ2: How Do Narratives Constructed By Media Producers Impact Public Perceptions of Disabled Veterans' Gendered Identities?

This analysis revealed that *Without Limits* provoked 28 responses in the "*inspirational*" category, whilst *Strictly* had only 11. A larger proportion of the responses to *Strictly* focused simply on the fact that Little was an *inspiration*, often without any attempt to qualify their evaluation of him and his performance: "Absolutely stunned by Cassidy and Natalie. So inspiring! Wow!! #peoplesstrictly" (Anonymous contributor D, 2015). Similar comments were posted in response to the veterans on *Without Limits*: "Get #withoutlimits on bbc1 on Now! These guys are a true inspiration #H4H #InvictusGames #INVICTUS" (Anonymous contributor E, 2018). For the most part, the responses to *Without Limits* tended to be more specific and contributors attempted to support their claims, indicating that the producers of *Without Limits* constructed overcoming narratives which reinforced the SPC and ER components of GRC.

It is essential to consider the impact that genre has on the narrative constructed for disabled veterans. As a prime-time reality talent show, the purpose of *Strictly* is to entertain audiences. The remit of *Without Limits* as a documentary is to interrogate a subject, promote debate, and evoke emotion from the audience. Moreover, the central focus of *Without Limits* is on disabled veterans and their overcoming narratives. For *Strictly*, however, the disabled veteran's journey is just one distinct narrative arc in an already established show. As such, the narratives of the veterans featured on *Without Limits* are designed to evoke emotion from the audience and showcase veterans' achievements in overcoming their disabilities. Consequently, it is perhaps unsurprising that the responses to *Without Limits* more explicitly claim the veterans to be *inspirational*.

Many of the audience responses frame the veterans as setting an example to others through their overcoming narrative:

One of my best friends @keanietrick was on BBCs #WithoutLimits last night and I'm so proud of her! She persisted through chronic pain and mental health issues. And I'm sure she had helped many people with the same problems realise you can follow your dreams. #armyveteran #bbc. (Anonymous contributor F, 2018).

This tweet makes the claim that Trick has *inspired* many people with disabilities by overcoming chronic pain and mental health issues. It relies heavily on the fact that Trick has overcome her mental health issues by restricting her emotionality (RE in GRC terms). Her journey will provide *inspiration* for many. However, it is important to recognise that for some, it is not possible to overcome similar health issues. In the following tweet, the civilian viewer has not been *inspired* in a positive way, but rather she feels guilty for not being able to overcome depression:

Watching the final episode of #Without Limits on @BBC I had a bad day today with my #depression and #mentalhealth but I feel so bad for moaning when they all have been through what they have been through! I feel like a mardy bitch and have nothing to feel bad about #perspective. (Anonymous contributor G, 2018)

In this instance, the overcoming narrative serves to reinforce the idea that bodies and minds should be mended, therefore positioning those who cannot overcome their disability as failures. For veterans unable to restrict their emotionality or "overcome" their injuries, their masculinised military identity could be jeopardized by a failure to secure success, power, and compete effectively, thus reinforcing their emasculation and separation from their military identities (this includes female veterans since military identity remains heavily dependent on notions of masculinity). As Nelson (2000) summarises, the "supercrip" is known in the disability community as "someone who has excelled so much in spite of his or her handicap that others who do not measure up are regarded as inadequate" (p. 185–187). These are the disabled veteran figures that remain absent from prime-time television shows. The invisibility of injured bodies and minds is an issue which must be addressed if the BBC and other programme makers are to claim fair representation of disabled veterans and responsibly inform the perceptions of able-bodied civilian audiences.

Ryan (2016) criticises the production of what she terms "*inspiration* porn," or stories of disabled people overcoming physical, psychological, and social barriers to achieve something. Disabled people do not wish to be seen as *inspirational*, but rather able-bodied people expose themselves to such stories to feel as though they are being inclusive (Ryan, 2016). *Without Limits* in particular provoked some responses which were problematic in the way that they discussed inspiration: "You think you're having a bad day but you should always think how lucky you are. The folks on #WithoutLimits are amazing, inspiring people! #invictusgames #bbc" (Anonymous contributor H, 2018). Another wrote: "In awe of these vets on BBC #WithoutLimits Australia. Huge courage. Hugely inspiring. I will never moan about commuting again." (Anonymous contributor I, 2018) These tweets have an element of self-reflection, but furthermore, they situate the veterans' experiences as undesirable, "lesser" existences, prompting the contributors to congratulate themselves on their own able-bodied lives.

These comments highlight the contributors' interpretation that the veterans do not conform to societal expectations of military masculinity, or even civilian masculinity. As Patterson and Hughes (2000) claim, "the hegemonic notion of the disabled body constructs it in terms of corporeal or intellectual 'deficit'" (p. 39). The veterans avoid GRC in as much as they meet the requirements for success, power, and effectively competing in terms of overcoming their disabilities to complete the *Without Limits* challenge. However, their positioning as supercrip implies deficit in everyday situations. If they are unable to achieve "ordinariness," then they cannot achieve SPC, leaving them vulnerable to GRC.

RQ3: To What Extent Does Military Status Influence Audience Perceptions of Masculinity?

In the "*Heroism/Deserving*" category we see a degree of interplay between the different influences on audience perception. Reality talent shows are constructed around the "hard work" narrative (Bonner, 2011), and audiences base their votes on who is the most "*deserving*." Whilst this could mean the person who dances best, audiences usually vote for the person who has made the biggest improvement, faced the biggest adversity, or who constructs the most convincing "hard work" narrative. In the case of the disabled veterans in *Strictly* and (although not a reality talent show) *Without Limits*, their participation in the programmes enables them to achieve success, power, and competitiveness, thus securing their masculinised identities. Whilst much of the audience reaction can be attributed to the veterans' achievement through the hard work narrative, the responses indicate that the veterans provoked emotional responses from the audience members simply by virtue of their veteran statuses:

> Just catching up on @BBC #Without Limits—hero is a word and term so over-used these days—these are the real heroes in life. These and the many other serving, those that have served and those preparing to serve. Inspirational group. A must watch. (Anonymous contributor J, 2018)

As one contributor suggests in their response to Little's performances in *Strictly*, the emotional reaction provoked by his veteran status and overcoming narrative arguably gave him an advantage over his fellow competitors: 'Cassidy HAD to be the people's choice, though. Well done for Natalie too ☺ #SCD' (Anonymous contributor K, 2015). This tweet suggests that the very presence of a disabled veteran on *Strictly* emotionally manipulates the audience to the point at which Little is the only acceptable winner. The public do not watch reality talent shows to witness a soldier "failing" to overcome their physical injuries or PTSD (so they achieve SPC), or becoming openly emotional (so they perform RE). As Cree and Caddick (2019) observe, "the story must exclude veterans whose bodies have not been remade—or are too broken—for these would bring not redemption but despair" (p. 7).

This presents a dilemma for the producers of these shows. It is necessary for them to create narratives for the veterans which simultaneously construct engaging and emotive stories whilst maintaining fair representation. In constructing such strong overcoming narratives, the programmes' produc-ers are actively avoiding engagement with what Scarry (1985) identifies as the primary purpose of war: injuring (pp. 80–81). Achter (2010) claims that social order is maintained through "discourses that manage the representation of injured veterans, constituting them as normal or 'proper' bodies" (p. 48). Cree and Caddick build on Achter's observation, suggesting that "produc-ing the wounded soldier as *not less but more of a man* serves to blur out the violence of the sovereign state, and render the military subject governable and manageable again" (2019, p. 7). Cree and Caddick (2019) claim that "the politics of wounded veteran narratives hinges on the tensions between ideals of patriotism, heroism, sacrifice, and masculinity on the one hand, and perceptions of victimhood, disability, despair and betrayal on the other" (p. 259). I develop this suggestion further to argue that media audiences form perceptions of disabled veterans which further complicate the tensions that Cree and Caddick (2019) identify.

The veterans are immediately presented as "*deserving*" due to both their heroic military statuses and the fact that they overcome disability to compete

in the competition. In other words, the very fact that the veterans are competing at all immediately propels them to "superhuman" status. The sense that
these veterans are on a journey of recovery is essential in order to make the
programmes enticing to audiences. The viewer wishes to be part of each veteran's journey, to witness the remaking of the warrior. Although the veterans'
bodies cannot be restored to their previous forms, the powerful overcoming
narratives constructed by the programmes work to restore their heroic statuses and warrior identities, whether that is by dancing the Jive or climbing
rocks in Australia.

CONCLUSION: TOWARD A NEW NARRATIVE

By conducting a detailed analysis of audience responses to *Without Limits*
and *Strictly*, I have established that whilst the tweets can be grouped into
many different categories with a few emerging as dominant, essentially the
responses are determined by the *overcoming* narratives constructed for the
veterans. These narratives are intimately bound up with veterans' ability
to achieve success, power, and compete effectively (SPC) and restrict their
emotions (RE). Although it would be possible to present these veterans as
victims of trauma (especially in light of the British military's recent drive to
increase awareness of PTSD and address mental health issues), both shows
make strategic decisions to create narratives which position the veterans as
"supercrips" who have sacrificed for their countries, therefore elevating them
to unquestionable heroic status. Both programmes acknowledge the physical and mental health implications of military service, but ultimately, they
focus on constructing strong *overcoming* narratives for the veterans, in terms
of both their physical disabilities and their PTSD (and related mental health
conditions).

Whilst the programme producers aim to be inclusive, the decision to focus
on *overcoming* narratives poses possible dangers for fair representation and
has the potential to cause GRC crises for other disabled veterans in society.
If the responses analysed in this chapter are indicative of wider societal
trends, then these media representations of disabled veterans have created
societal expectations that all veterans (and potentially other groups of disabled people) can *overcome* their disabilities to achieve success, power, and
compete effectively. Consequently, those who cannot achieve this potentially
face GRC.

Ofcom's Annual Report in 2017/18 stated that more nuanced approaches to
programme making were required in order to reflect diversity within groups
as well as between them, thus making programmes feel more authentic

(Ofcom Annual Report, 2018, p. 30). This need for nuanced representation is especially true for veterans. Programme makers must acknowledge where there is a clear *overcoming* narrative, and also represent those who cannot *overcome* disability, in order to avoid triggering GRC for veterans. It is essential that the BBC and other media producers continue to develop their approach in terms of diversity and fair representation. Crucially, programme makers need to take significant steps toward involving disabled veterans (and the disabled community more widely) in their production process (Pitchford-Hyde & Parry, 2020). Media producers must lead the way in challenging damaging stereotypes and representations in order to avoid GRC and make a positive difference to veterans' identities, well-being, and chances of successful reintegration.

The focus of the study reported in this chapter on textual analysis of audience responses—together with its use of masculine GRC, disability, and media studies approaches in its analysis—enables it to make an original and significant intervention in debates on the real world impact of representations of veterans on British television programmes (especially in gender, media, disability, and veterans studies). It also has the potential to inform future policy making within the BBC, other media organisations, the government department for Digital, Culture, Media and Sport, and the new cross-government Veterans Unit. Ultimately, its aim is to improve public understanding of the issues facing veterans, and consequently, contribute to a positive experience for veterans reintegrating into society.

This chapter demonstrates the potential for using GRC theory in research which requires a nuanced analysis of audience responses in terms of masculinity and disability. It has illustrated how the core concepts from GRC can be invaluable to interdisciplinary research addressing complex and intertwined issues such as military identities, masculinity, and disability. Crucially, this study demonstrates the benefits of applying GRC components to textual analysis and opens the way for future projects in this area.

Limitations and Future Directions

It is important to acknowledge that Twitter is not fully representative of *The People's Strictly* or *Without Limits* audiences. As such, this chapter focuses on a self-selecting group who wish to share their reactions to the programmes with others via the use of hashtags. One of the limitations of this research is that the cohort of people who watch *Strictly* or *Without Limits* and respond to it via Twitter is fairly narrow. Although it is difficult to establish the exact demographic group each Twitter user belongs to, it is notable that (according to their profiles) most contributors are able-bodied, British, white, and over 25 years old.

There are a number of ways to develop the study explored in this chapter for future research: a wider range of genres could be examined, responses on other social media platforms could be analysed, and focus groups could be used instead of social media responses. The use of multiple coders and use of GRC formulas would offer other interesting routes through these future research topics. The most intriguing area with potential for development is how GRC approaches can be used to analyse veterans' own responses to media representations.

ACKNOWLEDGMENTS

Thank you to Professor Donnalyn Pompper and Dr. Filipa Antunes for their guidance, support, and feedback throughout the writing process.

REFERENCES

Achter, P. (2010). Unruly bodies: The rhetorical domestication of twenty-first-century veterans of war. *Quarterly Journal of Speech*, 96(1), 46–68. https://doi.org/10.1080/00335630903512697.
Anonymised contributor A. (2015, 11 March). [Tweet]. Twitter. www.twitter.com.
Anonymised contributor B. (2015, 25 December). [Tweet]. Twitter. www.twitter.com.
Anonymised contributor C. (2015, 12 March). [Tweet]. Twitter. www.twitter.com.
Anonymous contributor D. (2015, 11 March). [Tweet]. Twitter. www.twitter.com.
Anonymous contributor E. (2018, 24 October). [Tweet]. Twitter. www.twitter.com.
Anonymous contributor F. (2018, 17 October). [Tweet]. Twitter. www.twitter.com.
Anonymous contributor G. (2018, 24 October). [Tweet]. Twitter. www.twitter.com.
Anonymous contributor H. (2018, 24 October). [Tweet]. Twitter. www.twitter.com.
Anonymous contributor I. (2018, 17 October). [Tweet]. Twitter. www.twitter.com.
Anonymous contributor J. (2018, 25 October). [Tweet]. Twitter. www.twitter.com.
Anonymous contributor K. (2015, 13 March). [Tweet]. Twitter. www.twitter.com.
Ashcroft, M. (2017). Veterans' Transition Review, Third Follow-up Report: October 2017. Veterans' Transition Review website. http://www.veteranstransition.co.uk/vtrreport.pdf.
Attlee, J. (2018). Veterans Strategy: Background to Government Policy Debate on 15 November 2018 [research briefing]. Retrieved October 3, 2020, from https://lordslibrary.parliament.uk/research-briefings/lln-2018-0118/.
Bignell, J. (2008). *An introduction to television studies* (2nd ed.). Routledge.
Bonner, F. (2011). *Personality presenters: Television's cultural intermediaries with viewers*. Ashgate.

Bonner, F. (2013). Gaudy nights: dance and reality television's display of talent. In J. Jacobs and S. Peacock (Eds.), *Television Aesthetics and Style* (pp. 251–268). Bloomsbury.

Boyle, A. & Hamilton, A. (Executive Producers). (2015) The people's strictly for comic relief [TV Series]. BBC.

Caso, F. (2016). Sexing the disabled veteran: the homoerotic aesthetics of militarism. *Critical Military Studies*, 3(3), 217–234. https://doi.org/10.1080/23337486.2016.1 184420.

Crichton, B. (Executive Producer). (2018). *Without limits: Australia* [TV series]. BBC.

Corner, J. (2006). A fiction (un)like any other. *Critical Studies in Television*, 1(1), 89–96.

Cree, A., & Caddick, N. (2019). Unconquerable heroes: Invictus, redemption, and the cultural politics of narrative. *Journal of War and Culture Studies*, 13(3), 258–278. https://doi.org/10.1080/17526272.2019.1615707.

Der Derian, J. (2001). *Virtuous war: Mapping the military-industrial-media -entertainment network.* Westview.

Green, G., Emslie, C., O'Neill, D., Hunt, K., & Walker, S. (2010) Exploring the ambiguities of masculinity in accounts of emotional distress in the military among young ex-servicemen. *Social Science and Medicine*, 71, 1480–1488. https://doi .org/10.1016/j.socscimed.2010.07.015.

Guo, M. (2018). How television viewers use social media to engage with program-ming: The social engagement scale development and validation. *Journal of Broad-casting and Electronic Media*. 62(2), 195–214. https://doi.org/10.1080/08838151. 2018.1451856.

Haller, B. (2000). How the news frames disability: Print media coverage of the Amer-icans with Disabilities Act.' In B. M. Altman and S. N. Barnartt (Eds.). *Expanding the scope of social science research on disability (Vol. 1)* (pp. 55–83). JAI Press.

Hardin, M., & Hardin, B. (2004). The "supercrip" in sport media: Wheelchair ath-letes discuss hegemony's disabled hero. *Sociology of Sport Online*, 7(1). Retrieved October 21, 2020, from http://physed.otago.ac.nz/sosol/v7i1/v7i1_1.html.

Higate, P. R. (2003). *Military masculinities: Identity and the state.* Praeger.

Hill, S. (2017). Exploring disabled girls' self-representational practices online. *Girl-hood Studies*. 10(2), 114–130. https://doi.org/10.3167/ghs.2017.100209.

Howe, P. D., & Silva, C. F. (2017). The cyborgification of paralympic sport. *Move-ment and Sport Sciences*. 97, 17–25. https://doi.org/10.1051/sm/2017014.

Kelly, J. (2016). Western militarism and the political unity of sport. In A. Bairnier, J. Kelly and J. Woo (Eds.), *Routledge handbook of sport and politics* (pp. 277–292). Routledge.

Lorber, W., & Garcia, H. (2010). Not supposed to feel this: Traditional masculinity in psychotherapy with male veterans returning from Afghanistan and Iraq. *Psy-chotherapy: Theory, Research, Practice and Training*, 47(3), 296–305. https://doi .org/10.1037/a0021161.

McAllister, L., Callaghan, J. E. M., & Fellin, L. C. (2018). Masculinities and emotional expression in UK servicemen: "Big boys don't cry?" *Journal of Gender Studies*. 28(3), 257–270. https://doi.org/10.1080/09589236.2018.1429898.

McGillivray, D., O'Donnell, H., McPherson, G., & Misener, L. (2021). Repurposing the (super)crip: Media representations of disability at the Rio 2016 Paralympic Games. *Communication and Sport*, 9(1), 3–32. https://doi.org/10.1177/2167479519853496.

Melton, J., Miller, R., & Salmona, M. (2017). University student use of Twitter and Facebook: A study of posting in three countries. *Journal of Technical Writing and Communication*. 48(3), 331–358. https://doi.org/10.1177/0047281617724402.

Mills, B. (2010). Invisible television: The programmes no-one talks about even though lots of people watch them. *Critical Studies in Television*, 5(1), 1–16. https://doi.org/10.7227/CST.5.1.3.

Ministry of Defence. (April 26, 2018) Defence Secretary Launches First Ever Veterans Strategy and New Cross-Government Veterans Unit [Press release]. Retrieved October 19, 2020, from https://www.gov.uk/government/news/defence-secretary-launches-first-ever-veterans-strategy-and-new-cross-government-veterans-unit.

Mitchell, D. T. & Snyder, S. L. (Eds.), (1997) *The Body and Physical Difference: Discourses of Disability*. University of Michigan Press.

Nelson, J. A. (2000). The media role in building the disability community. *Journal of Mass Media Ethics*, 15(3) 180–93. https://doi.org/10.1207/S15327728JMME1503-4.

Ofcom. (October 25, 2018). Ofcom annual report 2017/18. Retrieved October 2, 2020, from https://www.ofcom.org.uk/__data/assets/pdf_file/0015/124422/BBC-annual-report.pdf.

———. (October 25, 2018). Ofcom representation and portrayal on BBC TV report. Retrieved October 2, 2020, from https://www.ofcom.org.uk/__data/assets/pdf_file/0022/124078/report-bbc-representation-portrayal.pdf.

O'Neil, J. M, Helms, B. J., Gable, R. K., David, L., & Wrightsman, L. (1986). Gender-role conflict scale: College men's fear of femininity. *Sex Roles*, 14(5), 335–350. https://doi.org/10.1007/BF00287583.

O'Neil, J., Good, G. E., & Holmes, S. (1995). Fifteen years of theory and research on men's gender role conflict: New paradigms for empirical research. In R. Levant and W. Pollack (Eds.). *The new psychology of men* (pp. 164-206). Basic Books.

O'Neil, J. M. (2008). Summarizing 25 years of research on men's gender role conflict using the gender role conflict scale: New research paradigms and clinical implications. *The Counseling Psychologist*, 36, 358–445. https://doi.org/10.1177/0011000008317057.

———. (2011). The psychology of men. In E., Altmaier and J., Hansen. (Eds.). *Oxford handbook of counseling psychology*. Oxford University Press.

Parmelee, J. H., & Bichard, S. L. (2012). *Politics and the Twitter revolution: How tweets influence the relationship between political leaders and the public*. Lexington Books.

Parsons, N. (Executive Producer). (2015). *Strictly Come Dancing Christmas Special* [TV special episode]. BBC.

Patterson, K. & Hughes, B. (2000). Disabled bodies. In: P. Hancock, B. Hughes, E. and Jagger (Eds.), *The body, culture and society: An introduction* (pp. 29–44). Open University Press.

Phillips, R. (2020). 'The stigmatized hero? A review of UK opinion polls and surveys on perceptions of British veterans in UK society. *Journal of Veterans Studies*. 6(1), 64–84. http://doi.org/10.21061/jvs.v6i1.150.

Pitchford-Hyde, J. & Parry, K. (2020). Veterans and the media: A pilot survey report on how UK veterans perceive media representations about military and post-military experiences. Report. University of Leeds. https://doi.org/10.5518/100/49.

Quinlan, M. M. & Bates, B. R. (2008). Dance and discourses of (dis)ability: Heather Mill's embodiment of disability on Dancing with the Stars. *Text and Performance Quarterly*, 28(1–2), 64–80. https://doi.org/10.1080/10462930701754325.

Richardson, N. (2016). "Whether you are gay or straight, I don't like to see effeminate dancing": effeminophobia in performance-level ballroom dance. *Journal of Gender Studies*, 2016, 27(2), 207–219. https://doi.org/10.1080/09589236.2016.1202105.

Ryan, F. (2016). It's time to stop calling disabled people "inspirational." *The Guardian*, September 7, 2016. Retrieved November 9, 2020, from https://www.the guardian.com/commentisfree/video/2016/sep/07/its-time-to-stop-calling-disabled -people-inspirational-video.

Scarry, E. (1985). *The body in pain: The making and unmaking of the world*. Oxford University Press.

Sloan, L. (2017). Who tweets in the United Kingdom? Profiling the Twitter population using the British social attitudes survey 2015. *Social Media and Society*. 3(1), 1–11. https://doi.org/10.1177/2056305117698981

Statista. (2019). Number of monthly active Twitter users worldwide from 1st quarter 2010 to 1st quarter 2019. Retrieved November 9, 2020, from https://www.statista .com/statistics/282087/number-of-monthly-active-twitter-users/.

Wester, S. R., & Vogel, D. L. (2012). The psychology of men: Historical developments, current research, and future directions. In N. A. Fouad, J. Carter, and L. Subich. (Eds.). *Handbook of counseling psychology*. American Psychological Association.

Chapter Eight

Nawaz Sharif

The Rise and Fall of a Pakistani Sher *(Big Cat)*

Sakina Jangbar

INTRODUCTION

Western media has stigmatized Muslim men as violent and deviant (Puar, 2007). In films and television, Muslim men are often depicted as "oversexed, degenerate . . . sadistic, treacherous, and low" (Said, 1979, p. 286). Narratives of Muslim women as "victims of male brutality who must be rescued" have constructed Muslim masculinity as the antithesis of democratic values of equality and respect for human rights (Ewing, 2008, p. 2). Because of these mediated representations, the West lacks a clear understanding of how masculinity is defined and perpetuated in Muslim countries. Even in scholarly literature, there are very few studies that make Muslim men visible as gendered subjects (Ouzgane, 2006). And when academics study Muslim men, they tend to focus on Arabic or Middle Eastern men, which creates an impression that Islam is a monolithic religion (De Sondy, 2015). My chapter focuses on Pakistani masculinity, which provides an opportunity "to read against the grain of mainstream Islamic tradition" and exposes Western audiences to the diversity within Islamic communities (De Sondy, 2015, p. 4). In the last 50 years, Pakistani politics has masculinized Islam "to the point of overwhelming its mystical-feminine expressions" even though the feminine side of Islam has functioned as its hidden backbone for centuries (Ahmed, 2006, p. 21). The Qur'an emphasizes five traits of believing men (submissiveness, altruism, steadfastness, righteousness, and combativeness); however, partial readings of the Qur'an are being used to create violent masculinities (Kabasakal Arat & Hasan, 2018). Suppression of Islam's feminine aspects has created a hypermasculine Pakistani identity that responds to the feminine form

Figure 8.1. Pakistan's Former Prime Minister Nawaz Sharif
Courtesy of Depositphotos Inc.

(symbolic or actual) with "horror/fear of that which seems alien and which then must be eliminated" (Ahmed, 2006, p. 22). In this chapter, I study manhood in Pakistan through the lens of GRCS model. Using Nawaz Sharif as my case study, I examine how hegemonic masculinity was reinforced with memes that humiliated Nawaz Sharif for being publicly emotional and therefore unmanly. See Figure 8.1.

REVIEW OF LITERATURE

Background Information on Pakistan's Former Prime Minister —
Nawaz Sharif

Once a three-term Prime Minister, Mian Mohammed Nawaz Sharif, born in 1949, now is a wanted man in Pakistan since he lives in exile in London after he failed to return home to face corruption charges (Associated Press, 2020). Nawaz Sharif was Pakistan's Prime Minister for three non-consecutive terms. Pakistan's Constitution outlines a parliamentary form of government in which powers are divided between the legislative, executive, and judicial branches. The President is a ceremonial figure head as the Prime Minister is the chief executive, responsible for running the federal government. Nawaz Sharif was first elected in 1990; however, he did not complete his term because the President of Pakistan dissolved the National Assembly—the lower house of the Parliament—in 1993. From 1993–1996, Nawaz Sharif was the opposition leader during Benazir Bhutto's administration. Nawaz Sharif was reelected as Prime Minister in 1997, but his government was dissolved in 1999 when the army took over in a bloodless coup (Dugger, 1999). After imprisonment and exile, Nawaz Sharif was reelected in 2013, but removed from office in 2017 by the Supreme Court of Pakistan on the basis of accusations of corruption stemming from the Panama Papers (Specia, 2017). The Panama Papers was a name given to the leak of 11.5 million files from the database of an offshore law firm, which implicated twelve national leaders (including Nawaz Sharif) and 143 politicians in illegal accumulation of wealth (Harding, 2016). Not only was Nawaz Sharif removed from office in 2017, he was also sentenced to 10 years in prison, fined $10.6 million, and received a life-time ban from politics (Alecci, 2018). The lifetime ban verdict was given because Nawaz Sharif had violated the articles of Pakistan's Constitution that dictate that national leaders should be people of good character (Hadid et al., 2018). Nawaz Sharif was released on bail in November 2019 for four weeks to receive medical treatment in the UK from which he never returned ("Pakistani court," 2020). Nawaz Sharif has been declared a fugitive by Pakistani courts and the government has approached UK for his extradition (Khan, 2020).

Sher (Big Cat) Imagery Employed by Nawaz Sharif

When Nawaz Sharif was Prime Minister, he branded himself as a *sher*. In Urdu, *sher* is a general term that refers to both tigers and lions, and Nawaz Sharif used feline imagery to situate himself as a powerful, courageous leader. Although their chubby, balding leader hardly represented a ferocious feline predator, Nawaz Sharif's supporters chanted *kon aya, sher aya* (who's here, a *sher* is here) in rallies and held aloft large stuffed tigers. At his home, two taxidermized lions, imported from Zimbabwe, flanked the staircase (Sethi, 2013). In the election campaign of 2013, Nawaz Sharif's daughter rented a rare white tigress from a party official and paraded her in rallies, chained inside the bed of a truck (Khan, 2013). In a country where most people are not literate, a symbol can play a key role in winning an election (Ghosh, 2013). Since masculinity is a cultural construct, the symbolism employed by Nawaz Sharif underscores cultural expectations of masculinity in Pakistan.

Significance of the Sher (Big Cat) Symbol in Islamic Cultures

The *sher* symbol occupies a prominent place in Islamic tradition. A *sher* represents a version of masculinity that is courageous and wise. The most famous Muslim associated with *sher*-like qualities is Ali ibn Abi Talib, cousin and son-in-law of Prophet Mohammed (Haylamaz, 2013). For his courage on the battlefield, Prophet Mohammed gave him the title of *Hyder-e-Karrar*—the lion who attacks swiftly (Saeed, 2019). Among South Asian Muslims, Ali is known as *Sher-e-Khuda* (Lion of God) and Shia Muslims invoke his name whenever embarking on tasks that are difficult—physically or psychologically (Saeed, 2019). In art, Ali is often portrayed with a lion and his famous double-bladed sword, Zulfiqar. As a symbol of Ali's strength, the figure of a lion or a tiger performs during Ashura—an annual event that commemorates the martyrdom of Ali's son, Hussain, and his family in fourteenth-century Iraq (Saeed, 2019).

Besides Ali, many Muslim warriors are remembered as lions and tigers. Saladin (1137–93), who led the Islamic forces during the crusades, was known as the Tiger of Islam. Omar al-Mukhtar (1860–1931), who led the Libyan resistance against the Italian colonial rule, was named the Lion of the Desert (Saeed, 2019). Tipu Sultan (1750-1799), the ruler of Mysore (South India), used the emblem of the tiger on his coins, wall decorations, soldiers' uniforms, and constructed a mechanical tiger intended to swallow the colonial soldiers (Brittlebank, 1995). Even contemporary Muslim leaders are associated with feline predators. Yasser Arafat, the Palestinian leader, was known as the Lion of Jerusalem and Muammar Ghaddafi, the Libyan leader, was photographed with lions and tigers, "making them masculine heroes for many young Muslims in occupied or disputed lands" (Saeed, 2019, p. 6). Thus, Nawaz Sharif tapped deep into the roots of Islamic culture when he adopted the *sher* imagery for his political party. Although this symbol provided him with the ethos of a strong, fearless leader, it also placed tremendous pressure on him to live up to the standards set by the legendary Muslim heroes. When Nawaz Sharif's masculine mask cracked under pressure, he became the laughing stock of the entire nation.

Unmasking of the Sher (Big Cat)

On August 10, 2017, a few days after the Supreme Court removed Nawaz Sharif from the office of the Prime Minister, he gave a speech in which he asked 22 times—*mujhey kyun nikala* (why was I removed). From behind a green bullet-proof screen, he stated, "I lost my government. In one minute, five judges dismissed me even though millions of people voted for me" (Ailaan TV). He threw up his hands in the air and shook his head to non-verbally indicate that the Supreme Court's decision was beyond his comprehension. He reiterated, "Five judges with a stroke of their pen sent your Prime Minister packing" (Ailaan TV). He asked the audience, "Can you bear this insult" (Ailaan TV)? His voice became high pitched as he continued to ask, "And why, why? Did I do corruption? Answer me, did I do corruption" (Ailaan TV)? The audience responded with, "no." Then, he asked again, "Why was I removed, why? I want to ask, why was I removed? When there is no stain of corruption on me, when there is no stain of kickbacks on me, there is no taint of commissions on me, thank God, then someone explain to me, someone explain to me, was I removed because I was responsible for Pakistan's progress" (Ailaan TV)? He stated that he is not worried about himself, but worried about the youth of the country, and advised his young supporters to not lose hope. Then he turned toward Pakistan's history and stated that for 70 years, no Prime Minister has finished his/her term, yet the dictators stay in power for 10 years and are supported by the judges. He said, "If we want a better future, we have to change. I have not come here to be reinstated. I am going home, I am being sent home. I am not here to beg. I only seek to improve your future" (Ailaan TV). Then he absurdly simplified the details of his corruption case and stated that he is being removed only because he did not take a salary from his son's company. He asked, "Do you understand any proper reason for removing me" (Ailaan TV)? As he paused, the camera captured an audience member waving a large stuffed tiger in the air. Nawaz Sharif ended his speech with this question, "Will you stand with me in changing Pakistan's destiny" (Ailaan TV)?

There were other topics in his speech such as the power of the Supreme Court to remove an elected Prime Minister, the history of military coups in Pakistan, the fact that no Prime Minister of Pakistan has been allowed to finish their term, and jobs for the youth. However, the audience became hyper focused on the *mujhey kyun nikala* (why was I removed) question as evidenced by the flood of memes and videos on social media on this topic. This fixation reveals a collective anxiety about masculinity and low tolerance for a display of male emotionality in public. Members of the Pakistani public were quick to punish this display of femininity in order to maintain cultural norms of manhood.

By repeating the question, *mujhey kyun nikala* (why was I removed) over and over in a high-pitched voice breaking with emotion, Nawaz Sharif became a caricature in Pakistan's politics. The *sher* (big cat) imagery of his campaign was based on hegemonic masculinity that valorizes the masculine aspects of Islam at the expense of feminine qualities that balance the faith. The *mujhey kyun nikala* (why was I removed) speech represents a rupture in the hyper-masculine image as feminine energy erupted in a vulnerable moment. Such moments present a challenge to hegemonic masculinity (Gesualdi, 2013), which is why Pakistanis were quick to question Nawaz Sharif's manliness. A "real man" in Pakistan is expected to handle pain and stress without complaining (Aurat Foundation, 2016) and gender norms are enforced rigidly for men who are in leadership positions (Gesualdi, 2013). Therefore, when Nawaz Sharif became emotional, he was severely punished for deviating from cultural expectations of masculine behavior. Social media was flooded with videos and memes on the *mujhey kyun nikala* (why was I removed) theme. The onslaught of humiliating material was relentless. The legendary humorist, Anwar Maqsood, wrote a 70-minute play titled, *Kyun Nikala*, that was performed at the Arts Council of Pakistan for weeks (Rizvi, 2018). The phrase has become so popular that the American comedian, Jeremy McLellan, used it to compare Donald Trump to Nawaz Sharif and also captioned it under a photo of his new born baby ("Mujhay kyun nikala," 2020; "Jeremy McLellen," 2018). Three years after the incident, I still receive forwards of memes and videos that have gone viral.

Utility of Studying Memes

Memes are useful to look at because they blend pop culture with politics and have become a primary expression of public participation in politics (Shifman, 2014). The term "meme" was first introduced by Richard Dawkins in 1976 to refer to small units of cultural information that spread through imitation just like human genes do (Dawkins, 2006). The "tag 'internet meme' is commonly applied to describe the propagation of items such as jokes, rumors, videos, and websites from person to person via the Internet" (Shifman, 2014, p. 2). Memes often recombine content to provide new perspectives. For example, the "I have a drone" meme challenged the rhetorical equivalence of Martin Luther King Jr. and U.S. President Barack Obama by calling out Obama's policy of drone attacks (Howley, 2016). This emerging form of participatory culture is significant as it permits citizens to challenge mainstream media narratives (Jenkins, 2006). This chapter also utilizes memes to see how Pakistani citizens challenged the narrative provided by their ousted Prime Minister and recombined his own words and images to humiliate him as unmanly.

This chapter focuses on how Nawaz Sharif was ridiculed for deviating from normative masculinity when he was removed from the office of the Prime Minister. Lacking competence in verbalizing emotions, Nawaz Sharif found himself repeatedly uttering the phrase—*mujhey kyun nikala* (why was I removed)—in a speech given after the dissolution of his government. I analyze the memes and videos created around the *mujhey kyun nikala* (why was I removed) phrase. My analysis highlights three themes: cognitive dysfunction, feminization, and homophobia, which I discuss in detail with examples. These themes show that masculinity in Pakistan is embedded in the negation of vulnerable beings, namely, women, children, animals, and members of the LGBTQ community. In the discussion section, I advance a proposal to expand the GRCS model. My study shows that fear of femininity and homosexuality, which are positioned at the center of the model, do not represent a comprehensive view of the fears that shape masculinity. The model would be more nuanced if "fear of cognitive dysfunction" were added to the heart of the GRCS model.

Theoretical Framework: GRCS

Research shows that masculinity is precarious. Men are not only expected to achieve and maintain their high status as men, but also suffer consequences if they fall short of strict masculine standards (Vandello & Bosson, 2013; Vandello et al., 2008). Although prescriptive masculine behavior can vary from culture to culture, men are expected to act in ways that align with cultural ideals of what it means to be a man. When men are unable to consistently perform masculinity, they often experience inner conflict and stress. Next, I examine four patterns of men's GRCS, types of role stress men experience because of discrepancies between the ideal and actual masculine self, and fear of femininity that lies at the heart of the model.

Patterns of Men's GRCS

GRCS occurs when "rigid, sexist, or restrictive gender roles result in restriction, devaluation, or violation of others or self" (O'Neil et al., 1995). O'Neil (2008) described four patterns of men's GRCS with the help of a model. On the right side of the model is restrictive emotionality (RE), which is "defined as having restrictions and fears about expressing one's feelings as well as restriction in finding words to express basic emotions" (p. 367). Not only do men worry about being judged for displaying their emotions, but they also lack the language skills for expressing basic emotions. Holmes (2015) pointed out that there is remarkably little research on how heterosexual men interpret emotions (their own as well as others') and how they act upon their interpretations. Since emotions are central to how we operate in the world, it is helpful to focus on the societal factors that shape emotional expressions of men, rather than visualize men's emotionality as a "biological or psychological given" (Holmes, 2015, p. 189). On the left side of the model is "personal attitudes about success pursued through competition and power," concisely labeled as "success, power, and competition issues" (SPC) (p. 367). On the top side of the model is the category of conflicts between work and family relations (CBWFR), which reflects the health problems and stress men suffer from when they are unable to balance work with family time and leisure activities. On the bottom of the model is the category of restrictive and affectionate behavior between men (RABBM), which represents "restrictions in expressing one's feelings and thoughts with other men and difficulty touching other men" (p. 367).

Types of Role Stress

When men are unable to meet the cultural expectations of masculine behavior, they experience condemnation and negative evaluations from others (Pleck, 1981). There are three types of role stress: discrepancy, trauma, and dysfunction. Discrepancy stress results when individuals try to conform to gender roles with varying degrees of success, and compensate for the discrepancies with hypermasculine behavior (Pleck, 1995). Trauma stress occurs when boys and men undergo difficult experiences as part of the socialization process, and these experiences shape their identities and future relationships. Although men as victims of sexism is a contentious subject, there is research that discusses the trauma men experience during gender role socialization (Brooks & Good, 2001; Lisak, 2001). Dysfunction is the third type of stress identified by Pleck (1995) and it is connected to negative consequences of restrictive gender norms. Negative consequences entail dysfunctional behaviors that either harm the male himself or others associated with him. The three stressors identified by Pleck (1995) affect men's relationships, career, and health, and therefore expand our understanding of the role conflict and their consequences on men's identities and behaviors.

Fear of Femininity

At the heart of the GRCS model lies a fear of femininity (Pompper, 2010). Fear of femininity consists of "negative emotions associated with stereotypic feminine attitudes, values, and behaviors" (O'Neil, 2008, p. 367). Construction of a masculine identity is a relational process in which to be a man is to not be a woman (Gutterman, 1994). Men are socialized early in life to not be feminine, which leads some men to counter their fear of femininity by becoming hypermasculine—acting aggressively, resolving conflicts through violence, developing their muscles or asserting dominance over what is perceived as weak (MacKinnon, 2003; Brod, 1987).

This chapter is devoted to studying masculinity in Pakistan. The goal is to discover how masculinity is defined in Pakistan by studying the memes and videos that were made in response to the infamous speech. Since masculinity is a cultural construct, this analysis sheds light on why a break in expected decorum of a public official led to such a strong and sustained response from the Pakistani public. My research question is as follows:

RQ: Which themes are embedded in the memes and videos that were made in response to the *mujhey kyun nikala* (why was I removed) speech?

METHOD

The method employed in this chapter is thematic analysis of the memes and videos associated with Nawaz Sharif's speech. Thematic analysis is a research technique that codes and interprets texts (speeches, pictures, documents) in order to uncover patterns or themes. This method is employed when the researcher is concerned with social meanings embedded in texts (Hesse-Biber & Leavy, 2011). A thematic analysis entails six steps: becoming familiar with the texts; generating initial codes; examining the codes for patterns or themes; reviewing the themes to ensure that data supports the themes; defining the themes; and writing a report on the findings (Braun & Clarke, 2006).

Data Collection

I searched for memes and videos on Google with the phrase *mujhey kyun nikala (*why was I removed) for any hits prior to December 15, 2020. The results were organized into groups based on how each image or video represented Nawaz Sharif. An initial categorization yielded several themes: Nawaz Sharif depicted as an infant or child, represented as an animal or interacting with animals, linked with filthy substances like sewer or trash, represented as a female dancer, associated with traditional symbols of femininity (henna, jewelry, make-up) or emotionality (tears), depicted as a devil, portrayed as a drag queen or shown as receiving a beating. If a particular category had only one image, I searched on Google with more precise phrases such as "Nawaz Sharif baby" or "Nawaz Sharif animal." Some images and videos were excluded as they were not relevant to my focus on masculine social identity. Now that I have explained my method, I will move on to my analysis.

Data Analysis

I analyzed the memes and videos that I had collected on this topic. I refined the categories of memes and videos that I had collected and grouped earlier and arrived at three themes—cognitive dysfunction, feminization, and homophobia. The images that depicted Nawaz Sharif as a baby, child, or animal were grouped into one theme—cognitive dysfunction—because these images depicted loss of agency, mental acuity, and judgment. The images and videos that incorporated female dancers and feminine symbols such as tears, henna, jewelry, and make-up were classified into one theme—feminization. The final theme was homophobia and it included images that showed Nawaz Sharif as a drag queen or as transgendered.

FINDINGS

My analysis includes 15 memes and one video. Three elements emerged from reviewing the memes and videos on the topic of *mujhey kyun nikala* (why was I removed): (a) cognitive dysfunction, (b) feminization, and (c) homophobia. See Table 8.1.

Table 8.1. Thamatic Distribution of 16 Texts (15 Memes and 1 Video)

Infants & Children	Filth	Adult Acting as Child	Animals	Women	Feminine Symbols	Homophobic
2	1	1	7	2	1	2

Theme One: Cognitive Dysfunction

Two memes depict Nawaz Sharif as an infant or a school-aged child, which shows that after the *mujhey kyun nikala* speech, he was perceived as not having the mental capacity or agency to be a leader. In Pakistan, masculinity is associated with rationality, objectivity, aggressiveness, and assertiveness (Aurat Foundation, 2016). These attributes imply that male leaders are expected to respond to stressful situations in a rational rather than emotional manner and take decisive actions rather than complain about unfair procedures. When Nawaz Sharif was unable to maintain the masculine façade, he was humiliated in memes and videos as a baby or a child lacking in agency, objectivity, and judgment. One meme simply superimposed Nawaz Sharif's face onto a baby whereas the other meme was more complex. In the more complex meme, we are shown a schoolboy standing outside the classroom with this caption—"When the entire class was making noise but the teacher only throws you out and you are like: *Mujhey kyun nikala*." In his speech, Nawaz Sharif repeated several times that he does not understand why he was removed from office. Thus, the meme depicts him as an undisciplined child who not only breaks the rules, but also fails to understand what the rules are and that there are consequences for breaking them. Moreover, the meme shows that Nawaz Sharif felt singled out for punishment when it seems to him that all politicians engage in corruption.

One meme paints a picture of Nawaz Sharif as a dirt-covered child to highlight his crimes and a lack of good sense. The meme I examined includes a photo of a young boy covered in filth from head to toe with an open drain behind him. The caption reads—*mujhey kyun nikala*. The filth in the meme stands for corruption, but the interesting thing is that the child seems unaware that he should not play with trash swimming in sewage, and is complaining about being removed from his dirty play area. Once again, the meme depicts Nawaz Sharif as unable to tell the difference from clean sources of income versus criminal activities, and implies that he wants to return to his illegal business schemes.

I examined one video in which Nawaz Sharif is portrayed as an adult male who is acting like a child. The video is set up like a short play which begins with Nawaz Sharif showing up at the door of a party leader in the middle of the night asking *mujhey kyun nikala* (why was I removed). The party leader comforts Nawaz Sharif and tells him to lie down and get some sleep. Nawaz Sharif puts his head on the party leader's lap and the party leader soothes him like a mother would comfort an upset child. Once Nawaz Sharif has fallen asleep, the party leaders have a meeting to decide how to treat the former Prime Minister. The loss of agency depicted in the video is a form of infantilization even though Nawaz Sharif was shown as an adult male rather than an infant or a child.

I examined seven memes which portray loss of agency and mental capacity by depicting Nawaz Sharif as an animal culturally not associated with wisdom or masculinity. One meme shows Nawaz Sharif riding a donkey, another shows him addressing a group of donkeys, and yet another meme shows a donkey looking in a mirror and seeing a lion in the reflection. To be called a donkey is an insult in Pakistan because donkeys are visualized as unintelligent, and are often used to pull carts for transporting good across the city. Some memes depict Nawaz Sharif with lions but in unflattering ways. For example, in one meme, a lion is held captive on the operating table by a medical team, and the caption reads PML-N at Lahore ICU ward. (Nawaz Sharif was a candidate of the PML-N party.) In another meme, a dog is photoshopped with a lion's mane with a caption that reads *babar kutta*. *Kutta* means dog and *babar sher* is a male lion. This meme reduces the *sher* imagery employed by Nawaz Sharif to that of a dog masquerading as the king of the jungle. Moreover, some Muslims believe dogs to be ritually impure (Mikhail, 2017), which adds another layer of complexity to the meme. Another meme shows a male lion walking away while Nawaz Sharif tugs its tail, and the caption states that the lion has abandoned the PML-N party. One meme depicts a male lion with Nawaz Sharif's face superimposed on the lion's face and the caption reads "Bald Lion: Mate, believe me, I am a *sher*." Physical attractiveness is the second most important trait to Pakistani men, second only to their provider identity (Aurat Foundation, 2016). One reason a male lion looks magnificent is because he has a mane that makes him look kingly. To depict Nawaz Sharif as a bald lion is to highlight his distance from a lion, not only in behavior but also in appearance. Moreover, the meme emphasizes that the *sher* identity was always a pretense.

Theme Two: Feminization

Two memes portray Nawaz Sharif as a woman, which shows that after the *mujhey kyun nikala* speech, he lost the high-value position given to males in patriarchal societies. For Pakistani men, a "real man" is not effeminate; he behaves differently from a woman (Aurat Foundation, 2016). A study found that Pakistani college men tend to endorse traditional masculine ideology to a greater extent than American college students (Rashid et al., 2016). Although both men and women in Pakistan embrace positive aspects of femininity, the superior position of men is perpetuated through the institutions of family, religion, laws, and popular culture (Aurat Foundation, 2016). Therefore, memes and videos that depict Nawaz Sharif as a woman seek to demote him from his high-status position. In this category of memes, there is no simple super-imposition of Nawaz Sharif's face on a woman's body. Instead, the message is multi layered as memes depict him as a particular kind of a woman. In one meme, Nawaz Sharif is portrayed as an exotic dancer in a bright green outfit decorated with embroidery and sequins and a bodice constructed to emphasize the breasts. The shade of the dancer's outfit is similar to the green tint created by the bullet proof screen used during the *mujhey kyun nikala* speech. The dancer is wearing heavy bridal jewelry and henna, which are feminine symbols of fertility and beauty. The image is not only of a woman, but a woman who dances for money. In Pakistani culture, sex work is illegal and taboo, therefore, memes that depict Nawaz Sharif as a sex worker highlight not only his illegal money grabbing moves, but also a lack of shame regarding his conduct.

A twist in the feminized depictions of Nawaz Sharif is a meme in which his face is super imposed on the Mona Lisa portrait. The caption under the Mona Lisa meme reads—*Choona Lisa*. In Urdu, *choona* literally means chalk, but the figurative meaning is to cover up one's crimes and pretend to be innocent of all wrong doings. This meme not only feminizes Nawaz Sharif, but also associates him with the deception of Western colonizers who destroyed the economies and cultures of the nations they colonized and now pretend that they are a benevolent and freedom-loving force in the world.

In one meme, Nawaz Sharif is portrayed as a woman, not through super imposition of his face on women's bodies, but through symbols typically associated with women. For example, the meme I examined had a picture of a male lion on a coffee mug. The lion is curled up in a fetal position on the floor, shedding rivers of tears that have pooled around his body. Once again, the caption reads: *Mujhey kyun nikala*. The fetal position indicates fear or child-like behavior, and tears portray an emotional response traditionally considered to be feminine or childish.

Theme Three: Homophobia

Two memes depict Nawaz Sharif as a transgender woman, which highlights that masculinity not only entails a rejection of femininity, but also dictates a heterosexual identity. Transgender women are a marginalized community in Pakistan although laws have been passed recently to protect their interests (Khan & Greene, 2013). They are often ostracized by the society and abandoned by their families, which leaves them with fewer options for education and legal employment. Transgender women typically end up as entertainers and sex workers and are often subjected to scorn and ridicule (Real Stories, 2016). To portray Nawaz Sharif as a transgender woman is to place him in the lowest social category in Pakistan. This meme shows Nawaz Sharif as a woman in bright red clothing with a light scarf around her head and a blue handbag slung over her shoulder. His facial image has been altered to add lipstick, blush, eye make-up, and hair. The caption reads: *Day dana dan: Mujhey kyun nikala*. *Day dana dan* is a slang term, and it refers to an action being performed repeatedly and consecutively. Another meme shows Nawaz Sharif dancing in a yellow-colored woman's outfit, surrounded by drag queens. Production quality is low in these memes and no effort is made to blend in his facial features. Instead, his face is garishly and inartistically superimposed on the bodies of colorfully dressed transgender women.

The themes of cognitive dysfunction, feminization, and homophobia in the memes created after Nawaz Sharif's *mujhey kyun nikala* speech show that masculinity in Pakistan is constructed negatively. In other words, to be a man is to be not a child, not a woman, not an animal, and not a member of the LGBTQ community. Nawaz Sharif became associated with "unmanly" attributes because he was unable to contain his emotional response after being removed from his position as Prime Minister and also because he lacked the linguistic capacity to express disappointment in a competent manner. Like a broken record, he found himself asking the same question over and over. The audience immediately turned his question into a catchy phrase that denoted his fall from a *sher*-like manhood and punished him by creating memes and spoof videos meant to humiliate him by associating him with babies, children, animals, women, and the LGBTQ community.

DISCUSSION AND CONCLUSION

My chapter on Nawaz Sharif concurs with most aspects of the GRCS model but proposes an addition that would make the model more nuanced. First, I will discuss the aspects of the model that align with my study and then propose a revision to the model based on my findings.

Findings that Expand the GRCS Model

The GRCS model posits that men's behavior is constrained by sexist values, which dictate that men should contain their emotions even in challenging circumstances. In the event that emotions leak out, men are shamed for being too sensitive or feminine. My study on Pakistani masculinity concurs that deviations from cultural standards of masculinity result in loss of status, and the wayward person is punished to prevent future infractions and to preserve traditional norms of behavior deemed appropriate for men.

The GRCS model also illustrates that masculine standards are created around rejection of femininity and homosexuality. Results from my study also suggest that manliness in Pakistan is defined in oppositional terms—a man is not a woman or a child, nor does he display any behavior that deviates from heterosexuality.

The GRCS model explains that men's emotional responses are socially constrained and men lack words for expressing emotions appropriately. Findings reported in this chapter also suggest that Nawaz Sharif was overcome with emotion, but he lacked the words with which he could communicate his distress and chagrin at being removed from his high post of Prime Minister. His linguistic incompetence led to repetition of a phrase, which in turn led to loss of respect and status. I will now move on to discuss one way in which the GRCS model could be improved.

Proposed Revision: Fear of Cognitive Dysfunction

The GRCS model posits that men fear being perceived as feminine and homosexual; however, the model does not account for fear of cognitive dysfunction. My study on Pakistani masculinity suggests that men are expected to be rational, intelligent, and display sound judgment. In fact, the dominant theme in the memes and video that I analyzed was cognitive dysfunction. When Nawaz Sharif expressed that he did not understand why he was removed from the office of the prime minister, he was perceived as lacking in intelligence. Not only did Nawaz Sharif admit that he could not grasp the reasons for his removal, he also repeatedly asked why he was removed, which implies immaturity. The manner in which he was ridiculed after that speech shows that when men fail to demonstrate mental acuity and judgment, they are perceived as lacking the sense of mature adults. Currently, the GRCS model does not accommodate intelligence, rationality, and sound judgment. These traits can be grouped under "fear of cognitive dysfunction." Cognitive dysfunction includes fear of being perceived as mentally ill, unintelligent or lacking in agency and judgement, and needs to be included in the center of the model, along with fear of femininity and homosexuality. This addition has significant implications for masculinity studies. It can perhaps explain why men find it difficult to seek help for mental health issues, feel the need to mansplain in situations where a woman has more expertise on the subject or hesitate to admit that they were wrong or might have misunderstood the situation.

For male political leaders, the issue of mental acuity becomes magnified as their actions are monitored and covered by the news media as well as archived for posterity. This level of exposure perhaps makes it difficult to admit mistakes or propose a change of course as the public might perceive that as being "weak" or "unmanly." A good example of this is the issue of mask wearing during the COVID-19 public health crisis. Initially, the U.S. president, on the advice of experts on infectious diseases, took the stance that wearing masks was not necessary to stop the spread of the virus. However, when experts began to realize their mistake and encouraged people to wear masks, President Trump found it difficult to retract his position. Thus, wearing masks not only became a political issue, but also presented a challenge for navigating cultural ideas of masculinity. Could the president admit that he was wrong or change his position on wearing masks without appearing weak to his supporters? A revised GRCS model could explore these questions as a crisis in the performance of masculinity.

In conclusion, men internalize masculinity standards to their own as well as societal detriment. It is already difficult to break away from problematic cultural constructs, but when the media becomes involved, it becomes even harder. Boys and men learn from movies and video games that men must be tough and hard, both physically and psychologically. These standards are difficult to maintain as they require men to negate many aspects of their emotions and deny their vulnerabilities. In a crisis, it becomes almost impossible to live up to those standards, as Nawaz Sharif found out. Total control over emotions and tone is unrealistic. Men are human beings who have a right to develop their capacity to feel and express a wide range of emotions in an appropriate manner so that they can receive the support they need to carry them through the various challenges that life presents. Eve Ensler (2009), the playwright, notes that when men are not allowed to embrace their feminine sides, they become violent. Indeed, bullets are tears that hardened because they were not allowed to fall (Ensler, 2009). Similarly, intelligence and scientific thinking requires admission of errors so that we can make progress, but masculinity standards perhaps communicate a different message to boys and men. When fear of cognitive dysfunction controls men's behaviors, it becomes difficult to respond to crises in dynamic ways.

Limitations and Future Directions

My findings are limited as my research was focused on a single case study of a politician in Pakistan and a small data set. Future studies could study fear of cognitive dysfunction in different cultural contexts to verify its prevalence and impact and chart how it influences decisions made by men.

REFERENCES

Ahmed, D. S. (2006). Gender and Islamic spirituality: A psychological view of 'low' fundamentalism. In L. Ouzgane (Ed.), *Islamic masculinities* (pp. 11–34). Zed Books.

Ailaan TV. (2017, August 10). *Nawaz Sharif speech 10 August 2017 @pmln_org* [Video]. YouTube https://youtu.be/O1YMkXCfbRY.

Alecci, S. (2018, July 6). Former Pakistan PM Sharif sentenced to 10 years over Panama Papers. *International Consortium of Investigative Journalists* https://www.icij.org/investigations/panama-papers/former-pakistan-pm-sharif-sentenced-to-10-years-over-panama-papers/.

Associated Press. (2020, December 2). Pakistani court declares ex-PM Sharif fugitive from justice. ABC News. Downloaded March 31, 2021, from https://rb.gy/qe54f9.

Aurat Foundation, Gender Equity Program. (2016). *Comparative analysis of masculinity and femininity in Pakistan: A qualitative study.* http://af.org.pk/gep/images/GEP%20Gender%20Studies/Comparative%20Analysis%20of%20Masculinity%20and%20Femininity%20in%20Pakistan.pdf.

Braun, V., & Clarke, V. (2006). Using thematic analysis in psychology. *Qualitative Research in Psychology, 3,* 77–101.

Brittlebank, K. (1995). Sakti and barakat: The power of Tipu's tiger: An examination of the tiger emblem of Tipu Sultan of Mysore. *Modern Asian Studies, 29*(2), 257–269.

Brod, H. (1987). Introduction: Themes and theses of men's studies. In H. Brod (Ed.), *The making of masculinities: The new men's studies* (pp. 1–17). Allen and Unwin.

Brooks, G. R., & Good, G. E. (2001). Introduction. In G. R. Brooks and G. E. Goods (Eds.), *The new handbook of psychotherapy and counseling with men: A comprehensive guide to settings, problems, and treatment approaches* (pp. 3–21). Jossey-Bass.

Dawkins, R. (2006). *The selfish gene: 30th anniversary edition.* Oxford University Press.

De Sondy, A. (2015). *The crisis of Islamic masculinities*. Bloomsbury.

Dugger, C. W. (1999, October 13). Coup in Pakistan: The overview; Pakistan army seizes power hours after prime minister dismisses his military chief. *New York Times*. https://www.nytimes.com/1999/10/13/world/coup-pakistan-overview-pakistan-army-seizes-power-hours-after-prime-minister.html.

Ensler, E. (2009). Embrace your inner girl. *TED: Ideas Worth Spreading*. https://www.ted.com/talks/eve_ensler_embrace_your_inner_girl/transcript?language=en.

Ewing, K. P. (2008). *Stolen honor: Stigmatizing Muslim men in Berlin*. Stanford University Press.

Gesualdi, M. (2013). Man tears and masculinities: News coverage of John Boehner's tearful episodes. *Journal of Communication Inquiry, 37*(4), 304–321.

Ghosh, P. (2013, May 16). Nawaz Sharif, the lion (or tiger?) of Pakistan. *International Business Times* https://www.ibtimes.com/nawaz-sharif-lion-or-tiger-pakistan-1262417.

Gutterman, D. S. (1994). Postmodernism and the interrogation of masculinity. In H. Brod and M. Kaufman (Eds.), *Theorizing masculinities* (pp. 219–238). Sage.

Hadid, D., Sattar, A., & Neuman, S. (2018, April 13). Pakistan's high court bans ousted Prime Minister Sharif from politics. *NPR* https://www.npr.org/sections/thetwo-way/2018/04/13/602092137/pakistans-high-court-bans-ousted-prime-minister-sharif-from-politics.

Harding, L. (2016, April 5). What are the Panama Papers? A guide to history's biggest data leak. *Guardian* https://www.theguardian.com/news/2016/apr/03/what-you-need-to-know-about-the-panama-papers.

Haylamaz, R. (2013). *Ali Ibn Abi Talib: Hero of chivalry*. Tughra Books.

Hesse-Biber, S. N., & Leavy, P. (2011). *The practice of qualitative research* (2nd ed.). Sage.

Holmes, M. (2015). Men's emotions: Heteromasculinity, emotional reflexivity, and intimate relationships. *Men and Masculinities, 18*(2), 176–192.

Howley, K. (2016). 'I have a drone': Internet memes and the politics of culture. *Interactions: Studies in Communication and Culture, 7*(2), 155–175.

Jenkins, H. (2006). *Fans, bloggers, and gamers: Exploring participatory culture*. New York University Press.

"Jeremy McLellen welcomes daughter with tribute to Nawaz Sharif." (2018, May 19). Tribune Express https://tribune.com.pk/story/1714088/jeremy-mclellen-welcomes-daughter-tribute-nawaz-sharif

Kabasakal Arat, Z. F., & Hasan, A. (2018). Muslim masculinities: What is the prescription of the Qur'an? *Journal of Gender Studies, 27*(7), 788–801.

Khan, R. S. (2013, May 17). The mysterious case of the white tigress. *Dawn*. https://www.dawn.com/news/1011661/the-mysterious-case-of-the-white-tigress.

Khan, S., & Greene, J. (2019, January 31). What Pakistan gets right and the US gets wrong on trans rights. *CNN* https://www.cnn.com/2019/01/31/opinions/united-states-pakistan-transgender-rights-khan-greene/index.html.

Lisak, D. (2001). Male survivors of trauma. In G. R. Brooks and G. E. Goods (Eds.), *The new handbook of psychotherapy and counseling with men: A comprehensive guide to settings, problems, and treatment approaches* (pp. 263–277). Jossey-Bass.

McKinnon, K. (2003). *Representing men: Maleness and masculinity in the media.* Oxford University Press.

Mikhail, A. (2017, July 26). The moment in history when Muslims began to see dogs as dirty, impure, and evil. *Quartz India* https://rb.gy/ultgxr.

"Mujhay kyun nikala, Jeremy McLellan mocks Donald Trump." (2020, November 6). Global Village Space https://www.globalvillagespace.com/mujhay-kyun-nikala -jeremy-mclellan-mocks-donald-trump/.

O'Neil, J. M. (2008). Summarizing 25 years of research on men's gender role conflict using the Gender Role Conflict Scale: New research paradigms and clinical impli- cations. *Counseling Psychologist, 36*, 358–445.

O'Neil, J. M., Good, G. E., & Holmes, S. (1995). Fifteen years of theory and research on men's gender role conflict: New paradigms for empirical research. In R. F. Levant and W. S. Pollack (Eds.), *A new psychology of men* (pp. 164–206). Basic Books.

"Pakistani court issues arrest warrant for former PM Sharif." (2020, September 15). *ABC News* https://abcnews.go.com/International/wireStory/pakistani-court-issues -arrest-warrant-pm-sharif-73024846.

Ouzgane, L. (2006). The rape continuum: Masculinities in Ben Jelloun's and El Saa- dawi's works. In S. M. Whitehead (Ed.), *Men and Masculinities: Critical Concepts in Sociology*, vol. V. Routledge.

Pleck, J. H. (1981). *The myth of masculinity.* MIT Press.

Pleck, J. H. (1995). The gender role strain paradigm: An update. In R. F. Levant and W. S. Pollack (Eds.), *A new psychology of men* (pp. 11–32). Basic Books.

Pompper, D. (2010). Masculinities, the metrosexual, and media images: Across dimensions of age and ethnicity. *Sex Roles, 63*, 682–696.

Paur, J. K. (2007). *Terrorist assemblages: Homonationalism in queer times.* Duke University Press.

Rashid, T., Yasin, M., & Massoth, N. (2000). Pakistani males: An example of tra- ditional masculine socialization. *Society for the Psychological Study of Men and Masculinity Bulletin, 5*(3), 25–26.

Real Stories. (2016, December 30). *Pakistan's transgenders: Hidden lives.* YouTube https://www.youtube.com/watch?v=cvehhXaFh8Uandfeature=youtu.be.

Rizvi, A. (2018, August 15). Review: Anwar Maqsood's new play uses 'black face' for cheap laughs. *Cutacut* https://cutacut.com/2018/08/15/review-anwar-maqsoods -new-play-uses-blackface-for-cheap-laughs/.

Saeed, Y. (2019). Lions of Islam: Symbols of masculine power in the devotional art of India and Pakistan. *Tasveer Ghar* http://www.tasveergharindia.net/essay/lions -islam-manly-sufis.

Said, E. W. (1979). *Orientalism*: Random House.

Sethi, M. (2013, April 1). Watch the throne: Nawaz Sharif on the cusp of power. *Caravan* https://caravanmagazine.in/reportage/watch-throne.

Shifman, L. (2014). *Memes in digital culture.* The MIT Press.

Specia, M. (2017, July 28). How the Panama Papers changed Pakistani politics. *New York Times* https://www.nytimes.com/2017/07/28/world/asia/panama-papers -pakistan-nawaz-sharif.html.

Vandello, J. A., & Bosson, J. K. (2013). Hard won and easily lost: A review and synthesis of theory and research on precarious manhood. *Psychology of Men and Masculinity, 14*(2), 101–113.

Vandello, J. A., Bosson, J. K., Cohen, D., Burnaford, R. M., & Weaver, J. R. (2008). Precarious manhood. *Journal of Personality and Social Psychology, 95*(6), 1325–1339.

Chapter Nine

The Machismo Conflict of Bad Bunny's *Yo Perreo Sola* in Reggaetón

Nathian Shae Rodriguez

INTRODUCTION

Grammy Award winning artist Bad Bunny is a Puerto Rican rapper, singer, and songwriter. Although his musical origins in music began in Latin Trap and reggaetón, Bad Bunny's music has crossed over musical genres and global audiences. His music addresses racism, politics, gender, identity, and often questions the toxic masculinity entrenched in Latinx/a/o culture. His personal style also has bended traditional gender norms of machismo— a strong, exaggerated sense of manliness that assumes virility, courage, strength, and entitlement to dominate are attributes of masculinity. Bad Bunny often is shown in media with painted nails and feminized clothing. He identifies as a straight cisgender male and a proud ally of the LGBTQ community. In his music video, *Yo Perreo Sola*, released 2020, Bad Bunny dresses as a woman and dances seductively. The song's message centers on consent and challenges harassment against women. The video drew praise from some and criticism from others, including many who berated Bad Bunny for being effeminate and gay (Cepeda, 2018).

Bad Bunny's performance in *Yo Perreo Sola* serves as a counterhegemonic portrayal to traditional gender roles. Violations or deviation from patriarchal male gender roles may cause negative outcomes, particularly for men, known as GRC/GRS (Levant, 1996). This chapter's research findings explore social media discourse around the release of the video *Yo Perreo Sola*, employing a textual analysis using a lens of Gender Role Conflict (GRC). The study examines how individuals used Twitter to create meaning around machismo identity in Latinx/a/o pop culture, specifically when it deviates from traditional cultural norms in reggaetón. This chapter examines how a mediated pop culture text can serve as a situational source for GRC, helping to better understand how pop culture icons provide both a space to challenge hegemonic notions of masculine ideologies and a space of conflict for gender identity formation. This chapter first will provide background information on Bad Bunny and *Yo Perreo Solo*, followed by a review of literature on GRC, GRS, reggaetón, and machismo before revealing findings and implications.

El Conejo Malo. Bad Bunny, born Benito Martínez Ocasio to working-class parents in Puerto Rico, identifies as a cisgender heterosexual recording artist who combines the aesthetics of Latin trap and reggaetón in his music. He first burst onto the música urbana [urban music] scene at the age of 22 in 2016 and, since then, has had several Spanish-language chart-topping hits and an English-language crossover hit with Cardi B and J Balvin. He also is well known for his nail art and renouncement of gender norms, particularly in fashion. Bad Bunny openly has called out homophobia and preconceived notions on how women should look, dress, and act, redefining the masculine genre of reggaetón with his emotional vulnerability in lyrics that highlight depression, and mental illness (Cepeda, 2018). In the 2019 video to *Caro* [*Expensive*], Bad Bunny opens the video getting his nails painted. Then, within seconds, transforms into a woman who performs the rest of the rap verses. The video also highlights a variety of women not typically seen in reggaetón, rap, or Latinx/a/o videos, including a pregnant woman, a drag queen, and a girl with Down Syndrome. Bad Bunny's artistry, however, is not without criticism. Bad Bunny has been called out for his objectification-of-women lyrics by many.

This study highlights reaction to a single from Bad Bunny's second album entitled *YHLQMDLG*, an acronym for *Yo Hago Lo Que Me Da La Gana* [*I Do Whatever I Want*], released on February 29, 2020. The album debuted at number one on the Billboard Top Latin Albums Chart, number 2 on the Billboard 200 Albums Chart, and is the highest-charting Spanish-language album ever on Billboard to-date (Yglesias, 2020). To promote the album, Bad Bunny performed one of the album's tracks *Ignorantes* [*Ignorants*] on *Late Night With Jimmy Fallon* wearing a pink jacket, flowing skirt, earrings, and a t-shirt that read "Mataron a Alexa, no a un hombre con falda [They killed Alexa, not a man in a skirt]," condemning the murder of Alex Negrón Luciano, a Puerto Rican transwoman who was shot and killed for using a woman's bathroom.

Despite Bad Bunny's highly visible nail polishing, gender-bending fashion, and LGBTQ advocacy, many were surprised when the reggaetón artist dressed in drag for the *Yo Perreo Sola* video, which loosely translates to *I Twerk Alone*, a single off the *YHLQMDLG* album (Cepeda, 2018). In the video, released on March 27, 2020, he appears in drag three times. In his first appearance, he is dressed in a shiny ruby red shirt, skirt, and matching boots. In the second, he dawns a mixed-print pant suit with a long-haired wig. In his final appearance, he is in a black bodysuit with a long blonde wig. In all instances he wears fake breasts, makeup, and earrings. Throughout the video he perreas [dances] and sings about empowering women and respect. He also appears out of drag wearing bright colors while dancing. In one scene Bad Bunny is bare chested, chained, and surrounded by women on thrones (two of which hold his chains). The video closes with a black screen and red text that reads: "SI NO QUIERE BAILAR CONTIGO, RESPETA, ELLA PERREA SOLA [IF SHE DOESN'T WANT TO DANCE WITH YOU, RESPECT HER, SHE TWERKS ALONE]."

Bad Bunny told *Rolling Stone* magazine that he wrote it from the perspective of a woman, stating he sometimes feels like the women he sings about (Exposito, 2020). In the article he reveals "I have always felt like there [was] a part of me that is very feminine, but I never felt as masculine as I did the day I dressed up like a drag queen" (para. 38). His video, and his performance in it, was met with mixed reviews from fans and other musicians alike. International popstar and Grammy-winner Ricky Martin praised Bad Bunny, stating he "resonates with a generation that is, at the moment, discovering who they really are. It is very refreshing to witness in an industry known for its machismo" (Exposito, 202, para. 40). Fellow Puerto Rican rapper, and one-time collaborator, Anuel AA, however, was not a fan. Hours after the video premiered, Anuel posted on Instagram, a disparaging remark of "El conejo malo jugando a los transformers [The Bad Bunny playing transformers.]" followed by ten vomiting emojis. Seemingly, the tweet was part of a series of Instagram comments Anuel made calling out other artists in the music industry for being "tontos e hipócritas [fools and hypocrites]." He specifically named fellow Latin music artists Daddy Yankee, Nicky Jam, Farruko, Ñengo Flow and Kendo (as well as tagged Residente, Lunay, J Balvin, and Jhay Cortez) as the only artists he wanted to remain friends with, by writing "No puedo irme más na en contra de mis ideales por un negocio!!!!!!! [I can no longer go against my ideals for a business!!!!!!!]" Many fans of Bad Bunny noted Bad Bunny's name was visibly absent from the posts and Anuel did not follow him on any social platforms. The fans, as well as LGBTQ activists and allies, immediately replied to Anuel on various social media platforms for being homophobic and machista. Anuel quickly became a trending topic on Twitter under the hashtag #AnuelIsOverParty. Anuel's commentary emphasized the machismo ethos of reggaetón. It also places a spotlight on Bad Bunny's performance in *Yo Perreo Sola* as a source of GRC/GRS among its viewers, a majority of them Latinx/a/o, as it disrupts traditional gender norms of machismo in reggaetón.

REVIEW OF LITERATURE

Three subsets of literature provide the foundation for this study: 1) Gender role conflict and stress: Theoretical foundations, 2) Reggaetón: Music y machismo and 3) Machismo and male Latinx/o identities, leading to a formal research question. This study is designed to expand O'Neil's (2008) *Gender Role Conflict Model: Patterns of Men's Gender Role Conflict* by focusing on race, ethnicity, culture, and sexual orientation. Specifically, I use the model as a lens through which to examine Bad Bunny's video *Yo Perreo Sola,* a media representation which serves as a situational source for expanding the center of O'Neil's (2008) model illustrating men's gender role socialization as a product of masculinity ideology and norms.

Gender Role Conflict and Stress: Theoretical Foundations

Gender Role Stress (GRS) and Gender Role Conflict (GRC) are types of discrepancy-strain, which "results when one fails to live up to one's internalized manhood ideal, which among contemporary adult men, is often a close approximation of the traditional code" (Levant, 1996, p. 261). GRC is defined as a "psychological state in which socialized gender roles have negative consequences for the person or others" (O'Neil, 2008, p. 362). These gender roles are learned within a heteronormative, patriarchal society and cause cognitive, affective, unconscious, and behavioral issues—which make up the four domains of GRC (O'Neil, Good, & Holmes, 1995). O'Neil et al. (1993) conceptualized gender role transitions and the gender role journey, components of GRC, to develop a concept that with greater specificity to the gender role change process. Gender role journey is comprised of three phases: acceptance of traditional roles; anger, ambivalence, confusion, and fear; and personal-professional activism. These phases describe the cognitive, affective, and behavioral self-evaluations an individual experiences in their gender role growth and can be applied to both men and women.

Pleck (1981) rooted his theorization about gender role strain in social constructionism to help explain contemporary tensions of gender roles as they are shaped and reshaped by prevailing gender ideologies in society and imposed by cultural transmitters (such as parents, clergy, peers, and media). GRS/GRC posits that contemporary gender roles are often contradictory and inconsistent with traditional gender roles—which dictate that men are supposed to be dominant, aggressive, sexual, and not show emotion. Deviations, or violations, of gender roles can result in negative ramifications and condemnation, particularly in men (Levant, 1996, p. 260). Pleck (1995) updated his original conceptualization with a typology that reflected the research on three varieties of male gender role strain inspired by the paradigm: discrepancy-strain, dysfunction strain, and trauma strain (see Levant, 1996 for a detailed outline of each variety and the major research programs within each).

Gender role strain is correlated with masculinity ideology—"beliefs about the importance of men adhering to culturally defined standards for male behavior" (Pleck, 1995, p. 19). Masculinity ideology is grounded in the construct of masculinity, measured in characteristics that are socially constructed as desirable for men; such as autonomy, self-confidence, assertiveness, and instrumentality (Bem, 1974). Gender role stress (GRS), as theorized by Eisler and Skimore (1987), builds upon these foundations and creates a cognitive appraisal of specific situations that may cause stress for men. GRS is the resulting anxiety, fear, or other negative outcomes caused by an individual's perceived inability to conform to their patriarchal male gender role or when a situation is perceived as requiring unmasculine or effeminate behavior that plays out in social interactions with others.

Measurement of GRS typically has been conducted through quantitative questionnaires that assess stress related to gender role expectations, such as the Masculine Gender Role Stress Scale (see Eiseler & Skidmore, 1987) and the Feminine Gender Role Stress Scale (see Gillespie & Eisler, 1992). GRC has been previously measured quantitatively using the Gender Role Conflict Scale (O'Neil et al., 1986) and qualitatively using interviews to examine intersections of culture, gender, and masculinity (Pompper, 2010). Previous application of GRC in research has demonstrated that GRC significantly impacts psychological, emotional, and interpersonal issues in men (O'Neil, 2008) and may vary based on demographics, personality, mental health, and other relational variables (O'Neil, Good, & Holmes, 1995). GRC has been associated to abusive behaviors in men (Schwartz et al., 2005), substantiating the consequences of GRC have a societal effect.

There also is evidence that media may also be a contributing factor to GRC/GRS. Movies, television shows, and video games reify rigid and exaggerated patriarchal gender roles (Blackburn & Scharrer, 2019; Sink & Mastro, 2017). Social media, particularly Instagram, have also been spaces that not only reinforce gender roles, but also foster objectification and machismo behavior (Feltman & Szymanski, 2018; Rodriguez & Hernandez, 2018). Despite the aforementioned research in GRC/GRS, there has been few studies that focus on international media and traditionally marginalized identities. This chapter's study builds upon these foundations and qualitatively examines the relationship of globally mediated pop culture, in this instance Bad Bunny and his music, Latinx/a/o audiences, and GRC/GRS through a thematic textual analysis of tweets.

Machismo and Male Latinx/o Identities

This chapter's study is designed to expand upon the center of O'Neil's (2008) *Gender Role Conflict Model: Patterns of Men's Gender Role Conflict* model. To date, our understanding of men's gender role socialization—as rooted in masculinity ideology and norms—has presumed a Caucasian/White and het-eronormative racial identity (Carter et al., 2005; Pompper, 2010). By using this model as a lens through which to examine a situational source—a music video of a cross-dressing Latinx/o performer—I seek to discover ways that his artistry disrupts norms and expands opportunities for members of the Latinx community to avoid the stress, strain, and conflict that accompanies traditional ideas about masculinity and male gender roles. This approach of using a media representation as a situational source is consistent with the rec-ommendation of O'Neil (2008) who suggested that "qualitative research may first need to identify situational areas where boys and men violate or conform to masculine norms" (p. 407).

It is also important to note that the Latinx/a/o community, although used here as an umbrella term for the concession of research, is not a monolithic group and encompasses a variety of nationalities, ethnicities, geographies, histories, and other intersectional identities. There are multiple ways of per-forming a singular racial/ethnic identity (Hernández, 2012). I use Latinx as an identifier for those born in the U.S. with Latin American descent and Latino/ Latina for anyone of Latin American descent or from Latin America. Mascu-linities among Latinx/o men most often reference dimensions of machismo that are linked to traditional gender ideologies such as power, sexual prow-ess, homophobia, and competition (Hirai et al., 2018; Levant, 1996; Ramirez, 1993).

In Latin American spaces, in particular, machismo produces a rigid dichotomy (often referred to as *machista*) that contrasts men as dominate, powerful, and strong with an inferior femininity that is obedient, passive, and domestic (Freidus and Romero-Daza, 2009). Machismo is made up of aggres-siveness and hypersexuality that produce a system of patriarchal authority reified by gendered sexual and societal dominance (Ingoldsby, 1991). The concept of machismo in Latinx/a/o culture is "typically characterized as being strong, violent, phallocentric, heterosexual and hyper-masculine" (Hernán-dez, 2012). Additionally, machismo produces anti-gay attitudes and effemi-phobia (Hirai et al., 2018). Men who deviate from traditional machismo archetypes are viewed as gay or lesser than and socially othered. Bad Bunny's lyrics and genderbending performances are counter the concept of machismo and, through their examination, can provide insight into the intersections of culture, gender, sexual orientation, and masculinities.

Machismo ideologies may be perpetuated and reinforced by both men and women and can be tied to societal gendered labor roles, both inside and outside of the home, often in poor communities of color (Ingoldsby, 1991). Machismo has been linked to negative consequences such as anti-gay prejudice, misjudgments about cultures, reinforcement of stereotypes, aggression, and violence (Hernández, 2012; Hirai et al., 2018). Higher levels of machismo and GRC/GRS have also been found to be significant predictors of higher levels of depression and stress in Mexican-American men, specifically (Fragosa & Kaskubeck, 2000). It is, however, also important to note that although reggaetón contributes and reinforces machismo culture and issues of gender, it is not solely to blame. Society, advertising, religion, and shortcomings in education systems and government youth programs are also at fault (Martínez Noriega, 2014). Performance of machismo, particularly for Latinx/o men, "is necessary to give voice to a portion of the Latino culture that specifically feels marginalized and disempowered" (Hernández, 2012, p. 105). Despite the negative implications of machismo, there are positive implications such as honor and family responsibility (Neff, 2001; Pompper, Soto, & Piel, 2007). There has also been an increase in social diversity into the genre through Christian lyrics, gender tolerance, and a cultivation of feminism by female artists such as Ivy Queen, La Bruja, and Camille, among others (Samponaro, 2009).

Reggaetón: Music y Machismo

The musical genre of reggaetón traditionally has been typified by a hyper masculine ethos that most often reifies objectification of women, violence, and homophobia (Zenit Dizney-Flores, 2008). Bad Bunny disrupts this machismo ethos, which makes him and his music particularly important to examine. Reggaetón has been called the "defining music of Latino youth culture" and, although originating in Panamanian artists called *raperos Panameños* in 1903, gained its popularity in the Panamanian dance halls in the late 1980s (Samponaro, 2009, p. 489). The first Latin American reggaetón recordings "merged Colombian cumbia with Trinidadian soca, Jamaican reggae, calypso, and Haitian kompa" (p. 490). Much like hip-hop, reggaetón is a genre created out of marginalization and solidarity amongst groups with shared historical experiences, both genres are "fluid cultural spaces, zones whose boundaries are adaptable" (Garcia, 2016). Reggaetón's sound is one of urban marginalization, stigmatization of youth, and a response to segregation that mixes rhythms of various socioeconomic classes— "un collage socio-musical [sociomusical collage]" (Martínez Noriega, 2014, p. 64). Reggaetón spread to other areas of the Caribbean in the mid-1990s, particularly in Puerto Rico, with the help of El General, who is credited as the principal figure of the genre, and by the mid-2000s it was being played on U.S. radio airwaves (see Samponaro, 2009). In 2020, the Latin Recording Academy added the category Best Reggaetón Performance to the list of GRAMMY Awards—which was won by Bad Bunny for *Yo Perreo Sola.*

Reggaetón is built upon "both dancehall traditions and Caribbean notions of machismo" where "artists routinely celebrate a virulent masculinity" (Samponaro, 2009, P. 498), and is hallmarked by its implicit and explicit sexual innuendos manifested in its song lyrics and music video images, as well as in the twerk-like sexually suggestive grinding-style dance called "perreo" that many of its listeners perform (Martínez Noriega, 2014). The most popular themes of the genre center on "sex, dancing and partying, experiencing love, lyrical prowess, violence, and heartache" (Zenit Dizney-Flores, 2008, p. 47). Reggaetón, and the imagery it spreads of both of men and women, has been criticized as a manifestation of machismo culture that reinforces the dominant gender role of men and establishes specific gendered stereotypes in younger listeners; such as men are aggressive, violent, dominant, and rude, whereas women are sensual, seductive, and sexual objects (Martínez Noriega, 2014).

Reggaetón, much like hip-hop, has also become highly popularized around and commercialized around the world (Samponaro, 2009). Silva (2016) outlined the many examples of neoliberal commodification that helped propel reggaetón to the international stage in her perspective on the genre. Among those are Kellogg's international ad campaign that redesigned Tony the Tiger as ReggaetónTony; Daddy Yankee's endorsements with Pepsi and Reebock; and Tego Calderon's appearances in advertisements for Hennessy, Verizon, and First Bank Mortgage of Puerto Rico. Most recently, in 2020, J Balvin teamed up with McDonalds for a J Balvin namesake meal. Also in 2020, Bad Bunny collaborated with Crocs for a limited-edition Bad Bunny X Crocs glow Classic Clog and spearheaded Cheetos' *Deja Tu Huella* Campaign. These commercial examples not only highlight the lucrative potential of reggaetón, but also the ubiquity of the genre and its artists. As the genre continues to be critiqued for its gendered and sexualized nature, its popularity continues to increase and spread across the globe. The target audience of the genre, however, remains Spanish-speaking Latinx/a/o.

Examining examples of situational sources of GRC/GRS within the genre of reggaetón is imperative, particularly for those who identify as Latinx/a/o. Previous research has found race/ethnicity to either moderate or mediate GRC/GRS. The effects of racial/ethnic identity have been evidenced in Asian-American men (Kim et al., 1996; Shek, 2012), African-American men (Wade, 1996), Mexican-American men (Fragosa & Kaskubeck, 2000), and Chinese-Canadian men (Wester, Kuo, & Vogel, 2006). Two studies have compared and contrasted GRC/GRS in Black, Latinx/o, and Asian men and found a strong ascription to race/ethnicity in regards to Latinx/o men (Carter et al., 2005; Pompper, 2010). The findings highlight the more affinity Latinx/o men have with their racial/ethnic group, the more they subscribe to gender role norms and GRC, particularly psychological issues and a fear of being perceived as feminine.

The goal of the research in this chapter is to broaden the scope of masculinities research in GRC/GRS, which has predominately focused on U.S./Euro-centric white identities. Bad Bunny's drag performance in the video clearly violates masculine norms (as outlined above). Exposure to contradictory perspectives of traditional gender roles may cause an individual to perceive a disparity between their gender role and societal norms of said gender role, resulting in GRC/GRS (Eisler & Skimore, 1987; O'Neil, 2008; Pleck, 1981, 1995). Because Bad Bunny is a reggaetón/Latin trap artist that sings in Spanish, it is important to examine the reactions of the viewers from a cultural context, placing particular interest on reggaetón and machismo ideals. Thus, this chapter's study argues Bad Bunny's video *Yo Perreo Sola* is a situational source of GRC/GRS. This study will explore:

RQ: How does *Yo Perreo Sola* disrupt traditional heteronormative gender norms of machismo in reggaetón?

METHOD

Viewers of the video expressed their reactions to the performance, as it relates to their cultural interpretation of masculine ideology, on social media platforms, particularly Twitter. Twitter was used to examine audience reaction to Bad Bunny's *Yo Perrea Sola* video. Twitter is a ubiquitous social media platform that connects millions of users around the globe. For minorities such as Latinx/a/o, Twitter is purposefully used to express opinions that may not be present in mainstream media, echoing collective agency (Rodriguez, 2016). Twitter is well-suited for data collection and analysis on how meaning is crafted around machismo identity in Latinx/a/o pop culture, specifically when it deviates from traditional cultural norms, such as in the *Yo Perrea Sola* video.

Data Collection

Data were collected using Advanced Twitter Search. Tweets that contained the words/phrases "Bad Bunny" and "Yo Perrea Sola," as well as the hasghtag #AnuelIsOverParty, between March 27, 2020 (the day the video premiered) and April 3, 2021 (a week after the premiere) in both Spanish or

English were selected. A random sample of 500 tweets per day for the week were selected over the seven-day period, resulting in 3,500 tweets. Of those, a second random sample of 2,000 tweets were selected for analysis on. Each tweet's text comprised the unit of analysis.

Data Analysis

Tweets were extracted and placed in NVivo, a qualitative analysis software. A textual analysis was conducted in a process according to Corbin and Strauss (2008) in which data is analyzed for themes and patterns and then compared to theory to draw conclusions. First, raw data were reduced into smaller units by grouping levels of meaning (data that can stand on its own as an individual theme) together in order to construct linkages between data. Second, themes within the subsamples were identified and reexamined to determine if they need to be expanded or whether a new theme had been created. The final themes were compared to GRC/GRS to ensure they were not only data-driven, but also were aligned with the theoretical underpinnings to reveal context, causal conditions, and consequences.

FINDINGS

In response to RQ1, four essential themes emerged that address ways in which Bad Bunny's *Yo Perrea Sola* served as a situational source for GRC/GRS. The themes are: (1) reforming reggaetón; (2) heteronormative policing; (3) LGBTQ ally and appropriation; and (4) feminism and gendered stereotypes.

Theme One: Reforming Reggaetón

The first theme uncovered in the tweets was the reformation of reggaetón by Bad Bunny "desde la raiz [from the roots]." The genre of reggaetón includes machismo ideologies, such as violence and sexual objectification. Many tweets credited the video for disrupting the paradigm of macho alfa pelo en pecho rodeado de 1,000 mujeres "[macho alpha hair on chest surrounded by 1,000 women]." Another tweet read: ". . . The same industry that talk shit about women, treats us like object. Thank you for being you. 'Yo Perreo Sola' is now history . . ." Other tweets were quick to mention that reggaetón has come a long way, "por no hablar de la impresionante evolución que ha tenido con los años [not to mention the impressive evolution it has had over the years]."

Some tweets argued the video goes beyond reforming reggaetón, and helps us reframe how we think about gender in general: "bad bunny en perrea sola cuando se perrea a sí mismo quiere exponer que a feminidad no es una dimensión contraria de su personalidad sino que es un complemento sin duda a través de su performance nos hace una invitación a revaluar los arquetipos de género en nuestro pensamiento [Bad Bunny, in *Perrea Sola,* when he himself twerks, he wants to expose that femininity is not a contrary dimension of his personality, but undoubtedly compliments it. Through his performance he invites us to re-evaluate the gender archetypes in our thinking]." However, many individuals called out Bad Bunny for his past peccadillos in prior song lyrics such as: "yo te lo meto, te lambo toaa, meue ese culto, to parto toaa [I'll stick it in you, I'll lick it all, move that ass, I'll break it all]" and "ma puta que Betty Boop [more whore than Betty Boop]." One individual tweeted "Que doble moral la de BAD BUNNY en todas sus canciones denigra a la mujer y fomenta el machismo y ahora va a lavarse las manos con esa CANCIÓN . . . [What a double standard that of BAD BUNNY in all his songs denigrates women and encourages machismo and now he is going to wash his hands with that SONG]".

Theme Two: Heteronormative Policing

A second theme that demonstrated how *Yo Perreo Sola* served as a situational source of GRC/GRS was heteronormative policing. Some individuals simply called Bad Bunny gay with no context. Tweets like "100 yard penalty for being gay as fuck," "bad bunny hella gay," and "BAD BUNNY IS GAY ASF FOR THAT VIDEEO IDGAFFF #teammanuel" were abound. Some individuals classified dressing as a woman, for any reason, as "gay stuff" and tweeted "Yes any man that dress like a women is gay!" And others claimed Bad Bunny "quiso ser mujer [wanted to be a woman]" in tweets such as ". . . If you are straight, that's just not some straight shit to do. that's some gay shit Man but, if you are gay or trans then that's okay, do you Man."

Some tweets stated, "Bad Bunny has a girlfriend and cannot be gay," exhibiting GRC/GRS, but still supporting the artist. Many tweets were quick to police these justifications: "You do realise [sic] there are faggots that have had wives. So this bad bunny character being gay has nothing to do with having a girlfriend." Others blamed the reggaetón genre: "Bad bunny is gay . . . that girl he's with is a cover up because of all the fake ass homophobia that's in the music industry." His supporters were persistent and replied to these tweets, creating a back-and-forth: "y'all who saying bad bunny gay on the low be proving his point in what he tryna fight and they don't even see it Face with tears of joy." Another individual called it fragile masculinity: "Lmao ever since bad bunny released his music video mens machismo has really spiked yalls masculinity really hurt HUH."

In the case of Bad Bunny, some policing manifested as jokes such as "ya se porque perrea sola [I know why he twerks alone], bad bunny an ugly girl bruh

ROFL" and "puta, ahora no puedo escuchar ella perrea sola, sin imaginarme a bad bunny con tetas [Fuck, now I can't listen to *ella perrea sola*, without imagining a bad bunny with tits." Others' policing was a bit more extreme, including tweets with slurs such as "puto asco [fucking disgusting]" and "Por mi qie se vista de lo qie quiera pero ese 'artista' si se le puede llamar así estaría mejor muerto [For me, dress as you want, but that 'artist' if you can call him that would be better off dead]."

Theme Three: LGBTQ Ally and Appropriator

A third theme that emerged from the data was *LGBTQ Ally and Appropriator*. Twitter was also a space for praise of LGBTQ support and advocacy and argued the video "fue con mucho respeto, resaltando un mensaje de orgullo tanto para las mujeres como para la comunidad trans [was with great respect, highlighting a message of pride for both women and the trans community]." Another tweeted "Wey estuvo chido, ayudando a las feministas y los trans [dude was cool, helping feminists and trans]." Individuals called Bad Bunny an advocate and an "aliado [ally]." Some of the tweets praising LGBTQ support, however, concurrently reinforced traditional masculine gender roles sometimes found in the gay community, "Can we please make Bad Bunny a gay icon but for tops?" A top is the insertive partner and viewed as a more machismo role, whereas the bottom is the man who is penetrated and is seen as a more feminine role.

Although some praised Bad Bunny for his LGBTQ support, others were more critical. Some accused him of appropriating LGBTQ culture: "What bad bunny did was, breaking of machismo gender roles and toxic masculinity however he DID steal from a community that he is not a part of." Some accused him of queerbaiting:

> Bad Bunny has confirmed multiple times that he is a straight cis man. We love him as an ally, but that does not forgive the constant queer-baiting he's done his entire career. I'm 100% here for dismantling machismo, but where's the fucking line.

Bad Bunny was also criticized for not "having a trans women star in the mv instead," and one individual tweeted: "It's terribly ironic if his point es que Alexa no era un hombre vestido como mujer [is that Alexa wasn't a man dressed as a woman] when he himself is literally a man dressed as a woman in this video."

Others used Bad Bunny's video to call out his admirers and question their support for LGBTQ masculinities in everyday life, asking: "where is that same energy for your average fem gay men every day. Y'all can't even handle a high-pitched voice. Don't be a hypocrite do better." Another individual tweeted: "Todos esos que apoyan a Bad Bunny en su video yo perreo sola después bardean a un gay que se viste como quiere y con las uñas pintadas, en fin la hipoteca [All those who support Bad Bunny in his video *Yo Perrea Sola* then berate a gay who dresses as he wants with painted nails, alas the hypocrisy]."

As in other themes, people spared back and forth with other Twitter users. One defender of Bad Bunny's performance tweeted: "love bad bunny for being so comfortable in his sexuality and standing up for the trans community and homophobic stereotypes You don't have to be gay to stand up for transphobic/homophobic stereotypes . . ." Others commented on the role of race in their defenses: "so twitter will cream their pants when a white boy says 'gay rights' but when bad bunny actually does something to bring awareness to trans hate crimes and uses his privilege for good he gets called out . . ." In these instances, individuals directly called out GRC/GRS that they saw displayed in tweets about the video.

Theme Four: Feminism and Gendered Stereotypes

The final theme that answered how *Yo Perreo Sola* served as a situational source of GRC/GRS was *feminism and gendered stereotypes*. Respect for women was the main message of Bad Bunny's video and it was directly echoed in the tweets, many directly tweeting the tagline from the video word-for-word followed by "tomen nota [take note]," "ya young men need to feel this," "some guys need to do that," and "PERIODT." He was also praised for "dando un mensaje de empoderamiento de la mujer por medio del perreo [gives visualization in his gender, giving a message of empowerment of women through perreo]." Many tweets, however, claimed his perreo actually reinforced stereotypic gender role norms of a hypersexualized Latina, exclaiming "las mujeres no somos tetas uñas y pelo largo, bad bunny es otro varoncito q se cuelga de nuestra y ustedes lo tienen como feminist icon [women are not tits, nails and long hair, bad bunny is another little boy who hangs on us and you have him as a feminist icon]." Another tweet read: "Hola gente, por si todavía no sabían es 2020 y pues como ya deberían saber que ser mujer no es un maldito disfraz hipersexualizado. Las mujeres no somos tetas, cabello largo y maquillaje [Hello people, in case you still did not know it is 2020 and as you should already know that being a woman is not a damn hypersexualized costume. Women are not boobs, long hair and makeup]."

Bad Bunny was also accused of "capitalizando [capitalizing]" feminism, stating music should support feminist ideas, "sino distorsionarlas, pink-washearlas y vender un producto diluido que poco o nada tiene que ver con los principios originales [not distort them, pink-wash them and sell a diluted

product that has little or nothing to do with the original principles]." Many
admitted Bad Bunny's voice and platform were important, but the delivery of
the messages was inappropriate, arguing such messages "representa la lucha
contra los feminicidios, no es slogan de video musical [represent the fight
against femicides, it is not a music video slogan]." Some men were quick to
attack the women who brought up feminism, called them "feminazis" and
stated the video "demuestra que las feministas son tan manipulables [shows
that feminists are so manipulable]". The tweets also accused Bad Bunny's
performance as satire that poked fun at women and argued he employed
"estereotipos femeninos como los q dices 'tetas grandes, culo y cabello largo'
para demostrar q son solo eso, tetas culo y cabello, relájate un chingo y perrea sola [used his male body, with female stereotypes like the ones you say
"big tits, ass and long hair" to show that they are just that, tits, ass and hair,
fucking relax and twerk alone]."

DISCUSSION

Masculinity ideology and norms, as well as men's gender role socialization,
contribute to GRC/GRS as a result of societal influences and cultural transmitters, such as media (O'Neil, 2008). Bad Bunny's performance of gender
in his international music video *Yo Perreo Sola* serves as a mediated situational source of masculine gender socialization that is counter-hegemonic
and violates machismo ideologies and norms of reggaetón. This violation, as
evidenced by the tweets, created GRC/GRS in some viewers. Bad Bunny's
positionality as a Puerto Rican reggaetón and Latin Trap artist cannot be
understated. "Reggaetón from Puerto Rico is considered the authentic representation of the genre due to the massive commercial success enjoyed by this
variant since the turn of the century" (Samponaro, 2009, p. 492). Bad Bunny
has become the global ambassador for the genre and his messages and his
popularity continues to rise. He was named the world's most streamed artist
in 2020 by Spotify with over 8.3 billion streams on Spotify alone, has won
several Latin Grammy Awards, and one Grammy Award. Thus, his message
of respect, gender, and masculinity weighs heavy and influential.

The chapter evidences patterns of machismo ideology in reggaetón mirror
those found in masculinity ideology (Levant, 1996). Bad Bunny is helping to
usher in a new era of gender equity and respect in reggaetón, but is still operating within the confines of personal and institutional sexism and gender role
conflict and strain (O'Neil et al., 995). He pushes some boundaries and settles
within the space of others" (Cepeda, 2018, para. 12). Individuals expressed
GRC/GRS on social media, evidencing that Twitter is a space where men

devalue and restrict each other as a form of policing masculinity ideology, as well as crafting hegemonic hierarchies against women. The back-and-forth nature of Twitter allows for iterative negotiation of GRC/GRS and provides an opportunity for global audiences to engage in debate on gender roles.

Contemporary Reformation of Masculinities

Bad Bunny disrupts traditional male gender norms of machismo in reggaetón and offers new dimensions to the masculinities concepts that incorporates and blends gender and sexuality. This disruption is positive as Bad Bunny's counter hegemonic portrayal demonstrates that a broader definition of masculinities may reduce GRC/GRS; rather than viewing the video as a violation or deviation of constricted delineations of masculinities (Pompper, 2010, p. 688). Findings highlight more contemporary and acceptable interpretations of both masculinities and reggaetón. Bad Bunny is not alone, other Latinx/o and reggaetón artists like Residente and J Balvin have spoken out in support of the LGBTQ community and promoted mental health awareness, helping to modernize the genre. In a similar fashion, hip-hop artists such as Young Thug and Lil Uzi Vert have also bended gender through wearing nail polish, makeup, and skirts (Cepeda, 2018). Both genres are similar in many aspects and are undergoing a gender role renaissance of sorts, mediated through pop culture and social media. Although many tweets evidenced deviation from traditional gender norms in reggaetón as positive, other tweets highlighted objectifying lyrics in other songs by Bad Buddy. Bad Bunny's performance in *Yo Perreo Sola* is helping to change masculinity ideology and norms in reggaetón. However, it is a slow and incomplete process.

Heteronormativity and Hegemony

Many individuals tweeted negative reactions to the video and used Twitter as a space to police masculine ideologies of machismo, heteronormativity, and gender roles. Machismo in reggaetón centers on heterosexual experiences (Freidus & Romero-Daza, 2009). Such tweets suggest the video could have contributed to GRC/GRS due to a fear of femininity. Verbal sparring amongst tweeters, although indicative of patterns of masculinity ideology (Levant, 1996), demonstrated that Bad Bunny himself, and not just his video, is a source of GRC/GRS. Policing of masculinity and hegemony (referred to as hegemonic masculinity) often occurs on social media and ranges in intensity (Rodriguez and Hernandez, 2018). Tweets containing anti-gay slurs and fraternal jokes evidence gender role devaluations, which are personal experiences of GRC/GRS that devalue or negatively critiques oneself or others when "conforming to, deviating from, or violating stereotypic gender role

norms of masculinity ideology" (O'Neil, 2008, p. 363). All of these tweets
were from men, evidencing that Twitter is space where men devalue each
other as a form of policing machismo ideology and norms.

Queering Reggaetón

Findings evidence that GRC/GRS generated from a counter portrayal of
machismo norms, not commonly found in the reggaetón genre, particularly
genderbending and queering masculinities. Reggeatón privileges heterosexuality and normative assumptions of male dominant sexual relationships and
experiences (Freidus & Romero-Daza, 2009). Some of these tweets, albeit
queer, still reinforced heteronormative social structures through a bottom/top
dichotomy. Many of the men who tweeted, regardless of sexual orientation,
were socialized in a patriarchal society that culturally transmitted masculinity ideology and norms. Individuals may unconsciously have reinforced
these socializations. The unconscious domain of GRC/GRS has gone largely
unexplored (O'Neil, 2008). It's also important to note that Bad Bunny was
sexualized by non-heterosexual men, but identifies as heterosexual. The
interpersonal expression of GRC/GRS places Bad Bunny in a rigid sex role
that is in support of, but not included in, the LGBTQ community. It limits
Bad Bunny's potential to be a fully functioning, androgynous whole human
being (O'Neil, 1981). LGBTQ tweeters also highlighted the hypocrisy of
heterosexuals who supported Bad Bunny's queering of reggaetón online, but
not the LGBTQ community offline. Bad Bunny (because of his cisgender
heterosexual positionality, celebrity status, and removal from physical prox-
imity), may be a safe and acceptable deviation from masculinity ideology
and norms, whereas deviations experienced face-to-face in the physical world
may not be.

Gendered Stereotypes

Bad Bunny was accused of GRC/GRS himself and imposing gender role
restrictions, which are personal experiences of GRC/GRS that "confine
oneself or others to stereotypic norms of masculinity ideology" on women
(O'Neil, 2008, p. 363). His genderbending performance highlighted women
as hypersexual and hyperfeminine stereotypes. Some tweets extended this
accusation into capitalizing on feminism. Capitalism, along with the music
industry and popular culture, have been faulted with generating the socialization, subjectivities, and sexualization of the reggaetón (Martínez Noriega,
2014). In response to these accusations, men, specifically, tweeted pejorative
slurs like "feminazis," another example of gender role devaluations (O'Neil,
2008) and a way to reinforce masculine hierarchies over women through

digital means (Rodriguez & Hernandez, 2018). The retweeting and replying also demonstrated the back-and-forth nature of social media and its ability to help individuals negotiate GRC/GRS.

Limitations and Future Study

Although the findings are not generalizable to a larger population, the study provides a nuanced perspective on a cultural sources of GRC/GRS. O'Neil (2008) argues that diversity variables have gone mostly unexplored and the degree to which they may moderate or mediate GRC/GRS is mostly unknown. This chapter evidences that Latinx/a/o may experience GRC/GRS from Latinx/a/o popular culture, particularly through music videos. Future research should examine more closely the ways in which various intersectional identity categories affect the ways in which masculine ideologies and gender role norms are conformed to or violated in relation to masculinities at-large in racial and ethnic spaces around the globe.

REFERENCES

Bern, S. L. (1974). The measurement of psychological androgyny. *Journal of Personality and Social Psychology 42*, 155–162. https://doi.org/10.1037/h0036215.

Blackburn, G., & Scharrer, E. (2019). Video game playing and beliefs about masculinity among male and female emerging adults. *Sex Roles, 80*(5–6), 310–324. https://doi.org/10.1007/s11199-018-0934-4.

Carter, R. T., Williams, B., Juby, H. L., & Buckley, T. R. (2005). Racial identity as mediator of the relationship between gender role conflict and severity of psychological symptoms in Black, Latino, and Asian men. *Sex Roles, 53*, 473–486. https://doi.org/10.1007/s11199-005-7135-7.

Cepeda, E. (2018). Latin trap rapper Bad Bunny is redefining masculinity in a genre steeped in machismo. *The ARTery*. Retrieved from https://www.wbur.org.

Corbin, J., & Strauss, A. (2008). *Basics of qualitative research: Techniques and procedures for developing grounded theory* (3rd ed.). Sage.

Eiseler, R. M., & Skidmore, J. R. (1987). Masculine gender role stress: Scale development and component factor analysis in the appraisal of stressful situations. *Behavior Modification, 11*(2), 123–136. https://doi.org/10.1177/01454455870112001.

Exposito, S. (2020, May 14). How does a Latin-pop superstar spend lockdown? Hanging out with his girlfriend, watching 'Toy Story' and surprising the world. *Rolling Stone*. Retrieved from https://www.rollingstone.com.

Feltman, C. E., & Szymanski, D. M. (2018). Instagram use and self-objectification: The roles of internalization, comparison, appearance commentary, and feminism. *Sex Roles, 78*(5–6), 311–324. https://doi.org/10.1007/s11199-017-0796-1.

Freidus, A., & Romero-Daza, N. (2009). The space between: globalization, liminal spaces and personal relations in rural Costa Rica. *Gender, Place and Culture, 16*(6), 683–702. https://doi.org/10.1080/09663690903279146.

Garcia, W. (2016). Rethinking Hip-Hop ED Through Intersectional Collective Identities. In V. Nadal-Ramos and D. Smith Silva (Eds), Perspectives on reggaetón (pp. 67–75). Universidad de Puerto Rico.

Gillespie, B. L., & Eisler, R. M. (1992). Development of the feminine gender role stress scale: A cognitive-behavioral measure of stress, appraisal, and coping for women. *Behavior Modification, 16*(3), 426-438. https://doi.org/10.1177/01454455920163008.

Hirai, M., Dolma, S., Popan, J. R., & Winkel, M. H. (2018). Machismo predicts prejudice toward lesbian and gay individuals: testing a mediating role of contact. *Sexuality Research and Social Policy, 15*(4), 497–503. https://doi.org/10.1007/s13178-017-0308-7.

Hernández, J. C. (2012). Machismo: the role of Chicano rap in the construction of the Latino identity presented at WSCA (Monterey, CA, 2011). *International Journal of Humanities and Social Science, 2*(20), 98–106.

Ingoldsby, B. B. (1991). The Latin American family: Familism vs machismo. *Journal of Comparative Family Studies, 22*(1), 57–62. https://doi.org/10.3138/jcfs.22.1.57.

Levant, R. F. (1996). The new psychology of men. *Professional psychology: Research and practice, 27*(3), 259. https://doi.org/10.1037/0735-7028.27.3.259.

Marshall, W. 2009. From música Negra to reggaetón Latino: The cultural production of nation, migration, and commercialization. In R. Z. Rivera, W. Marshall, and D. Pacini Hernández (Eds), *Reggaetón,* (pp. 19–76). Duke University Press.

Martínez Noriega, D. A. (2014). Música, imagen y sexualidad: el reggaetón y las asimetrías de género. *Cotidiano—Revista de La Realidad Mexicana, 29*(186), 63–67. https://doi.org/ 10.1037/0735-7028.27.3.259.

Miller, J. L., & Levy, G. D. (1996). Gender role conflict, gender-typed characteristics, self-concepts, and sport socialization in female athletes and nonathletes. *Sex roles, 35*(1–2), 111–122. https://doi.org/10.1007/BF01548178.

Neff, J. A. (2001). A confirmatory factor analysis of a measure of "machismo" among anglo, African American, and Mexican American male drinkers. *Hispanic Journal of Behavioral Sciences, 23*(2), 171–188. https://doi.org/10.1177/0739986301232004.

O'Neil, J. M. (1981). Male sex role conflicts, sexism, and masculinity: Psychological implications for men, women, and the counseling psychologist. *The Counseling Psychologist, 9*, 61–80. https://doi.org/10.1177/001100008100900213.

———. (2008). Summarizing 25 years of research on men's gender role conflict using the Gender Role Conflict Scale: New research paradigms and clinical implications. *The Counseling Psychologist, 36*(3), 358-445. https://doi.org/10.1177/0011000008317057.

O'Neil, J. M., Good, G. E., & Holmes, S. (1995). Fifteen years of theory and research on men's gender role conflict: New paradigms for empirical research. In R. Levant and W. Pollack (Eds.), *The new psychology of men* (pp. 164-206). Basic Books.

O'Neil, J. M., Helm, B., Gable, R., David, L., & Wrightsman, L. (1986). Gender Role Conflict Scale (GRCS): College men's fears of femininity. *Sex Roles, 14*, 335–350. https://doi.org/10.1007/BF00287583.

O'Neil, J. M., Egan, J., Owen, S. V., & Murry, V. M. (1993). The gender role journey measure: Scale development and psychometric evaluation. *Sex Roles, 28*, 167–185. https://doi.org/10.1007/BF00299279.

Pleck, J. H. (1981). *The myth of masculinity*. MIT Press.

———. (1995). The gender role strain paradigm: An update. In R. F. Levant and W. S. Pollack (Eds.), *A new psychology of men* (pp. 11–32). Basic Books.

Pompper, D. (2010). Masculinities, the metrosexual, and media images: Across dimensions of age and ethnicity. *Sex roles, 63*(9–10), 682–696. https://doi.org/10.1007/s11199-010-9870-7.

Pompper, D., Soto, J., & Piel, L. (2007). Male body image and magazine standards: Considering dimensions of age and ethnicity. *Journalism and Mass Communication Quarterly, 84*(3), 525–545. https://doi.org/10.1177/107769900708400308.

Ramirez, R. (1993). *Dime capitán: Reflexiones sobre la masculinidad*. Ediciones Huracán.

Rodriguez, N. S. (2017). # FIFAputos: A Twitter textual analysis over "puto" at the 2014 World Cup. *Communication and Sport, 5*(6), 712–731. https://doi.org/10.1177/2167479516655429.

Rodriguez, N. S., & Hernandez, T. (2018). Dibs on that sexy piece of ass: Hegemonic masculinity on TFM girls Instagram account. *Social Media+ Society, 4*(1), https://doi.org/10.1177/2056305118760809.

Schwartz, J. P., Waldo, M., & Daniel, D. (2005). Gender-role conflict and self-esteem: Factors associated with partner abuse in court-referred men. *Psychology of Men and Masculinity, 6*(2), 109–113. https://doi.org/10.1037/1524-9220.6.2.109.

Shek, Y. L., & McEwen, M. K. (2012). The relationships of racial identity and gender role conflict to self-esteem of Asian American undergraduate men. *Journal of College Student Development, 53*(5), 703–718. https://doi.org/10.1353/csd.2012.0065.

Sink, A., & Mastro, D. (2017). Depictions of gender on primetime television: A quantitative content analysis. *Mass Communication and Society, 20*(1), 3–22. https://doi.org/10.1080/15205436.2016.1212243.

Smith Silva, D. (2016). More than just a beat: The phenomenon of reggaetón. In V. Nadal-Ramos and D. Smith Silva (Eds), Perspectives on reggaetón (pp. 8–17). Universidad de Puerto Rico.

Wester, S. R., Kuo, B. C., & Vogel, D. C. (2006). Multicultural coping: Chinese Canadian adolescents, male gender role conflict, and psychological distress. *Psychology of Men and Masculinity, 7*, 83–100. https://doi.org/10.1037/1524-9220.7.2.83.

Wade, J. C. (1996). African American men's gender role conflict: The significance of racial identity. *Sex Roles, 34*, 458–464. https://doi.org/10.1007/BF01544793.

Yglesias, A. M. (2020). Bad Bunny's 'YHLQMDLG' breaks records, is the highest-charting spanish language album ever. *The Recording Academy*. Retrieved from https://www.grammy.com.

Zenit Dizney-Flores, Z. (2008). De la disco al caserío (from the disco to the projects): Urban spatial aesthetics and policy to the beat of reggaetón. *CENTRO Journal, 20*(2), 34–69.

Unit III

MASCULINITIES & EMOTIONALITY

Chapter Ten

"Bitch-Ass Pussy!"

Perceptions of Abused Men Predicted by Media, Educational, and Experiential Topic Exposure

Jessica Eckstein and Jessica Cherry

INTRODUCTION

In the United States, over 32.2 million men will be physically victimized in their lifetimes, with exponentially more psychologically abused by female partners (Black et al., 2011). Abuse outcomes typically include direct and indirect/chronic physical injury and major, chronic psychosomatic trauma symptoms. These outcomes are further compounded as they interact with the relational violence itself, societal judgment, *and* internal identity threats (Choudhary et al., 2015; Hines & Malley-Morrison, 2001). Because sexed-females long have been viewed as the "appropriate" or typical victims of intimate violence (Dobash & Dobash, 1978; George, 1994; Hammock et al., 2015; Russell et al., 2019), abused men face additional challenges when victimized. Men have fewer support resources and are more likely to be stigmatized for their victimization than are women (Hammock et al., 2015; Hines et al., 2007; Lehman & Santilli, 1996). Believed to result from a variety of sources, societal rhetoric—as expressed by individuals' narratives—has the potential to affect public impressions and effect social change (e.g., Baker & Bevacqua, 2017). However, particularly with partner abuse, sources' relative influences in and manner of perpetuating stigma remain unclear; our study was designed to determine these influences.

We examine "abused man" topical information-exposure sources as predictors of stigmatizing perceptions known to contribute to gender role stress and/or conflict (GRS/C) for abused men. In this chapter, we begin by addressing factors prior research identified as shaping masculinity-tied abuse perceptions connected to abused men's GRS/C. Our literature review introduces the context of abused men's stigma by looking at the nature and sources of their potential GRS/C. We then present the methods of our community-sampled survey study, followed by our data on info-sources' respective roles in influencing people's "abused man" narratives. Finally, we discuss these findings in terms of implications for O'Neil's (1981a) gender role conflict model and practical suggestions for reducing abused men's stigma.

LITERATURE REVIEW

To our ground our study, in this section, we present 1) key concepts related to men's gender role stress and conflict, 2) apply these concepts to the context of abused men's stigmatization, and 3) review potential sources influencing stigmatization of abused men.

Nature of Gender Role Stress and Conflict

The roles expected of particular *sexes* (i.e., normatively binary categorical differences based on observable physical traits; male/female) in our society are intrinsically tied to their *gender*, or socially constructed expectations for interpersonal performance (Bem, 1981; Muehlenhard & Peterson, 2011). Because gender is presumed by many to directly correspond to sex (e.g., masculine males and feminine females), expectations are highly ingrained both societally and personally. Whether conforming or challenging, people's lived identities are subject to constant monitoring and regulation for their "fit" with expected norms. As such, *gender roles* involve the constant challenges and social pressures (presented by media and individual others) to conform to societally accepted, often sex-typed, macro-norms (Bem, 1981). Unsurprisingly, such pressures can result in *gender role stress/conflict*, or the detrimental outcomes of these burdens on individuals perceiving restrictions to their preferred gender enactments (Eisler & Skidmore, 1987; O'Neil, 1981b).

Originally hypothesized by O'Neil (1981a, 1981b), GRS/C is believed to hinder identity-performance abilities and is observable via limitations on emotional expression and "control, power, and competition issues" resulting from the "masculine mystique and value system" pushed by the "masculine socialization process" in a particular culture (O'Neil, 1981a, p. 63). These factors closely align with hegemonic masculinity components (Connell, 2000) frequently discussed in studies of men abused by women. Abused men in heterosexual relationships are frequently stigmatized (and thus, avoid seeking support) for not meeting masculinity expectations that they deny or ignore pain, refuse assistance, and maintain control over others in their lives (Eckstein, 2009; Migliaccio, 2001). As a result, internalization of identity failure (i.e., GRS/C) for abused men remains a primary barrier to their psychological, physical, and behavioral health.

Nature of Stigmatizing GRS/C for Abused Men

According to O'Neil's model, through *gender role socialization*, which begins early and continues throughout life, individuals learn to adopt behaviors, values, and attitudes that constitute masculinity and femininity (O'Neil 1981a, 1981b). This process is hypothesized to directly affect norms associated with a particular gender enactment. In the case of masculinity, stereotype-based cultural ideals inform what "manhood" is, or at least, "should" be (Connell, 2000; Courtenay, 2000), which lends to the *masculine mystique*. In the past, this value system was thought to be beneficial and aspirational for men (see Kimmel, 2006). However, research consistently finds these values are detrimental to all sexes because they devalue women and deny men opportunities to embody feminine styles (e.g., Helgeson, 1994; Kaplan & Marks, 1995). Thus, even when identifying attributes of masculinity or femininity positively, a masculine mystique remains harmful to everyone.

The masculine mystique implies that femininity and femaleness are inferior, which then contributes to men's overall "fear of femininity" (see Gallagher & Parrott, 2011). This is seen in boys' striving to be stoic, self-reliant, dominant—to avoid having others identify them as feminine (Connell, 2000). Deviating from this normative masculinity, as do men in abusive relationships, is significantly stigmatizing. Abused men are frequently subject to others' viewing them as possessing feminine attributes (Eckstein & Cherry, 2015; George, 1994; Migliaccio, 2001), aspects which become negative or identity-threatening to men, even when the attributes are otherwise "positive" in nature. When men in abusive heterosexual relationships face this stigma, it can contribute to their GRS/C. For example, Eckstein (2009, 2010) found that although abused men deviated from masculine ideologies, when interpreting their own victimization, these men still clung to dominant cultural narratives in attempts to avoid GRS/C and to reinforce or re-establish their masculinity (e.g., "I'm not a victim of *her*; it's the system.") in norm-congruent ways.

This GRS/C management is not only internal for abused men. Cultural rhetoric is distributed and reinforced both by media and via interpersonal encounters. In the initial stage of this project, we explored the nature of the cultural rhetoric surrounding abused men and found that people's stigmatizing messages were entirely based on stereotypical, hegemonic masculine role expectations. Overwhelmingly (99.5 percent), and in keeping with O'Neil's (1981a) "masculine mystique," people denigrated abused men for failing at masculinity while also derogating femininity as a "lesser" personality or relational characteristic (Eckstein & Cherry, 2015). Almost 94 percent of all messages, which were often accompanied by emasculating slurs, directly blamed the man for his own victimization; the additional 25.3 percent of responses that excused or gave a rationale for the man's abuse did so only in the process of blaming him for not subsequently fixing those issues himself (Eckstein & Cherry, 2015). Clearly, victimized men's stigma is directly related to their potential GRS/C. What remains unexamined are its specific contributors, which our current study was designed to explore.

Sources of GRS/C Socialization

O'Neil's (1981a) GRS/C model included multiple contributors to gender socialization processes. Specifically, his model showed the ways biological sex, "environment" (i.e., family, peers, and school), and the interactions of these sources were purported to affect the manner in and degree to which GRS/C would exist for individual men. Our study explored (and this section previews) three of these information-sources for their influence on the socialization processes described by O'Neil (1981a). Their relative contributions are as yet unclear, but three main sources in O'Neil's (1981a, 1981b) model are typically discussed in gender relations literature (e.g., Babarskiene & Gaiduk, 2018): social interactions, media, and educational outlets.

Interpersonal Exposure

Labeled "environment" by O'Neil (1981a), interpersonal interactions shape relational communication and gender understandings both indirectly and directly. For example, people may learn about partner violence from family and peers *indirectly*, by observing others' behaviors or hearing messages regarding someone else's experiences with abuse, or they may learn *directly* by experiencing abuse (e.g., as victim or perpetrator) themselves. Both learning methods involve facing others' *attributions*, or underlying beliefs about causes, regarding abuse victims (Harris & Cook, 1994; Koepke et al., 2014). In other words, any message inherently communicates a meta-message or value statement about a condition and people with that condition.

Both direct and indirect learning experiences influence people's lives, but actually encountering violence distinguishes victims' perceptions. Certainly, those without personal abuse experience can rely on both interpersonal- and media-disseminated cultural rhetoric to make sense of the topic (e.g., see Hockett et al., 2016; Koepke et al., 2014). But having gone through abuse oneself also may personally bias any alternate understandings of the same experience happening to someone else (e.g., see Khan & Rogers, 2015). For example, Eckstein and Quattro (2021) found that those who previously experienced technology-mediated abuse were less likely to understand this abuse type in its full complexity. No matter how they encounter it, those who experience violence—whether through first-hand victimization or supporting a victimized loved one—are likely to understand it differently than someone with no personal experience (Davies, 2019). Our study was designed to test this assumption. Although people may not (knowingly) have personal experience with abused men, other exposure sources shape the larger rhetoric of abused men's masculinity.

Media Exposure

Although the extensive media-influence field is beyond the scope of this chapter, we acknowledge a 50+ year history of cultivation analysis. It is important to note that media clearly shape and/or reflect societal communication of cultural "norms" that reinforce beliefs and behaviors (Carlyle et al., 2014; Coyne et al., 2011; Kretz, 2019; Paluck, 2009). Scholars and policymakers generally agree that media influence perceptions, but remain divided on its ability to *directly*/immediately change values and beliefs (e.g., direct effects versus cultivation models), particularly those related to gender and relational norms, which are established early in socialization (Galloway et al., 2015; Jesmin & Amin, 2017; Lippman, 2018; Oliver et al., 1998). O'Neil (1981a) hypothesized that mass media contribute to GRS/C by supporting sex-stereotypes and reinforcing masculine norms. But before examining how media affect perceptions regarding abused men, it is first necessary to determine if they actually might, as we do in this study.

Educational Exposure

Finally, educational outlets are touted as the primary means by which people are "taught" their understandings of masculinity and its accompanying social norms. Being "educated" on a topic is directly related to people's knowledge type and understanding extent, with attributional, attitudinal associations included (Mansoori-Rostam & Tate, 2017). As a result, education is frequently used in attempts to reduce stigma; and these interventions show some success in eliciting positive attitudes and/or healthy behaviors *when* pupils do not experience contradictory messages in their daily lives outside of school (Corrigan & Penn, 1999). For example, this is the main assumption of *primary prevention education*, which holds that early-socialized attitudes and knowledge foster sensitivity to damaging behaviors otherwise taught by family or society. However, despite knowing that first impressions are highly influential, gender- and abuse-related topics are often avoided when teaching children (Monsoori-Rostam & Tate, 2017).

Increased topic-exposure frequency, a tactic highly conducive to (but not often practiced in) educational settings, generally positively affects gendered attitudes when that information is consistent and reinforced over time (Anderson & Whiston, 2005). However, what people actually learn in school or other formally taught/delivered programs may not always be that which is intended by educators. For example, Eckstein and Sabovik (2021) found that despite ostensibly being taught gender equality, some students in a primary prevention program aimed at addressing interpersonal violence remained unchanged in, and in some cases increased, their negative attitudes toward victims. Thus, formal curricula's efficacy in shaping gendered attitudes, beliefs, and behaviors remains uncertain and dependent on many factors (Mansoori-Rostam & Tate, 2017), a primary concern being that of content. Education can reinforce *or* challenge societal myths contributing to GRS/C. Both the presence *and* manner (e.g., situated in what course/academic discipline, framed by which educator/s) must be examined.

Ultimately, to begin countering negative messages for abused men, whose victimization life-context affects and is e/affected by physical, interpersonal, home/family, and work life (all aspects of O'Neil's GRS/C model), it is necessary to determine the source/s of cultural narratives driving the masculine socialization process. After the source/s of these narratives are determined, we can begin exploring the relative role of different information sources in shaping people's perceptions of men abused in heterosexual relationships. Thus, we proposed the following:

RQ1: What are the primary sources of public gender narratives regarding people's perceptions of abused men?

H1: Personal experience will predict male abuse perceptions, such that those with/out interpersonal exposure will differ in describing abused men.

H2: Media sources will predict male abuse perceptions, such that those with/out topical media exposure will differ in describing abused men.

H3: Educational sources will predict male abuse perceptions, such that those with/out topical education exposure will differ in describing abused men.

METHODS

Sampling, Participants, and Procedures

After obtaining our university's IRB approval, we implemented community-based (i.e., not a college-student sample) social network sampling in midwestern and northeastern U.S. states. Specifically, trained research assistants and colleagues at other universities recruited anyone less than 18 years old who was willing to share their perceptions of abused men. Data were obtained in-person at locations convenient for participants (e.g., homes, libraries). Recruiters collected/stored consent forms separately from questionnaires, which we then identified only by reference numbers (i.e., no master matching-list).

On the survey form, participants first read the following: *"Imagine one of your current male friends was being abused by his wife or girlfriend . . . "* Next, they were instructed to write all of their perceptions of this man, with no additional prompts or examples provided to guide those responses. Finally, participants indicated via open-response any prior exposure to the topic of men abused by women. Exact wordings of these items are provided in the Appendix.

Analyses

Results discussed in this chapter were part of a larger data collection project in which we (Eckstein & Cherry, 2015) used a constant comparative open-coding method to analyze the qualitative data from the first (i.e., "Describe this man") survey question. In that study, we observed concept-indicators to note re-emerging themes based on participants' specific phrasing and word choice. Additional information on the coding process and resulting traits used to describe an abused man are discussed in that qualitative-focused article (Eckstein & Cherry, 2015). In the present analysis, we quantitatively coded those eleven qualitative categories as dependent, outcome variables; they included: perceiving the abused man as possessing (a) a Passive Personality, (b) a Weak Physicality, or being (c) an overly Positive Relator, (d) Physically Beaten, (e) Stigmatized, (f) a Past Abuse Victim, (g) a Substance Abuser, (h) Negatively Internalizing, (i) Negatively Externalizing, (j) Normal, and (k) actually using Emasculating slurs (e.g., "bitch-ass pussy") against the man (see Table 10.2 for representative category exemplars). This category "master list" (Strauss, 1987) was applied to data by two coders—one of us (author) and an advanced student trained to independently assess each response, allowing for co-occurring codes within participants (inter-rater agreement $\kappa > .81$ across all categories). Further descriptions of coding and resulting themes are described in Eckstein and Cherry (2015) and in this chapter's following discussion.

FINDINGS

A total of $N = 1{,}957$ participants (42.3 percent male, 56.9 percent female identified), ranging in age from 18 to 93 years old ($M = 30.74$ years, $SD = 13.38$), completed the survey study. Educational achievement ranged from completing some high school (1.1 percent), a high school diploma (26.6 percent), some college (35.1 percent), a college degree (29.3 percent), to a graduate degree (8.0 percent) of study.

In the following subsections, we present results according to each research question/hypothesis; these generally took the form of topic-exposure trends, followed by effects of influence (i.e., each stigmatizing descriptive category as dependent variable) from each info-source/independent variable. We describe each finding without replicating Tables' statistics.

Exposure Trends

For two-tailed significance tests ($\alpha = .05$), statistical power to detect effect sizes was .96 for small ($d = .20$) and 1.00 for medium ($d = .50$) and large ($d = .80$) t-tests effects, and over .99 for all complete-sample regression effects. Out of the overall sample, 77.2 percent ($n = 1{,}510$) indicated having no prior exposure to the notion of an abused man. Abused-man topic-exposure was reported by 1.5 percent of the overall sample.

RQ1: What are the primary sources of public gender narratives regarding people's perceptions of abused men?

Those who reported prior exposure ($n = 447$, 22.8 percent of all participants) indicated their exposure sources, including a college or high school class, via media, or through personal experience. Overall educational attainment predicted having had some form of exposure to the concept of abused men, $b = .22$, $SE = .06$, Wald $= 13.35$, $p < .001$, 95 percent CI [1.11, 1.41]. People with any kind of exposure to the topic of abused men tended to be significantly younger, more likely female, and higher educated overall than those with no prior exposure (see Table 10.1).

Of those exposed to the topic of abused men, 6.6 percent reported male abuse personal experience, which included victimized friends or family or a male participant reporting it himself (although these were not distinguished in this study, in an effort to maintain privacy and minimize potential trauma in this large community-sampled study). Those with personal experience with/as an abused man were significantly older than those not reporting this exposure type. There were no educational attainment differences in terms of personal experience (see Table 10.1).

Table 10.1.   Distribution of Exposure-Group Effects by Sex, Age, and Educational Attainment

Distributions of Exposure-Group Effects by Sex, Age, and Educational Attainment

	Sex			Age			Education		
	Males	Females	Difference	Had	None	Difference	Had	None	Difference
	n (%)	*n (%)*	χ^2	*M (SD)*	*M (SD)*	*t (df)*	*M (SD)*	*M (SD)*	*t (df)*
ANY EXPOSURE	145 (17.5)	294 (26.4)	21.40 ***	27.49	31.68	6.58 (869.04) ***	2.32	2.12	3.68 (1772) ***
N = 447			φ = .11	(10.94)	(13.87)	*d* = .34	(.90)	(.95)	*d* = .22
ANY EDUCATION	93 (64.1)	193 (65.6)	.10	26.06	30.29	3.46 (220.51) **	2.38	2.21	1.71 (383)
n = 287				(9.29)	(13.20)	*d* = .37	(.89)	(.92)	
Health class	17 (11.7)	25 (8.5)	1.16	23.79	27.89	3.50 (71.16) **	2.16	2.34	1.18 (383)
				(6.73)	(11.24)	*d* = .44	(.95)	(.90)	
WS class	2 (1.4)	19 (6.5)	5.51 *	25.29	27.60	0.95 (430)	2.50	2.31	0.91 (383)
			φ = .11	(9.22)	(11.02)		(.89)	(.90)	
Abuse class	12 (8.3)	41 (13.9)	2.94	24.47	27.91	3.22 (103.07) **	2.20	2.34	1.03 (383)
				(6.52)	(11.37)	*d* = .37	(.86)	(.91)	
Other class	60 (41.4)	101 (34.2)	2.14	27.37	27.55	0.17 (430)	2.51	2.21	3.27 (383) **
				(10.53)	(11.19)		(.90)	(.88)	*d* = .34
Women's Center	4 (2.8)	17 (5.8)	1.95	25.52	27.59	0.84 (430)	2.21	2.33	0.55 (383)
				(9.07)	(11.03)		(.79)	(.91)	
ANY MEDIA	23 (15.9)	69 (23.5)	3.39 ¹	33.86	25.76	5.11 (111.10) ***	2.30	2.33	0.27 (383)
n = 92			φ = .09	(14.44)	(9.07)	*d* = .67	(.97)	(.88)	
Read	12 (8.3)	37 (12.6)	1.82	33.82	26.68	3.39 (54.51) **	2.35	2.32	0.26 (383)
				(14.29)	(10.18)	*d* = .58	(1.00)	(.89)	
Viewed	13 (8.9)	39 (13.3)	1.78	34.22	26.59	3.72 (57.03) ***	2.32	2.32	0.02 (383)
				(14.17)	(10.12)	*d* = .62	(.96)	(.89)	
PERS. EXPER.	14 (9.7)	15 (5.1)	3.30 ¹	32.81	27.13	2.63 (430) **	2.19	2.33	0.76 (383)
n = 29			φ = .09	(12.70)	(10.74)	*d* = .48	(.98)	(.90)	

Notes. *p < .05. **p < .01. *** p < .001. ¹p ≤ .07. All percentages are within-sex %s.
Created by Authors.

Next, those indicating topic exposure via any media (4.7 percent of total sample, 20.6 percent of those with any abused-man topic-exposure) reported $M = 0.22$ ($SD = .46$, *range* = 0 to 2 sources) types of media exposure—either reading a book or article (2.5 percent of the total sample) or viewing a film or TV show (2.7 percent of the total sample) mentioning the topic. The distribution of media types was relatively equal among those with any topical media exposure (see Table 10.2 for these statistics), who were typically older than those without this exposure (see Table 10.1 for these statistics). Sex and educational attainment were not significantly associated with overall or individual media exposure types.

Finally, exposure via formal education was reported by 14.7 percent of the total sample. Over 64 percent of the exposed subsample reported $M = 0.67$ ($SD = .53$, *range* = 0 to 3) sources of topical education, including mention of abused men in a high school or college-level general health class (2.2 percent of overall sample), women's studies class (overall sample = 1.1 percent), abusive relationships class (overall sample = 2.7 percent), or via an invited guest-speaker (e.g., local women's center/shelter) presentation not specific to abused men (overall sample = 1.1 percent), and/or an "other" (not abuse/gender/health-specific) class (overall sample = 8.2 percent). Tables 10.1 and 10.2

Table 10.2. Stigmatization Use by Exposure (Source type and Frequency) to Abused Men

Stigmatization Use by Exposure (Source Type & Frequency) to Abused Men

Stigma Type	Any exposure	Education						Media			Personal Experience
		Any Education class	Health class	WS class	Abuse class	Other class	WC Present	Any Media	Read	Viewed	
	N = 447	*n* = 287	*n* = 43	*n* = 21	*n* = 53	*n* = 161	*n* = 21	*n* = 92	*n* = 49	*n* = 52	*n* = 29
		64.2	*9.6*	*4.7*	*11.9*	*35.9*	*4.7*	*20.6*	*11.0*	*11.6*	*6.5*
PASSIVE PERSONALITY *n* = 1,222 *(62.4%)*	282	180	27	9	37	98	14	51	29	25*	21
"Weak-minded, no backbone"	*63.1*	*62.7*	*62.8*	*42.9*	*69.8*	*60.9*	*66.7*	*55.4*	*59.2*	*48.1*	*72.4*
NEGATIVE INTERNALIZER *n* = 563 *(28.8%)*	152**	93	18	6	16	49	11*	30	15	17	11
"Edgy, sad, lonely"	*34.0*	*32.4*	*41.9*	*28.6*	*30.2*	*30.4*	*52.4*	*32.6*	*30.6*	*32.7*	*37.9*
WEAK PHYSICALITY *n* = 540 *(27.6%)*	122	77	13	4	13	45	6	23	10	13	7
"Thin, a little nerdy around the edges"	*27.3*	*26.8*	*30.2*	*19.0*	*24.5*	*28.0*	*28.6*	*25.0*	*20.4*	*25.0*	*24.1*
POSITIVE RELATOR *n* = 237 *(12.1%)*	66*	43	5	4	11	25	0	14	9	9	2
"Forgives anything, stays in bad situation"	*14.8*	*9.6*	*11.6*	*19.0*	*20.8*	*15.5*		*15.2*	*18.4*	*17.3*	*6.9*
NEGATIVE EXTERNALIZER *n* = 165 *(8.4%)*	39	21	6	2	4	8*	1	8	5	4	2
"Outwardly rude to females"	*8.7*	*7.3*	*14.0*	*9.5*	*7.5*	*5.0*	*4.8*	*8.7*	*10.2*	*7.7*	*6.9*
EMASCULATED *n* = 134 *(6.8%)*	31	21	3	1	4	12	1	9	6	3	1
"Bitch ass pussy"	*6.9*	*7.3*	*7.0*	*4.8*	*7.5*	*7.5*	*4.8*	*9.8*	*12.2*	*5.8*	*3.4*
PAST ABUSE VICTIM *n* = 43 *(2.2%)*	12	4*	0	0	0	4	0	1	1	1	0
"Probably abused as child"	*2.7*	*1.4*				*2.5*		*1.1*	*2.0*	*1.9*	
STIGMATIZED *n* = 23 *(1.2%)*	4	3	0	0	1	2	1¹	1	1	0	0
"Shame" & "Humiliation"	*0.9*	*1.0*			*1.9*	*1.2*	*4.8*	*1.1*	*2.0*		
PHYSICALLY BEATEN *n* = 18 *(0.9%)*	4	1	0	0	0	1	0	0	0	0	0
"Unexplained-cuts & bruises"; "flinchy"	*0.9*	*0.3*				*0.6*					
SUBSTANCE ABUSER *n* = 17 *(0.9%)*	4	3	0	0	0	3	0	1	1	0	0
"Probably a drunkard" & "Druggie"	*0.9*	*1.0*				*1.9*		*1.1*	*2.0*		
NORMAL *n* = 159 *(8.1%)*	32	20	4	2	5	10	0	7	3	6	2
"No specif. character. Any man can be abused"	*7.2*	*7.0*	*9.3*	*9.5*	*9.4*	*6.2*		*7.6*	*6.1*	*11.5*	*6.9*

Notes. First column (Stigma Type) values are descriptive of total reports (*N* = 3,099) from the entire sample (*N* = 1,957). Second column (Any Exposure) values are percent of total (*n* = 447) participants for each stigma category with types of exposure to abused men. All percentages, except first row (which are % of each exposure type out of total participants indicating *any* topic-exposure) are % *within* each exposure type who indicated a particular stigma category and may be > 100% due to participants identifying more than one category in their descriptions of the abused men.
*p < .05. **p < .01. *** p < .001. ¹p < .06.

Created by Authors.

show those who reported educational topic-exposure primarily experienced this in "other" classes (i.e., those not distinguished by participants). Among the topically-exposed subsample, those reporting "any" educational exposure, in a health class, and/or in an abuse class were significantly younger than those who were not introduced to it via these sources. Those whose educational exposure occurred in an "other" class had higher educational achievement than those without this exposure source. Exposures via women's center presentations or women's studies classes were unrelated to age or educational attainment (see Table 10.1).

Exposure Influence

Participants characterized the abused man using descriptors ranging from 0 to 4 categories; *n* = 3,099 characteristics coded into *M* = 1.60 (*SD* = 0.70) categories per respondent. Abused-man descriptions were overwhelmingly (over 93.7 percent of all descriptors) negative and derogatory (see Eckstein & Cherry, 2015 and Table 10.2 for participant-quoted examples of each category). Thus, with the exception of the Normal (e.g., "just like any other man") category, analyses showing use of particular traits refer to likelihood of stigmatizing the man as blameworthy for causing and/or not stopping his own victimization due to a variety of his own physical, personality, and communicative traits/tendencies.

Chi-square proportion-differences across the entire sample found that those reporting any kind of prior exposure to the topic differed from those without prior exposure; exposed participants were more likely to identify the man as a Negative Internalizer ($\chi^2 = 7.75$, $p < .01$, $\varphi = .06$) and an overly Positive Relator ($\chi^2 = 3.84$, $p < .05$, $\varphi = .04$). Next, to test comparative influences among the exposed subsample, we ran Wilcoxon ranked-sign tests whereby each exposure source was paired with every other source type to determine which had greater influence in predicting category-use (i.e., each source-type pairing repeated for all 11 descriptors, with each iteration including only the subsample who used a particular descriptor). We discuss these results in the following, respective source-type sections.

H1: Personal experience will predict male abuse perceptions, such that those with/out interpersonal exposure will differ in describing abused men.

Across the entire sample, personal experience with an abused man did not predict likelihood of describing him using particular categories (see Table 10.2). However, when limited to the exposed subsample, comparative-influence results showed that personal experience played a significantly higher role than all formal education sources (except Health classes) in predicting use of the Positive Relator category (see Table 10.3). Further, experience was a consistently stronger predictor than "other" classes and most other exposure sources (i.e., education and media types, except women's studies classes) of labeling the man as Passive Personality, Negative Internalizer, Weak Physicality, Positive Relator, Past Abuse Victim, and using actual Emasculating slurs against him. Thus, H1 was not supported across the entire sample, but was supported in nuanced ways for the topic-exposed subsample.

H2: Media sources will predict male abuse perceptions, such that those with/out topical media exposure will differ in describing abused men.

Supporting H2, among those with any topical exposure, group-difference results showed those reporting viewed media were significantly less likely to view abused men as having blameworthy, Passive Personalities than were those who received their exposure from other sources, $\chi^2 = 5.58$, $p < .05$, $\varphi = .11$ (Table 10.2). Comparative findings reveal that media types did not significantly differ from each other; they were statistically similar to one another in predicting people's perceptions (Tables 10.2 and 10.3) across the whole sample and in the exposed subsample.

Overall media exposure did comparatively differ from other exposure types for those reporting any topical exposure. Media sources were less influential than women's studies classes and more influential than every other educational source in predicting using the following categories to describe abused men: Passive Personality, Negative Internalizer, Weak Physicality, Positive Relator, and using Derogatory/Emasculating phrases against them.

H3: Educational sources will predict male abuse perceptions, such that those with/out topical education exposure will differ in describing abused men.

Table 10.3. Comparison Among Exposure Types in Predicting Characteristics Used to Describe Abused Men

Comparisons Among Exposure Types in Predicting Characteristics Used to Describe Abused Men

	Education (class types)								Media				Personal Experience	
	Health		Abuse		Other		WC Prsnt.		Read		Viewed			
Descriptor Used	z	r	z	r	z	r	z	r	z	r	z	r	z	r
PASSIVE														
WS Class	-3.00**	.18	4.13***	.25	8.60***	.51	ns		3.24**	.19	2.74**	.16	2.04*	.12
Abuse Class	ns		---		5.20***	.31	3.08**	.18	ns		ns		-2.25*	.14
Other Class	-6.40***	.38	-5.29***	.32	---		7.91***	.47	-6.38***	.38	-6.69***	.40	-7.31***	.44
WC Present.	-2.08*	.12	-3.22**	.19	-8.01***	.48	---		-2.29*	.14	ns		ns	
NEG. INTERN.														
WS Class	-2.45*	.20	2.13*	.17	5.72***	.46	ns		2.07*	.17	2.29*	.19	ns	
Other Class	-3.75***	.30	-4.06***	.33	---		4.90***	.40	-4.30***	.35	-3.97***	.32	-4.90***	.40
WEAK PHYS.														
WS Class	-2.18*	.20	2.18*	.20	5.98***	.54	ns		ns		2.18*	.20	ns	
Other Class	-4.20***	.38	-4.21***	.38	---		5.57***	.50	-4.81***	.44	-4.28***	.39	-5.49***	.50
RELATOR														
WS Class	ns		ns		3.90***	.48	2.00*	.25	ns		ns		ns	
Other Class	-3.92***	.48	-2.33*	.29	---		5.00***	.62	-3.02**	.37	-3.02**	.37	-4.43***	.55
WC Present.	-2.24*	.28	-3.32**	.41	-5.00***	.62	---		-3.00**	.37	-3.00**	.37	ns	
Pers. Exper.	ns		2.50*	.31	4.43***	.55	ns		-2.11*	.26	-2.11*	.26	---	
NEG. EXTERN.														
WS Class	ns		ns		1.90^i	.30	ns		ns		ns		ns	
Other Class	ns		ns		---		2.33*	.37	ns		ns		-1.90^i	.30
WC Present.	-1.89^i	.30	ns		-2.33*	.37	---		ns		ns		ns	
EMASCULAT.														
WS Class	ns		ns		3.05**	.55	ns		1.89^i	.34	ns		ns	
Other Class	-2.32*	.42	-2.00*	.36	---		3.05**	.55	ns		-2.32*	.42	-3.05**	.55
WC Present.	ns		ns		-3.05**	.55	---		-1.89^i	.34	ns		ns	
Pers. Exper.	ns		ns		3.05**	.55	ns		-1.89^i	.34	ns		---	
PAST VICTIM														
WS Class	ns		ns		2.00*	.58	ns		ns		ns		ns	
Other Class	-2.00*	.58	-2.00*	.58	---		2.00*	.58	ns		ns		-2.00*	.58
NORMAL														
WS Class	ns		ns		2.31*	.41	ns		ns		ns		ns	
Other Class	ns		ns		---		3.16**	.56	-2.11*	.37	ns		-2.31*	.41
WC Present.	-2.00*	.35	-2.24*	.40	-3.16**	.56	---		ns		-2.24*	.40	ns	

Note. Table shows only those pairings for which results were significant using Wilcoxon signed-ranks test z-scores. Negative scores indicate that exposure source in header row was more influential than exposure source in first column (e.g., Health class influenced more than WS Class), whereas positive scores indicate column source to be more influential than header row source (e.g., WS Class influenced more than Read Media).
*p < .05. **p < .01. *** p < .001. ^{i} p < .06. r = z/√N$_{pairs}$, per Rosenthal (1994).

Created by Authors.

Among the exposed subsample, those with any educational exposure were less likely to describe the abused man as Previously Abused than those with any other exposure types, $\chi^2 = 5.11, p < .05, \varphi = .11$. People whose educational exposure was via a women's center presentation were more likely to describe abused men as Negative Internalizers ($\chi^2 = 3.82, p < .07, \varphi = .09$) and as Stigmatized ($\chi^2 = 3.71, p < .06, \varphi = .09$) than those receiving exposure via any other sources, whereas those educated via an "other" class were less likely to identify the man as a Negative Externalizer, $\chi^2 = 4.42, p < .05, \varphi = .10$. Thus, H3 was generally supported.

Comparative results among education types (see Table 10.3) show a decreasing order of influence ranging from health (most influential), women's studies, abuse, and "other" classes to the women's center presentation (least influential), respectively. This trend was found for those using descriptive categories of Internalized Negativity, Previously Abused, Passive Personality, Weak Physicality, and using actual Emasculating slurs against him; describing the man as Normal was similarly influenced by these educational sources. Of note for deviating from this trend was the role of women's studies classes, which (typically in the top two education influencers) were *most* predictive of using Negative Externalizer and Negative Internalizer labels. These classes were the only education type more influential than media in predicting these descriptions, as media was generally more influential than the other education sources.

Interactive Influences

We concluded by examining potential confounding variables and interactions. As discussed in Eckstein and Cherry (2015), sex was largely insignificant across most outcome-perceptions; although sex predicted prior topical exposure in our current study (i.e., females more exposed), it did not predict likelihood of using particular descriptive categories. Women were slightly more likely to report prior media exposure and slightly less proportionally likely than men to report personal experience, though these only approached significance (see Table 10.1).

Notably, however, a significantly higher proportion of women (than men) indicated topic-exposure via a women's studies class; no sex-differences emerged for other education sources. Thus, in sex-segregated subsamples, we re-ran regression tests of women's studies classes' influence; combined with logistic interaction (sex × WS_{class}) models, results showed sex did not predict using any categories where women's studies classes influenced those results.

Next, we focused on potential age and educational attainment confounders. Youth was a significant predictor of labeling Weak Physicality: $b = .01$, $SE = .00$, Wald $= 11.20, p < .001$, 95 percent CI [.98, .99], with those who perceived him this way significantly younger (M = 29.09 years, SD = 12.46) than those who did not employ this descriptive trait (M = 31.37, SD = 13.68), $t(1061.36)$ = 3.52, p < .001, d = .17. Youth also predicted using actual Emasculating slurs against the hypothetical man, though this only approached significance: b = .01, SE = .01, Wald = 3.17, p = .08, 95 percent CI [.97, 1.00]. Age did not independently predict any other descriptors.

Finally, across the total sample, those who described the abused man as Physically Beaten had significantly less overall educational attainment (M = 1.62 on a 5-point scale, SD = 1.26) than those who did not use this description of the man (M = 2.17, SD = .94), $t(1772)$ = 2.11, p < .05, d = 49. Thus, higher levels of educational attainment predicted *not* perceiving the abused man in terms of this (non-culpable) victimization experience: b = .69, SE = .33, Wald = 4.22, p < .05, 95 percent CI [.26, .97]. Because age typically accompanies educational attainment, we ran regression models to determine the influence of age, education level, and their interaction in predicting use of Physically Beaten. The final model suggested that, although they influenced interactively (β_{Intaxn} = .20, p < .05), this was largely a function of youth (β_{Age} = .18, p < .001) accounting for "lower" education levels (β_{Edu} = .08, *ns*) relating to use of this descriptor. However, as noted previously, age on its own (i.e., outside of the interactive model) did not predict the binary logistic outcome of identifying the man as Physically Beaten. No other characteristic categories were predicted by overall educational attainment level.

DISCUSSION

In our previous work, we explored the nature of stigmatizing reactions people have when asked to describe a man abused by a female partner (Eckstein & Cherry, 2015). In this current study, we went further to examine the impact of topical education, media exposure, and personal experience on the tendency to describe these men in particular ways. Understanding how exposure to the topic of abused men affects people's likelihood (or not) of stigmatizing abused men themselves has theoretical implications for a GRS/C model and practical implications for educators and activists dealing with this issue.

Implications for GRS/C: Abused Men, Masculine Mystique,
and Fear of Femininity

Many GRS/C studies importantly focus on the degree of GRS/C in particular samples and various outcomes associated with experiencing it. In other words, a lot of research looks at the "resulting," right-hand side of O'Neil's (1981a) model. This study contributes to the GRS/C literature by examining the "environmental influences" (i.e., the left-hand side) of the model. As such, this study furthers an understanding of socialization sources influencing masculinity as it is valued and experienced by individuals.

Participants in this study overwhelmingly perceived a hypothetical abused man negatively. Highly stigmatizing, blaming, derogating descriptions (e.g., "What a pussy!") of this man predominated. This is notable not for the fact that abused men were stigmatized by the people in our sample (not surprising, as found in prior research), but because perceptions are highly likely to guide people's actual real-world behavior, particularly in violent situations (Stratmoen et al., 2020; Yule & Grych, 2020). In the current study, people consistently framed the abused man as gender- and relationally-deviant. Further, people blamed the man himself (rather than other potential environmental or interpersonal factors) for his own deviant condition. This tendency to blame victims not only for experiencing abuse, but also for being supposedly "complicit" in its continuation lends itself to explanation via O'Neil's model. Masculine mystique patterns of socialized control and competition require men to constrain not only themselves, but also to regulate and restrict others' genders (O'Neil, 1981b). Therefore, by attributing otherwise positive, yet feminine, characteristics (e.g., Positive Relator, Passive Personality) to abused men, this sample suggested that males unable (or unwilling) to end their own victimization violate masculine normativity and are thus worthy of stigmatization.

In general, prior topical exposure to abused men did not correspond to less stigmatization of them. All types of educational exposure predicted using a variety of blaming, derogating terms to describe abused men, but for those who indicated having had them, women's studies classes were most strongly related to people's perceptions—in largely negative, biased ways. This speaks to the importance of verifying—not just theorizing/assuming—that topical exposure (particularly education) is accurate and positive. Confirming the (positive or negative) effects of exposure can reduce risk of further perpetuating topical stigma.

The fact that women's studies courses (primarily taught at the college-level) generally exerted the most influence across exposure types lends further credence to O'Neil's (1981a) model and its emphasis on the fear of femininity as a driving force of GRS/C. In this study, people whose educational exposure included women's studies courses largely exhibited fear of femininity—as shown in their use of Emasculation, Passive Personality, and overly Positive Relator (attributes associated with femininity and thus, deviant gender norms for sexed-males) categories. Use of these descriptors illustrates maintenance of a "masculine mystique" in which men are expected to be stoic, strong, and controlling of (not controlled by) others (Connell, 2000). Accordingly, these perceptions (especially when communicated) not only harm the abused man, but denigrate the exact traits supposedly "valued" in women. These negative views of abused men, reinforced through education (but in this study, primarily women's studies courses), hurt both men and women. Gender itself may be explored in positive, sex-affirming ways, but it is clear that even courses intended to redress inequalities may be sources of negativity for men who are abused by women. The fact that overwhelmingly stigmatizing perceptions were associated with many and varied topical exposure sources suggests there are very few outlets currently portraying abused men in realistic or supportive ways. These sources, particularly influential on people's perceptions, suggest opportunities for improvement in anti-stigma education.

Applications to Lived Stigmatizing Exposure

Formal education environments are believed prime locales for advancing not only information, but also opinions and attitudes surrounding a topic (Connell, 2000; O'Neil, 1981a, 1981b). Given that attitudes (based on formative perceptions) are typically formed early, targeting children's school curricula is a common tactic (Hust et al., 2017). However, this early-education or primary-prevention approach assumes that what is being taught is accurate, free of discriminatory bias, and does not further perpetuate stigma. Our results suggest that education sources were not particularly helpful, from a post-hoc statistical standpoint, in minimizing use of stigmatizing labels to describe an abused man. In fact, many education sources were affiliated with particularly derogatory labeling of this victim. Because the classroom plays a significant role in not only education, but also boys' and girls' socialization from childhood into adulthood (O'Neil, 1981a, 1981b), it is worrisome that additional exposure *to* education may increase men's stigma.

Far from helping, courses where people typically receive exposure to the topic (e.g., health and abuse-specific coursework) were tied to actually enhanced (or more implicit) stigmatization of these men. For example, the Physically Beaten theme still blamed abused men (i.e., for not stopping their own abuse) but focused a bit more on abuse outcomes than on the man's supposed internal flaws. People who used this theme tended to focus on describing bruises or scars visibly observable on such a man (see Eckstein & Cherry, 2015 for more), but then went on to attribute even these external results to internal characteristics of the man. Notably, and supporting the notion that educational sources were largely *un*helpful in reducing stigma, those who used this seemingly less obviously stigmatizing label had achieved *less* education than those who used other, more derogatorily emasculating labels. However, this was also found to be a function of those with higher educational attainment being older and perhaps of a different generation;

older participants (with more education completed) were less likely to use this *relatively* sympathetic theme.

Demographic factors were of further interest when viewed across the entire sample. A majority of respondents had no prior exposure to this topic; they had not studied, experienced, read, or viewed anything related to abused men. That in itself is alarming, given the prevalence of men in the U.S. who actually report abuse. As a reminder, 25.7 percent (roughly 1 in 4) of men in the U.S. reported physical abuse from a romantic partner, with 13.8 percent of U.S. men (roughly 1 in 7) reporting severe violence, and psychological abuse victimization experienced by almost half of U.S. men (Black et al., 2011). In our current study, those most likely to have heard about men being abused were younger participants, those who had achieved higher education levels, and/or those identifying as female. The fact that so few reported "personal experience" (either personally or via friends/family) is not surprising because abuse is typically underreported (e.g., Othman et al., 2014). However, it also demonstrates the validity of the GRS/C model's inclusion of *restrictive emotionality*, whereby men find it difficult to express emotion and demonstrate vulnerability—an emotional restriction caused by fear of femininity and of lacking masculinity (O'Neil, 1981b). It is possible male abuse personal experience was underreported due to this GRS/C pattern.

Noted by O'Neil (1981a), media are another main source of socialization. Although personal experience (either self or other) and media sources certainly played a role in forming some people's negatively stigmatizing perceptions, it was also these two sources (and not as much education) that predicted describing the man in ways that did not obviously discriminate. This finding lends credence to work that endorses positive encounters with stigmatized individuals to reduce associated stigma (Corrigan & Kosyluk, 2013; Corrigan & Penn, 1999). Basically, positive contact via personal interactions with a potential stigma target allows for perspective-taking and accompanying stigma-reduction. The primary barrier to this exposure source is the circular causality of stigma: to reduce it through interaction with a victim, those victims must disclose their stigmatized trait, which they are unlikely to do while stigma exists.

Taken together with the known role of schooling in socialization, the fact that media sources such as films/shows, newspapers/magazines, and online content related to some of the less stigmatizing characterizations points to the potential for future educators to rely more on cultural (as opposed to theoretical) tools in their topical education. Distributing non-stigmatizing messages through media such as television, online social media, and film may be crucial for not only activists outside academia, but also for those within the education system. Education on the topic should not cease, as these sources potentially reinforcing stigma may be the very ones needed to fight or resist it (Corrigan & Kosyluk, 2013).

Additionally, media may overlap and be mediated/moderated by/with other information sources. For example, entertainment education, although it has shown mixed results (Hoffman et al., 2017), may raise awareness of health and interpersonal issues when tailored to specific audiences (Hust et al., 2017). Even when not intentionally educational, media still expand awareness (e.g., Kahlor & Eastin, 2011). However, scholars and activists (i.e., typical advocates of progress) may have comparatively little influence on media content. The sources over which educators and activists have the most control are usually more formal educational settings such as school classrooms and community programs. The influence of peers at school, in the community, and/or within families is clearly established as a (if not *the*) primary shaper of people's gendered understandings (Arbeit, 2018; Brutsaert, 2006; DeKeseredy et al., 2018; Hertzog & Rowley, 2014; Lobel et al., 1999; Marcell et al., 2011; to name just a few). Thus, potential remains for individual educators to incorporate media and to tailor their formal curricula according to particular students to also harness peers' influence (Rogers et al., 2018). Even the incorporation of *current* research, rather than outdated misconceptions related to controversial (or *seemingly* uncontroversial) topics, can help distinguish ideas "commonly believed" versus "actually practiced" (Hertzog & Rowley, 2014) or clarify when media portrayals are/not accurate (Kahlor & Eastin, 2011).

Finally, it is important that the influence of cultural rhetoric also be countered among those purporting to teach gender/sex equality. Clearly illustrating O'Neil's (1981b) discussed patterns of socialized control, power, competition, and homophobia (all GRS/C contributors), the labels attributed to abused men in this study emphasized a "masculine mystique" by drawing on cultural narratives that fear feminine attributes, particularly when embodied by males supposed to be "opposite" from females—in gender expressions and sexuality. These common perceptions of masculinity as a stoic, strong, control-based gender can be harmful if perpetuated as "actual/embodied" versus "idealistic/normative" concepts. For example, where it may be necessary for women's studies courses to establish the larger concepts of patriarchy and masculine hegemony, it is equally important for professors in those courses to discuss the ways those forces limit both males and females in our culture. No one man can fully embody hegemonic masculinity; and, as shown in our study, many men *and* women embody or communicate complicit masculinity forms that reinforce harmful, essentializing stereotypes (e.g., see Connell, 1995; Eckstein, 2010). Acknowledging this, though perhaps challenging for those advancing particular worldviews, is but one step in showing the complexity of gender as it operates in all our lives.

Limitations and Directions for Future Research

A primary limitation of our study was the lack of knowledge regarding the specificity (e.g., education level, media titles/programs) and extent (e.g., exposure hours across what time periods) of people's various exposure types. Due to the exploratory nature of this project, and to avoid priming participants, we used an open-ended question to assess prior topical exposure. This meant we were unable to standardize the extent to which people responded to particular exposure types. For example, if they reported exposure via a Women's Center guest presentation, we had no way of knowing if that occurred as part of a health, abuse, or "other" class. As such, we were unable to assess how/when the abused-man topic was covered in each class.

Similarly, participants with experiential exposure did not always differentiate between personal experience types (e.g., self, relative, friend, or acquaintance victimization). Establishing the differences in personal experience types could provide richer understanding of how they impact perceptions of abused men. Future research should establish both the type and nature of relationship among those with personal experience exposure. Many in this study reporting "personal experience" were among the most derogatory, victim-blaming, and emasculating slur-users. If only positive interactions reduce stigma (Corrigan & Penn, 1999), it is important to know whether the victimized man they know is liked, respected, and/or off-putting.

Finally, respondents may have reported only their most memorable exposure sources. Using a checklist level-indicator (as done by Eckstein & Quattro, 2021, for example) would aid in identifying more specific parameters to measure exposure. Now that we know prior exposure affects perceptions, future research must explore factors like receiver-attention (e.g., interest in) and exposure intensity (i.e., duration/length, and frequency) across varying sources.

CONCLUSION

Stereotypes and judgments initially help us make sense of the world around us; the application of stigma during that process may happen automatically and without ill intent (Barrett, 2017). Indeed, some of the themes associated with abused men in this study were not *intended* to be derogatory, as they included "excuses" for the man's condition. Nonetheless, they still served to reduce the abused man to something other than masculine (i.e., stoic, strong, controlling), reinforcing the potential for GRS/C experienced by so-called deviant abused males. Unfortunately, it appears that education in its current state may further reinforce stigmatizing characterizations. This is particularly problematic in that GRS/C and damaging gender-beliefs about masculinity do not only harm males. The larger belief system that sets up masculinity as oppositional to femininity reinforces women as "appropriate" abuse victims. By targeting deviant men, male-abuse stigmatizers (a potential majority in the U.S. today) actually attack men *and* women.

REFERENCES

Anderson, L., & Whiston, S. (2005). Sexual assault education programs: Meta-analytic examination of effectiveness. *Psychology of Women Quarterly, 29*, 374–388. https://doi.org/10.1111/j.1471-6402.2005.00237.x.

Arbeit, M. (2018). Student leadership in sex violence intervention & response at West Point. *Journal of Community Psychology, 46*, 598–615. https://doi.org/10.1002/jcop.21961.

Babarskiene, J., & Gaiduk, J. (2018). Implicit theories of marital relationships: A grounded theory of socialization influences. *Marriage & Family Review, 54*, 313–334. https://doi.org/10.1080/01494929.2017.1347547.

Baker, C., & Bevacqua, M. (2017). Challenging narratives of the anti-rape movement's decline. *Violence Against Women, 24*, 350–376. https://doi.org/10.1177/1077801216689164.

Barrett, L. F. (2017). *How emotions are made: The secret life of the brain.* Houghton Mifflin.

Bem, S. (1981). Gender schema theory: A cognitive account of sex typing. *Psychological Review, 88*, 354–364. https://doi.org/10.1037/0033-295X.88.4.354.

Black, M., Basile, K., Breiding, M., Smith, S., Walters, M., Merrick, M., Chen, J., & Stevens, M. (2011). *NISVS: 2010 summary report.* National Center for Injury Prevention & Control. www.cdc.gov/violenceprevention/pdf/nisvs_report2010-a.pdf.

Brutsaert, H. (2006). Gender-role ID & perceived peer acceptance among early adolescents in Belgian mixed & single-sex schools. *Gender & Education, 18*, 635–649. https://doi.org/10.1080/09540250600980204.

Carlyle, K. E., Scarduzio, J., & Slater, M. D. (2014). Media portrayals of female perpetrators of IPV. *Journal of Interpersonal Violence, 29*, 2394–2417. https://doi.org/10.1177/0886260513520231.

Choudhary, E., Coben, J., & Bossarte, R. M. (2010). Adverse health outcomes, perpetrator characteristics, and sexual violence victimization among U.S. adult males. *Journal of Interpersonal Violence, 25*, 1523–1541. https://doi.org/10.1177/0886260509346063.

Connell, R. W. (1995). *Masculinities: Knowledge, power & social change.* UC Press.

Connell, R. W. (2000). *The men and the boys.* University of California Press.

Corrigan, P., & Kosyluk, K. A. (2013). Erasing stigma: Where science meets advocacy. *Basic & Applied Social Psychology, 35*, 131–140. https://doi.org/10.1080/01973533.2012.746598.

Corrigan, P., & Penn, D. L. (1999). Lessons from social psychology on discrediting psychiatric stigma. *American Psychologist, 54*, 765–776. https://doi.org/10.1037/0003-066X.54.9.765.

Courtenay, W. (2000). Constructions of masculinity & influence on men's well-being. *Social Science & Medicine, 50*, 1385–1401. https://doi.org/10.1016/S0277-9536(99)00390-1.

Coyne, S., Nelson, D., Graham-Kevan, N., Tew, E., Meng, K., & Olsen, J. (2011). Media depictions of physical & relational aggression. *Aggressive Behavior, 37*, 356–362. https://doi.org/10.1002/ab.20372.

Davies, C. (2019). Young women's perspectives of "OK" & "not OK" in intimate relations. *Journal of Family Violence, 34*, 479–491. https://doi.org/10.1007/s10896-019-00038-2.

DeKeseredy, W., Hall-Sanchez, A., & Nolan, J. (2018). College campus sexual assault: Contribution of peers' proabuse info support & attachment to abusive peers. *Violence Against Women, 24*, 922–935. https://doi.org/10.1177/1077801217724920.

Dobash, R. E., & Dobash, R. P. (1978). Wives: The "appropriate" victims of marital violence. *Victimology: An International Journal, 2*(3–4), 426–442.

Eckstein, J. (2009). Exploring communication of men revealing abuse from female romantic partners. In D. Cahn (Ed.), *Family violence* (pp. 89–111). SUNY.

———. (2010). Masculinity of men communicating abuse victimization. *Culture, Society & Masculinity, 2*, 62–74. https://doi.org/10.3149/csm.0201.62.

Eckstein, J., & Cherry, J. (2015). Perceived characteristics of men abused by female partners: Blaming, Resulting, Blaming-Excuses, or Normal? *Culture, Society, & Masculinities, 7*, 140–153. https://doi.org/10.3149/CSM.0702.140.

Eckstein, J., & Quattro, R. (2021). Does exposure matter?: Media, education, & experience affecting technology-mediated abuse knowledge, understanding, & severity-perceptions. In J. Weist (Ed.), *Theorizing criminality & policing in digital age* (pp. 3–24). Emerald.

Eckstein, J., & Sabovik, E. (2021). Still just hegemonic after all these years?: "Worst thing s/he thinks about me" predicts attitudinal risk factors for high school healthy relationships program. *Boyhood Studies, 14*(1), 6-24. https://doi.org/10.3167/bhs.2020.140102.

Eisler, R., & Skidmore, J. (1987). Masculine gender role stress: Scale development & component factors in the appraisal of stressful situations. *Behavior Modification, 11*, 123–136.

Gallagher, K., & Parrott, D. (2011). What accounts for men's hostile attitudes toward women?: Influence of hegemonic male role norms & masculine gender role stress. *Violence Against Women, 17*, 568–583. https://doi.org/10.1177/1077801211407296.

Galloway, L., Engstrom, E., & Emmers-Sommer, T. (2015). Does movie viewing cultivate young people's unrealistic expectations about love and marriage? *Marriage & Family Review, 51*, 687–712. http://doi.org/10.1080/01494929.2015.1061629.

George, M. (1994). Riding donkey backwards: Men as unacceptable victims of marital violence. *Journal of Men's Studies, 3*, 137–159. https://doi.org/10.1177/106082659400300203.

Hammock, G., Richardson, D., Williams, C., & Janit, A. (2015). Perceptions of psychological & physical aggression between heterosexual partners. *Journal of Family Violence, 30*, 13–26. https://doi.org/10.1007/s10896-014-9645-y.

Harris, R. J., & Cook, C. A. (1994). Attributions about spouse abuse: It matters who the batterers and victims are. *Sex Roles, 30*, 553–565. https://doi.org/10.1007/BF01420802.

Helgeson, V. (1994). Relation of agency & communion to well-being. *Psychological Bulletin, 116*, 412–428. https://doi.org/10.1037/0033-2909.116.3.412.

Hertzog, J., & Rowley, R. (2014). My beliefs of my peers' beliefs: Exploring gendered nature of social norms in adolescent romantic relationships. *Journal of Interpersonal Violence, 29*, 348–368. https://doi.org/10.1177/0886260513505145.

Hines, D., Brown, J., & Dunning, E. (2007). Characteristics of callers to Abuse Helpline for Men. *Journal of Family Violence, 22*, 63–72. https://doi.org/10.1007/s10896-006-9052-0.

Hines, D., & Malley-Morrison, K. (2001). Psychological effects of partner abuse against men. *Psychology of Men & Masculinity, 2*, 75–85. https://doi.org/10.1037/1524-9220.2.2.75.

Hockett, J. M., Smith, S. J., Klausing, C., & Saucier, D. A. (2016). Rape myth consistency and gender differences in perceiving rape victims: A meta-analysis. *Violence Against Women, 22*, 139–167. https://doi.org/10.1177/1077801215607359.

Hoffman, B., Shensa, A., Wessel, C., Hoffman, R., & Primack, B. (2017). Exposure to fictional television and health. *Health Education Research, 32*, 107–123. https://doi.org/10.1093/her/cyx034.

Hust, S., Adams, P., Willoughby, J., Ren, C., Lei, M., Ran, W., & Marett, E. (2017). E-E strategy in sexual assault prevention. *Journal of Health Communication, 22*, 721–731. https://doi.org/10.1080/10810730.2017.1343877.

Jesmin, S., & Amin, I. (2017). Impact of mass media in changing attitudes towards violence against women in Bangladesh. *Journal of Family Violence, 32*, 525–534. https://doi.org/10.1007/s10896-016-9837-8.

Kahlor, L., & Eastin, M. (2011). TV's role in culture of violence toward women: Study of TV viewing & cultivation of rape myth acceptance in the U.S. *Journal of Broadcasting & Electronic Media, 55*, 215–231. https://doi.org/10.1080/08838151.2011.566085.

Kaplan, M. S., & Marks, G. (1995). Appraisal of health risks: The roles of masculinity, femininity, and sex. *Sociology of Health & Illness, 17*, 206–221. https://doi.org/10.1111/1467-9566.ep10933391.

Khan, R., & Rogers, P. (2015). The normalization of sibling violence: Does gender and personal experience of violence influence perceptions of physical assault against siblings? *Journal of Interpersonal Violence, 30*, 437–458. https://doi.org/10.1177/0886260514535095.

Kimmel, M. S. (2006). *Manhood in America* (2nd ed.). Oxford University Press.

Koepke, S., Eyssel, F., & Bohner, G. (2014). Effects of sexism norms, type of violence, and victim's pre-assault behavior on blame attributions toward female victims and approval of aggressor behavior. *Violence Against Women, 20*, 446–464. https://doi.org/0.1177/1077801214528581.

Kretz, V. (2019). TV/movie viewing predict adults' romantic ideals and relationship satisfaction. *Communication Studies, 70*, 208–234. https://doi.org/10.1080/105109 74.2019.1595692.

Lehmann, M., & Santilli, N. R. (1996). Sex differences in perceptions of spousal abuse. *Journal of Social Behavior and Personality, 11*(5), 229–238.

Lippman, J. (2018). Effects of media portrayals of persistent pursuit on beliefs about stalking. *Communication Research, 45*, 394–421. https://doi.org/10.1177/ 0093650215570653.

Lobel, T. E., Gewirtz, J., Pras, R., Shoeshine-Rokach, M., & Ginton, R. (1999). Relationship between self-endorsement of traits & gender-related judgments of female peers. *Sex Roles, 40*, 483–498. https://doi.org/10.1023/A:1018827827921.

Mansoori-Rostam, S., & Tate, C. (2017). Peering into the 'black box' of education interventions. *Journal of Social Psychology, 157*, 1–15. https://doi.org/10.1080/00 224545.2016.1152211.

Marcell, A., Eftim, S., Sonenstein, F., & Pleck, J. (2011). Associations of family & peer experiences with masculinity attitude trajectories at individual & group level in adolescent & young adult males. *Men & Masculinities, 14*, 565–587. https://doi .org/10.1177/1097184X11409363.

Migliaccio, T. A. (2001). Marginalizing the battered male. *Journal of Men's Studies, 9*, 205–226. https://doi.org/10.3149/jms.0902.205.

Muehlenhard, C., & Peterson, Z. (2011). Distinguishing between sex & gender. *Sex Roles, 64*, 791–803. https://doi.org/10.1007/s11199-011-9932-5.

O'Neil, J. (1981a). Male sex-role conflict, sexism & masculinity. *The Counseling Psychologist, 9*, 61–80. https://doi.org/10.1177/001100008100900213.

———. (1981b). Patterns of gender role conflict & strain: Sexism & fear of femininity in men's lives. *Personnel & Guidance Journal, 60*, 203–210. https://doi.org/ 10.1002/j.2164-4918.1981.tb00282.x.

Oliver, M., Sargent, S., & Weaver, J., III. (1998). Impact of sex and gender role self-perception on affective reactions to different film types. *Sex Roles, 38*, 45–62. https://doi.org/10.1023/a:1018760427785.

Othman, S., Goddard, C., & Piterman, L. (2014). Victims' barriers to discussing domestic violence in clinical consultations: A qualitative enquiry. *Journal of Interpersonal Violence, 29*, 1497-1513. https://doi.org/10.1177/0886260513507136

Paluck, E. L. (2009). What's in a norm?: Sources and processes of norm change. *Journal of Personality & Social Psychology, 96*, 594-600. https://doi.org/10.1037/ a0014688

Rogers, M., Rumley, T., & Lovatt, G. (2018). The *Change Up* project: Using social norming theory with young people to address domestic abuse and promote healthy relationships. *Journal of Family Violence, 34*, 507-519. https://doi.org/10.1007/ s10896-018-0026-9

Rosenthal, R. (1994). Parametric measures of effect size. In H. Cooper & L. V. Hedges (Eds.), *The handbook of research synthesis* (pp. 231-244). Russell Sage Foundation.

Russell, B., Kraus, S. W., Chapleau, K. M., & Oswald, D. (2019). Perceptions of blame in IPV: The role of the perpetrator's ability to arouse fear of injury in the victim. *Journal of Interpersonal Violence, 34*, 1089-1097. https://doi.org/10.1177/0886260516646999

Stratmoen, E., Rivera, E. D., & Saucier, D. A. (2020). "Sorry, I already have a boyfriend": Masculine honor beliefs and perceptions of women's use of deceptive rejection behaviors to avert unwanted romantic advances. *Journal of Social and Personal Relationships, 37*, 467–490. https://doi.org/10.1177/0265407519865615

Strauss, A. L. (1987). *Qualitative analysis for social scientists.* Cambridge University Press.

Yule, K., & Grych, J. (2020). College students' perceptions of barriers to bystander intervention. *Journal of Interpersonal Violence, 35*(15-16), 2971-2992. https://doi.org/10.1177/0886260517706764.

APPENDIX

Imagine one of your current male friends was being abused by his wife or girlfriend . . .

What would be the characteristics of this man?

Have you ever received education (read a book about, received a lecture or class) that discussed male abuse victims? If so, what was it (what class, book, etc.) and what did it cover?

Chapter Eleven

It's Not Unusual, or Is It?

Tom Jones' Unique Blend of Heteromasculine Emotionality

Donnalyn Pompper

INTRODUCTION

Masculinity is a complex concept that seems bereft of meaning unless it is contrasted with emphasized femininity (Connell, 2005) or framed as fear of femininity (Blazina, 2003). Specifically, while girls and women are allowed to express a wide range of emotions, the emotion mostly acceptable for boys and men is anger. Masculinity is a dynamic set of processes according to time, culture, norms, values, and is more useful when considered in its plural form of *masculinities* (Kimmel, 2001). Despite significant social changes with women's massive paid workforce entry this past century, men still occupy higher status jobs and earn more money than women in those jobs (Bhatia & Bhatia, 2021). These outcomes continue to shape our expectations about both women and men and inform stereotypes we use to make meaning about gender groups (Ellemers, 2018). Still, there is only one *hegemonic masculinity;* a cultural form of idealized manhood dominant over gay men, women, children, and the elderly that men use to compare themselves and check one another (Connell, 2005) against behaviors considered un-masculine (Messerschmidt, 2010) within in-groups and across out-groups (Tajfel & Turner, 1986; Turner, 1985). Traditional masculine narratives, or hypermasculinity involving exaggerated musculature or anxiety about masculinity (MacKinnon, 2003), can become toxic if praised as a form of conflict resolution or when harmful behaviors like misogyny and homophobia negatively impact women and marginalized groups (Kimmel, 2017). Many men struggle to communicate their inner emotions, having learned as boys to "divest their emotional selves" or risk characterization as "mama's boy," creating men "unprepared to sustain and nurture themselves or others" (Dvorkin, 2015, p.

245). Today, perhaps the word *masculine* is used more as a verb than a noun. For example, *Man Up!* demands masculine men and boys be tough.

A gateway concept for revealing multiple narratives, *masculinity* (Roubal & Cirklová, 2020) is immersed in conditions of late modern consumer culture. Culture is produced by the entertainment industry (Kidd, 2018) and supported by advertising and media. For men, the metrosexual look was coined in 1994; a combination of metropolitan and heterosexual (but can refer to gay and bisexual men) to describe an upwardly mobile urban man meticulous about his appearance (Simpson, 2002). Through consumerism, males are offered choices for presenting themselves (Pompper et al., 2007). Twenty years later, metrosexualism went "mainstream" and Simpson (2014) introduced a new term—spornosexual—to characterize "a new, more extreme, sex- and body-obsessed version" of a single man who contributes to growing male grooming consumer services and goods industries which have increased 4.5 percent each of the past 20 years (Bano & Sharif, 2015). Sectors includes body practices (e.g., hair removal, face/eye cream) and fashion (e.g., cologne, tailoring), for an expanded window on evolving ways to consider masculinity. For some, however, these consumer trends contribute to a crisis in masculinity (e.g., Zimbardo & Coulombova, 2016) which involves degrees of submission and marginalization which many heterosexual men reject (Roubal & Cirklová, 2020). In the U.K. for example, *laddism* characterizes young men who reject the metrosexual (Benwell, 2003)—even though the metrosexual poster man may be former Manchester United footballer, David Beckham, who inspired a "masculine revolution" (Simpson, 2014).

Marketers know that sex sells and women buy it. Academic research findings about how sex operates or functions in media suggest that the dynamic is subjective, defies measurement, and bears an implied "assumption that sex is used to attract the attention of certain audiences—those people who find sexual information pleasurable and arousing" (Reichert & Lambiase, 2006, p. 3). Sexual appeal seems to depend on four characteristics of race/ethnicity, age, and masculinity-femininity, and the sexual orientation of audience (Mackaronis et al., 2005). Magazines, websites, social media, and other outlets publish images of *sexiest man alive* and hot lists and male sex appeal is used to finance and promote films. Male celebrities' erotic appeal is linked to bodily display and availability/resistance to a theorized gaze (Gallagher, 2014). Mulvey (1975) introduced the male gaze concept to film spectatorship critique—examining the privileged male point of view—and the concept has become a general template for gaze theory to accommodate perspectives across gender groups.

The portal through which I examine the Tom Jones case study is supported by male gender role conflict/stress (GRC/S) theory (O'Neil, 2008) from psychology and the theory of erotic capital (Hakim, 2010) from sociology. I combine perspectives from gender studies, psychology, and sociology to offer a call for eliminating restrictive emotionality (RE) and restrictive affectionate behavior between men (RABBM) which contribute to toxic masculinity as I ask:

RQ: What can we discover about Tom Jones and his career to learn more about male emotionality and further contextualize the male Gender Role Conflict/Stress model?

THE TOM JONES PHENOMENON

These foundations for the case study—1) Males and Gender Roles Conflict/Stress Theory (GRC/S), 2) Popular culture fame and flexibility, and 3) Erotic capital for panty magnetism—lead up to a call for further contextualizing the GRC/S theory model for future hypothesis testing.

Males and Gender Role Conflict/Stress Theory (GRC/S)

Violated gender roles carry greater consequences for men than for women (Pleck, 1981), with masculinity perceptions among men staying "more stagnant" than femininity perceptions linked to women (Bhatia & Bhatia, 2021). Masculinity, when hegemonic, represents the "most powerful version of manhood" and typically is thought of as White, fit, upper middle class, and heterosexual (Allen, 2011, p. 46). When men feel their masculinity being threatened, they may choose to assert their masculine social identity to disprove the threat and protect their manhood through hyper-masculine behavior (Cohn et al., 2009). Masculinity threat increases bias and negative emotions toward feminine gay men (Wellman et al., 2021). Because *emotional* is a word more often associated with women or feminine traits (Bhatia & Bhatia, 2021), boys and men are socialized to restrict emotions other than anger and simultaneously are taught not to cry (Gesualdi, 2013; Pompper et al., 2007; Robinson & Hockey, 2011). Masculinities are reproduced through institutional practices that often rely on images, ideals, and representations of roles, behaviors, and emotions (Connell, 2005). Yet, social norms as standards or rules, often constrain males' ability to express emotions (Mahalik, 1999; Pompper, 2010). Restrictive Emotionality (RE) is operationalized as "having restrictions and fears about expressing one's feelings as well as restrictions in finding words to express basic emotions" (O'Neil, 2008, p. 367). Boys and men experience GRC when they deviate from, conform to, or violate male gender role norms of masculinity ideology (O'Neil, 2008). Males who suppress their emotions act out with anger, aggression, or violence to compensate for their repressed feelings (O'Neil, 1981). Effects negatively impact males' health, interpersonal relationships, career, and family life, including feelings of victimization and abuse that cause psychological and physical pain linked to perceptions of loss in personal status or positive regard, being compared to negative stereotypes, and experiencing limited or decreased potential (O'Neil, 2008). Similarly, GRC theory explains how males are socialized to restrict affectionate behavior between men (RABBM) as another outcome of fear of femininity that can play out in bullying behaviors directed toward other men, as well as women. In sum, males are socialized to RE and RABBM when they encounter gender role devaluations, restrictions, and violations (O'Neil, 2008; O'Neil, Good, & Holmes, 1995). Men also avoid showing appreciation for other men or risk being ridiculed as gay (Lotz, 2014).

I combine these two similar concepts—into male GRC/S—to fortify my argument that the actual context for RE and RABBM matter and can play out in terms of both conflict and stress. The mix also offers a means for examining disruptions of toxic masculinity conditions and an opportunity to accommodate expanded forms of masculinity for further contextualizing the GRC/S model. By examining RE and RABM in the life of an iconic popular culture entertainer like Tom Jones, I offer a case study illustrating how hypermasculine heterosexual male norms may be disrupted to accommodate unrestrictive displays of emotion and avoid contributing to GRC/S. Encouraging men to show emotions has been deemed beneficial for everyone in terms of supporting equality, as well as for men who stand to suffer mental and physiological harm if they hold emotions inside. I join other researchers who suggest that men increasingly are practicing "softer or more emotional forms of masculinity" (de Boise & Hern, 2017, p. 779, Holmes, 2015) which may positively correlate emotional communication with greater gender equality. I suggest that Tom Jones has been practicing heteromasculine emotionality for nearly six decades now.

Popular Culture Fame and Flexibility

Born Tom Woodward, the self-professed Teddy Boy teen in the 1960s recognized benefits of male flexibility early on. He loved rock 'n roll music and avoided dressing like older men by modifying his dad's discarded jacket with velvet accoutrements that he asked his mom to sew to the collar in order to more closely resemble the dandy, Edwardian feminized Teddy Boy style: "I want—and in fact need—to be a Teddy boy, with the drainpipe trousers and the beetle-crusher shoes" (Jones, 2015, p. 54). His autobiography recounted marrying at age 16 after impregnating his 15-year old girlfriend, Melinda

Trenchard, and earning money singing in workingmen's pubs with piano players, which he humbly described: "I didn't seem to have too much trouble getting people to listen" (Jones, 2015, p. 83). Such humility is inconsistent with the traditional male gender role and more consistent with femininity (Dvorkin, 2015) or religiosity (Yoo, 2020).

Fifteen million Americans watched Tom Jones' debut performance on *The Ed Sullivan Show*. He performed "It's Not Unusual," his first Decca Records recording with "the Squires" produced in November 1964 and released the following year. Decca's publicity machine wrote: "He's 22, he's single and he's a coal miner" but Jones wrote in his autobiography ". . . I was 24 going on 25, I had a wife and a son and I had never been down a coal mine in my life . . ." (Jones, 2015, p. 159). It's the song that forever changed Jones' life, according to his 2015 autobiography, *Tom Jones Over the Top and Back*. He explained that Sullivan's producers warned him during rehearsals "to keep my hips in check or face immediate and irrevocable censorship . . . This is a family show . . . So, easy on the grinding" (Jones, 2015, p. 6). He characterized "It's Not Unusual" as the song "that has catapulted me to stardom in Britain and Europe and spun my life around . . . brought me out here to America—put me on a plane for only the second time in my life, seen me collected from the airport in a big black town car . . ." (Jones, 2015, p. 7). Jones ultimately appeared on the Ed Sullivan Show in 1965, 1968, and 1970.

Figure 11.1. Tom Jones albums
Courtesy of Depositphotos Inc.

This exposure lead Tom Jones to his own syndicated one-hour TV variety show, *This is Tom Jones* on ABC-TV, debuting February 7, 1969. In the mid-1960s, networks began broadcasting most of prime-time schedules in color and color TV sales exceeded black and white TV sales by 1972 (Kidd, 2018). In the late twentieth century, television was *the* popular culture form (Storey, 1996), when the average American spent two-thirds of their waking hours watching TV (Allen, 1992). The Tom Jones image became larger than life on this highly-produced show, with king-sized letters "TOM" as set backdrop, costumed dancers, colorful psychedelic scenery typical for the 1960s, and Tom Jones wearing his trademark tuxedo with bowtie. He launched each of the 65 episodes over 2.5 seasons by singing "It's Not Unusual" and a solo finale under dimmed lights and a moving stage which surrounded him with an orchestra. Sandwiched in between, Tom Jones sang duets with popular artists of varying styles, genres, and ethnic social identities, including: Janis Joplin, Stevie Wonder, Tina Turner, Jerry Lee Lewis, Donny Osmond, Cher, Chaka Khan, Joe Cocker, Wilson Pickett, Little Richard, CSNY, Ella Fitzgerald, Chet Atkins, Aretha Franklin, and more. Like Ed Sullivan, Tom Jones respected artists across ethnic groups and promoted their talent—even working to modify his own singing style so that he might complement them (Jones, 2015).

Even though toughness through inflexibility is a traditional male gender role quality, the form of masculinity Tom Jones has represented for decades in his personal life and as a performer ruptures that code in three main ways. First, Jones called his *This Is Tom Jones* TV program the ". . . biggest deal that had ever been struck for a singer-led variety show" (Jones, 2015, p. 233) and he wrote extensively throughout his autobiography about opportunities to perform duets with dozens of diverse talented guests, singing across multiple genres from rock and roll to folk to blues, and more. Jones (2015) wrote in his autobiography, "I could do the ballads, rip the shit out of rock'n'roll numbers and meet and swing with these great people. And I didn't seem to be afraid of it. I thought I could do it all. Why not? . . . Why not be versatile?" (p. 237). Second, each episode of the show was shot in the U.K. twice; once for British audiences and once for Americans to accommodate network censorship in the United States. Third, flexibility eventually became the marker of Tom Jones' career as he worked extensively in Las Vegas through the 1980s and hired his son, Mark Woodward to manage him. Biographer Smith (2015) wrote about how 16-year-old Mark missed his traveling, absentee father, so Tom Jones allowed his son to leave school at 16 to go on the road with him (p. 168). In addition to restricted emotionality (RE), another key component of GRC/S theory is restricted affectionate behavior between men (RABBM) (O'Neil, 2008). Writing in his autobiography, Jones (2015) noted: "A lot of sons don't want to be associated with what their fathers do. Fortunately, mine does. And I know that he's doing what he wants to do" (p. 408). It was son Mark who introduced Tom Jones to MTV audiences when he teamed up with Art of Noise and recorded Prince's dance tune, "Kiss," in 1987.

The Tom Jones image was at its zenith by the late '60s and early '70s and it may be argued that flexibility enabled Tom Jones to capitalize on fame. Building upon and expanding human capital theory of the 1960s, Bourdieu (1986) defined *social capital* on a foundation of relational reality, exploring ways individuals become capable of generating certain advantages over other people—so that relations across our social world are steeped in forms of capital that organize and define social positions and lifestyles. Across the three sources of *cultural capital*—objective (e.g., books, works of art), embodied (language, mannerisms, preferences), and institutionalized (e.g., qualifications, education credentials), the labor of artists contributes tangible cultural capital artifacts like music, art, literature, poetry, and other forms of expression to world (Bourdieu, 1984). As a popular artist, Tom Jones profited from his talent as he subscribed to the masculine code as breadwinner; a social role that enables men to display and embody dominance and socioeconomic success (Levant, 1997). Tom Jones' heterosexual masculinity was characterized in press coverage and at least a dozen biographies in terms of taking care of his family while living the jet set lifestyle. Biographer Russell (2007) wrote that Tom Jones is a "family man" (p. 207) and Smith (2015) also wrote that he is "a wonderful provider for his family" (p. 168).

Erotic Capital for Panty Magnetism

Tom Jones also possessed *erotic capital*, a concept I borrow from psychology (Roubal, 2019), involving physical attractiveness, sexual attractiveness, as well as "social competence, temperament, sexuality, and a capacity for self-presentation" (grooming) (Roubal & Cirklová, 2020, p. 19). Erotic capital plays out in relationships with partners and others, as well as in one's professional life, or career (Hakim, 2010). Physical beauty and sexual attractiveness connote social prestige which translate to social capital through social networks that can evolve into higher income, or real economic and social capital. Erotic capital contributes positively to a person's identity and self-concept. Physical attractiveness and self-presentation are important components that give men positive psychological effects such as increased self-confidence and self-concept. Yet, when these attributes are absent, men can experience low self-esteem associated with male gender role stress or feeling strained to measure up to expectations of a masculine code for behavior (Pleck, 1995). For Tom Jones, erotic capital played out in his talent, charm, and animal magnetism (Elis & Sutherland, 2000), which included a "hairy chest" (MacFarlane, 2020, p. 14).

The shift from Teddy Boy to "Panty Magnet" was not one Tom Jones could have anticipated (Smith, 2015, p. 131; Jones, 2015, p. 227). Of his image in 1965, he shared in his autobiography an anecdote about what happened to a raincoat gifted by his manager: "I was able to see fame coming . . . Bam! I'm on the pavement under a pile of screaming girls . . . Their mission was clearly to gather souvenirs . . . Also to land kisses on my face if possible . . . They ripped the shit out of it—left it in strips . . . By the time Tom Jones was performing at the Copacabana New York nightclub in 1968, a woman in the audience stood up, wriggled out of her panties, bent down to pick them up and handed them to Tom Jones to wipe his forehead. The event attracted a newspaper columnist's attention. Explaining this event in his autobiography, Jones (2015) said: "I dab my brow with them. And then I say, 'You want to watch you don't catch cold'" He added: "[A]lmost my entire image . . . It becomes a thing . . . A carpet of donated underwear" (p. 226). Whereas night-clubbing women earlier handed Jones a white linen napkin or towel, after the Copa incident, women began throwing their panties at the stage—with those in Las Vegas also tossing their room key. *This Is Tom Jones* producers capitalized upon the phenomenon and routinely planted the first three rows of the TV audience with attractive women. When Tom Jones loosened his bowtie, he sent women into "paroxysms of lust" (Elis and Sutherland, 2000, p. 113) and actually encouraged their behavior by accepting the articles and offering full-mouth kisses. In a 2013 interview with Terry Gross on NPR's "Fresh Air," Jones said the ritual was complicated: ". . . I don't think any woman had ever thrown underwear at a singer before . . . it was very sexy at the time. But then it—you know, it became a bit of a joke because people would bring their underwear, you know, in handbags . . . So it backfired on me a bit" (Gross, 2021).

Research findings long have suggested that investments in cultivating one's beauty pay off with attractive women and men earning more and achieving leadership positions earlier in their career by 20 percent as compared to less attractive people (Wong & Penner, 2016). For Tom Jones, actual capital enabled him to buy multiple mansions, Rolls Royces, sports cars, and have his nose fixed after it had been broken in youthful barroom brawls. According to multiple biographies and tabloids, Tom Jones' erotic capital fueled tabloid coverage of extramarital affairs of varying durations, as well as arguments with his childhood bride-wife. Amidst the media spectacle of the affairs, he consistently expressed being committed to his wife—if only spiritually, given that he's been called a "serial adulterer (Ellis & Sutherland, 2000, back cover). In his autobiography, Jones (2015) recounted a question that Elvis Presley him ". . . all those years ago: 'What do you take to stay sane'? . . . 'It's easy. I have Linda'" (p. 410).

By 2016, Tom Jones expressed another emotion in a very public way and earned significant media coverage. When his wife passed from cancer, *The Independent* newspaper reported on her death and offered an extensive context of their 59-year marriage, including Jones' "famed womanizing" — juxtaposed with text and photographs of a weeping Jones under the headline: "Tom Jones breaks down in first public appearance since wife's death" (Tom, 2016). *The Independent* featured a grown man crying in public as atypical hegemonic heterosexual male behavior with language such as: "overcome with emotion as he insisted he never considered leaving his childhood sweetheart" (Tom, 2016). MacFarlane's (2020) biography of Tom Jones also included a photograph of the pop star crying at the funeral of his long-time manager, Gordon Mills, in 1986. Public crying violates a key tenet of masculinity, or, what it means to be a man (Connell & Messerschmidt, 2005; Gesualdi, 2013) and is more typically associated with femininity.

By the time he reached his 50s and 60s, with erotic capital in check, Jones found new ways to be flexible, reinvent himself, and address his vanity. Jones performed many highly promoted and publicized benefits and tributes, recorded "You Can Leave Your Hat On" for *The Full Monty* (1997), and recorded disco hit, *Sex Bomb* (1998), but changed the original lyrics from "I'm a" sex bomb to "You're my" sex bomb. He secured a cameo on the TV cartoon, *The Simpsons,* and became a staple of *The Voice U.K.* for four seasons. Explaining how he gave up dyeing his hair in 2009, Jones (2015) offered in his autobiography: "Don't get me wrong: if I didn't think the gray looked better, I'd still be dyeing my hair. Vanity doesn't just vanish" (p. 395). Knighted in 2006 by Queen Elizabeth II and performing at her Diamond Jubilee in 2012, Jones (2015) explained that appearing on "The Voice U.K." was an opportunity to mentor others: "[I] liked the way the show talked about 'coaches' and 'coaching' rather than 'judges' and 'judging . . . wasn't in the game of humiliating people for pleasure, as on some other talent shows" (p. 400). I posit that this sentiment also is inconsistent with traditional hegemonic masculinity tenets of aggressive competition.

Summary and Case Study Research Method

This exploratory case study relied on combining male GRC/S theory with erotic capital theory to examine the career of Tom Jones as I took a closer look at a unique blend of heteromasculine emotionality that un-restricts male expressions of emotion. The case study research method supports investigations of contemporary phenomena in context and addresses descriptive or explanatory questions (Yin, 2018). In conjunction with the formal case study method, I used a descriptive analysis form of inquiry to map out the "prominent landmarks of a given social world" to see patterns or themes (Kidd,

2018, p. 123). Suitable for the case study research method are *what happened* investigations (Yin, 2018). My concerns include formation and outcomes of toxic masculinity which continue to plague men and boys throughout the life course and play out negatively—impacting everyone. Reading Tom Jones autobiography (Jones, 2015) and several biographies, sifting through news coverage of Tom Jones and his career over nearly 60 years, and watching clips of *This is Tom Jones*, I explored:

RQ: What can we discover about Tom Jones and his career to learn more about male emotionality and further contextualize the male Gender Role Conflict/Stress model?

What I discovered is that this international pop star entertainer illustrated emotions inconsistent with masculine ideology, such as being humble and flexible, respecting and embracing diversity/equity/inclusion (DEI), crying in public, and demonstrating affectionate behavior between men—all of which may contribute much to alleviating toxic masculinity and its effects. Altogether, Tom Jones' career involved using his sexuality to amplify a Teddy Boy and "Panty Magnet" image, sell more than 100 million records, accrue 36 Top 40 hits in the U.K. and 19 Top 40 hits in the United States, and ultimately net a worth of $250 million (Tom, n.d.) Such emotive expressiveness by a man who built a successful career over nearly six decades suggests that masculine ideology's restriction on emotion can be ruptured to accommodate greater flexibility and minimize GRC/S inherent in hegemonic and toxic masculinity tenets.

FURTHER CONTEXTUALIZING THE GRC/S MODEL

The purpose of this case study has been to discover new means for inspiring a reflexive shift in hegemonic masculinity by advocating for further contextualizing the male gender role conflict/stress model. Accommodating context of men working as entertainers who are unafraid to infuse emotion into their image or brand supports reducing emphasis on categorizing emotionality as either feminine or masculine. The GRC/S model (O'Neil, 2008) is a sphere fortified by walls consisting of GRS/C and sexism (personal and institutional) surrounding the conflict/stress quadrants which include Restrictive Emotionality (RE) and Restrictive Affectionate Behavior Between Men (RABBM). The outcome of this case study about Tom Jones suggests ways to contextualize RE and RABBM as rupturing toxic masculinity conditions when a man is an entertainer. Thus, I pose the rhetorical question of *Why not extend such conditions to all males?* to support social acceptance of boys and men who cry in public, nurture others, promote DEI (e.g., actively working to break down biases such as racism, sexism, homophobia), are humble and flexible, and demonstrate affectionate behavior between men. At the model's center is fear of femininity as it plays out in terms of male gender socialization and masculinity ideology/norms. I posit that once we, as a society, become more flexible in adapting to and embracing new forms of masculinity that include acceptance of a wider range of emotions, this fear of femininity core may begin fading as emotions become less categorized as either feminine or masculine.

Global popular culture icon and sex symbol, Tom Jones carefully cultivated his performances and media interviews to project a confident-yet-humble talent who realized early on that his performances, charm, and physical appearance are hits with heterosexual women. Tom Jones' erotic capital (Hakim, 2010) in the form of physical attractiveness (Hamermesh & Biddle, 1994) played out in song delivery and body movement for success in cultural capital (Bourdieu, 1984) as a popular culture icon and for success in economic capital, as he became a multi-millionaire. Lipovetsky (2002) explained that human physicality becomes eroticized and commercialized—with physical beauty taking on an additional economic dimension due to demand associated with its scarcity.

Tom Jones' live performances and screen sexual charisma were amplified on his TV show's camerawork, lighting, and sound. We know that marketers use sex appeals in advertising —as persuasion based on words, images, actions delivering an explicit or implicit sexual message (Reichert et al., 2001). This strategy has been popular in the U.S., Europe, and Asia for many years (e.g., Reichert and Carpenter, 2004), but evidence on whether or not sex appeals sell has been mixed (Wirtz et al., 2018). Magazine covers are another space often occupied by sex symbols. Over the years, Tom Jones' image appeared on covers of numerous published television program schedule guides, *Life* magazine, *Amateur Photographer*, and magazines produced for women (*My Weekly*), newspaper magazine sections, souvenir magazines, *50 Plus Magazine*, *The Big Issue* magazine, and *Music Week* (Jones, 2015). Advertising's visuals help us to understand ways masculinity is constructed (e.g., Bordo, 2000; Connell, 2005), so over time, it is easy to see how Tom Jones' emotive expression as part of his heteromasculine-emotional persona contributed to his popularity and success.

Masculine ideology suggests that males simultaneously (and contradictorily) are socialized to be powerful and competitive—yet warned to not demonstrate any weaknesses in emotions. However, Holmes (2015) contended that today's relational complexity demands emotional reflexivity. So reflecting on Tom Jones' long successful career as a heteromasculine- emotional man offers a window on viewing just one way masculinity may be reshaped to accommodate males' range of emotionality. Imagining a wider expression of male emotions, beyond just anger, ruptures hegemonic masculine ideology at a time when White males, in particular, push back against feminism as delimiting male power. Increasingly more women enter the workforce, increase their economic power, and raise their voices for political change; actions that potentially increase men's fear of women's gains. Around the world in recent years, large numbers of women across social identity groups have pushed back on traditional female gender role stereotypes of non-agency (Bhatia & Bhatia, 2021) with protests against racial injustice, police brutality, federal government (in)action, and trends to exclude voters and roll back Roe vs. Wade— such as with the #MeToo movement, #BLM movement, and reaction to the election of Trump in 2016. Observing people acting contrary to stereotypes and norms has an important part to play in affecting social change.

DISCUSSION

It's no secret that the masculinity concept is deeply embedded across social structures and resistant to change. I argue, however, that we must reconfigure a White-fit-upper-middle-class-heterosexual default for a more dynamic and inclusive conception of masculinity. Even "arguably the most privileged people on the planet" (Kimmel, 2017; Kimmel and Wade, 2018, p. 236) stand to gain multiple benefits once we can accept a wider range of male emotions. To begin, boys and men can avoid physical and psychological trauma associated with toxic masculinity so long researched by GRC/S investigators who seek to support clinical treatment for boys and men. Other benefits of a male emotionality continuum include emotionally competent people engaging in more successful relationships across gender groups for more positive outcomes that play out at home and at work (Holmes, 2015), a wider range of interest/study/occupation arenas for men (Chaffee et al., 2020), improved clinical treatment for men battling cancer (Hoyt, 2009) and navigating military service conditions (McAllister et al., 2018), and management of organizations (Petrenko et al., 2017). Overall, acts of emotional labor by and for males—like self-disclosure, compassion, and vulnerability—must become normalized over time.

For decades, Tom Jones' heterosexuality has comfortably fit with masculinity tenets and the pop star's extramarital affairs have provided much tabloid fodder. In his personal life, Tom Jones' *ladies man* persona also fueled arguments about extramarital affairs with his wife (e.g., Ellis and Sutherland, 2000). Biographer Russell (2007) wrote of an interview with Tom Jones, who explained: "Normally men are the predators, the chasers . . . When you become a celebrity, the role is reversed . . . you have these women wanting to be with you. Men are men and if you're a real man, then . . ." (p. 209). Biographers also have written extensively about Tom Jones' affairs with groupies and celebrities such as Miss World Marjorie Wallace and Mary Wilson of The Supremes—and subsequent domestic disputes. Celebrity biographer Smith (2015) told of wife Linda's regret that her husband had grown so famous and tossing of her "expensive gold jewellery" out a limo window after her husband retorted, "You've not done too badly on it" (p. 164). Yet, in his autobiography, Tom Jones wrote of devotion to wife, Linda, claiming that he never thought of divorce, couching his commitment in an anecdote about conversing with another ladies-man-persona pop star, Elvis Presley. (Jones, 2015). Tom Jones' sex appeal is something that biographer MacFarlane (2020) suggested any man would desire, even though "to the men in the audience Tom Jones is a parody, a caricature of what a real man should be" (p. 15).

Like Holmes (2015), I concur that today's relational complexity demands emotional reflexivity and invite expulsion of the phrase *real man* whenever it perpetuates toxicity. While possessing the greatest amount of social power, men simply don't *feel* powerful (Kimmel and Wade, 2018). Enabling men to express emotions other than anger could give them power to feel more comfortable talking about and expressing their emotions so that they may support a new kind of power-sharing gender equality system. The Tom Jones' case study, with its unusual violations of hegemonic masculinity through expressing emotionality provides an opportunity to reject accepted norms of restrictive masculinity and replace them with more evolved and equitable behaviors.

REFERENCES

Allen, B. J. (2011). *Difference matters: Communicating social identity* (2nd ed.). Waveland Press.

Allen, R. (1992). *Channels of discourse, reassembled.* Routledge.

Bano, S., & Sharif, M. A. M. (2015). Metrosexual: Emerging and lucrative segment for marketers. *International Review of Management and Marketing*, 6(4), p. 117. doi: http://www.econjournals.com/.

Benwell, B. (2003). Introduction: Masculinity and men's lifestyle magazines. In B. Benwell (Ed.), *Masculinity and men's lifestyle magazines* (pp. 6–29). Blackwell Publishing.

Bhatia, N, & Bhatia, S. (2021). Changes in gender stereotypes over time: A computational analysis. *Psychology of Women Quarterly*, 45(1), 106–125. doi: https://doi.org/10.1177/0361684320977178.

Blazina, C. (2003). *The cultural myth of masculinity*. Praeger.

Bordo, S. (2000). *The male body: A new look at men in public and in private*. New York: Farrar, Straus and Giroux.

Bourdieu, P. (1984). Distinction a social critique of the judgement of taste, Routledge.

———. (1986). The forms of capital. In Richardson, J. (Ed.): *Handbook of theory and research for the sociology of education* (pp. 241–258). Greenwood.

Chaffee, K. E., Lou, N. M., Noels, K. A., & Katz, J. W. (2020). Why don't "real men" learn languages? Masculinity threat and gender ideology suppress men's language learning motivation. *Group Processes and Intergroup Relations*, 23(2), 301–318. doi: 10.1177/1368430219835025.

Cohn, A., Seibert, L. A., & Zeichner, A. (2009). The role of restrictive emotionality, trait anger, and masculinity threat in men's perpetration of physical aggression. *Psychology of Men and Masculinity*, 10, 218–224. doi: 10.1037/a0015151.

Connell, R. W. (2005). *Masculinities*. Cambridge: Polity.

Connell, R. W., & Messerschmidt, J. W. (2005). Hegemonic masculinity: Rethinking the concept. *Gender and Society*, 19(6), 829–859. doi: https://doi.org/10.1177/0891243205278639.

de Boise, S., & Hearn, J. (2017). Are men getting more emotional? Critical sociological perspectives on men, masculinities and emotions. *The Sociological Review*, 65(4), 779–796. doi: https://doi.org/10.1177/0038026116686500.

Dvorkin, K. (2015). Working with men in therapy. *Group*, 39(3), 241–250. doi: https://www.jstor.org/stable/10.13186/group.39.3.0241.

Elis, L. E., & Sutherland, B. (2000). *Tom Jones close up*. Omnibus Press.

Ellemers, N. (2018). Gender stereotypes. *Annual Review of Psychology*, 69(1), 275–298. doi: https://doi.org/10.1146/annurev-psych-122216-011719

Gallagher, M. (2014). On Javier Bardem's sex appeal. *Transnational Cinemas*, 5(2). doi: http://dx.doi.or/10.1080/20403526.2014.959296.

Gesualdi, M. (2013). Man tears and masculinities: News coverage of John Boehner's tearful episodes. *Journal of Communication Inquiry*, 37(4), 304–321. doi: https://doi.org/10.1177/0196859913505617.

Glass, L. L. (1984). Man's man/ladies' man: Motifs of hypermasculinity. *Psychiatry*, 47(3), 260–278. doi: https://doi.org/10.1080/00332747.1984.11024247.

Gross, T. (2021, March 14). Tom Jones remembers when audiences threw underwear and room keys at him. [Radio broadcast transcript]. NPR. https://rb.gy/rb8lyz.

Hakim, C. (2010). Erotic capital, *European Sociological Review*, 26(5), 499–518. doi: https://doi.org/10.1093/esr/jcq014.

Hamermesh, D. S., & Biddle, J. E. (1994). Beauty and the labor market. *The American Economic Review*, 84(5), 1174–1194. doi: 10.3386/w4518.

Holmes, M. (2015). Men's emotions: Heteromasculinity, emotional reflexivity, and intimate relationships. *Men and Masculinities*, 18, 176–192. doi: https://doi.org/10.1177/1097184X14557494.

Hoyt, M. A. (2009). Gender role conflict and emotional approach coping in men with cancer. *Psychology and Health*, 24(8), 981–996. doi: 10.1080/08870440802311330.

Jahn, M. (1971, June 15). Tom Jones excels at Garden recital. *New York Times*, p. 49.

Jones, T. (2015). *Tom Jones over the top and back: The autobiography.* Blue Rider Press.

Kidd, D. (2018). *Pop culture freaks: Identity, mass media, and society,* 2nd ed. Routledge.

Kimmel, M. S. (2001). Global masculinities: Restoration and resistance. In B. Pease and K. Pringle (Eds.), *A man's world: Changing men's practices in a globalized world* (pp. 21–37). Zed Books.

Kimmel, M. S. (2017). *American masculinity at the end of an era: Angry white men.* Nation Books.

Kimmel, M. S., & Wade, L. (2018). Ask a feminist: Michael Kimmel and Lisa Wade discuss toxic masculinity. *Signs: Journal of Women in Culture and Society,* 44(1), 233–254. doi: https://doi.org/10.1086/698284.

Levant, R. F. (1997). The masculinity crisis. *Journal of Men's Studies,* 5(3), 221–231. doi: https://doi.org/10.1177/106082659700500302.

Lipovetsky, G. (2002). *The empire of fashion: Dressing modern democracy.* Princeton University Press.

Lotz, A. D. (2014). *Cable guys: Television and masculinities in the 21st century.* New York University Press.

MacFarlane, C. (2020). *Sir Tom Jones: 80.* Colin MacFarlane.

Mackaronis, J. E., Strassbert, D. S., Cundiff, J. M., & Cann, D. J. (2005). Beholder and beheld: A multilevel model of perceived sexual appeal. *Archives of Sexual Behavior,* 44, 2237-2248. doi: 0.1007/s10508-015-0517-1.

MacKinnon, K. (2003). *Representing men: Maleness and masculinity in the media.* Oxford University Press Inc.

Mahalik, J. R. (1999). Interpersonal psychotherapy with men who experience gender role conflict. *Professional Psychology, Research and Practice,* 30, 5–13. doi: 10.1037/0735-7028.30.1.5.

McAllister, L., Callaghan, J. E. M., & Fellin, J. C. (2019). Masculinities and emotional expression in UK servicemen: Big boys don't cry? *Journal of Gender Studies,* 28(3), 257–270.

Messerschmidt, J. (2000). Becoming real men: Adolescent masculinity challenges and sexual violence. *Men and Masculinities,* 2, 286–307. doi: https://doi.org/10.1177/1097184X00002003003.

Messerschmidt, J. W. (2010). *Hegemonic masculinities and camouflaged politics: Unmasking the Bush dynasty and its war against Iraq.* Paradigm.

Mulvey, L. (1975). Visual pleasures and narrative cinema. *Screen,* 16(3), 6–18. doi: https://doi.org/10.1093/screen/16.3.6.

O'Neil, J. M. (1981). Patterns of gender role conflict and strain: Sexism and fear of femininity in men's lives. *Personnel and Guidance Journal, 60,* 203–210. doi: 10.1002/j.2164-4918.1981.tb00282.x.

———. (2008). Summarizing 25 years of research on men's gender role conflict using the Gender Role Conflict Scale: New research paradigms and clinical implications. *Counseling Psychologist,* 36, 358–445. doi: https://doi.org/10.1177/0011000008317057.

O'Neil, J. M., Good, G. E., & Holmes, S. (1995). Fifteen years of theory and research on men's gender role conflict: New paradigms for empirical research. In R. Levant and W. Pollack (Eds.), *The new psychology of men* (pp. 164–206). Basic Books.

Petrenko, O. V., Aime, F., Recendes, T., & Chandler, J. A. (2017). The case for humble expectations: CEO humility and market performance. *Strategic Management Journal*, 40(12), 1938–1964. https://doi.org/10.1002/smj.3071.

Pleck, J. H. (1981). *The myth of masculinity*. MIT Press.

———. (1995). The gender role strain paradigm: An update. In R. F. Levant and W. S. Pollack (Eds.), *A new psychology of men* (pp. 11–32). Basic Books.

Pompper, D. (2010). Masculinities, the metrosexual, and media images: Across dimensions of age and ethnicity. *Sex Roles: A Journal of Research*, 63(9), 682–696. Doi: https://doi.org/10.1007/s11199-010-9870-7/

Pompper, D., Soto, J., & Piel, L. (2007). Male body image and magazine standards: Considering dimensions of age and ethnicity. *Journalism and Mass Communication Quarterly*, 84(3), 525–545. doi: https://doi.org/10.1177/10776990070840030 8.

Reichert, T., & Carpenter, C. (2004). An update on sex in magazine advertising: 1983 to 2003. *Journalism and Mass Communication Quarterly*, 81, 823–837. doi: https://doi.org/10.1177/107769900408100407.

Reichert, T., & Lambiase, J. (2006). Peddling desire: Sex and the marketing of media and consumer goods. In R. Reichert and J. Lambiase (Eds.), *Sex in consumer culture: The erotic content of media and marketing* (pp. 1–10). Lawrence Erlbaum Associates, Publishers.

Robinson, V., & J. Hockey (2011). *Masculinities in transition*. Palgrave Macmillan.

Roubal, O. (2019). The erotic capital of men from the perspective of the sociology of marketing communication. Conference Proceedings from the International Scientific Conference, in Kusa, A., Zauskova, A., and Buckova, Z. (Eds.) Marketing identity 2019: Offline is the new online (pp. 706–717), Slovakia.

Roubal, O., & Cirklová , J. (2020). Crisis of masculinity, erotic capital and male grooming in the sociology of marketing communications. *Communication Today*, 11(2), 19–34. doi: 10.1007/s11294-020-09779-z.

Russell, G. (2007). *Arise Sir Tom Jones the biography*. John Blake.

Simpson, M. (2002, July 22). Meet the metrosexual. Salon. Downloaded June 7, 2021, from https://www.salon.com/2002/07/22/metrosexual/.

Simpson, M. (2014, June 11). Spornosexual is the new metrosexual. The Telegraph. Downloaded June 7, 2021, from https://rb.gy/rjktdy.

Smith, S. (2015). *Tom Jones the life*. Harper Collins Publishers.

Storey, J. (1996). *Cultural studies and the study of popular culture: Theories and methods*. University of Georgia Press.

Tajfel, H., & Turner, J. C. (1986). The social identity theory of intergroup behavior. In S. Worchel and W. G. Austin (Eds.), *Psychology of intergroup relations* (2nd ed.), pp. 7–24. Nelson.

Tajfel, H., Turner, J. C., Austin, W. G., & Worchel, S. (1979). An integrative theory of intergroup conflict. In M. J. Hatch and M. Schultz (Eds.), Organizational identity: A reader, (pp. 56–65). Oxford University Press..

Tom Jones' net worth (n.d.) Downloaded June 8, 2021, from https://rb.gy/13diav.

Tom Jones breaks down in first public appearance since wife's death (June 6, 2016). *The Independent.* Downloaded June 25, 2021, from https://rb.gy/dio34c.

Turner, J. C. (1985). Social categorization and the self-concept: A social cognitive theory of group behavior. In E. J. Lawler (Ed.), *Advances in group processes* (Vol. 2, pp. 77–122). JAI Press.

Wellman, J. D., Beam, A. J., Wilkins, C. L., Newell, E. E., & Mendez, C. A. (2021). Masculinity threat increases bias and negative emotions toward feminine gay men. *Psychology of Men and Masculinities.* doi: https://doi.org/10.1037/men0000349.

Wirtz, J. G., Sparks, J. V., & Zimbres, T. M. (2018). The effect of exposure to sexual appeals in advertisements on memory, attitude, and purchase intention: A meta-analytic review. *International Journal of Advertising*, 37(2), 168–198. doi: 10.1080/02650487.2017.1334996.

Wong, J. S., & Penner, A. M.: Gender and the returns to attractiveness. *Research in Social Stratification and Mobility*, 44, 113–123.

Yin, R. K. (2018). *Case study research and applications: Design and methods*, 6th ed. Sage.

Yoo, W. (2020). Constructing soft masculinity: Christian conversion and gendered experience among young Chinese Christian men in Beijing. *Chinese Sociological Review*, 52(5), 539–561. doi: https://doi.org/10.1080/21620555.2020.1799347.

Zimbardo, P., & Coulombova, N. D. (2016). *Man, interrupted: Why young men are struggling and what we can do about it.* Red Wheel.

Chapter Twelve

Retire *Like a Man*

Peyton Manning, Andrew Luck, and Competing Masculinities

Anthony LaStrape and Ann Burnette

INTRODUCTION

The sport of football features dramatic elements including speed, force, and strategy. But the most dramatic element of the game may be the bodies of the players themselves as they personify and symbolize valued aspects of masculinity. As the game has developed from its origins to the twenty-first century, players' bodies have become bigger, stronger, and body parts have become more specialized in the football context. Field positions that require the most muscle mass and strength provide one benchmark for examining ways meaning has been made about players' bodies—and ways male athletes' body parts are objectified. Wells (2019) observed that today's NFL players "are drastically different" than they were earlier in the league's history and explained, "Competition for a spot is fierce. This means that players start training, using diet and exercise to build their bodies into highly specialized machines." Describing offensive linemen, Gaines (2015) noted, "Of the 159 players who have started at least four games as an offensive lineman since the start of the 2014 season, only 23 weigh less than 300 pounds and 39 weigh at least 320 pounds." The pressure for NFL players to be hypermasculine in terms of size, strength, and competitiveness, creates a fertile environment for expanding our understanding of Gender Role Stress/Conflict (GRS/C).

This chapter examines the discursive tensions embodied in the construct of masculinity as expressed by retiring NFL players Peyton Manning and Andrew Luck. Both athletes reached the pinnacle of the NFL as award-winning quarterback—Manning for the Indianapolis Colts and Denver Broncos, and Luck for the Indianapolis Colts. When each man retired after a successful career—Manning in 2016 and Luck in 2019—they delivered retirement statements that reflected on their accomplishments as NFL players and their perspectives on the game. In analyzing these texts, we found that the words offer contrasting interpretations of masculinity, and that each athlete navigated gender role conflict/stress (GRS/C) in a profoundly different way. Moreover, reactions to each athlete's statement opens revealing windows onto the role and outcome of hegemonic masculinity in professional football culture. The case study reported in this chapter was designed to investigate how Manning and Luck negotiated hegemonic masculinity tenets and implications for GRS/C.

LITERATURE REVIEW

To illuminate the expression of GRS/C in public discourse by male athletes, first we need to understand: (1) rhetorical construction of masculinity, (2) bodies as sites of interpretation, (3) policing function of hegemonic masculinity, and 4) Manning, Luck, and the Pain Principle.

Rhetorical Construction of Masculinity

Masculinity, as a rhetorical construct, has many dimensions. While it is common to speak of an individual's masculinity, the various components of the construct can produce masculinities in the plural to acknowledge intersections of gender with other social identity dimensions such as age, ethnicity, sexual orientation, and more (Connell & Messerschmidt, 2005). Masculinities function at sociological and psychological levels and are expressed through symbols and messages, which means that they also function rhetorically. Boys and men (as well as girls and women) face a lifetime of messages about what constitutes *appropriate* masculine behavior. These messages come from interpersonal relationships, public arguments, and mass media. What makes these tenets of masculinity *hegemonic* is that they are rhetorically constructed and widely communicated and accepted (Connell, 1990; Trujillo, 1991). The hegemonic, rhetorical construction of masculinity serves as an ideal model for people to use as they judge the masculine performances of men on and off the football field. Connell (1990) observed that hegemonic masculinity is "culturally exalted and . . . its exaltation stabilizes a structure of dominance" (p. 94). This construction of masculinity places immense pressure on those who want to be seen as masculine.

The sport of American football is an especially powerful locus of hegemonic masculinities. In the NFL, athletes conform to a masculine ideal because their athletic career and livelihood depends on it. Because of a need for speed, power, and full body contact, football is a natural venue for the communication of masculinity. Sports, both amateur and professional, have long served as a proving ground for socially approved manhood. As Whitson (1990) explained, "Sport has become, it is fair to suggest, one of the central sites in the social production of masculinity" (p. 19). Trujillo (1995) wrote that football is "one of the most appropriate sports in which to find reproductions of hegemonic masculinity" (p. 405). Similarly, Foote and colleagues (2017) argued that football, in particular, is "commonly upheld as the standard of American masculinity" (2017, p. 270). Butterworth (2012) opined that football has a compelling effect on Americans' imaginations, even among people who are not football fans. Masculinity's hegemonic import—as an ideal and norm—offers an important lens through which to view Manning's and Luck's retirement statements.

Bodies as Sites of Interpretation

Sports media coverage often focuses on and objectifies football players' bodies. Oates (2007) argued, "extensive media-facilitated public display of the athletic body, presented as entertainment, has become a staple of sports media coverage" (p. 78). The NFL organization amplifies these practices, too. In late February 2020 the league's official website featured detailed coverage of the 2020 NFL Combine event. Taking place annually in Indianapolis, this invitation-only event is for NFL draft prospects who are measured, tested, and timed for the benefit of NFL coaches and scouts. The NFL website posts performance results of physical tests such as the bench press, the 40-yard dash, and the broad jump, as well as each participant's measurement of his height, weight, arms, and hands (NFL, 2020). This practice not only highlights players' bodies in motion, but breaks down men's body parts for display—or objectification. Among many takeaways, this website's treatment subsequently invites sports media coverage and fuels disturbing outcomes with implications about class and race, as Oates (2007) observed:

> In an age when blacks are perceived to be dominant, especially in macho team sports like football and basketball, the draft, and the looking it enables, serves to reassert the white male power structure by positioning increasingly non-white athletic bodies as commodities. (p. 88)

Hence, male bodies are more than physical frames. They are also sites of expression, performance, interpretation, and objectification.

NFL athletes are male. They also are considered highly masculine and this framing is amplified by mediated images of professional athletes. Performative gender does not necessarily organically follow from a body's biological attributes. As Connell (1990) argued, "Masculinity is not inherent in the male body; it is a definition given socially to certain characteristics" (p. 89). O'Neil

(2008) posited that the more rigid a depiction of masculinity, the more likely gender role conflict and stress will exist. It is within the cognitive social construction of masculinity that devaluation can occur. This is especially evident when those who look like strong, potent representatives of hegemonic masculinity act in a way that expressly violates these norms.

The Policing Function of Hegemonic Masculinity

Hegemonic masculinities serve an ordering function for regulating men's behaviors. In professional football, athletes regulate their behavior to conform to NFL expectations and collectively this dynamic perpetuates a certain brand of hegemonic masculinity. Connell and Messerschmidt (2005) observed that men must be policed in order to conform with hegemonic masculinity. A critical way in which football players are policed is through the expectation that they do not allow injury or pain to interfere with their play. Executives, coaches, sports media, and fans all contribute to this policing function to ensure that appropriate standards of masculinity are upheld within the sport (see Foote et al., 2017).

Patriarchy, or relationships among men, is a feature of hegemonic masculinity and of football culture (Trujillo, 1991). It plays out in two ways: 1) players are celebrated as "brothers" and 2) male authority figures such as coaches and owners are cast as the *fathers* of football *families*. Professional football players operate within a brotherhood code which maintains a patriarchal order in football. We characterize this dynamic as patriarchal because masculinities are socially constructed and ultimately serve a disciplining function. Football players enable masculinity in football to remain hegemonic and culturally dominant—while they're simultaneously policed by authorities and others to remain disciplined. This is how hegemonic patterns of masculinity endure (Connell & Messerschmidt, 2005). GRS/C for football players may manifest itself in ways players, sports media, and fans qualify a football player in terms of his team spirit—degrees to which a male athlete endorses, personifies, and perpetuates team spirit. The bonds created in training and on the field constitute a brotherhood wherein team camaraderie is nurtured and supported. As part of it, they support their fellow players, at least publicly. One of the harshest judgments that can be made about a player is labeling him *not a team player*. When a player violates this expectancy for being a team player, he may be summarily marginalized and even shunned by players, sports media, and fans.

In particular, coaches are compelling forces in the maintenance of the patriarchal order in football through discipline. Foote and colleagues (2017) described a "specific mythology associated with football" that privileges "the celebration of coaches as moral authority figures" (p. 273). One area where coaches exert their authority is in the articulation and management of others' pain. Many coaches push players to play through their physical pain and become psychologically stronger for the experience. Foote and colleagues (2017) noted: "football cultivates its own version of 'tough love'" (p. 279). This philosophy of disciplining athletes to accept pain also fortifies the principles of masculinity as applied to players' bodies, and the ethos of football (Furness, 2016; Mangold & Goehring, 2018). The NFL's patriarchal order is maintained through both formal and informal means and the degree to which players become disciplined to meet expectations of hegemonic masculinity tenets has serious implications for an athlete's career and legacy.

Discourse is central to the policing function of hegemonic masculinity when an athlete is perceived to deviate from or to violate expectations for normative masculinity. Adams and colleagues (2010) found that coaches use bullying techniques of ridiculing weakness, questioning genitalia, and exhibiting blatant misogyny in order to motivate players they consider to be underperforming. Beyond individual ability or the ability of an opponent, poor performance is framed as a player not being *man enough* to overcome and dominate his opponent. In men's sports, victory comes to whomever channels traditional masculinity tenets, while defeat is reserved for those who are not man enough. The sports context can foster a pattern of gender role stress or conflict (GRS/C) (O'Neil, 2008) and men fear loss of privilege when social norms around masculinity appear to be changing (Pompper, 2010). Sport serves as one of the few spaces where men can reject weakness in any form. Winning, above all, is the principle that matters. So, policing masculinity involves severe outcomes for men who do not conform to its tenets. Reigeluth and Addis (2016) found that adolescent boys reported 55-85 percent of the insults they experienced as part of masculinity policing episodes attacked their intelligence, ability, and manifested in misogyny and homophobia. Disciplined boys routinely moderate their behavior to put on an acceptable façade, having had their masculinity policed. The policing of manhood is prevalent on campus and in locker rooms and it is effective. Yet, there is more to discover about how negative effects contribute to GRS/C.

A critical way in which football players are policed is through the expectation that they do not allow injury or pain to interfere with their play. The gender role stress and conflict (GRS/C) outcome of men feeling pressured to appear and be masculine is under-explored territory in research about the sport of football. O'Neil (2008) noted that men caught within a "rigid gender role socialization processes" experience GRS/C that can "limit them from being fully functioning human beings" (p. 359). Hence, GRS/C can contribute to health and emotional problems among men. Physical manifestations of pain, such as crying, rupture tenets of hegemonic masculinity and are socially disdained because they disrupt gender norms rigidly enforced for male lead-ers (Gesualdi, 2013). In the NFL, the emphasis on players' ability to play through pain is fertile ground for negative outcomes such as GRS/C.

Fear of losing out on a perceived or justifiable benefit also functions as an implicit method of policing masculinity (O'Neil, 2008). Professional athletes must play through pain or risk losing their position on a team and the status that comes with it. Thus, fear motivates athletes to hide injuries and play even though they're injured—in order to be considered a reliable and accepted part of the team (Faure & Casnova, 2019). Professional athletes who admit injury and pain stand to lose financial rewards since NFL contracts are not guaranteed and a player can be removed from the team for any reason includ-ing being injured too often (Nieh, 2017). Perhaps one of the most prominent accounts of a star athlete losing out on fame and endorsements due to injury was Washington Redskins quarterback Robert Griffin III. He had endorse-ments with Adidas, Subway, and Gatorade among others as the face of the team in 2012 (Rovell, 2012). Four years later, after multiple knee injuries, Griffin was neither a starting quarterback nor an advertising pitch man. Grif-fin was unable to regain the status he commanded before his injuries and he currently is on no NFL roster.

Manning, Luck, and the Pain Principle

The construct of hegemonic masculinity is powerfully expressed and reified across NFL franchises by professional football players and their bodies. NFL players are expected to withstand significant pain, subordinate their personal needs for the good of the team, and accept and perpetuate a patriarchal system of management and coaching. When NFL quarterbacks Peyton Manning and Andrew Luck retired in 2016 and 2019 respectively, both could look back on a career marked by national success. However, both had also struggled to play despite repeated serious injuries.

Power and representation is central to perpetuating hegemonic masculinity. Among the features of hegemonic masculinity are physical force and con-trol, which includes "physical strength, force, speed, control, toughness, and domination" (Trujillo, 1991, p. 291). "Real" or "masculine" men are physi-cally strong and able to marshal that strength in order to dominate situations and people. This aspect of masculinity also is expressed as power or control over one's own body. Connell (1990) argued that elite male athletes must "triumph" over their bodies (p. 95). One of the implications of defining mas-culinity in terms of physical strength is that physical pain challenges a man's ability to be forceful and in control and thus threatens his masculinity. Foot-ball culture embraces what some observers have called the Pain Principle, a belief that pain is an inevitable aspect of sport and that "enduring pain, rather than giving into it, is a vital step in one's character development and worth" (Sanderson et. al., 2016, p. 6).

Men are socialized to manage their physical and emotional pain within the hegemonic masculinity construct. While all humans experience pain, men are closely judged for their ability to withstand pain. Pain may be a universal experience shared by all living things. Emotional pain can come at the loss of loved ones, or the loss of the ability to perform tasks once considered routine (Apkarian et al., 2004; Leary, 2015). Physical pain can manifest in the dull ache of a hip, the stiffness of a knee when the weather changes, and the experience of heartburn and indigestion. Pain is what reminds humanity that life is not a simulation, that there are consequences for actions (Bastian et al., 2014). In many cultures, men who mask their pain are celebrated and those who cannot are ridiculed (Gesualdi, 2013). The ability to withstand injury and the pain that accompanies it is a key component of NFL players' masculinity. The normalized (unspoken) Pain Principle in football encourages players to disregard their own health for the good of the team and the franchise. This ability not only enables football players to remain competitive in a physically violent game, but it also has profound ethical implications and can contribute to GRS/C.

Negotiating, managing, and performing through pain is the norm for football play across recreational and professional settings. Helmets and shoulder pads are standard equipment required for playing football in order to minimize injury and to reduce painful outcomes (Orchard, 2002; Cottler et al., 2011). Football teams that play in organized leagues from Pop Warner to the NCAA all have trainers and medical professionals charged with teaching athletes how to avoid injury and pain. In professional football, there are team doctors, trainers, specialists, nutritionists, and surgeons all tasked with getting players ready to play with and through the pain associated with football. Football players establish themselves as athletes who can be counted on to play even while enduring pain. Playing through pain is the sort of sacrifice a leader makes to show his teammates that he is to be trusted (Foote et al., 2017).

Active NFL players feel pressure of the Pain Principle and retired players have become valorized for sacrificing their body to the sport so that pain masking is a defended value in football. Former Oakland Raider Jim Otto called his autobiography, co-authored with Dave Newhouse, *Jim Otto: The Pain of Glory* (Fainaru-Wada & Fainaru, 2013). Otto's playing injuries resulted in fusions of his back vertebrae, shoulder replacements, multiple knee replacements on both knees, and the eventual amputation of his right leg. In the book, Otto reflected on the physical price he paid as an NFL center for 14 years, saying, "I take responsibility for everything that happened to my body" (quoted in Fairanu-Wada & Fairanu, 2013, p. 352). Celebrated football players perform their masculinity by showing others that they're physically and mentally tough, enduring pain and debilitation without complaint.

There are only 32 NFL quarterback jobs in America, so the pressure is on for men playing quarterback who are immediately thrust into the spotlight as the face of the franchise. These young men experience gender role stress as they strive to hold on to their quarterback job for as long as possible. One such man is Peyton Manning. The Manning family is NFL royalty (Glass, 2013) as Peyton's father, Archie Manning, was a quarterback for the New Orleans Saints for 15 years and Peyton's younger brother, Eli Manning, is a two-time Super Bowl Champion with the New York Giants who recently retired from the NFL after 16 years. In his own right, Peyton Manning is a two-time Super Bowl champion, winning one with the Indianapolis Colts and the other with the Denver Broncos. He retired in 2016 after playing 18 years in the NFL and will go down as one of the greatest quarterbacks to ever play (Richards, 2017). Pain fails to respect NFL royalty status, however. An 18-year NFL veteran, Manning once was considered an NFL Iron Man—a description given to players who never miss a game. He experienced a neck injury in 2010 and had four neck surgeries the following year and missed the entire 2011 season for physical recovery (Jenkins, 2013; Bell, 2015; Stites, 2015). Peyton Manning's neck pain and his missed season due to injury inspired the announcement we analyze in this chapter while comparing and contrasting it with Andrew Luck's retirement statement.

Similarly, Andrew Luck also is considered NFL royalty. His father, Oliver Luck, was an NFL quarterback for the Houston Oilers in the 1980s and currently serves as XFL commissioner, a burgeoning professional football league that plays during the spring instead of the fall (Schilken, 2018). Luck went to Stanford University and was the starting quarterback as a freshman. By his junior season he was the consensus first pick in the NFL draft, but Luck stayed in college for his senior year. Thamel (2011) chronicled the process by which Luck made his decision to stay in school. Part of that process was reaching out to Peyton Manning for counsel, as he also remained in college for his senior year. So, Luck stayed in college an extra year while Manning healed in the 2011 season, resulting in Indianapolis losing so many games that they had the first pick in the 2012 NFL draft. Instead of using that draft pick to continue to build around Peyton Manning, the Colts released their four-time NFL MVP, and Super Bowl champion quarterback. This move was made to make room for Andrew Luck and his potential to provide another 15 years of quarterback play.

With Manning in Denver and Luck at the helm in Indianapolis, the future looked exceedingly bright for the Colts organization. During his rookie season, Luck set records for individual passing yards by a rookie in a single game with

Figure 12.1. Peyton Manning (18), quarterback Indianapolis Colts, 1998–2011
Courtesy of Depositphotos Inc.

Figure 12.2.   Andrew Luck (12), quarterback Indianapolis Colts, 2012–2018
Courtesy of Depositphotos Inc.

433 yards and led seven game-winning drives (Tredinnick, 2012; Kacsmar, 2012; Kacsmar, 2013). Yet, injury and pain found Luck, too, when he sprained his shoulder in 2015 but kept playing even when he lacerated his kidney and pulled several abdomen muscles. Stites (2018) chronicled how injuries kept Luck from much of the 2015 season. In 2016 Luck suffered a frayed labrum and in 2017 underwent surgery on the shoulder injured two years before. Luck played through many games while injured, but he used January 2017–2018 to stop playing and to recover from shoulder surgery. Luck returned to the field in 2019, but announced his retirement when pain became unbearable (Erickson, 2019; Haislop, 2019). As Luck walked off the field at Lucas Oil Stadium in Indianapolis for the last time as a starting quarterback for the Colts, fans cascaded him with boos from the stands (Nesbit, 2019).

Upon this foundation of the hegemonic masculinity construct and the Pain Principal at play in the professional work of Peyton Manning and Andrew Luck, the study reported in this chapter was designed to examine two retirement statements to see how masculinity interplays with experiences with injury and pain in football. Both athletes come from football families, were number one picks in the NFL draft, and were regarded as elite. Insights that emerge in conjunction with career end clarify one's chosen profession and can amplify ways masculinity is constructed. Thus, we pose these questions.

RQ1: To what extent does Peyton Manning's retirement statement uphold the construct of hegemonic masculinity?

RQ2: To what extent does Andrew Luck's retirement statement uphold the construct of hegemonic masculinity?

METHOD

A case study technique involving close textual analysis was used to examine how tenets of hegemonic masculinity are perpetuated or violated in professional football with regard to athletes' experiences with injury and pain. Namely, transcripts from Peyton Manning and Andrew Luck's retirement addresses were obtained from ESPN.com to critically read how each framed his retirement decision. We also examined the athletes' lived experiences (Van Manen, 1990) against ways the public reaction to the announcements—as reported in sports media.

First, we first identified statements that indicated the rhetor's position with regard to the Pain Principle. We assessed whether each rhetor made statements that endorsed or contradicted the assumption that a football player should play through the pain. Second, we identified statements that indicated the rhetor's position in relation to traditional norms of being expected to mask pain. We considered the degree of GRS/C that Manning and Luck implicitly or explicitly conveyed. Finally, we noted the immediate reaction to each announcement across popular sports media.

FINDINGS

RQ1: To what extent does Peyton Manning's retirement statement uphold the construct of hegemonic masculinity?

Manning, a 6'5", 230-pound athlete at the time of his retirement in 2016, referred to an ability to withstand pain as a prerequisite for success among professional football players during the first minute of his retirement announcement. He shared a short anecdote about completing a pass in his first NFL game: "Somebody hit me really hard and after I got up, I told myself, 'I know I can play in this league.'" Playing among a league of professional male athletes and taking hits while still doing the job is a sign of success in professional football. Manning concluded the announcement with another physicality reference, saying: "Well, I've fought a good fight. I've finished my football race and after 18 years, it's time."

Sandwiched between these two references to pain and fight[ing], Manning used the retirement announcement to express gratitude, to recall legendary players who influenced him, and to paint a sweeping picture of his achievements across membership on two teams—the Indianapolis Colts, and the Denver Broncos. He thanked coaches, teammates, rivals, and staff who supported him. Manning recalled charming anecdotes about his grandfather, thanked his wife, children, and extended family members. He also thanked fans and cities where he played throughout his career, and he wished luck to athletes still playing football.

To some, Manning's announcement represents what is expected of men. The announcement resonates with hegemonic masculine ideals emphasizing physical strength, skill, and the ability to withstand pressure, as well as respect and good manners with nostalgia and optimism thrown in. In the NFL, players are susceptible to gender role conflict or stress if they cannot withstand pain. In his farewell announcement, Manning's message was one of succeeding and meeting expectations.

Messages about the need to withstand pain are inherent in ways fathers communicate with sons across generations. Early in his announcement, Manning mentioned influences of legendary quarterbacks Dan Marino and Johnny

Unitas, revering both as symbols of a patriarchy to which he also belongs. Manning recalled a throw Marino made during his first ever regular season game that he described as the "damndest throw I'd ever seen." Marino's example also taught Manning what to do with pain since Marino played in the NFL for 17 years, continuing play for six seasons after rupturing his achilleas tendon and using up all the cartilage in his left knee, wearing large support braces on both legs while playing and practicing to compensate for the damage done to his body (Carucci, 1994). Marino taught Manning that if your throwing arm still works, then you can play. In his retirement announcement, Manning described how he once shook Unitas' hand as an honor, saying "He told me, 'Peyton, you stay at it. I'm pulling for you.'" Nack (2001) once described Unitas' right arm as the most dangerous right arm in the entire NFL, an important observation to share in this case study because three decades after retirement, the nerve damage in Unitas' right arm was so severe that he could no longer close his right hand.

RQ2: To what extent does Andrew Luck's retirement statement uphold the construct of hegemonic masculinity?

In stark contrast to Manning's retirement announcement, Luck's news conference statement announcing retirement at age 29 as Indianapolis Colts quarterback in 2019 explicitly tied his decision to retire to the frustration and pain that his injuries had caused. Qualifying his press statement as "the hardest decision of my life," he explained the high degree of physical pain he had endured: "For the last four years or so, I've been in this cycle of injury, pain, rehab, injury, pain, rehab, and it's been unceasing, unrelenting, both in-season and offseason, and I felt stuck in it. The only way I see out is to no longer play football." Moreover, Luck detailed "mental and emotional toll" associated with playing football: "I feel tired, and not just in a physical sense."

Luck's statement included expressions of appreciation for teammates, coaches, family, and the opportunity to play football, calling it "the greatest game in the world . . . There are times last year I'd have to pinch myself, am I allowed to have this much fun on a football field?" Luck conveyed admiration for his teammates, saying: "There are things that people need to know about the men in that locker room: They're great, they're honest, they're real, and there's no bigger fan of them than me." He declared that choosing to stay on the team would be the selfish decision and it would be unfair to his teammates: "I know that I am unable to pour my heart and soul into this position, which would not only sell myself short but the team in the end as well." Luck also shared short anecdotes thanking his father for taking him to see legendary freeagent placekicker Adam Vinatieri and then later joining him on the field: "I'll tell my grandkids I got to play with him."

Luck also showed emotion as part of his retirement announcement when a reporter asked him to comment on the recent episode when fans booed Luck at a 2019 pre-season game when they heard Luck had planned to retire. Breech (2019) reported Colts fans "savagely" booed Luck when he exited the field following a 27–17 loss to news of his retirement broke during the pre-season game's fourth quarter. Luck said: "I'd be lying if I didn't say I heard the reaction. It hurt; I'll be honest."

DISCUSSION AND CONCLUSION

As NFL quarterbacks who retired within three years of one another and both experienced a frequent succession of injury and pain that is so common for professional football players, Peyton Manning and Andrew Luck qualified their experiences very differently in their retirement announcements. The way each framed his retirement decision tells much about the masculinity construct and gender role conflict and stress as the dynamic plays out in professional sports. Next, we discuss how athletes who violate masculinity norms become targets for masculinity policing or are rewarded for silence about pain, injury, and hiding their emotions. Finally, we conclude with recommendations for further expanding masculinities' continuum to further help reduce male gender role conflict and stress.

Policing Hegemonic Masculinity

A male athlete who violates gender role norms is perceived as less masculine and opens himself to becoming a target for hegemonic masculinity policing. In this way, a well-recognized code of masculinity is invisibly protected and enforced. In the context of the case study examined in this chapter, whereas Manning upheld the traditional masculinity code shaped by stoicism in the face of pain and even appreciation for the opportunity to prove himself through the experience of pain, Luck conversely identified injury and pain as the reason why he felt the need to retire. Clearly, Luck deviated from central tenets of hegemonic masculinity and acknowledged the male gender role conflict and stress he felt leading up to the decision that included an emotional reaction to being booed by fans. Manning felt embraced by his team and fan base, but Luck felt that he had let down his team and fans because they had policed him with a negative reaction to his retirement decision. An NFL player who admits pain, seeks to avoid pain, and puts his needs above those of his team violates a central feature of hegemonic masculinity and opens himself to scrutiny with targeted policing.

When the news of Andrew Luck's retirement reached the sports media landscape, the masculinity policing began. Matthews (2019) chronicled some of the responses Andrew Luck received via Twitter and Doug Gottlieb from Fox Sports wrote that "Retiring cause rehab is too hard is the most millennial thing ever" (Matthews, 2019). Retired NFL quarterback Steve Beuerlein wrote, "I am a HUGE Andrew Luck fan . . . always have been. NO scenario where retirement is defensible. To do this to his teammates, organization, fans, and the NFL 2 weeks before the season is just not right. I love the guy but this will haunt him" (Matthews, 2019). It seems that real male athletes do not leave their teammates or highly exceptionally competitive positions, and they certainly do not articulate or complain about physical or emotional pain. Those who felt betrayed by Luck for succumbing to pain felt compelled to lash out with booing and mediated criticism.

The hegemonic masculinity policing of Andrew Luck's decision to retire from professional football is one rooted in gender role conflict and the stress enjoined with conflict. Physical manifestations of masculinity include images of large muscles, firm jaws, and strong backs which produce false, fantastical, and unattainable representations—and men who do not achieve those can become subject to ridicule. In addition, masculinity demands that men do not show emotion or they risk being labeled as feminine since the two constructs are binary dualisms and some scholars have argued that masculinity cannot exist without femininity (e.g., Connell, 1995; Pompper, 2017). Hence, male athletes trying to live up to impossible standards experience conflict and stress (O'Neil, 2008). Both media and audiences rely on common understandings of manhood and masculinity as integral components of enjoying violent male sports like football. Andrew Luck had to be devalued, and his personal status had to be lessened because his actions directly challenged how we cognitively perceive masculinity (O'Neil, 2008). To let Luck's actions stand as normal and acceptable behavior, other players might start to consider their own wellbeing over their teammates and the fans who watch might question why we pay people to run into each other as hard as they can for our entertainment.

Rewarding Hegemonic Masculinity

Not only are boys and men policed to ensure they live up to hegemonic masculinity tenets, but they also can be rewarded for silence about pain, injury, and hiding their emotions—as the case study explored in this chapter has illustrated. NFL players who take the pain, applaud the sport of football, support their team, and uphold the masculine ideals that undergird the NFL in the popular imagination stand to be celebrated. Furthermore, such retired players may anticipate further involvement in football as coaches, media commentators, or work in NFL-related business opportunities. This is how the code of masculinity is protected without having to be articulated.

Andrew Luck's time away from the game has been lived in relative obscurity. When he is not reading books to kids virtually amid the Coronavirus pandemic, Luck keeps a low profile (Gentry, 2020). In contrast, Peyton Manning's spotlight has only grown in retirement. He has continued his close relationship with the NFL through media and promotion and has sustained his personal brand identity as a spokesperson for corporate America. He achieved this status by reifying conventional standards of masculinity through his exceptional play, but also his handling of pain on and off the field. Having such a clear ethos with regard to masculinity is a valuable commodity and sponsors within as well as outside the game of football have taken notice.

Manning remains as connected to football as any retired player can be. In 2016 when he retired, Manning had garnered endorsement deals with Nike, Buick, DirecTV, Gatorade, Nationwide Insurance, and Papa John's Pizza, netting upwards of $15 million (Heath, 2016). *Forbes* magazine released a list of the most marketable athletes in 2016 and Manning ranked first on this list, beating out Olympic athletes that year, as well as LeBron James who had just been named NBA Finals MVP. Corporations are in the business of making money and do not spend money without an expected return on investment. Manning recently wrapped up hosting *Peyton's Places,* a 30-episode, ESPN documentary series, in celebration of the NFL's 100th season. In the show Manning crisscrossed the nation to interview and highlight the people who made professional football into the pastime we celebrate today (Fonseca, 2019). The extended and perpetual success of Peyton Manning is dependent on his ability to continue holding up the values of hegemonic masculinity. Manning's likability in the minds of Americans around the country is the reason for this investment and that likability is tied to Manning's masculinity.

Recommendations

Finally, we conclude with recommendations for accommodating acceptance of new forms of masculinity that are less apt to cause conflict and stress. In his retirement address, Manning minimized the pain he had suffered while extolling the sport of football—and seems to have been rewarded for it. Luck, however, cited his cycle of injuries and pain as the reason he was retiring and explicitly stated that he was privileging his own physical and mental wellbeing over the needs of his team. While Manning upheld hegemonic masculinity tenets in announcing his retirement, Luck tried to negotiate a different vision of masculinity that violated the expectations of NFL officials and fans, as well as the greater entertainment market. We argue that further expanding hegemonic masculinities' tenets to include a more humane acceptance that all humans experience pain and that professional athletes like football quarterbacks probably experience a disproportionate share of pain due to injury. When prominent men like Andrew Luck are willing to admit something that opens them to scrutiny, it's time to break down and reshape our ideas about masculinity so that there are multiple ways to negotiate the conflict surrounding the performance of manhood. Luck reacted differently to gender role conflict and stress than his peers and was negatively policed for it and certainly has not been rewarded for it. Luck's willingness to expose his emotional vulnerability is unmasculine within the NFL paradigm and in describing his experience with play-related injuries and emotional repercussions so frankly, Luck violated hegemonic masculinity norms and professional football's ideal.

Limitations and Future Study

The main limitation is that this case study analysis focused on only two texts. The lived experiences of these two quarterbacks were chosen because their narratives are uniquely symbiotic. An analysis of other franchise quarterback retirement addresses from the likes of John Elway, Dan Marino, or Troy Aikman also could be most revealing. Future studies also could involve examining non-elite athletes, various age groups, as well as experiences and outcomes across cultures. Indeed, the rhetoric of sport should continue to be studied with respect to GRS/C. Specifically, how do athletes in women's professional sports negotiate pain and aggressive behavior? Sports is a space that codes as masculine regardless of who the participants are. It would stand to reason that women who are professional athletes also experience high levels of GRS/C as they negotiate how to compete at the highest levels of athletics.

REFERENCES

Apkarian, A. V., Sosa, Y., Krauss, B. R., Thomas, P. S., Fredrickson, B. E., Levy, R. E., Harden, R. N., & Chialvo, D. R. (2004). Chronic pain patients are impaired on an emotional decision-making task. *Pain, 108*(1–2), 129–136. https://doi.org/10.1016/j.pain.2003.12.015.

Bastian, B., Jetten, J., Hornsey, M. J., & Leknes, S. (2014). The positive consequences of pain: A biopsychosocial approach. *Personality and Social Psychology Review, 18*(3), 256–279. https://doi.org/10.1177/1088868314527831.

Bell, S. (2015, January 13). *Peyton Manning not the iron man he was.* ESPN.com Stephania Bell Blog. https://www.espn.com/blog/stephaniabell/post/_/id/3030/peyton-manning-notthe-ironman-he-was.

Butterworth, M. L. (2012). Militarism and memorializing at the Pro Football Hall of Fame. *Communication and Critcal/Cultural Studies, 9*(3), 241–258. https://doi.org/10.1080/14791420.2012.675438.

Carucci, V. (October 7, 1994). *Dan still dangerous despite 2 bad legs Marino refuses to submit to injuries.* The Buffalo News. https://buffalonews.com/1994/10/08/dan-still-dangerous-despite-2-bad-legs-marino-refuses-to-submit-to-injuries/.

Connell, R. W. (1990). An Iron Man: The body and some contradictions of hegemonic masculinity. In *Sport, men, and the gender order: Critical feminist Perspectives*, pp. 83–95. Messner, M. A., and Sabo, D. F., eds. Human Kinetics Books.

Connell, R. W., & Messerschmidt, J. W. (2005). Hegemonic masculinity: Rethinking the concept. *Gender & Society, 19*(6), 829–859. https://doi.org/10.1177%2F0891243205278639.

Cottler, L. B., Abdallah, A. B., Cummings, S. M., Barr, J., Banks, R., & Forchheimer, R. (2011). Injury, pain, and prescription opioid use among former National Football League (NFL) players. *Drug and alcohol dependence, 116*(1–3), 188–194. https://doi.org/10.1016/j.drugalcdep.2010.12.003.

Dellenger, R. (Februrary 11, 2020). *All eyes on Arch Manning to extend family's qb dynasty.* Sports Illustrated. https://www.si.com/high-school/2020/02/11/arch-manning-next-generation-eli-peyton.

Erickson, J. A. (August 25, 2019). *The joy Andrew Luck felt in 2018 wasn't enough to break the vow he made after pain of 2016.* IndyStar. https://www.indystar.com/story/sports/nfl/colts/2019/08/25/why-did-andrew-luck-quit-indianapolis-colts-andrew-luck-frank-reich-jim-irsay-chris-ballard-injury/2051549001/.

Fainaru-Wada, M., & Fainaru, S. (2013) *League of denial: The NFL, concussions, and the battle for truth.* Random House.

Fonseca, B. (July 29, 2019). *Peyton Manning's ESPN+ documentary series is live| how to watch 'Peyton's Places' online.* NJ.com. https://www.nj.com/sports/2019/07/peyton-mannings-espn-documentary-series-is-live-how-to-watch-peytons-places-online.html.

Foote, J. G., Butterworth, M. L., & Sanderson, J. (2017). Adrian Peterson and the "wussification of America": Football and myths of masculinity. *Communication Quarterly, 65*(3), 268–284. https://doi.org/10.1080/01463373.2016.1227347.

Furness, Z. (2016). Reframing concussions, masculinity, and NFL mythology in *League of Denial. Popular Communication, 14*(1), 49–57. https://doi.org/10.1080/15405702.2015.1084628.

Gaines, C. (September 13, 2015). *NFL Linemen weren't always so enormous—see how much they've grown over the years.* Business Insider. https://www.businessinsider.com/nfl-offensive-lineman-are-big-2011-10/.

Gentry, J. (March 23, 2020). *Former colts qb Andrew Luck reads book to kids virtually amid COVID-19 outbreak.* Fox59 Indianapolis. https://fox59.com/news/coronavirus/former-colts-quarterback-andrew-luck-reads-kids-book-virtually-amid-covid-19-outbreak/.

Gesualdi, M. (2013). Man tears and masculinities: News coverage of John Boehner's tearful episodes. *Journal of Communication Inquiry, 37*(4), 304–321.

Glass, A. (2013, September 24). *Growing up Manning: A look inside football's first family*. Forbes. https://www.forbes.com/sites/alanaglass/2013/09/24/growing-up -manning-a-look-inside-footballs-first-family/#a0810e27b69e.

Haislop, T. (2019, December 16). *Why did Andrew Luck retire? Colts qb's decision to end NFL career, explained*. The Sporting News. https://www.sportingnews.com/ us/nfl/news/why-did-andrew-luck-retire-colts-qb/1nta6urevjrpi1p4wm8dy4pops.

Heath, J. (2016, September 17). *Peyton Manning is making just as much from endorsements as he did on the field*. BroncosWire.USA Today. https://broncoswire .usatoday.com/2016/09/17/peyton-manning-net-worth-making-as-much-from -endorsements-as-nfl/.

Jenkins, S. (2013, October 21). *Peyton Manning on his neck surgeries rehab— and how he almost didn't make it back*. The Washington Post. https://www .washingtonpost.com/sports/redskins/peyton-manning-on-his-neck-surgeries -rehab-and-how-he-almost-didnt-make-it-back/2013/10/21/8e3b5ca6-3a55-11e3 -b7ba-503fb5822c3e_story.html.

Kacsmar, S. (2012, December 5). *Andrew Luck outclasses Robert Griffin III and Russel Wilson in the clutch*. Bleacher Report.https://bleacherreport.com/ articles/1433559-how-do-nfls-2012-rookie-qbs-stack-up-in-the-clutch.

———. (2013, January 9). *Ignore the raw numbers, Andrew Luck had a great rookie season*. Bleacher Report. https://bleacherreport.com/articles/1477009 -ignore-the-raw-numbers-andrew-luck-had-a-great-rookie-season.

Leary, M. R. (2015). Emotional responses to interpersonal rejection. *Dialogues in clinical neuroscience, 17*(4), 435–441. https://doi.org/10.31887/DCNS.2015.17.4/ mleary.

Luck, A. (2019 August 25). *Transcript of retirement speech*. ESPN.com. https://www .espn.com/blog/indianapolis-colts/post/_/id/24738/transcript-of-andrew-lucks -retirement-news-conference.

Mangold, E., & Goehring, C. (2018). Identification by transitive property: Inter- mediated consubstantiality in the N.F.L.'s Salute to Service campaign. *Criti- cal Studies in Media Communication, 35*(5), 503-516. https://doi.org/ 10.1080/ 15295036.2018.1504166.

Manning, P. (2016 March 7). *Transcript of retirement speech*. ESPN.com. https://www .espn.com/blog/denver-broncos/post/_/id/19274/transcript-of-peyton-mannings -retirement-speech.

Matthews, I. (2019, August 28). *Why Andrew Luck's decision to retire from the NFL was so shocking*. Forbes.com. https://www.forbes.com/sites/ian mathews/2019/08/28/why-andrew-lucks-decision-to-retire-from-the-nfl-was-so -shocking/#eee46995c57d.

Nack, W. (2001, May 7). *The wrecking yard as they limp into the sunset, retired NFL players struggle with the games grim legacy: A lifetime of disability and pain*. The Sports Illustrated Vault. https://vault.si.com/vault/2001/05/07/the-wrecking-yard -as-they-limp-into-the-sunset-retired-nfl-players-struggle-with-the-games-grim -legacy-a-lifetime-of-disability-and-pain.

Nesbitt, A. (2019, August 24). *Andrew Luck booed by colts fans as he left field after retirement news broke.* USA Today. https://www.usatoday.com/story/sports/ftw/2019/08/24/colts-fans-boo-andrew-luck/40006821/.

NFL (2020, 7 April). *NFL scouting combine.* NFL.com. http://www.nfl.com/combine

Oates, T. P. (2007). The erotic gaze in the NFL draft. *Communication and Critical/Cultural Studies, 4*(1), 74–90. https://doi.org/10.1080/14791420601138351.

O'Neil. J. M. (2008). Summarizing 25 years of research on men's gender role conflict using the gender role conflict scale: New research paradigms and clinical implications. *The Counseling Psychologist, 36,* 358–445. https://doi.org/10.1177/0011000008317057.

Orchard, J. W. (2002). Benefits and risks of using local anesthetic for pain relief to allow early return to play in professional football. *British journal of sports medicine, 36*(3), 209–213. https://doi.org/10.1136/bjsm.36.3.209.

Pompper, D. (2010). Masculinities, the metrosexual, and media images: Across dimensions of age and ethnicity. *Sex Roles, 63,* 682–696. https://doi.org/ 10.1007/s11199-010-9870-7.

———. (2017). *Rhetoric of femininity: Female body image, media, and gender role stress/conflict.* Lexington Books.

Richards, P. (2017, September 29). *Celebrating Peyton Manning: He leaves a legacy far beyond the field in Indianapolis.* IndyStar. https://www.indystar.com/story/sports/nfl/colts/2017/09/29/celebrating-peyton-manning-he-leaves-legacy-far-beyond-field-indianapolis/714970001/.

Sanderson, J., Weathers, M., Grevious, A., Tehan, M., & Warren, S. (2016). A hero or sissy? Exploring media framing of NFL quarterbacks' injury decisions. *Communication & Sport, 4*(1), 3–22. https://doi.org/10.1177%2F2167479514536982.

Schilken, C. (2018, June 5). *Oliver Luck, father of Indianapolis Colts qb Andrew Luck, is named XFL commissioner.* Los Angeles Times. https://www.latimes.com/sports/nfl/la-sp-xfl-commissioner-luck-20180605-story.html.

Stites, A. (2015, August 24). *Peyton Manning hasn't had feeling in his fingertips for years.* SBNation. https://www.google.com/search?q=sb+nation&rlz=1C5CHFA_enUS759US759&oq=SB+NATION&aqs=chrome.0.0l6j69i60l2.1612j0j7&sourceid=chrome&ie=UTF-8.

Stites, A. (2018, October 4). *Andrew Luck's injury history, a timeline.* SBNation. https://www.sbnation.com/2017/10/16/16469416/andrew-luck-shoulder-injury-history-timeline-colts-return.

Thamel, P. (2011). *A diploma. Then the draft.* The New York Times. https://www.nytimes.com/2011/02/13/sports/ncaafootball/13luck.html.

Tredinnick, A. (2012, November 5). *Andrew Luck is quietly having one of the best seasons of any rookie quarterback in history.* Business Insider. https://www.businessinsider.com/andrew-lucks-amazing-rookie-season-2012-11.

Trujillo, N. (1991). Hegemonic masculinity on the mound: Media representations of Nolan Ryan and American sports culture. *Critical Studies in Mass Communication, 8*(3), 290–308. https://doi.org/10.1080/15295039109366799.

Trujillo, N. (1995). Machines, missiles, and men: Images of the male body on ABC's Monday Night Football. *Sociology of Sport Journal, 12*(4), 403–423. https://doi.org/10.1123/ssj.12.4.403.

van Manen, M. (1990). *Researching lived experience: Human science for an action sensitive pedagogy*. State University of New York Press.

Wells, L. (2019, September 21). *Would your body type succeed in the NFL?* Sportscasting. https://www.sportscasting.com/would-your-body-type-succeed-in-the-nfl/.

Whitson, D. (1990). Sport in the social construction of masculinity. In *Sport, men, and the gender order: Critical feminist Perspectives*, pp. 19–29. Messner, M. A., and Sabo, D. F., eds. Human Kinetics Books.

Chapter Thirteen

A Critical Exploration of Pandemic Protection as a Threat to Masculinity

Facemask Usage and Male Gender

James Carviou and Jennifer Jackson

INTRODUCTION

Hegemonic masculinity remains a form of gender-based negotiation that changes over time, but we posit that it must be more flexible in times of a health crisis. Political action reinforces a female-male gender divide by shoring up the existence of hegemonic masculinity steeped in power and control of those involved in governing (Bourdieu, 2001). While the COVID-19 pandemic started in 2020, it took an executive order after President Joe Biden started his term in January 2021, to enforce more consistent face mask mandates nationwide (Biden, 2021). The masculine ideal suggests that men should be the superheroes who save the day—to demonstrate their manliness. However, by refusing to wear face masks, some men's behavior during the COVID-19 pandemic demonstrated that hegemonic masculinity can lead to toxicity that threatens society's health and well-being rather than de-escalating a health crisis.

Who would have thought that following recommended health guidelines during a pandemic could be viewed as a sign of weakness? In everyday casual observation throughout the 2020 COVID-19 pandemic, we typically saw more women than men wearing face coverings and the *BBC World Service* confirmed in a report from July 19, 2020 that this observation was not a figment of the imagination (Duarte, 2020). In fact, it has been documented that men are less likely than women, world-wide, to don a face mask during the pandemic—a trend that is on par with previous epidemics and health crises (Duarte, 2020). In a study conducted in the U.K. and the U.S., researchers found that men seemed more likely than women to agree that "wearing a face covering is shameful," that it is a "sign of weakness," and that a "stigma attached to wearing a face covering is preventing them from wearing one as often as they should" (Capraro & Barcelo, 2020, p. 14). The same gender split was observed in Mexico City during the 2009 swine flu pandemic when commuters observed, "a higher proportion of women than men were seen wearing face masks on the metro system" (Duarte, 2020). Ironically, some men seem willing to risk their lives and the lives of those around them to continue to assert their dominance, while also being twice as likely to die of COVID-19 than women (Rabin, 2020; Pearce, 2020). To add to the irony, men also were found to be less likely to comply with simple hand washing standards while being more seriously impacted by COVID-19 (Pearce, 2020).

A federal government's role and political party ideologies can play significant roles in the unfolding of health crises in terms of gender-specific behaviors (Hamel, et al, 2020), as demonstrated in previous pandemics. During the 1980s HIV/AIDS health crisis, the U.S. federal government was slow to respond, contributing to the widespread pandemic (Valdiserri & Holtgrave, 2020). It wasn't until major public figures were fighting for their lives that the federal government took action (Francis, 2012) beyond framing the pandemic as an issue for one group of people, with men largely resisting taking preventative measures to avoid contracting HIV (Parker, et al, 2000). Flash forward to the 2020 COVID-19 pandemic, only half of U.S. men who identify as Republican were likely to wear a face mask during outings outside of their homes as compared to 70 percent of women who identify as Republican (Hamel et al., 2020). Beyond the U.S., men in Asia also seem less likely to wear face coverings as compared to women, with law-mandated mask wearing seemingly the dominant prescription for erasing the gender divide (Hamel et al., 2020).

Rhetorically, this chapter investigates the gender divide surrounding a face covering and why some men feel that their hegemonic masculinity is threatened by wearing one. We investigate this phenomenon of male gender behaviors associated with face covering through a GRC/S theory lens to explain that learned gender roles can lead to negative outcomes (O'Neil, 1981). GRC/S theory provides a foundation for understanding how high levels of hegemonic masculinity may become toxic and life threatening when amplified by opinion leaders—such as in 2020 when former President Trump (in office when the COVID-19 pandemic began) took to Twitter to assert his version of a socially constructed ideal of "what it means to be a man" (Grogan, 2010, p. 762). After exploring the fear-based phenomenon that facemasks threaten one's masculinity, this chapter will reflect on how this discourse works within the realm of toxic masculinity and male supremacy and resulting social impacts.

REVIEW OF LITERATURE

As a foundation for the study presented in this chapter, it is important to look at three areas of scholarship: 1) Gender role conflict/stress theory, 2) Masculinities and the male body, and 3) Twitter and the power of opinion leaders. This section concludes with the research question that guided the analysis.

Gender Role Conflict/Stress Theory

Many people believe that gender roles come from some natural dichotomy between men and women (Cislaghi & Heise, 2020) and that these are not fluid. It is this natural dichotomy that leads to the basis for gender role conflict/stress (GRC/S) theory. The projection of gender roles as binary dualisms can have adverse effects—when men are supposed to be and act certain ways *as men*. When looking through this lens at extremes of toxic hegemonic masculinity, Pompper (2010) explained that "masculinity is a slippery notion of what is expected of men that varies through the life course" (p. 683). If a man does not act according to this expectation, it can cause dissonance for those who believe that gender roles are natural and clearly defined. Pascoe's (2011) *Dude You're A Fag* highlights the way in which high school boys police manliness based on masculine ideals and label as homosexual those who appear to deviate from these norms. Such outcomes can lead to men limiting their own abilities to communicate their feelings, needs, or concerns because of the fear of being labeled *feminine* (Shepard, 2002). Such outcomes have been found to occur among gender and sexual minorities and has been termed *femmephobia* (Hoskin, 2020).

Men are threatened to find security in a culture where they feel their agency is being constantly threatened and compromised. Much of it is linked to traditional masculinity and the social construction of what ultimately defines manhood. Broadly speaking, the focus of masculinity in GRC/S theory is defined as "what it means to be a man" (Grogan, 2010, p. 762). This definition means evading physical and verbal expressions of emotions, feelings, or other modes of showing weakness, because that is a sign of masculinity's opposite, femininity (O'Neil, 1981). This theory is used to explain how gender roles, especially if understood as a binary dualism, creates sexism and oppression (Pompper, 2010). O'Neil (1981) posited that outcomes harm everyone, though, because "men's gender role socialization and the values of the masculine mystique produce a devaluation of feminine values and learned fear of femininity in men's lives" (p. 203). Social construction theorists posit that men in a patriarchal culture like the U.S. learn their norms from socialization and then attempt to live up to those expectations with their actions and words (Wade, 1996). This results in a sexist attitude toward certain behaviors and perpetuates sexism that is overtly rampant in the U.S. (O'Neil, 1981). Some men involve themselves in the *macho paradox* wherein they define their masculinity based on dominance over women (Katz, 2006), resulting in behaviors problematic to both men and the women across their life course.

Consequences of violating male gender role norms may be severe and last a lifetime. According to O'Neil (1981), gender role conflict is a "psychological state . . . The ultimate outcome of this conflict is the restriction of the person's ability to actualize their human potential or the restriction of someone else's potential" (p. 203). In a traditional hegemonic framework, men should be rigid, invulnerable, resolute; a superhuman without weakness (O'Neil, 1981). Even if a masculine man has a moment of feeling afraid, needs help, or is sick, he must respond with the accepted gender norm behavior of not appearing to be in such a vulnerable state (Gibar, Wester, & Ben-Porat, 2020). Males are socialized early in life to avoid any display of weakness because to do so risks displaying helplessness and vulnerability to others (O'Neil, 1981).

Masculinities, Male Bodies, Hegemony, and Toxicity

Defining masculinity and ways it has become hegemonic—and sometimes toxic—is a complex exercise of power. Masculinity must be considered in its plural form of *masculinities* (Kimmel, 2001), always in flux, and linked to levels of agency provided to a person at a given moment in time (Connell, 2005). Overall, defining masculinity is further complicated by concepts of the male body ideal/athleticism (Bordo, 1999), economic success, and familial legacy (Kimmel, 2017). Media play a significant role in representing masculinities to the degree that men may suffer an identity crisis when they feel they cannot measure up to images of a male body ideal that is thrust upon them through media depictions of men in marketing and advertising representations (Bordo, 1999).

There are cyclical moments of agency and regression in how masculine identities are defined within the U.S. mainstream (Kimmel, 2017). *Hegemonic masculinity* refers to the social ascendancy of a particular version or model of masculinity that becomes "common sense," legitimizing men's dominant social position and justifying subordination of women and some men (Connell, 1995; Hanke, 1990, p. 232) often including family breadwinning role and muscularity displays (Pompper et al., 2007); a concept proven highly resistant to change across many cultures. What makes certain forms of masculinity hegemonic is some men's power displays designed to secure their male gender identity through abuse of women (e.g., misogyny) and gay men (e.g, homophobia) (e.g., Kimmel, 2001). Discrepancy between a man's lived experience and some ideal can result in impossible body expectations characterized as GRC/S (O'Neil, 2008). In the U.S., where male gender identity is re-defined against the mainstream, patriarchal privilege is secured through hegemonic masculinity. In the time of Trump's presidency, masculinity often played out in increased male violence (DiMuccio & Knowles, 2020) and greater levels of misogynistic, racist, and homophobic discourse across the public domain such as on social media (Jackson and Carviou, 2020). These dynamics have inspired greater consciousness of toxic masculinity—and in some quarters, greater levels of power and acceptance (Marron, 2020). Former President Trump eschewed wearing a face mask early on in the pandemic and used Twitter to amplify his opinions about it (Yaqub, 2020).

Hence, toxic masculinity within patriarchy has become outwardly visible in the U.S. mainstream as an outcome of individual men *not* feeling powerful within a system that empowers men (Kimmel & Wade, 2018). Men seeking to regain power they perceive has been lost due to gains by feminism was reinforced by the now former president who used Twitter to amplify his ideologies and political agenda (Johnson, 2017). Historically, masculinity has been used as a tool to threaten and coerce societies into avoiding change or deviating from established norms supported by opinion leaders (Hooper, 2001). Solutions to breaking toxicity associated with masculinity include creating new models steeped in reality rather than fantasy (Connell, 1987).

Twitter and the Power of Celebrity

The emergence of Twitter as a new social media platform in 2006 created a whole new culture of celebrity on social media that already had begun on social media sites like Facebook and YouTube. However, Twitter provides an instant forum about the everyday lives of celebrities, revealing details about their personal lives, political positions, and religious affiliations. Twitter offers a platform for gaining an up-close glimpse into celebrity lives (Marwick & boyd, 2011b). Former President Trump used Twitter as his prominent form of communication, likely inspired by his run as a reality TV host. Twitter occupies a gray area between traditional mainstream news media and social media, defining itself as a news organization with a direct line of important information from a source to its public (Jackson & Carviou, 2020). While people flocked to Twitter for information about COVID-19 and the public health crisis, they perhaps were likely to accept opinion leaders' perceptions at least on par with traditional mainstream news (Edgerly & Vraga, 2020).

The complexities of digital communication have created a world in which messages can be sent to the masses without repercussion and, often, without necessarily knowing how they were produced or understanding the impact those messages may have on audiences. Hence, outcomes of new technologies largely remain unknown in their complexity and impact: "Digital media raise a variety of issues as we try to understand them, their place in our lives, and their consequences for our personhood and relationships with others . . . lead[ing] to social and cultural reorganization and reflection" (Baym, 2010, p. 2). When a celebrity or political/community leader, the most likely type of user to have a certified Twitter account, tweets misinformation or confirms health risk behaviors such as an anti-mask position, it may inspire followers to adopt similar behaviors, to amplify those messages, and to build communities of like-minded individuals. This backdrop is important when trying to understand ways masculinity and GRC/S interplay during a health crisis. Communication is widely known as a catalyst for cultivating community and through this process, opinion leaders emerge as purveyors of information. Like journalists establish interpretive communities surrounding news events (Zelizer, 2007), Twitter is considered an interpretive community for breaking news and communicating it to a wide audience, along with their perspectives about news events, entertainment, social movements, and more. Twitter use can represent a singular (individual) view or a broader (collective) communal or societal view (Marwick & Boyd, 2011a).

Due to the potential influence of opinion leaders on Twitter and the severity of the risks to society caused by refusal to wear a mask during a pandemic, this 2020 moment in time offers a case study for examining GRC/S theory, masculinity (especially toxic hegemonic masculinity), and Twitter communication of powerful opinion leaders as a basis for studying relationships between mask wearing behaviors and masculinity during a health crisis. For the study reported in this chapter, we posed the following research question:

RQ1: In what ways may opinion leaders' Twitter messages about mask wearing have contributed to a culture of hegemonic masculinity during the COVID-19 pandemic?

METHOD

We used critical discourse analysis (CDA) as a method for exploring language used to disseminate information about mask wearing on Twitter during one year, January 1, 2020–January 1, 2021, to discover themes that emerged in the Twitter discourse. We define *discourse* as the tweets about mask wearing, focusing on the use of Twitter to disseminate messages, which resulted in formation of an interpretive community (Fairclough, 1995; Wood & Kroger, 2000). This is a timely investigation given the popularity of social media, the former president's attachment to Twitter, and socio-political power inherent in its ubiquity. In other words, we engaged with CDA to discover "what [Twitter] means for the dissemination of discourses" (Bouvier & Machin, 2018, p. 179) so that we might expand GRC/S theory. The CDA method's strength in exploring language has potential for revealing gendered political power and its implications for contributing to GRC/S.

Data Collection

The specific steps taken to collect data were:

1. We isolated the period of the pandemic tweets according to a timeline of January 1, 2020–January 1, 2021.
2. Units of analysis were tweets during this time period which amplified opinion leaders' resistance to mask wearing in response to preventing the spread of COVID-19.
3. We collected a convenience sample of tweets from political and celebrity leaders who had certified Twitter accounts and at least 100,000 followers. We looked for tweets that went viral and attracted news media coverage, knowing that these would have a larger reach and increased likelihood of influence. We did not use key words/phrases to derive a convenience sample, but rather selected tweets that emerged from these opinion leaders. We two authors served as investigators and coders, using a constant comparison technique.

Data Analysis

The specific steps taken to analyze the data are as follows:

1. Tweets were examined for discourse related to anti-mask behaviors and resistance to public safety measures.
2. Notes were taken and compared throughout the coding and data analysis process to illustrate tweets with potential for larger social influence. Direct quotes of the selected tweets were used to demonstrate the discourse being discussed.

FINDINGS

Our convenience sampling procedures resulted in five tweets over the course of one year and involved six different opinion leaders that were analyzed to respond to our research question.

RQ1: In what ways may opinion leaders' Twitter messages about mask wearing have contributed to a culture of hegemonic masculinity during the COVID-19 pandemic?

As co-researchers, we compared notes throughout the analysis to derive two themes/patterns: *Theme One: Ideologically branding the hegemonic masculine gender role during a pandemic*; and *Theme Two: Non-mask wearing as asserting a hegemonic masculine gender role behavior*. Collectively, these themes suggest that during the one-year period studied, resistance to mask wearing was used as a political tool for unifying Trump supporters by framing it as a threat to masculinity and civil liberties. It is important to look at influences of opinion leaders and how that influence fueled toxic hegemonic masculinity—in harmful ways. Overall, we use the themes that emerged to expand understanding of GRC/S theory.

Theme One: Ideologically Branding the Hegemonic Masculine Gender Role During a Pandemic

In 2020, President Trump represented the masculine ideal as straight, white, and Protestant (Kimmel, 2017). As Trump announced he wouldn't wear a mask during an April 3, 2020, White House media briefing (Reuters Staff, 2020) the pandemic hit its surge across the country and unfortunately, many people followed his lead despite information released to the public by Drs. Fauci (U.S. physician-scientist and immunologist, director of the U.S. National Institute of Allergy and Infectious Diseases and the chief medical advisor to the president) and Birx (U.S. physician and White House Coronavirus Response Coordinator in 2020), the CDC/NIH, and countless others. Specific language that was geared toward educating the U.S. public about how to protect people and reduce the spread of COVID-19 was ignored and repeatedly retaliated against by Trump and his supporters. Trump persisted in non-mask wearing until July 11, 2020 (BBC News, 2020). According to *BBC News* (2020), Trump had "previously said that he would not wear a mask" and even took the time to "mocked Democratic rival Joe Biden for doing so." He was not the only federal government opinion leader who resisted the CDC guidelines, supporting Trump's performance of an ideologically branded hegemonic masculine gender role.

Trump re-asserted his anti-mask stance when he visited a Ford plant on May 21, 2020, after the factory halted car manufacturing to convert to producing personal protective equipment (PPE). While that factory had a mask requirement, media images on Twitter failed to capture Trump publicly wearing a mask during his tour. When asked about it, Trump explained: "I wore one (a mask) in the back area. I didn't want to give the press the pleasure of seeing it" (Reuters Staff, 2020). Instead of leading by example and showing the nation that mask wearing complies with CDC guidelines, Trump resisted by not wearing a mask and actively avoiding any display of weakness that would be a violation of his brand of hegemonic masculine male identity.

Throughout 2020, Trump's hegemonic masculinity displays of resistance grew to toxic levels and evolved into increasingly dangerous levels of misinformation contradicting medical and scientific experts trying to help the country fight the virus. Trump and others not only publicly announced they would not be wearing a mask, but also mocked others who wore masks at several large-scale events that eventually came to be known as "superspreaders" —political rallies and fundraisers—because the attendees were not socially distanced or wearing masks. On May 27, 2020, Trump quote-tweeted conservative political commentator Brit Hume's condescending tweet about then presidential candidate Biden wearing a mask. Trump added a comment that was a simple, and not-so-subtle insult of Biden's physical appearance: "He looks better!" (Trump, 2020). Even after suffering from COVID-19 himself, Trump did not publicly call for wearing masks in a way that acknowledged the misinformation he had given for months (BBC News, 2020).

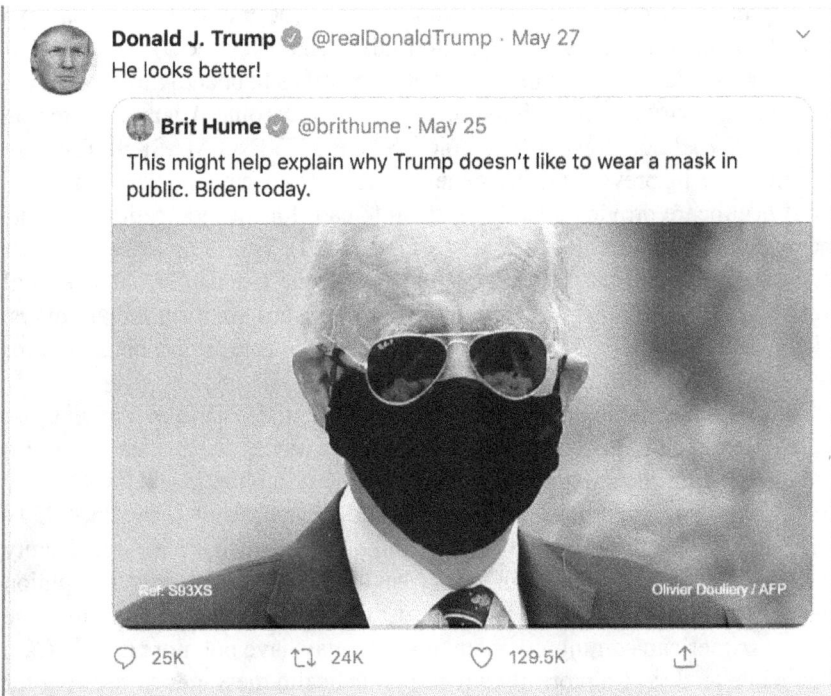

Figure 13.1. Tweet from President Trump from the @realdonaldtrump account on May 27, 2020, mocking presidential candidate Joe Biden for wearing a facemask.
Screenshot by Authors.

Perhaps the most influential anti-mask messaging came from former Vice President Mike Pence, as chair of Trump's Coronavirus Task Force. When the person charged with chairing the nation's response to the virus refused to follow CDC guidelines and also happened to be a white male of privilege in the second highest position of power in the free world, his anti-mask example sent a powerful global message. On April 28, 2020, political news source *Politico* tweeted the most damning evidence of Pence's inability to adhere to guidelines. The tweet read: "Mike Pence refused to wear a mask on Tuesday as he toured the Mayo Clinic and met with hospital staff and a patient, rejecting the famed hospital's policy that all visitors cover their faces to reduce #Covid-19 risks" (Politico, 2020) and included a video of Pence elbow-bumping with hospital officials and patients. Pence clearly violated the CDC's and Mayo Clinic's social distancing and mask guidelines. In the process, Pence implied that real men not only don't need protection, but should be defiant in all circumstances and avoid masks.

Theme Two: Non-Mask Wearing as Asserting a Hegemonic Masculine Gender Role Behavior

From prominent opinion leaders using Twitter, the message of being man enough to *not* wear a mask was easy to find, as characterized by tweets resisting mask mandates and community/state shutdowns happening to prevent the spread of the virus. Former Surgeon General Dr. Jerome Adams tweeted on February 29, 2020: "Seriously people—STOP BUYING MASKS! They are not effective in preventing the general public from catching #coronavirus, but if healthcare providers can't get them to care for the sick patients, it puts them and our communities at risk!" (Adams, 2020). The surgeon general later attempted to delete his February 29, 2020 tweets; it took Dr. Adams until April 14, 2020 to tweet a change in attitude toward wearing facial covers, allowing the falsehood to continue to negatively impact health behaviors for over two months while the pandemic surged.

Similarly, businessman and 2012 GOP presidential hopeful, Herman Cain, joined Trump and Pence in denouncing mask wearing on Twitter. Cain also attended a Trump campaign rally and was photographed maskless. On July 30, 2020, Cain succumbed to the virus and passed away (Lincoln, 2020). The virus disproportionately impacted the African-American community (Marshall, 2020) and the refusal to wear a mask by a prominent opinion leader like Cain reinforced the spread of misinformation, especially to those African-American community members who may have put more trust in Cain than white leaders. Cain openly defied public health messages advocating for

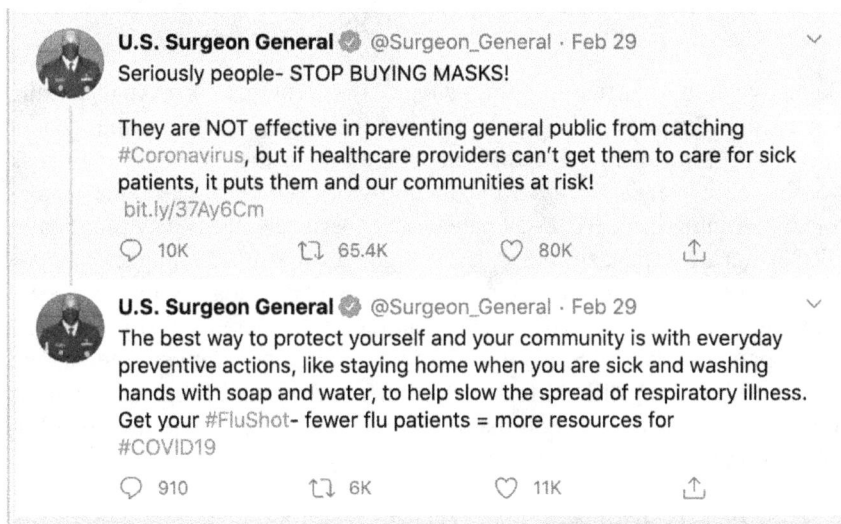

U.S. Surgeon General ✓ @Surgeon_General · Feb 29
Seriously people- STOP BUYING MASKS!

They are NOT effective in preventing general public from catching
#Coronavirus, but if healthcare providers can't get them to care for sick
patients, it puts them and our communities at risk!
bit.ly/37Ay6Cm

◯ 10K   ⟲ 65.4K   ♡ 80K   ⬆

U.S. Surgeon General ✓ @Surgeon_General · Feb 29
The best way to protect yourself and your community is with everyday
preventive actions, like staying home when you are sick and washing
hands with soap and water, to help slow the spread of respiratory illness.
Get your #FluShot- fewer flu patients = more resources for
#COVID19

◯ 910   ⟲ 6K   ♡ 11K   ⬆

Figure 13.2.   Tweets from Dr. Jerome Adams from the @Surgeon_General account on February 29, 2020 denouncing public use of masks.
Screenshot by Authors.

face mask wearing by instead falling in line with Trump, Pence, and other anti-maskers.

In June 2020 after Democratic Governor Gavin Newsom installed a mask mandate in California, additional celebrity voices of Ben Shapiro and Nick Searcy joined anti-mask messaging, inviting listeners to avoid masks for the sake of preserving manhood. Conservative political commentator and media host Ben Shapiro tweeted on June 18, 2020 in response to the California mask mandate: "I particularly look forward to Gavin Newsom attempting to enforce mask-wearing on my four-year-old son. Good luck with that" (Shapiro, 2020). Shapiro quipped about his four-year-old despite the fact that children learned to use masks with the support of adults modeling the proper behavior (Goudy, 2020). Rather, Shapiro expressed distaste for the California mandate and his resistance to wearing a mask. Similarly, Hollywood character actor Nick Searcy echoed Shapiro's reaction to the statewide mandate by tweeting: "This is not a law, @gavinnewsom. Therefore, we don't have to do what you say. Read up on that legislative process stuff" (Searcy, 2020). We suspect that Searcy felt his masculinity threatened by the mask mandate, considered mask wearing as a display of male weakness, so used non-mask wearing as a means for asserting a hegemonic masculine gender role behavior.

DISCUSSION

Collectively, this chapter's findings suggest that Trump, Pence, Adams, Cain, Searcy, and Shapiro ideologically branded the hegemonic masculine gender role during a pandemic, and this encouraged other men to adopt non-mask wearing as a means for asserting their own hegemonic masculine gender role. Examining the COVID-19 pandemic experience in this way illuminates GRC/S during a pandemic and sheds light on the overall impact of male power in health and policy making decisions with potential for life-and-death consequences. As other countries around the globe were able to prevent the virus spread, certain U.S. male leaders working in government, media, and Hollywood settings stifled life-saving efforts and worked to spread misinformation and advocated for non-mask wearing as an act of conservative political resistance to health and safety compliance.

Complicity in Endangering Public Health

Overall, we hypothesize that the 2020 course of events throughout the COVID-19 pandemic garnered significant influence in shaping behavior of followers of right-wing opinion leaders who failed to take proper precautions to protect themselves and others; actions which may have directly contributed to thousands of deaths. The CDC reports that in 2020, "COVID-19 was the underlying or a contributing cause of 377,883 deaths" in the U.S. (Ahmad et al., 2021). The anti-mask movement during the COVID-19 pandemic was supported by sets of Trump-following opinion leaders who sought to unite their base by using perceived masculinity threats as evidence of diminished civil liberties and freedoms (mask wearing) being inflicted upon U.S. citizens. Consequently, thousands of people were exposed to unhealthy and unsafe experiences at rallies and other public events without wearing masks and going on social media to declare their resistance to mask wearing. For example, Trump repeatedly went maskless—even after he had tested positive for COVID-19 on October 2, 2020, and spent three days at Walter Reed National Military Medical Center—and unceremoniously removed his mask in a televised stunt against having to wear it upon returning to the White House on October 5, 2020 (A timeline, 2020).

Through the lens of male GRC/S theory, we illuminate how these opinion leaders' misguided tweets may have contributed to male conflict and stress. Both Trump and Pence demonstrate a resistance to mask wearing by framing it as a behavior for the weak. Trump took on the defender of the toxic hegemonic masculine role by not only refusing to wear a mask, but also mocking his campaign rival in the tweet from May 27, 2020, saying "He looks better!" (Trump, 2020). Biden acted against the expectation of what it meant to be a man by wearing a mask and showing weakness, so Trump reacted in a condescending way. Trump's choice to mock Biden for wearing a mask during a public health crisis reinforced hegemonic masculinity—or, a belief that *being a man* is enough to avoid illness. We posit that this dynamic may have negatively impacted others by amplifying false information and creating GRC/S among men in the U.S. and perhaps globally.

Similarly, Pence—as leader of the nation's Coronavirus task force—perpetuated this dynamic when seen in the Politico tweet on April 28, 2020 not wearing a mask at the Mayo Clinic around its staff and patients. The tweet read: "Mike Pence refused to wear a mask on Tuesday as he toured the Mayo Clinic and met with hospital staff and a patient, rejecting the famed hospital's policy that all visitors cover their faces to reduce #Covid-19 risks" (Politico, 2020). By blatantly ignoring the policy set forth by this medical institution, Pence is asserting his manhood and disregard for any rule, regulation, or even recommendation that would make him appear weak.

Furthermore, Twitter attention to the pandemic included images of Trump's U.S. Surgeon General Jerome Adams, sending anti-mask-wearing messages. He stated in a February 29, 2020 tweet that the masks "are not effective" for the general public (Adams, 2020) and did not publicly renounce his inaccurate words, but attempted to subtly change his stance on April 14, 2020. Dr. Adams's stance in February devalued medical advice to wear a mask and reasserted hegemonic masculinity, resulting in many followers accepting Dr. Adams's words in February and being unwilling to accept his change in stance in April. *USA Today* reported many social media users continuing to promote the February 29, 2020 tweet in early 2021 and even questioning who forced Dr. Adams to delete the tweet (Fauzia, 2021).

Following Trump's lead, conservative political commentator Ben Shapiro and Hollywood actor Nick Searcy both articulated their opposition to wearing masks by tweeting condescending tweets about California Governor Gavin Newsom and the state-wide mask mandate he implemented. This mandate, to Shapiro and Searcy, forced other men to demonstrate weakness by asking them to help with curbing the spread of the pandemic by covering one's face in public. They used sarcasm, disdain, and were mocking as Shapiro quipped, "Good luck with that" (2020) and Searcy exclaimed, "This is not a law" (2020).

This chapter has explored the impact of mainstream opinion leaders using their privilege to spread misinformation and put the general public in danger while also shoring up their political agenda. As a medium, Twitter elevated the opinion leaders' reach during the pandemic, especially when people were isolated, quarantined at home, and spending time on social media. The culture of toxic masculinity under former President Trump generated misinformation which led to mask wearing being seen as weak and unpatriotic—despite CDC guidelines and historical precedent that mask wearing prevented spread of the Spanish flu during the pandemic of 1918 and Mexico's swine flu outbreak in 2009.

Male gender roles are socially constructed around male privilege and this dynamic received new agency in the U.S. under former President Trump with Twitter access, public appearances, and news media coverage. Ultimately, masks are not a threat to masculinity or a symptom of weakness, but rather were a sign used for a specific brand of political ideology that risked people's health during a pandemic. Yet, as earlier research findings interrogated a gender split on behaviors during health crises in the U.S., Mexico, and China (e.g., Capraro & Barcelo, 2020; Duarte, 2020; Hamel et al., 2020), clearly there is more to discover about masculinities and why men are so unwilling to wear face masks or to adopt other behaviors recommended by health authorities.

Limitations and Recommendations Moving Forward

The findings discussed in this chapter are limited by the examination of one medium and a small selection of male opinion leaders who used Twitter to advance their political agenda. Also, the analysis was supervised by two researchers who used a research method which does not involve reliability measures, but serves as a departure point for future hypothesis testing.

We offer recommendations for the future. Research findings reported in this chapter shed light on how a person's gender identity positions them to influence the general public regarding preventative measures such as mask wearing during the COVID-19 pandemic. This outcome was further complicated by mainstream media reliance on social media platforms for information—like Twitter during the COVID-19 pandemic—and suggests how influential opinion leaders such as leaders of political parties/organizations can be when positioned as authorities in decision-making processes. We believe that many lives could have been saved if these men had not fostered GRC/S conditions and used their position to elevate the science of mask wearing in an effort to prevent spread of COVID-19. Thus, both media and opinion leaders have image repair work ahead and must be responsible to the general public, especially during health crises. If more of the public could trust all media to provide accurate information during a pandemic, then they may be less influenced by those with a political agenda spreading dangerous falsehoods.

Future research on this dynamic could extend to:

1. Interviews with men of diverse social identity dimensions and political ideologies to ask them about their health risk behaviors.

2. Interviews with both men and women to compare their gendered behaviors and perceptions.
3. Content analysis of multiple media forms in addition to Twitter.
4. Interviews with women to examine roles they may play in supporting or resisting hegemonic masculine behaviors.
5. Content analysis of tweets by women opinion leaders and how their discourse reinforces or challenges existing hegemonic masculine ideologies.
6. Focus groups with men and women who work in healthcare settings to discover their perceptions of ways hegemonic masculinity impacts health education efforts.
7. Survey of the general public in the U.S. focused on information seeking practices of men and women interrogating how hegemonic masculinity plays a role specifically in information pertaining to their health that they perceive as trustworthy and credible.

REFERENCES

A timeline of Trump's battle with Covid-19. (2020, October 12). CNN. Downloaded May 23, 2021, from https://rb.gy/uxmnea.
Adams, J. [@Surgeon_General]. (2020, February 29). *Seriously people- STOP BUYING MASKS!* [Tweet]. Twitter. https://rb.gy/ehha8c.
Ahmad, F. B., Cisewski, J.A., Minino, A., & Anderson, R.N. (2021, April 9). Provisional mortality data—United States, 2020. *Center for Disease Control and Prevention.* https://rb.gy/mz0fj1.
Baym, N. K. (2010). *Personal connections in the digital age.* John Wiley & Sons.
BBC News (2020, July 12). Coronavirus: Donald Trump wears face mask for the first time. *BBC News.* https://rb.gy/ryty9a.
Biden, J. R. (2021, January 21). *Executive Order on Protecting the Federal Workforce and Requiring Mask-Wearing.* The White House. https://rb.gy/4uvr82.
Bordo, S. (2000). *The male body: A new look at men in public and in private.* Straus and Giroux.
Bourdieu, P. (2001). *Masculine domination.* Stanford University Press.
Bouvier, G. & Machin, D. (2018). Critical discourse analysis and the challenges and opportunities of social media. Review of communication, 18(3), 178–192. http://doi.org/10.1080.15358593.2018.1479881.
Capraro, V., & Barcelo, H. (2020, May 11). The effect of messaging and gender on intentions to wear a face covering to slow down COVID-19 transmission. https://doi.org/10.31234/osf.io/tg7vz.
Cislaghi, B., & Heise, L. (2020). Gender norms and social norms: differences, similarities and why they matter in prevention science. *Sociology of health & illness,* 42(2), 407–422. https://doi.org/10.1111/1467-9566.13008.
Connell, R. W. (1987). *Gender and power.* Stanford University Press.

DiMuccio, S. H., & Knowles, E. D. (2020). The political significance of fragile masculinity. *Current Opinion in Behavioral Sciences, 34*, 25–28. https://doi.org/10.1016/j.cobeha.2019.11.010.

Duarte, F. (2020, July 18). Coronavirus face masks: Why men are less likely to wear masks. *BBC News.* https://rb.gy/gyklg0.

Edgerly, S., & Vraga, E. K. (2020). That's not news: Audience perceptions of 'newsness' and why it matters. *Mass Communication & Society*, 23(5), 730–754. https://doi.org/10.1080/15205436.2020.1729383.

Fairclough, N. (1989). *Language and Power.* Longman.

———. (2000). Critical analysis of media discourse. In P. Morris and S. Thornham (Eds.), *Media studies: A reader* (pp. 308–325). New York University Press.

———. (1995). *Media discourse.* Edward Arnold.

Fauzia, M. (2021, February 17). Fact check: Trump surgeon general initially dismissed mask-wearing, but then endorsed. *USA Today.* https://rb.gy/p7xszx.

Francis, D. P. (2012). Deadly AIDS policy failure by the highest levels of the US government: A personal look back 30 years later for lessons to respond better to future epidemics. *Journal of Public Health Policy, 33*(3), 290–300. https://doi.org/10.1057/jphp.2012.14.

Gilbar, O., Wester, S. R., & Ben-Porat, A. (2021). The effects of gender role conflict restricted emotionality on the association between exposure to trauma, posttraumatic stress disorder and intimate partner violence severity. *Psychology of Men & Masculinities, 22*(1), 88–100. https://doi.org/10.1037/men0000266.

Goudy, M. (2020, June 24). Behind the mask: How to teach wearing a mask. *National Therapy Center.* https://rb.gy/7syvpr.

Grogan, S. (2010). Promoting positive body image in males and females: Contemporary issues and future directions. *Sex Roles 63*(9/10), 757–765. https://doi.org/10.1007/s11199-010-9894-z.

Haischer, M. H., Beilfuss, R., Hart, M. R., Opielinski, L., Wrucke, D., Zigaritis, G., Uhrich, T.D., & Hunter, S. K. (2020). Who is wearing a mask? Gender-, age-, and location-related differences during the COVID-19 pandemic. *PloS one, 15*(10), e0240785.

Hamel, L., Kearney, A., Kirzinger, A., Lopes, L., Munana, C., & Brodie, M. (2020, May 27). Kaiser Family Foundation health tracking poll—May 2020. *Kaiser Family Foundation.* https://rb.gy/oqjdp7.

Hanke, R. (1990). Hegemonic masculinity in thirty something. *Critical studies in media communication, 7*(3), 231–248. https://doi.org/10.1080/15295039009360176.

Hooper, C. (2001). *Manly states: Masculinities, international relations, and gender politics.* Columbia University Press.

Hoskin, R. A. (2020). "Femininity? It's the aesthetic of subordination": Examining femmephobia, the gender binary, and experiences of oppression among sexual and gender minorities. *Archives of sexual behavior*, 1–21. https://doi.org/10.1007/s10508-020-01641-x.

Howard M. C. (2021). Gender, face mask perceptions, and face mask wearing: Are men being dangerous during the COVID-19 pandemic?. *Personality and individual differences, 170*, 110417. https://doi.org/10.1016/j.paid.2020.110417.

Jackson, J. A. & Carviou, J. (2020). #MeToo and civic debate: The cultivation of toxic masculinity in twitter discourse. In M.B. Marron (Ed.), *Misogyny and Media in the Age of Trump* (131–147). Lexington Books.

Johnson, P. E. (2017). The art of masculine victimhood: Donald Trump's demagoguery. *Women's Studies in Communication, 40*(3), 229–250. https://doi.org/10.1080/07491409.2017.1346533.

Johnson, R. (1986/87). What is cultural studies anyway? *Social Text, 16*(1), 38–80. https://doi.org/10.2307/466285.

Katz, J. (2006). *Macho Paradox: Why some men hurt women and how all men can help*. Sourcebooks, Inc.

Kimmel, M. (2017). *Manhood in America*. Oxford University Press.

———. (2017). *Angry white men: American masculinity at the end of an era* (2nd ed.). Bold Type Books.

Kimmel, M. S. (2001). Global masculinities: Restoration and resistance. In B. Pease & K. Pringle (Eds.), *A man's world: Changing men's practices in a globalized world* (pp. 21–37). Zed Books.

Kimmel, M., & Wade, L. (2018). Ask a feminist: Michael Kimmel and Lisa Wade discuss toxic masculinity. *Signs: Journal of Women in Culture and Society, 44*(1), 233–254. https://doi.org/10.1086/698284.

Lincoln, R. A. (July 30, 2020). Herman Cain hospitalized for COVID-19 hours after tweeting 'People Are Fed Up' with masks: Former GOP presidential candidate was admitted to Atlanta-area hospital on Wednesday. *The Wrap*. https://rb.gy/bjen7j.

Marron, M. B. (2020). *Misogyny and media in the age of Trump*. Lexington Books.

Marshall, III, W. F. (August 13, 2020). Coronavirus infection by race: What's behind the health disparities? *Mayo Foundation for Medical Education and Research (MFMER)*. https://rb.gy/zho8kw.

Marwick, A., & boyd, d. (2011a). I tweet honestly, I tweet passionately: Twitter users, context collapse, and the imagined audience. *New Media & Society, 13*(1), 114–133. https://doi.org/10.1177/1461444810365313.

———. (2011b). To see and be seen: Celebrity practice on Twitter. *Convergence, 17*(2), 139–158. https://doi.org/10.1177/1354856510394539.

Morrison, V. (2020). Stand and Deliver [Recorded by E. Clapton]. The state51 Conspiracy (on behalf of Exile Records).

O'Neil, J. M. (1981). Patterns of gender role conflict and strain: sexism and fear of femininity in men's lives. *Personnel & Guidance Journal, 60*(4), 203. https://doi.org/10.1002/j.2164-4918.1981.tb00282.x.

———. (2008). Summarizing 25 years of research on men's gender role conflict using the Gender Role Conflict Scale: New research paradigms and clinical implications. *Counseling Psychologist, 36*, 358–445. doi: https://doi.org/10.1177/0011000008317057.

Parker, R., Barbosa, R. M., & Aggleton, P. (Eds.). (2000). *Framing the sexual subject: the politics of gender, sexuality, and power*. University of California Press.

Pascoe, C. J. (2011). *Dude, you're a fag: Masculinity and sexuality in high school*. University of California Press.

Pearce, K. (2020, June 17). Why COVID-19 poses greater risks for men than women. *Coronavirus Information and Resources for Johns Hopkins University.* https://rb .gy/gvojyn.

Politico [@politico]. (2020, April 29). *Mike Pence refused to wear a mask on Tuesday as he toured the Mayo Clinic.* [Tweet]. Twitter. https://rb.gy/tanzuq.

Pompper, D. (2010). Masculinities, the metrosexual, and media images: across dimensions of age and ethnicity. *Sex Roles, 63,* 682–696. https://doi.org/10.1007/ s11199-010-9870-7.

Pompper, D., Soto, J., & Piel, L. (2007). Male body image and magazine standards: Considering dimensions of age and ethnicity. *Journalism & Mass Communication Quarterly,* 84(3), 525–545. https://doi.org/10.1177/107769900708400308.

Rabin, R. C. (2020, April 7). In N.Y.C., the Coronavirus is killing men at twice the rate of women. *The New York Times.* https://rb.gy/393xgg.

Reuters Staff. (2020, July 21). TIMELINE-Masks and the future of the virus: Trump in his own words. *Reuters Healthcare Sector.* https://rb.gy/fi7mxi.

Searcy, N. [@yesnicksearcy]. (2020, June 18). *This is not a law @gavinnewsom. Therefore we don't have to do what you say.* [Tweet]. Twitter. https://rb.gy/osjho8.

Shapiro, B. [@benshapiro]. (2020, June 18). *I particularly look forward to Gavin Newsom attempting to enforce mask-wearing on my four-year-old son. Good luck with that.* [Tweet]. Twitter. https://rb.gy/kdzkd2.

Shepard, D. S. (2002). A negative state of mind: Patterns of depressive symptoms among men with high gender role conflict. *Psychology of Men & Masculinity, 3*(1), 3–8. https://doi.org/10.1037/1524-9220.3.1.3.

Stake, R. E. (2005). *Qualitative Case Studies.* In N. K. Denzin & Y. S. Lincoln (Eds.), *The Sage handbook of qualitative research* (p. 443–466). Sage Publications Ltd.

Trump, D. J. [@realdonaldtrump]. (2020, May 27). *He looks better!* [Tweet]. https:// rb.gy/bzm4nq.

Valdiserri, R. O., & Holtgrave, D. R. (2020). Responding to Pandemics: What We've Learned from HIV/AIDS. *AIDS and behavior,* 24(7), 1980–1982. https://doi .org/10.1007/s10461-020-02859-5.

Wade, J.C. (1996). African American men's gender role conflict: The significance of racial identity. *Sex Roles,* 34(1/2), 17–33. https://doi.org/10.1007/BF01544793.

Wood, L. A., & Kroger, R. (2000). *Doing discourse analysis: Methods for studying action in talk and text.* Sage Publications Ltd.

Yaqub, U. (2020). Tweeting during the COVID-19 pandemic: Sentiment analysis of twitter messages by President Trump. *Digital Government: Research and Practice,* 2(1), 1–7. https://doi.org/10.1145/3428090.

Zelizer, B. (2007). Introduction: On finding new ways of thinking about journalism. *Political Communication,* 24(2), 111–114. https://doi.org/10.1080/10584600701312829.

Chapter Fourteen

New Media Masculinities

How YouTube Influencers Incubate Masculine Ideologies and Mentor Males Through Gender Role Conflict/Stress

Gabriel Parks, Daniel Russo, and Jenni Simon

INTRODUCTION

Male gender role conflict/stress (GRC/S), often framed as a *crisis* of masculinity on social networking websites, has something to teach us about modern male identity negotiation and ways males struggle to embody or resist ideals of masculinity. Masculinity, like gender, is a social process in constant flux (Bridges & Pascoe, 2018). Masculinity and gender relations are historically prone to crises (Connell, 1995) due to their dynamic and unstable nature as socially constructed realities. Examining these dynamics is timely, given recent "major loss of legitimacy for patriarchy" which has resulted in "different groups of men now negotiating this loss in very different ways" (Connell, 1995, p. 202). The digital landscape of the early twenty-first century has created even more space for masculinity negotiation through social media. In this chapter, we suggest that the website YouTube functions as one of the most vital contemporary social media locations used by young men to shape their ideas about masculinity.

As modern young men cope with gender role conflict/stress (GRC/S), they are impacted by a variety of contingent social forces, such as media representations and parasocial relationships that may trigger GRC/S in patterned, cyclical ways (Brown, 2015; Mirrlees, 2018; O'Neil, 2008, 2015). With the emergence of Web 2.0 and social media used for entertainment purposes, millions of adolescents have flocked to YouTube channels, developing formative relationships with popular social and political influencers with varying perceptions of authenticity attributed to the content and other outcomes (Cunningham and Craig, 2017; Lewis, 2018, 2020; Marwick, 2015)—especially adolescents who use YouTube as part of their identity construction (Pérez-Torres et al., 2018). For males, interplay with YouTube includes encountering confusing messages traditionally directed to women about make-up, clothes and accessories (Haryanto & Suwito, 2017), populist resistance to dominant understandings of masculinity (Burgess, 2019), and what Ging (2019) called a "particularly toxic brand of antifeminism" (p. 638). To discover more about these dynamics with regard to GRC/S, we consider three popular channels by influencers: Elliot Hulse, Natalie Wynn (ContraPoints), and Charlie Houpert (Charisma on Command).

First, fitness-trainer-turned-masculinity-guru Elliot Hulse is situated in the manosphere's alpha wing—emphasizing hegemonic masculinity's tenets of emotionlessness, invulnerability, toughness, risk-taking (Burton & Nelson, 1994), and dominance/power over women. His video content is designed for men and includes topics like weightlifting and confidence. Recently, Hulse broadened his content to include tutorials on appropriate performances of alpha masculinity and commentary on the woes of being an alpha conservative male inhabiting a beta liberal world. Elliot Hulse has approximately 802k subscribers and 92.9 million video views (another channel of his, geared towards fitness and weightlifting, has 1.81 million subscribers) (Social Blade, 2021).

Second, Natalie Wynn operates a channel called ContraPoints, wherein she makes theatrical, political content on cultural issues often related to sex and gender. A trans woman often referring to her expertise as someone who has negotiated multiple gender identities and others' critique/bullying, ContraPoints has 1.25 million subscribers and 55.3 million video views (Social Blade, 2021). Her videos offer critical commentary as she aims to "counterbalance the hatred toward progressive movements that is so common online" (ContraPoints, 2019) and is commonly recognized as belonging to an informal group of online content creators constituting BreadTube or Left-Tube airing perspectives shaped by socialist, communist, anarchist, and other left-wing perspectives (Social Blade, 2021). Wynn's focus is to entertainingly help viewers "establish their own viewpoint" by providing "guidance, emphasizing practical individual and group involvement," through a dialectical process of engaging with multiple ideological perspectives on the same issue (Kuznetsov & Ismangil, 2020, p. 211–212). Wynn positions herself as a reference for examining gender discourses as a trans woman:

> I've spent a lot of the last of the last three years covering the manosphere . . . And from all the time I've tortured myself wading through these communities of incels, pick-up artists, men's rights slacktivists, intellectual dark web fanboys and alt-right racists, I've noticed that they all have one thing in

common—which is that they all recruit from the same massive pool of sad, young men (ContraPoints, 2019).

Third, Charisma on Command is a speech coaching business operated by Charlie Houpert to help young men develop greater confidence and charisma. Houpert has built a massive YouTube following—4.37 million subscribers and 394.8 million video views (Social Blade, 2021)—by producing videos on how to increase social skills and boost emotional intelligence. He typically borrows from pop culture icons (superhero characters, comedians, public intellectuals, and other entertainment figures) to teach his audience about arts of persuasion and reputation. For example, Houpert curated a channel playlist titled "Charismatic Leading Men," a collection of videos that teach tips/hacks—like flattering others and using emotions—for men to use in social situations to elevate their status.

In sum, whether framing their content through their own gender role conflict/stress or through the gender role stress that they perceive among others, Hulse, Wynn, and Houpert have amassed impressive online audiences in their roles as entertainers, mentors, and political commentators. Because content of the influencer's channels routinely invoke the masculinity construct and situates it as being somehow in crisis, we interrogate influencers' ideas and critiques as both performers and critics of gender role ideals in order to contribute to an expanded understanding of male GRC/S as it plays out in one variety of online social media entertainment space highly popular among young males.

LITERATURE REVIEW

The foundation for the study reported in this chapter is built on: 1) role of rhetoric in shaping masculinities, 2) male gender role conflict and stress, 3) YouTube influencers and the manosphere, and 4) closer look at three YouTube influencers.

Role of Rhetoric in Shaping Masculinities

Rhetorically-savvy opinion leaders like religious leaders and politicians existed long before the Internet. Today, opinion leaders in the form of social media influencers play an important role in creating social cohesion when persuading others to adopt their point of view. Opinion leaders like spreading their opinions, are considered to be highly interested in and better informed about certain topics/issues than the average person, and are good organizers who can "get people to take action" (Furlow, 2013, p. 719). Consequently, anyone who has a following can become an opinion leader on social media and marketers support those who have the potential to shape public opinion and influence them. The more active opinion leaders are, the greater their likelihood to interpersonally communicate and become "superdiffusers" (Boster et al., 2012).

When the topic/issue is masculinity, an influencer's rhetoric may seek to persuade an audience to adopt their specific *version* of masculinity. Rhetoric proves a useful tool for encouraging people to "voluntarily agree with the communicator" (Kuypers, 2010, p. 288). For example, influencers using the YouTube social media platform may offer reasons for an audience to agree with their sense-making, their perspective, their vision, and their reality (Pérez-Torres et al., 2018). The YouTube influencer's rhetoric may prove so persuasive that audiences united in certain belief systems become socially bound together (Quigley, 1998) as an audience that uses online fora to promote a certain brand of masculinity rooted in misogyny strongly opposing feminism and amplifying hostility toward women. This is known as manosphere ideology and may be examined among the rhetoric of social groups such as Men Going Their Own Way Movement (MGTOW) and involuntary celibates (incels) (Kuznetsov & Ismangil, 2020; Lewis, 2018; Parks, 2020). Gender discourse in popular culture and media shapes how we make sense of masculinity and adopt perspectives on what constitutes a male ideal. This ideal becomes a benchmark against which men assess themselves and women evaluate the men they encounter. Hence, the ideal becomes a reference point for male identity negotiations, as well as for patterns of gender relations across the sexes (Craig, 1992; Halberstam, 1998; Macnamara, 2006; Messerschmidt and Messner, 2018; Moss, 2011).

Negative outcomes of ideal male gender roles fueling the masculinity concept may be best understood by incorporating core ideas from the masculinity studies field about *hegemonic, hybrid,* and *intersectional* masculinities. Hegemonic masculinities are those "constructed locally, regionally, and globally that legitimate an unequal relationship between men and women, masculinity and femininity, and among masculinities" (Messerschmidt & Messner, 2018, p. 41). Ideas about masculinities become hegemonic when socially constructed differences among men or between men and women evolve into stereotypes used to dominate and subordinate others (Connell, 2005). Men may resist masculinity ideals by developing their own hybrids, or "selective incorporation of identity elements typically associated with various marginalized and subordinated masculinities or femininities" (Bridges & Pascoe, 2018, p. 256). When privileged men use aspects of marginalized gender expressions in their gender performance or identity, this is known as hybrid masculinity (Hansen, 2019). Men also may shape their sense of identity based on their own intersecting social identity dimensions (gender plus age, ethnicity, sexual orientation, socio-economic status, and more) —further amplifying a need for a plural understanding of masculinities (e.g., Connell and Messerschmidt, 2005).

Hybrid male gender performances that include aspects of hegemonic masculinity also may end up perpetuating gender inequality. Even though symbolically subverting hegemonic masculinity by incorporating otherwise marginalized traits (like behavior considered effeminate) (Bridges & Pascoe, 2018), a more relaxed understanding appeals to some men who seek to resist traditional hegemonic masculinity. Yet, so long as they perpetuate damaging stereotypes about women and some men, they still support marginalizing behaviors supported by hegemonic masculinity tenets. Indeed, hybrid masculinity can gain traction and end up radicalizing young men when the ideas are amplified across the rhetoric of popular Internet figures (Lewis, 2018).

Male Gender Role Conflict and Stress

Use of GRC/S theory (O'Neil, 2008) to undergird examinations of gender discourse across media content promotes understanding of issues at the core of rhetorical framing of masculinity as in *crisis* or conflict. Those who perceive themselves and others as failing to perform appropriate gender roles or to live up to some masculine ideal are said to be in gender role conflict or stress that can include physical and emotional symptoms (O'Neil, 2008). For example, men considered to be outside of traditional masculine norms may be devalued or restricted because of their deviation from traditional male gender role and masculinity norms (O'Neil, 2008). There are rhetorical dimensions of such activities when language is put in the service of underscoring hegemony for social control purposes or when actual physical violence is involved (Mansbridge & Shames, 2008).

O'Neil (2008) teased out four stress-inducing categories characterizing GRC/S: 1) restrictive emotionality (RE); 2) restrictive and affectionate behavior between men (RABBM); 3) success, power, and competition issues (SPC); and 4) conflicts between work and family relations (CBWFR). Negative consequences among these categories may include hostile work and home environments for men across the life course. For example, stressors can result in marital conflict and intimacy issues, physical and psychological violence, workplace or social ostracism, and substance abuse, among other problems. In sum, these outcomes negatively impact everyone (O'Neil, 2008), so that recognizing the patterns and eradicating their sources can go a long way in reducing the conflict and stress that men feel about their own sense of masculinity and male gender roles—and ways they intersect with everyone else.

YouTube Influencers and the Manosphere

YouTube is one of the most popular and influential Internet platforms for aspiring influencers to express themselves (Cunningham & Craig, 2017). The platform reported 1.68 billion users in 2019 (Statista, 2021a) and falls just behind Google as the second most-used search engine (Statista, 2019). The initial appeal of YouTube came from its founding promise to give everyday people a voice, exemplified in their original slogan, "Broadcast Yourself™" (Jarett, 2008, p. 133). YouTube provides far-reaching alternatives to the experience of sharing and is "a different technology, a shift in [media] user routines, a new type of content, and a radical overhaul of the traditional broadcast industry, including its business models" (Dijck, 2013, p. 110). YouTube has become a haven for those seeking fame outside traditional mainstream media. Otherwise non-celebrity people become influential personalities online by attracting followers documented by algorithms (Wotanis and McMillan, 2014; Marwick, 2015). Influencers' social capital appeals to marketers looking to advertise on influencers' sites. YouTube raised over $19.77 billion in ad revenues for 2020, accounting for 10.9 percent of its owner Google's total annual revenue (Statista, 2021a).

As a produced content medium, YouTube functions as a gender performance space and socializing force—and is extremely popular among males. Statistically, the audience may be 50–50 along gender lines (Nielsen, 2020), but more generation Z and millennial men consider YouTube their favorite site for following influencers compared to Gen Z and millennial women, who favor Instagram (Statista, 2021b). Due to the variety of user-generated content and its popularity among coming-of-age men, women, trans, and non-binary persons, YouTube has been increasingly studied as a site for the production and consumption of gender ideologies (e.g., Pérez-Torres et al., 2018; Pullen & Cooper, 2010; Wotanis & McMillan, 2014).

Influencers become well known among certain population segments who reward influencers with their attention, association, and their admiration. Audiences often consider popular YouTube influencers (sometimes referred to as micro-celebrities) as both peers and idols (Brown, 2015; Cunningham & Craig, 2017; Marwick, 2015). Popularity on YouTube usually is measured through content subscribers, views, and/or likes. Nouri (2018) noted that micro-celebrities are "seen as normal everyday people who have attained . . . millions of followers on these social media platforms" (p. 2). Generally, YouTube's interactive interface with both visual and audio promotes a level of intimacy (Nouri, 2018).

Some researchers have found that these social media dynamics are strong enough to mobilize individuals and build social movement or social backlash infrastructures (Thrall et al., 2008). YouTube and other social media spaces (e.g., Reddit, 4Chan, *Incels.is*, *RooshV, A Voice for Men*) have become home to the manosphere phenomenon. The manosphere constitutes a collection of websites, online fora and blogs that promote masculinity and oppose feminism—amplifying a form of exaggerated misogyny (Horta Ribeiro et al., 2020). In these spaces, male hegemony is a "preoccupation" (Ging, 2019, p. 16) and the goal is to push back against feminism (Ironwood, 2013; Nagle, 2015). Male audience members characterize themselves as alphas, betas, and incels/involuntarily celibate males, with some believing that their masculinity has become devalued in today's world—a justification for their "political position of anti-feminism" (Jones, 2020, p. ii). Critical discourse analysts suggest that the manosphere undergirds radicalization of men against women and hypothesize that such an Intellectual Dark Web (IDW) uses algorithmic recommendations to nudge users toward politically extreme content (e.g., Horta Ribeiro et al., 2020; Lewis, 2018). According to Hermann (2020), the manosphere maximizes use of rhetorical devices like metaphor (e.g., taking the Red Pill), hyperbole (e.g., claims of systemic male victimization and subjugation or suffering under women), condensed but emphatic enthymemes (e.g., declaring degradation of the West), and appropriation of feminist arguments (e.g., victimhood, rights, and oppression).

Thus, outcomes of YouTube influencers' impact may not necessarily be supportive across gender identity groups—especially among men coming to terms with what masculinity means for them. Women, of course, experience effects of misogyny. Those who refuse to accept that there are multiple ways to consider masculinity may be successful in convincing others to adopt a similar worldview—and this could perpetuate GRC/S for men who refuse to adapt to dominant hegemonic views on masculinity in manosphere communities or otherwise.

Research Question

With the understanding that YouTube has risen as a site for gender role performance and shaping of hegemonic masculinity tenets—and with the understanding that gender role conflict/stressors have widespread negative impact—we seek to answer this research question:

RQ: What does each YouTube influencer's a) framing of male GRC/S look like, and b) what solutions do they offer?

METHOD

We connect rhetorical framing analysis (Kuyper, 2010) with GRC/S (O'Neil, 2008) as a framework for qualitative textual analysis in order to examine gender-related discourse among YouTube influencer messages. Linking their rhetorical parsing of ideas about masculinity with potential male GRC/S will enable us to better understand how hegemonic masculinity tenets—what it means to be masculine and/or manly—are reinforced, reformed, or resisted. Next, we provide details of how data were collected and analyzed.

Influencer and Clip Selection

The process of selecting influencers for analysis included a strategic attempt to review diverging constructions of the masculinity concept. We chose three influencers who have explicitly communicated their ideas about masculinity: Elliot Hulse amplifies the manosphere's hegemonic masculinity; Charisma on Command/Houpert amplifies a hybrid masculinity; and ContraPoints/ Wynn amplifies a counterhegemonic masculinity.

Among the three influencers' programming, there were (N=985) videos to consider for analysis from 2016–2020. To derive a systematic sample of clips for analysis, we began by inputting the key terms *men* and *masculinity* into each of each of the three YouTube channel's database. Preliminary viewing of each clip ensured the videos explored the theme of masculinity.

We chose clips that we think best capture each influencer's perspective on masculinity. Each Elliot Hulse and Charlie Houpert/Charisma on Command video ranges 5–15 minutes in length, so we chose three. Each Natalie Wynn/ ContraPoints video is nearly 60 minutes long, so we chose two. Specific videos selected for analysis were: Charisma on Command: "How to Be the Coolest Guy in The Room," "How to Become the Man You Want to Be," "How to Be Charming Without Trying;" Elliot Hulse: "How to be a Dominant Man in a World Full of Sissies," "Don't Get in Touch with Your 'Feminine Side,'" and "What Is Wrong with Men These Days?" and ContraPoints: "Incels," and "Men."

Data Analysis Technique

Each of the influencer videos in the sample constituted the unit of analysis. Several steps were involved in analyzing data used to answer this study's research question.

1. We transcribed each video.
2. We performed a rhetorical analysis of each YouTube influencer's framing of masculinity in each video in two steps.

   a. First, we closely examined rhetorical devices like metaphors, analogies, stories, ideographs (buzzwords), appeals to cultural mores, and other framing techniques (Kuypers, 2010)—to reveal patterns qualifying each influencer's ideas about masculinity and solutions.
   b. Second, once we discovered that Wynn/Contrapoints and Elliot Hulse framed masculinity as being in *crisis* and advocated for a solution, with Houpert/Charisma on Command framing conflicts of masculinity as a problem of confidence and charisma, we examined each video in search of stress-inducing categories characterizing GRC/S (RE, RABBM, SPC, CBWFR) that influencers may have either: i) experienced themselves or ii) perceived as being experienced among males. GRC/S performances included statements or remarks related to one's perceived stress or conflict levels (O'Neil, 2008). A rhetorical performance of RE might include statements supporting or opposing traditional femininity in men as well as statements promoting or resisting calls for stoicism and fearlessness. A rhetorical performance of SPC might include statements supporting or opposing superiority/ social control over males and females deemed emotional and weak, as well as statements generally promoting or resisting a survival of the fittest attitude. A rhetorical performance of CBWFR might include statements promoting or resisting traditional, patriarchal gender roles such as women as mother and housewife and men as provider and protector. Rhetorical performances of RE, RABBM, SPC, and CBWFR also may offer hybrid alternatives. For example, a hybrid rhetorical performance of RE might include accepting less restriction on men expressing their emotions while simultaneously maintaining homophobic stances toward men displaying flamboyant (feminine) behaviors.

3. Finally, we three authors made our own notes individually and then extensively discussed readings of data at weekly meetings until interpretations were 100 percent agreed upon. Part of the agreement meant arriving at names for themes/patterns we had discovered among each influencer's content.

RESULTS AND DISCUSSION

RQ: What does each YouTube influencer's a) framing of male GRC/S look like, and b) what solutions do they offer?

Elliot Hulse: Making Hegemonic Men Strong Again by Conquering the Betas and Sissies

YouTube strength-coach-turned-masculinity influencer Elliot Hulse (805k subscribers) (Social Blade, 2021) called for a return to traditional gender roles by conquering betas and sissies as a solution to masculinity's crisis; a strategy that will result in peace for everyone. His YouTube channel's most recent branding and mission is encouraging men to be strong again—an homage to former President Donald Trump's 2016 campaign MAGA slogan—and make spaces safe for women and children by re-discovering traditional hegemonic masculinity where men are dominant, powerful, and respected leaders. Long-ing for a past with "be a man," he told men: "When our grandfathers were alive . . . men knew exactly what it meant to be a man" (Hulse, 2019). While Hulse acknowledged a mixed-race identity, he celebrated the "more dominant people" who conquered indigenous communities (Hulse, 2020a).

Yet, Hulse has warned viewers that masculinity is in crisis due to "easy times" (Hulse, 2020a). He advocated for strength and bravery and disdained mental and physical weakness—preferring patriarchal families with alpha male leadership. With utterances like, "Manly men are what created society . . . All the great things come from manly men who protect and then conquer." Hulse (2020a) has left little space for non-hegemonic views on masculinity because he perceives alternatives as jeopardizing hegemonic masculinity's tenets of dominance, self-reliance, independence, strength, and stoicism. In his show, "How to be a Dominant Man in a World Full of Sissies," Hulse (2020a) said: "I think it's a horrible idea for men to get in touch with their feminine side." For Hulse, then, the path to reclaiming privilege is a return to hegemonic masculinity's central tenets with traditional gender roles; a shift that requires masculinity reprogramming: "This is why our ancestors had rights of passages associated with boys becoming men . . . they have got to get away from that effeminate taste" (Hulse, 2020b).

A solution, in Hulse's manosphere, is to resolve the conflicts and stressors that today's men experience by turning back the clock. Rather than consider-ing GRC/S as a byproduct of hegemonic masculinity as O'Neil (2008) and others have theorized, Hulse turns the framework upside down to recapture hegemonic masculinity with elevated levels of respect and social status for men—while criticizing anything that threatens to diminish male privilege. For example, while O'Neil (2008) and others have theorized that hegemonic masculinity's tenet of restrictive emotionality (RE) means men hold in their emotions—which can lead to physical and mental health problems for men and domestic violence exacted on partners—Hulse (2020a) warned that showing emotions makes men "sissy" and therefore un-masculine. For Hulse, male success, power, and competition (SPC) can happen only when men embody hegemonic masculinity's tenets of dominance and high social status.

ContraPoints: Challenging Manosphere to Create an Inclusive Male Gender Community

This YouTube influencer challenged manosphere nihilism in "Incels" and "Men" by revealing the agenda of right-wing conservative and/or libertarian roots of certain men's groups. Wynn offered socio-political critique when exploring the degrees of gender role stress that men exhibit as an outcome of masculinity in crisis and advocated for a more inclusive male gender community. Overall, she characterized males' angst, loneliness, and yearning for purpose which cumulatively leads them to search for new gender role models and ends up alienating men in the process. Wynn framed a crisis of masculinity characterizing young men's struggle to find confidence and motivation— losses that stem from feeling invisible since they no longer fulfill social roles as warriors and providers. Wynn argued that these feelings drive males to nihilism: "most of these boys are not bad people," rather, they face a world that no longer requires or glorifies "the sacrificial role of men as warriors" (ContraPoints, 2019).

Wynn illuminated at least two GRC/S stressors driving her conclusion that masculinity is in crisis: 1) conflicts between work and family relations (CBWFR) emerge for men who see the career marketplace as a zero-sum game with opportunities on the rise for women in the West; and 2) success, power, and competition issues (SPC) leaving men feeling disenfranchised which manifests in feelings of low power levels as weak failures lacking purpose and motivation. According to Wynn, men who identify as incels lack confidence in their looks, sexual ability, and romantic skill for successful sexual conquest (ContraPoints, 2018).

As a solution, Wynn encouraged men to recognize the damage that nihilistic "lie down and rot" thinking can do by instead enhancing their social skills through interaction with people in person rather than online (ContraPoints, 2018). This advice is inconsistent with men's rights groups' mediated content that rarely advises audiences about "how to fix themselves" (ContraPoints, 2018). Hence, Wynn (ContraPoints, 2018) reasoned that "[m]aybe, the average man is also oppressed by the system that feminists call patriarchy." While remaining critical of the manosphere's sexism and dismissal of social justice solutions—as well as feminists who dismiss white male angst as a privileged position undeserving of sympathy—Wynn (ContraPoints, 2019) encouraged men to bond together to arrive at their own solutions as an inclusive male gender community.

Charisma on Command: Teaching Masculine Charm and Soliciting Success through Self-Branding

Houpert's Charisma on Command channel focuses on strategically performing masculinity to help men get what they want. He has suggested that men should strive to be likeable and the solution is to pay attention to one's habits and to adjust them accordingly. Houpert titles his videos using catchy self-help mantras, like "How to Become the Man You Want to Be," "How to be Charming without Trying," and "How to Be the Coolest Guy in the Room." These titles clearly reveal someone who is transfixed on male gender role stress and conflict-resolution, and explicitly notes that he tries to "deconstruct our culture's masculine ideal," because, "once you start to understand how you may have subtly been influenced by it, you don't have to unthinkingly accept" (2017a).

Charisma on Command illuminated two GRC/S stressors (SPC and RE) in the "How to Become the Man You Want to Be" video, as Houpert talked about the fictional character James Bond. Houpert characterized Bond as masculine, strategically using emotionality as a tool—as a balancing act depending on the situation. Rather than simply defaulting to hegemonic masculinity's tenet of restrictive emotionality (RE), or men holding in their emotions, Houpert offered a less-restrictive take on males showing emotions. Houpert examined Daniel Craig's masculine performance of James Bond, resolving that displays of emotion are masculine when they result in attracting a sexual partner, but that a stoic expression is more acceptable when facing violence or danger. Houpert noted that restrictive emotionality (RE) can be damaging: "By learning to trust no one and wall off emotionally, Bond finally becomes the guy that we've loved for 20+ movies, and of all the messages about masculinity and Bond, I think this is the most destructive" (Charisma, 2017a). In other words, Houpert warned men to act strategically where emotions are concerned but not to ignore or to suppress them.

In the same episode, Houpert emphasized the importance of control as a quality of masculinity by critiquing Bond's masculinity in a context of consumerism, or commodity fetishism, commonly evident in metrosexual masculinity representations. Houpert explained that having control enables men to dominate social situations: "[Bond] isn't a man because of what he has acquired or even because he has [male] parts . . . He's a man because of his actions in the face of adversity" (Charisma, 2017a). Thus, Houpert posited that simply possessing control enables masculine men to be successful, powerful, and competitive (SPC)—similar to men's lifestyle magazines' framing of masculinity in terms of consumption (Tan et al., 2013).

In "How to Be Charming Without Trying," Houpert suggests men be less restrictive and more "goofy" (Charisma, 2017b), implicitly reiterating the age-old Lucian mantra of 'Laugh at everything and take nothing seriously.' He argues that mental-emotional restriction is both bad for men's mental health and also leaves a poor first impression on people, which is not ideal if the goal is to be more likeable. Rather, for Houpert, positivity plus easygoingness results in a good first impression and subsequent positive reputation, with humor acting as a laudable tool for achieving such means and ends. As an explicit pedagogue, he teaches that "The best way to be amusing to others and to connect with them is by first having fun alone, by yourself. Then you can bring that energy and that mentality to whoever happens to be around you" (2017b). He argues that by practicing and allowing yourself to goof off alone, "you're going to become more clever, because you won't answer everything so seriously. Instead, you'll be in the habit of answering the random and boring parts of life in a sillier manner" (2017b).

Lastly, in "How To Be the Coolest Guy In The Room," Houpert compares the masculine performances of Robert Downey Jr.'s Ironman and Chris Evan's Captain America, characters both from the *Marvel* superhero series (2008–2020). Houpert is concerned with explaining the importance of the presentation of self in achieving optimal masculine performance. He suggests that a man's goal is to be likeable and the solution is to pay attention to your habits and adjust them if/when necessary (Charisma, 2016). In this sense, he recommends acting more like Captain America than Ironman. For him, Ironman demonstrates signs of elitism and pretention, where as Captain America promotes humble or reciprocal social interactions that place one as inferior, or at least on the same level as partner/s in conversation (Charisma, 2016). He concludes, "You are actually better off leaning towards being likeable than cool . . . pay attention to how your habits are making the people around you feel. Those habits are going to be the blueprint for the impression that you make most of the time" (Charisma, 2016).

CONCLUSIONS

These findings suggest that three prominent YouTube influencers use male conflict/stress as a tool to sell their entertainment programming. Wynn and Hulse articulate masculinity as a crisis screaming for a solution, invoking gender role stressors that they face in their lived experiences or perceive in others'. Houpert's rhetoric seems a bit less extreme as he frames masculinity as a diminishing return in a world where men have lost confidence. In the process of framing male GRC/S, each influencer amplifies their individual perspective, or agenda. Elliot Hulse's theme of *making hegemonic men strong again by conquering the betas and sissies* communicates about masculinity in terms of men conquering themselves and feminists by defeating weakness among men and across society. The ContraPoints channel, via Natalie Wynn, communicates about *challenging manosphere to create an inclusive male gender community* in terms of nihilistic worldviews threatening men's quality of life [opposite of "lay down and rot" (Wynn, 2018)]. And the Charisma on Command channel, via Charlie Houpert, communicates about *teaching masculine charm and soliciting success through self-branding* in terms of men charming others as a means for achieving success and social status.

Individually and collectively, these themes and each one's messages about masculinity could prove limiting and damaging. First, Hulse's heralding of hegemonic masculinity calls for a return to the America of the 1950s (Moss, 2011) and underscores just how easily discussions of masculinity can marginalize and bully certain groups of males and take political aim at progressive, liberal culture and politics. Hulse's ideal hegemonic masculinity perpetuates patriarchal work-home ideals (i.e., men protecting and providing for nuclear families), a nationalistic and ethnocentric social conscience (i.e., defending national borders and traditional Christian-American values), and an imperialistic view of power and success (i.e., expansion of American exceptionalism and hegemony). Second, the ContraPoints channel of Natalie Wynn advances a counterhegemonic masculinity by addressing intersectional and diverse gender topics, while refusing to acknowledge the manosphere's spectrum of members which she distills into a collection of "sad, young men" beyond help because they shun it (Wynn, 2019). Finally, Charlie Houpert of the Charisma on Command show advances a hybrid masculinity and frames masculinity in crisis as the need for strategic self-branding and manipulation. While Houpert does pushes back against hegemonic masculinity in some ways, he often reflects and reifies discourses of the neoliberal self (Hiramoto & Yanning, 2017) by offering an idea of cool, stoic, entrepreneurship driven by individualization. Houpert's seemingly neoliberal worldview emphasizes the heteronormative but fails to fully embrace diverse sexual orientations or social identity intersectionalities of his audience. Further, by placing more emphasis on relationships and self-improvement, his rhetoric differs from the explicitly Right- and Left-leaning ideological lessons from Hulse and Contrapoints, respectively. While Hulse and Houpert share an emphasis on personal success (i.e., making the strongest/best versions of oneself), they have different conceptions of it, and associate it with different ways of being male. Hulse advocates strength and traditional, hegemonic order, whereas Houpert's message is more politically ambiguous, offering tenable advice on presentation and persuasion.

Implications for GRC/S

Each YouTube influencer's program examined for this study follows the advertising industry's formula of illustrating a problem and then offering a solution (Ogilvy, 1985). Based on our analysis of some of their primary texts produced for audiences of predominantly young men, the lessons these influencers offer about how to deal with male GRC/S reflect both stubborn reactionary ideologies and hopeful dialogues about addressing and transforming hegemonic masculinity. Hulse's traditionalist philosophy with degrees of toxic masculinity-inspiring advice could serve to radicalize young males. Exposure to Wynn's videos could inspire young males to search for new male role models, or at least an understanding that males need to play a more active role in constructing twenty-first-century masculine ideals. Young male audiences of Houpert's Charisma on Command could learn about charming colleagues and romantic interests, criticizing hegemonic male behavior like "stonewall-ish" invulnerability or overindulgent suavity, and be influenced to consume certain media and to purchase products consistent with commercial visions of ideal male self-image and social status.

Our findings offer insight into current understandings and uses of GRC/S theory. When surveying transcript data to spot instances of male GRC/S patterns we focused on male emotionality as a component of the masculinity concept and ways restriction of emotionality can contribute to GRC/S. As O'Neil (2008) noted, "greater efforts are needed to inform the public about how men, women, boys, and girls are all potentially harmed by restrictive and sexist gender roles" (p. 424). O'Neil (2008) added that, "Many men can solve their problems outside of therapy if safe environments are created to explore their problems" (p. 422). We believe that the rise of YouTube influencers like Hulse, Wynn and Houpert highlights unique efforts outside of clinical settings wherein audiences are exposed to persuasive messages about handling male stress. Such pathways may lead to hegemonic interpretations of male success (SPC) predicated on restrictive emotions (RE), fixations with heteronormative image and status, and patriarchal power over family and community decision making. Overall, we support enabling adolescent audiences (in particular) to develop critical perspectives when engaging with these YouTube influencers' content so that they may develop their own critical examination of GRC constructs within mediated gender discourses and resist YouTube's radicalization pathways.

Limitations and Future Directions

The primary limitation of findings discovered as answer to our research question about how three YouTube influencers frame masculinity and address GRC/S by offering solutions is that we examined only three influencers and a handful of each influencer's programs—as a starting point for future hypothesis testing. Hence, findings are not generalizable. Future study of masculinities could include additional research methods that call for larger or broader data sets, such as interviews with influencers, focus groups to gather perceptions of viewers, experiments to test messaging effects, or content analyses to count frequencies.

REFERENCES

Bazerman, C. (1988). *Shaping written knowledge: The genre and activity of the experimental article in science.* University of Wisconsin Press.

Boster, F. J., Carpenter, C. J., Andrews, K. R., & Mongeau, P. A. (2012). Employing interpersonal influence to promote behavioral change. *Health Communication, 27,* 399-407. doi:10.1080/10410236.2011.595771.

Bridges, T., & Pascoe, C. J. (2018). On the elasticity of gender hegemony: Why hybrid masculinities fail to undermine gender and sexual inequality. In J. W. Messner et al. (Eds.), *Gender reckonings: New social theory and research* (pp. 254–273). New York University Press.

Brooks, M. (2020). *Against the web: A cosmopolitan answer to the new right.* Zero Books.

Brown, W. J. (2015). Examining four processes of audience involvement with media personae: Transportation, parasocial interaction, identification, and worship. *Communication Theory, 25,* 259–283. https://doi.org/10.1111/comt.12053

Burgess, S. (2011). YouTube on masculinity and the Founding Fathers: Constitutionalism 2.0. *Political Research Quarterly, 64,* 120–131. https://doi.org/10.1177/1065912909343580.

Charisma on Command. (May 10, 2016). "How to Be the Coolest Guy in The Room." [YouTube video]. Charlie Houpert. Retrieved from https://rb.gy/9lvi9i.

———. (September 18, 2017a). "How to Become the Man You Want to Be." [YouTube video]. Charlie Houpert. Retrieved from https://rb.gy/wafxff.

———. (May 4, 2017b). "How to Be Charming Without Trying." [YouTube video]. Charlie Houpert. Retrieved from https://rb.gy/mak1jz.

Connell, R. W. (1987). *Gender and power: Society, the person and sexual politics.* Stanford University Press.

———. (1995). *Masculinities.* University of California Press.

Connell, R. W. & Messerschmidt, J. W. (2005). Hegemonic masculinity: Rethinking the concept. *Gender & Society, 19*(6), 829–859. https://doi.org/10.1177/0891243205278639.

ContraPoints. (2018, August 17). Incels | ContraPoints. [YouTube video]. Natalie Wynn. Retrieved from https://www.youtube.com/watch?v=fD2briZ6fB0.

———. (2019, August 23). Men | ContraPoints. [YouTube video]. Natalie Wynn. Retrieved from https://www.youtube.com/watch?v=S1xxcKCGljY.

Cunningham, S., & Craig, D. (2017). Being 'really real' on YouTube: Authenticity, community and brand culture in social media entertainment. *Media International Australia, 164*, 71–81. https://doi.org/10.1177/1329878X17709098.

Dijck, J. (2013). The culture of connectivity: A critical history of social media. *Oxford University Press.*

Elliot Hulse. (2020a, March 29). How To Be A Dominant Man In A World Full of Sissies. [YouTube video]. Elliot Hulse. Retrieved from https://www.youtube.com/watch?v=HQoGscuQ-NI.

———. (2020b, March 28). MEN: Don't get in touch with your "feminine side". [YouTube video]. Elliot Hulse. Retrieved from https://www.youtube.com/watch?v=Ov6ahtIIgdY.

———. (2019, March 28). TOXIC: What is wrong with men these days? [YouTube video]. Elliot Hulse. Retrieved from https://www.youtube.com/watch?v=7QVH-cc8fZk.

Furlow, N. E. (2013). Public opinion and opinion leaders. In *Encyclopedia of public relations* (Vol. 2, pp. 719–720). Sage.

Ging, D. (2019). Alphas, betas, and incels: Theorizing the masculinities of the Manosphere. *Men and Masculinities, 22*(4), 638–657. https://doi.org/10.1177/1097184X17706401.

Halberstam, J. (1998). *Female Masculinity*. Duke University Press. https://doi.org/10.2307/j.ctv11hpjb1.

Hansen, K. (2019). The ambiguity of 'new' masculinities: Zayn Malik and disordered eating. *Celebrity Studies*, 1–5. https://doi.org/10.1080/19392397.2019.1639975.

Haryanto, N., & Suwito, K. A. (2020). Gender identity construction of male beauty vloggers on YouTube. *Talent Development & Excellence, 12*(2), 171–177. Retrieved from http://iratde.com/index.php/jtde/article/view/167.

Hiramoto, M., & Yanning, L. (2017). Building a body of followers: Neoliberalism and online discourse of fitness and masculinity. *Journal of Language and Sexuality, 6*(2), 262-291. https://doi.org/10.1075/jls.6.2.03hir.

Horta Ribeiro, M., Ottoni, R., West, R., Almeida, V. A. F., & Meira Jr., M. (2020). Auditing radicalization pathways on YouTube. In Conference on Fairness, Accountability, and Transparency, January 27–30, 2020, Barcelona, Spain. ACM, 131–141. https://doi.org/10.1145/3351095.3372879.

Horta Ribeiro, M., Blackburn, J., Bradlyns, B., De Cristofaro, E. Stringhini, G., Long, S., Greenberg, S., & Zannettou, S. (2020). The evolution of the Manosphere across the Web. In 15th International AAAI Conference on Web and Social Media (ICWSM 2021), AAAI, 1–12. Retrieved from https://arxiv.org/pdf/2001.07600v4.pdf.

Ironwood, I. (2013). *The Manosphere: A new hope for masculinity.* Red Pill Press.

Jones, A. (2020). Incels and the manosphere: Tracking men's movements online. University of Central Florida Electronic Theses and Dissertations, 2020-. 65. Retrieved from https://stars.library.ucf.edu/etd2020/65.

Khamis, S., Lawrence, A., & Welling, R. (2017). Self-branding, 'micro-celebrity' and the rise of social media influencers. *Celebrity Studies, 8*(2), 191–208. https://doi.or g/10.1080/19392397.2016.1218292.

Kuypers, J. (2010). Framing analysis from a rhetorical perspective. In P. D'Angelo and J. Kuypers (Eds.), *Doing news framing analysis: Empirical and theoretical perspectives* (pp. 286–311). Routledge.

Kuznetsov, D., & Ismangil, M. (2020). YouTube as praxis? On BreadTube and the digital propagation of socialist thought. *TripleC*, 18, 204–218. https://doi.org/ 10.31269/triplec.v18i1.1128.

The Latest YouTube Stats on Audience Demographics. (2021). Think with Google. https://www.thinkwithgoogle.com/data-collections/youtube-viewer-behavior -online-video-audience/.

Lewis, B. (2018). *Alternative Influence: Broadcasting the Reactionary Right on You-Tube.* Data & Society Research Institute.

Lewis, B. (2020). "This Is What the News Won't Show You": YouTube creators and the reactionary politics of micro-celebrity. *Television & New Media, 21*(2), 201–217. https://doi.org/10.1177/1527476419879919.

Macnamara, J. (2006). *Media and male identity: The making and remaking of men.* Palgrave Macmillan.

Maloney, M., Roberts, S., & Caruso, A. (2018). 'Mmm . . . I love it, bro!': Perfor-mances of masculinity in YouTube gaming. *New Media & Society, 20*(5), 1697–1714. https://doi.org/10.1177/1461444817703368.

Mansbridge, J., & Shames, S. L. (2008). Toward a theory of backlash: Dynamic resistance and the central role of power. *Politics & Gender, 4*(4), 623–634. https:// doi.org/10.1017/S1743923X08000500.

Marwick, A. (2015). You may know me from YouTube: (Micro-)celebrity in social media. In P. D. Marshall and S. Redmond (Eds.), *A companion to celebrity* (pp. 333–350). John Wiley & Sons.

Messerschmidt, J. W. & Messner, M. A. (2018). Hegemonic, non-hegemonic, and 'new' masculinities. In Messerschmidt, J. W. et al. (Eds.), *Gender reckonings: New social theory and research,* (pp. 35–56). New York University Press.

Mirrlees, T. (2018). The alt-right's discourse of "Cultural Marxism": A political instrument of intersectional hate. *Atlantis Journal, 39*(1), 49–69. https://doi.org/ 10.7202/atlantis.

Moss, M. H. (2011). *The media and the models of masculinity.* Lexington Books.

Naggar, S. E. (2017). 'But I did not do anything!'—analysing the YouTube videos of the American Muslim televangelist Baba Ali: delineating the complexity of a novel genre. *Critical Discourse Studies, 15*(3), 303–319. https://doi.org/10.1080/ 17405904.2017.1408477.

Nagle, A. (2015). Contemporary online anti-feminist movements. PhD thesis, Dublin City University, Dublin.

Nouri, M. (2018). The power of influence: Traditional celebrity vs social media influencer. *Advanced writing: Pop culture intersections, 32.* Retrieved from https:// scholarcommons.scu.edu/engl_176/32.

Ogilvy, D. (1985). *Ogilvy on advertising.* First vintage books.

O'Neil, J. M. (2008). Summarizing 25 years of research on men's gender role conflict using the Gender Role Conflict Scale: New research paradigms and clinical implications. *The Counseling Psychologist, 36*(3), 358–445. https://doi.org/10.1177/0011000008317057.

———. (2015). *Men's gender role conflict: Psychological costs, consequences, and an agenda for change.* American Psychological Association.

Parks, G. (2020). Considering the purpose of an alternative sense-making collective: A rhetorical analysis of the intellectual dark web. *Southern Communication Journal, 85*(3), 178–190. https://doi.org/10.1080/1041794X.2020.1765006.

Pérez-Torres, V., Pastor-Ruiz, Y. & Ben-Boubaker, S. A. (2018). YouTubers and the construction of adolescent identity. *Comunicar: Media Education Research Journal, 55*(26), 61–70. https://doi.org/10.3916/C55-2018-06.

Pompper, D. (2010). Masculinities, the metrosexual, and media images: Across dimensions of age and ethnicity. *Sex Roles, 63*(9), 682–696. https://doi.org/10.1007/s11199-010-9870-7.

Pullen, C., & Cooper, M. (2010). *LGBT Identity and Online New Media.* Routledge. https://doi.org/10.4324/9780203855430.

Quigley, B. L. (1998). Identification as a key term in Kenneth Burke's rhetorical theory. *American Communication Journal, 1*(3), 1–5. Retrieved from http://ac-journal.org/journal/vol1/iss3/burke/quigley.html.

Statista. (2019). U.S. population with a social media profile 2018. Retrieved from https://www.statista.com/statistics/273476/percentage-of-us-population-with-a-social-network-profile/.

———. (February 19, 2021a). YouTube—Statistics & Facts. Retrieved from https://www.statista.com/topics/2019/youtube/.

Statista. (January 14, 2021b). *U.S. teen and young adult favorite platforms for following influencers 2019.* https://www.statista.com/statistics/1092560/gen-z-millennials-platforms-follow-influencers-usa/.

Tan, Y., Shaw, P., Cheng, H. & Kim, K. K. (2013). The construction of masculinity: A cross-cultural analysis of men's lifestyle magazine advertisements. *Sex Roles, 69*, 237–249. https://doi.org/10.1007/s11199-013-0300-5.

Thrall, A. T., Lollio-Fakhreddine, J., Berent, J., Donnelly, L., Herrin, W., Paquette, Z., & Wyatt, A. (2008). Star power: Celebrity advocacy and the evolution of the public sphere. The International Journal of Press/Politics, 13(4), 362–385. https://doi.org/10.1177/1940161208319098.

Turner, F. (2018). Trump on Twitter: How a medium designed for democracy became an authoritarian's mouthpiece. In P. J. Boczkowski and Z. Papacharissi (Eds.), *Trump and the media,* (pp. 143–49). MIT Press.

28 YouTube influencer marketing statistics for 2020. (2021, January 20). ZINE Blog. https://blog.zine.co/brands-youtube-influencer-marketing-statistics/.

Wotanis, L. & McMillan, L. (2014). Performing gender on YouTube: How Jenna Marbles negotiates a hostile online environment. *Feminist Media Studies, 14*(6), 912–928. https://doi.org/10.1080/14680777.2014.882373.

Chapter Fifteen

Conclusion

Agency for All, Where It Counts

Donnalyn Pompper

Our sense of being masculine or feminine is part of a gender system constructed by humans and it is subject to change. Since the 1990s, men have responded to social change movements and a drive for equity in a variety of ways. About a decade after Betty Friedan (1963) published the book that launched contemporary feminism, *The Feminine Mystique* (1963), Warren Farrell published *The Liberated Man* (1975) after founding the NOW National Task Force in 1971—which became the organizational base of the men's movement working to eliminate oppressive male stereotypes. While some men have supported and embraced the waves of change, others have resisted in order to preserve their privilege—collectively known as patriarchy with hegemonic masculinity.

Considering that gender differences are natural, activist, and mythopoetic men's movement leader and best-selling author Robert Bly (1990) relied on ancient stories and legends to argue that modern men had lost touch with their *Zeus energy* and urged men to gather for all-male retreats and rituals to recapture the spirit of *deep and vigorous masculinity* (Bly, 1990). Throughout the 1990s, large-scale rallies saw men gathering to express their masculinity in the woods during retreats and on the streets to raise awareness about clinging to their "code of masculinity and to react with anger and defensiveness" (Levant, 1997, p. 226). The Wildman "is the healthy, wise, indigenous soul in all man . . . the union of the divine masculine within our bodies, hearts, and minds that seeks to do what is right and good for the betterment of all . . . to restore that which has been broken by brash irresponsibility of the tattered masculine" (Wildman Retreats, n.d.) Consortia of men's groups engage in workshops to navigate their way "through the labyrinth of the twenty-first century" (Wildman Retreats, n.d.) The Promise Keepers Men's Conference of Christian men gather at football stadia where "men of integrity—promise

keeping men—fulfill their destinies as godly husbands, fathers, and leaders
. . . to reunite, rebuild, re-imagine, and inspire the hearts of men" (About Us,
n.d.) and affirm seven promises: honor, brotherhood, integrity, family, serving, unity, and obedience (Experience the Seven Promises, n.d.) The Million
Man March on October 16, 1995, drew African-American men for a day of
reflection and atonement to "convey to the world a vastly different picture of
the Black male" (Madhubuti & Karenga, 1996, p. 152). Levant (1997) posited
that these events emerge from men's "growing sense that all is not well in
their world . . . awareness of the pain and isolation they experienced as men"
(p. 226). Hence, boys and men often are conflicted about what to do with a
"sense of disrespect from attempts to discuss their problems" (Levant, 1997,
p. 231) and too often media's use of comedy does little to advance conversations and seriously consider limits and negative impacts of male gender role
stereotypes which emerge from systemic patriarchy and hegemonic masculinity infrastructures.

WHAT THEN SHALL WE DO?

Nostalgia is a tricky concept because it can reinforce injustice by supporting
conservative forces that immobilize growth. Longing for a time *when men
were men* (Foxhall & Salmon, 1999) suggests some "continuous uniform
tradition" that's simply false (Brod, 1987, p. 48). As men experience greater
degrees of pain and discomfort associated with social change and transition-
ing to life where women enjoy increased financial independence from men,
what men *do* with this pain affects everyone. A global society, we must support males in moving away from destructive behaviors including anger, rage,
self-medication, and harmful silence. As gender role theory tells us, gender
stereotypes emerge among people's observations of adults in their social roles
(Eagly & Wood, 2012; Koenig & Eagly, 2014), so the old stereotypes must
give way to social change, too.

This means that media producers bear a significant responsibility to support social advancement by eradicating harmful gender stereotypes and
encouraging new, altered versions of masculinities. For example, media representations showing women and men in roles outside the home pursuing a
career (agentic) and working in the domestic sphere cooking and taking care
of children (communal) turn such behaviors into expectations so that traditional gender role stereotypes may become—not reversed—but equitably distributed so that all gender groups are viewed as both communal *and* agentic.
Because it is the "rigid role prescriptions that constrain male behavior" and
prevent men from expressing emotions and intimacy that makes them better

fathers, friends, and more sensitive lovers, media must go beyond producing pop self-help guides which end up reproducing the problems they supposedly remedy (Kimmel, 1987, p. 121).

Masculinity and femininity are relational constructs which must be disaggregated from one another so that one definition does not wholly rely on the definition of the other. In other words, one path to gender equity is the recognition that each person may embody and display degrees of both masculinity and femininity which vary over the life course. Judith Lorber (1986), founding editor of *Gender & Society*, posited that men and women should be socially interchangeable, thus "eradicating gender as an organizing principle of postindustrial society" (p. 568). To accommodate this goal for eliminating binary dualisms and thereby reducing gender's significance in everyday life, media must change internally so that their externally projected gender representations are truly diverse and equitable—from management leadership styles through hiring practices and content production involving storylines, actors, and graphics. Like Stern (2003), I anticipate the day that cultural studies of masculinity and femininity "connect under the same banner" (p. 227).

Collective View

Authors who joined this edited collection have investigated a number of phenomena in order to expand our understanding of masculinity, male gender role conflict/stress theory (GRC/S), its model, and ways these interplay with media.

Several authors interrogate complex dynamics associated with GRC/S and masculinity's tensions communicated via online spaces. Allison and Kristensen offer a cautionary tale about ways the internet is used to create and perpetuate specific forms of masculine ideology that fosters conflict/stress for men and threatens to forever exclude women from discourses. Yet, Mundy suggests that online fora offer men room to diffuse their personal male conflict/stress while staging their comeback after being accused of sexual misconduct—while women and men use social media to call out perpetrators and to increase awareness in support of victims. Rodriguez suggests that the video of a Latinx pop culture music video by reggaetón and Latin Trap artist Bad Bunny enables online audiences to engage with male GRC/S uniquely with new *situation sources* that may prove useful in expanding the masculinity concept to accommodate artists who identify as male but wear skirts, makeup, wigs, and false breasts. Carivou and Jackson examine online spaces for clues to understanding how toxic hegemonic masculinity threatens the health and safety of everyone when men refuse to wear a face mask during a pandemic because they perceive the behavior reduces their sense of masculinity by making them appear weak. Parks, Russo, and Simon compare/contrast ways that YouTube influencers characterize masculinity's problems and offer competing perspectives on and solutions to male GRC/S experienced by male viewers.

Other chapters address incomplete media representations of masculinity, which can contribute to male GRC/S. Bradley and Mullé posit that theorizing about sexuality's intersection with the masculinity concept will enhance utility of the GRC/S model and offer media producers advice to fully represent a broader spectrum of social identity intersections with masculinity by including asexuality representations. Mundy and De Moya offer recommendations to the advertising industry after conducting interviews with decision makers about which male images are amplified in ads with implied potential to contribute to male GRC/S. They recommend acting on corporate promises to shift away from persistent whiteness as the masculinity standard by authentically embracing DEI and social movements' demands for BIPOC justice. Cherry and Eckstein offer tangible outcomes of media's limited (and incorrect) representations of men abused by their female partners and resolve that male GRC/S is perpetuated by too few outlets portraying abused men in realistic, supportive, or otherwise positive ways.

Some chapters offer specific recommendations for enhancing/expanding the male GRC/S model. The traditional male gender role of breadwinner serves as a platform for Sai and Yamauchi's introduction of *dirty work masculinity* to the male GRC/S model as context for examining stigmatized employment. Jangbar recommends enhancing the GRCS model to accommodate *fear of cognitive dysfunction* as supplement to the model's attention to *fear of femininity and homosexuality*—for a more nuanced picture of fears at the heart of masculinity. Pompper offers the long career of a popular male music artist as context for further contextualizing the GRC/S model by adding heteromasculine-emotionality as pathway for avoiding restrictive emotionality (RE) and restrictive affectionate behavior between men (RABBM) that contribute to toxic masculinity and anger.

As a long-dominated space for males, sports and some other occupational arenas are rife for new ways of thinking about ways to avoid contributing to male GRC/S. Brooke offers concepts like flow, creativity, inclusivity, and modesty inherent in sports enjoyed in South East Asia as a means for expanding western views on sports with necessary adjuncts of violence and aggression. LaStrape and Burnette compare/contrast careers of two legendary NFL quarterbacks to examine how masculinity tenets shape storytelling at retirement time and contribute to male GRC/S throughout a football player's life course. Pitchford-Hyde examines ways that reality television producers rely on hackneyed narratives of disabled soldiers *overcoming* their disability through *hard work*. Paradoxically, this dynamic can contribute to male

GRC/S across disabilities communities, as well as fuel temporarily able-bodied audience members' perceptions which can contribute to male GRC/S when they frame their own interactions with people with disabilities as if one only needs to work harder to overcome one's disability.

Recommendations

Offered next are a handful of ideas for researchers to further study masculinity-GRC/S-media interplay:

1. Examine masculinities in non-Western societies, like Sai and colleagues' (2020) study of socio-cultural influences on the drive for muscularity among students and other men of various ages as represented across social media platforms to offer more inclusive views of masculinity.
2. Identify more spaces for men to explore changing gender roles and engage with emotional expression and connection. For example, critiquing cinema's historical masculine-as-silent-man-Gary-Cooper-style and masculine-as-John-Wayne-tough representations have given way in recent decades to multi-dimensional male characters in war narratives. How are these dynamics playing out today in terms of intersectional masculine identities in cinema as well as other media products such as video games and social media channels?
3. Examine ways advertisers perpetuate privileging of whiteness, hypermuscularity, aspirational middle-class, and other western masculine ideals and body aesthetics, comparable to Mishra's (2021) study of male lifestyle magazines in India.
4. Discover which practices and characteristics situate masculinity in comparison to femininity—superior, inferior, or complementary, how/why, and to what end? For example, what do these dynamics look like in terms of equality of power relations and distribution of resources? This recommendation is inspired by Schippers (2007), who builds on Connell's (2005) important work about multiple masculinities and hegemonic masculinity.
5. Engage in inter-disciplinarity and avoid gender-matching research. Borrowing a page from Brod's (1987) playbook, I share this intriguing thought to researchers of gender phenomena with a focus on masculinity. Men's studies is rooted in pro-feminism. Not all men's studies researchers are male and not all women's studies researchers are female.
6. Explore lived experiences of boys beyond simply focusing on juvenile delinquency by examining infrastructures and systems that produce context for boys' lives.
7. Theorize masculinities from both the center and from the margins.

8. Expand research suggesting that sports serve as a metaphor for the masculine male. How true is it that sports constitute a "special arena free of life's contradictions and contaminations, where a man can test himself and be tested" (Barthel, 1992)?
9. Continue calling out media representations that position male heterosexuality as some natural norm. For Foucault (1988), gender and sexuality are discourses that are entwined and mutually sustaining. There is much to discover about transgender lived experiences.
10. Dismantle fantasies of hegemonic masculinity which MacKinnon (2003) qualified as impacting social behavior "deeply influenced by commonsense beliefs about the fantasies of masculinity," p. 11).

Just in case my goal is not entirely clear, may I state it now? We each have a job to do in supporting boys and men through a transition in changing systems and infrastructures that currently support conflict/stress—to new systems undergirded by greater openness for discussing concerns about male GRC/S, more inclusive discussions that exclude no one, and supportive media that promote gender equity internally and in externally communicated gender representations. What I mean is, this goal means agency must override rhetoric alone and we all stand to gain much for ourselves and future generations.

REFERENCES

About us (n.d.) Promise keepers. Men of integrity. Downloaded June 27, 2021, from https://rb.gy/gtpmvd.
Barthel, D. (1992). When men put on appearances: Advertising and the social construction of masculinity. In S. Craig (Ed.), *Men, masculinity, and the media* (pp. 137–153). Sage.
Bly, J. (1990). *Iron John. A book about men*. Da Capo Press.
Brod, H. (1987). Introduction: Themes and theses of men's studies. In H. Brod (Ed.), *The making of masculinities: The new men's studies* (pp. 1–17). Allen & Unwin.
Connell, R. W. (2005). *Masculinities* (2nd ed.). University of California Press.
Eagly, A. H., & Wood, W. (2012). Social role theory. In P. van Lange, A. Kruglanski, and E. T. Higgins (Eds.), Handbook of theories in social psychology (pp. 458–476). Sage.
Experience the seven promises (n.d.) Promise keepers. Men of integrity. Downloaded June 27, 2021, from https://rb.gy/eewbb9.
Farrell W. (1975). *The Liberated Man*. Berkley.
Foucault, M. (1988). Power and sex. In L. D. Kritzman (Ed.), *Politics, philosophy, culture: Interviews and other writings*, 1977–1984 (pp. 110–124). Routledge.

Foxhall, L., & Salmon, J. (1999). *When men were men: Masculinity, power and identity in classical antiquity.* Routledge.

Friedan, B. (1963). *The feminine mystique.* Dell.

Kimmel, M. S. (1987). The contemporary "crisis" of masculinity in historical perspective. In H. Brod (Ed.), *The making of masculinities: The new men's studies* (pp. 121–153). Allen & Unwin.

Koenig, A. M., & Eagly, A. H. (2014). Evidence for the social role theory of stereotype content: Observations of groups' roles shape stereotypes. *Journal of Personality and Social Psychology,* 107(3), 371–392. https://doi.org/10.1037/a0037215.

Levant, R. F. (1997). The masculinity crisis. *The Journal of Men's Studies,* 5(3), 221–231. doi: https://doi.org/10.1177%2F106082659700500302.

Lorber, J. (1986). Dismantling Noah's ark. *Sex Roles,* 14, 567–580.

MacKinnon, K. (2003). *Representing men: Maleness and masculinity in the media.* Oxford University Press Inc.

Madhubuti, H. R., & Karenga, M. (Eds.) (1996). Million Man March fact sheet. *Million Man March / Day of Absence; A commemorative anthology, speeches, commentary, photography, poetry, illustrations, documents* (p. 152). Third World Press.

Mishra, S. (2021). Globalizing male attractiveness: Advertising in men's lifestyle magazines in India. *The International Communication Gazette,* 83(3), 280–298. doi: http://dx.doi.org/10.1177/1748048521992498.

Sai, A., Furusawa, T., Othman, M. Y., Tomojiri, D., Zaini, W. F. Z. W., Tan, C. S. Y., & Norzilan, N. I. B. M. (2020). Sociocultural factors affecting drive for muscularity among male college students in Malaysia. *Heliyon,* 6. doi: https://www.sciencedirect.com/science/article/pii/S2405844020312585.

Schippers, M. (2007). Recovering the feminine other: Masculinity, femininity, and gender hegemony. *Theory and Society,* 36(1), 85–102. doi: https://www.jstor.org/stable/4501776.

Stern, B. B. (2003). Masculinism(s) and the male image: What does it mean to be a man? In T. Reichert and J. Lambiase (Eds.), *Sex in advertising: Perspectives on the erotic appeal* (pp. 215–228). Lawrence Erlbaum Associates, Publishers.

Wildman retreats (n.d.) What is the Wildman? Downloaded June 27, 2021, from https://rb.gy/skf6c9.

Index

Note: Page numbers in *italics* refer to figures and tables.

About the Contributors

Donnalyn Pompper (PhD, media & communication, Temple University) is the endowed chair in public relations in the School of Journalism & Communication at the University of Oregon. She teaches courses in and researches public relations, corporate social responsibility, and social identity. She is an internationally recognized and award-winning teacher and scholar. Pompper holds the Accredited Public Relations credential from Public Relations Society of America. Prior to joining the academy, she worked as a public relations manager and journalist who brings 25 years of practical experience to the classroom and her research.

Marcia Allison is an assistant professor in rhetoric and an associate fellow at the Aarhus Institute for Advanced Studies at Aarhus University, Denmark. As an interdisciplinary scholar, her research explores social change as a rhetorical process in mediatised neoliberal societies, sitting at the intersection of political ideology, language, and cultural memory. Her work therefore examines the key social disparities of our time: social equality, deliberative democracy, and human-nature relations.

ben Brandley (pronouns: ben/ben's) is a graduate student of communication at Arizona State University interested in studying dissonant identities, nonhuman-human relationships, and organizational cultures. Recent projects have explored discursive issues relating to Mormon queerness and whiteness. ben has cherished the privilege of presenting at various conferences and the hopes of becoming a professor.

Mark Brooke is senior lecturer at the University Town Writing Programme, National University of Singapore. He designs and teaches undergraduate academic writing courses combining Sociology of Sport and English for Academic Purposes. He has authored a book entitled *Case Studies in Sport Socialisation* and published in journals such as *Sport in Society; Communication & Sport*; and the *Asia-Pacific Journal of Health, Sport and Physical Education*. On academic literacy development, he has co-authored a book entitled a *Practical Guide to Project-Based Learning* and numerous articles in international journals investigating practical classroom applications of Systemic Functional Linguistics and Legitimation Code Theory (LCT).

Ann Burnette (PhD, Northwestern University) is a Minnie Stevens Piper Professor and Regents' Teaching Professor of Communication Studies at Texas State University. Her research and teaching focus on American public address, political rhetoric, and freedom of expression issues. Her scholarship has appeared in national and international publications.

James Carviou (PhD, University of Iowa, 2017) is an assistant professor in the Department of Communication at Missouri Western State University who teaches journalism, public relations, and digital media. Carviou is the adviser for *Griffon Media*, which includes three student-run media outlets. He holds an MA in media studies from the University of Wisconsin-Milwaukee (2009), a BA in journalism and mass communication from UW-Milwaukee (2007). He also earned undergraduate certificates in Cultures and Communities (2007) and Digital Arts and Culture (2007). His research interrogates media narratives and audience response in areas surrounding public health and identity development.

Jessica Cherry (MA, Western Kentucky University) is currently a doctoral student in the School of Communication Studies at Ohio University. Her work focuses on interpersonal and family communication at the end of life. She is particularly interested in exploring trauma and healing of surviving family members after the loss of a loved one.

Maria De Moya (PhD, University of Florida) is an associate professor in DePaul's University College of Communication. She also serves as chair for the Public Relations and Advertising Program. She holds an MA in business and economic journalism from New York University, where she was a Fulbright scholar. Her research interests center on international and ethnic strategic communication, with a specific focus on questions of representation, community, identity, and advocacy.

Jessica Eckstein (PhD, University of Illinois, Urbana-Champaign) is professor of communication studies and director of the women's studies program at Western Connecticut State University. Her work focuses on interpersonal relationships and the under-studied and/or stigmatized aspects of communication, identity, and abusive relationships. She is particularly interested in the practical application of scholarship to the lives of individual victims.

Jennifer Jackson (Ph.D., University of Memphis, 2012) is an associate professor in the Department of Communication at Missouri Western State University and teaches public relations and journalism courses. Jackson holds a graduate certificate in women's and gender studies, an MA in communication from the University of Cincinnati (2007), and a BA in public relations with minors in speech communication and deaf language and culture from Otterbein University (2003). Her research interests are in rhetoric and public address; specifically the rhetorics of peace/anti-war protests, gender, women's public address, rhetorics of social justice, and first amendment studies.

Sakina Jangbar is an assistant professor at St. John's University in New York City, where she teaches courses in rhetorical theory and criticism. Her research focuses on the rhetoric of Pakistani activists, poets, politicians, religious leaders, and ordinary citizens in order to develop a more nuanced understanding of the discursive practices of South Asian Muslims. Her research examines not only words, but also silence as a mode of communication. When she's not writing, she replenishes her soul with art, music, poetry, and live shows. She is thankful for her children, who expand her capacity to love and live.

Jesper Greve Kristensen is a PhD student in cultural studies at the University of Iceland. His work focuses on social justice, gender, and sexuality, combining cognitive semiotics with social theory to explore online misogyny and men's rights communities online.

Anthony LaStrape (EdD Tarleton State University) is an assistant professor of practice in the College of Media and Communication at Texas Tech University. He has a background in rhetorical criticism, empirical methods, and motivational speaking. His research agenda currently includes emotional intelligence, adolescent to emerging adulthood mentoring, and the rhetoric of sports.

Katherine Mullé (she/her) is a graduate student of communication at the University of New Mexico. Her research interests include rhetoric, media, and intercultural communication. Her recent projects have explored these intersections through a critical disability studies lens with a focus on rhetorical ability.

Juan Mundel (PhD, Michigan State University) is an assistant professor of public relations and advertising at Arizona State University. His research looks at the unintended effects of advertising on vulnerable populations, particularly within the context of social media.

Robert Mundy is associate professor of English and writing program director at Pace University in Pleasantville, NY. His research focuses on composition theory and pedagogy, writing center theory and practice, and masculinity, literacy, and cultural studies. He contributed to and co-edited *Out in the Center: Public Controversies and Private Struggles* (2018), winner of the 2019 International Writing Centers Book Award. He also co-authored *Gender, Sexuality, and the Cultural Politics of Men's Identity: Literacies of Masculinity* (2019), a text that considers mass media and contemporary cultural trends to examine masculinity at a point of intense scrutiny and unprecedented change.

Gabriel Parks is a graduate student and instructional assistant in the Department of Communication Studies at the University of North Carolina at Greensboro. His debut research regarding online political communication won the *Mary E. Jarrard Award* for Top Undergraduate Paper at the Carolinas Communication Association convention in 2019. His research focuses on ways media and culture interplay to shape modern identities and beliefs. His work has been published in *Southern Communication Journal* in 2020.

Jenna Pitchford-Hyde is lecturer in humanities at the University of East Anglia, where she is Postgraduate Teaching Director, co-convenes an MA Gender Studies module "The Body, Gender, and Violence," and teaches undergraduate modules in cultural studies, literature, and research methods. Jenna's research focuses on contemporary war narratives in literature and media with particular interests in masculinity, technology, and disability studies. Her recent publications include "Bare Strength: Representing Veterans of the Desert Wars in US Media" (*Media, Culture & Society*, 2017) and "Veterans and the Media: A pilot survey report on how UK veterans perceive media representations about military and post-military experiences" (Pitchford-Hyde & Parry, 2020).

Nathian Shae Rodriguez is an associate professor in the School of Journalism & Media Studies at San Diego State University and core faculty in the Area of Excellence: Digital Humanities and Global Diversity. He specializes in critical-cultural and digital media studies, critical communication pedagogy, and pop culture pedagogy. His research focuses on minority representation in media, specifically LGBTQ and Latinx portrayals and intersectional identity negotiation, as well as pop culture, identity, radio broadcasting, and issues of masculinity. He also has 10 years of professional radio experience in on-air talent, sales, promotions, and social media marketing.

Daniel Russo is a graduate student in media studies at the University of Wisconsin-Milwaukee. In his master's thesis, he explores how popular standup comedian podcasters made sense of the #MeToo movement and why their discourse mattered for audiences trying to make sense of the movement. He generally is interested in how alternative information networks frame social reality relative to mainstream narratives. He has also worked as a video editor and researcher for documentary films related to environmental sustainability.

Akira Sai (PhD, Area Studies, Hokkaido University) is a research fellow at the Faculty of Health Sciences, Hokkaido University, Japan. His research focuses on body image, particularly in the context of social media and ethnicity in Malaysia. Recently, he has expanded his interest to exploring the values and self-esteem of sanitation workers through his fieldwork and participation in waste separation with garbage workers in an urban slum in Indonesia. His current work is part of an ongoing international project on global sanitation in conjunction with Research Institute for Humanity and Nature, Japan.

Jenni Simon (PhD, University of Denver) is the director of undergraduate studies for the Communication Studies Department at the University of North Carolina, Greensboro. Simon's research focuses on the intersectionality of gender, culture, and social movements. She is the co-editor of *Michelle Obama: First Lady, American Rhetor, An Ideological Analysis of Breastfeeding in Contemporary America: Disciplining the Maternal Body,* and the author of *Consuming Agency and Desire in Romance: Stories of Love, Laughter, and Empowerment.* Simon is editor of the Carolinas Communication Association's *Annual* and past chair of the Southern States Communication Association's Gender and Women's Studies Division.

Taro Yamauchi (PhD, health sciences, University of Tokyo) is a professor at the faculty of health sciences, Hokkaido University. He does intensive fieldwork in hunter-gatherer society, rural villages, and urban slums in developing countries (e.g., Papua New Guinea, Solomon Islands, and Cameroon) to understand the lifestyle and health of local populations and adaptation to their living environments. Through his position as the project leader for the Sanitation Value Chain Study under the Research Institute of Humanity and Nature, Japan, his research interests also include sanitation, participatory action research, and waste management.

www.ingramcontent.com/pod-product-compliance
Lightning Source LLC
Chambersburg PA
CBHW050627280326
41932CB00015B/2555